THE SOCIOLOGY OF BULLYING

CRITICAL PERSPECTIVES ON YOUTH
General Editors: Amy L. Best, Lorena Garcia, and Jessica K. Taft

Fast-Food Kids: French Fries, Lunch Lines, and Social Ties
Amy L. Best

White Kids: Growing Up with Privilege in a Racially Divided America
Margaret A. Hagerman

Growing Up Queer: Kids and the Remaking of LGBTQ Identity
Mary Robertson

The Kids Are in Charge: Activism and Power in Peru's Movement of Working Children
Jessica K. Taft

Coming of Age in Iran: Poverty and the Struggle for Dignity
Manata Hashemi

The World is Our Classroom: Extreme Parenting and the Rise of Worldschooling
Jennie Germann Molz

The Homeschool Choice: Children, Parents, and the Privatization of Education
Kate Henley Averett

Growing Up Latinx: Coming of Age in Time of Contested Citizenship
Jesica Siham Fernández

Unaccompanied: Immigrant Youth and the Dilemmas of Humanitarianism in the Immigration System
Emily Ruehs-Navarro

The Sociology of Bullying: Power, Status, and Aggression Among Adolescents
Edited by Christopher Donoghue

The Sociology of Bullying

Power, Status, and Aggression Among Adolescents

Edited by
Christopher Donoghue

NEW YORK UNIVERSITY PRESS
New York

NEW YORK UNIVERSITY PRESS
New York
www.nyupress.org

© 2022 by New York University
All rights reserved

References to Internet websites (URLs) were accurate at the time of writing. Neither the author nor New York University Press is responsible for URLs that may have expired or changed since the manuscript was prepared.

Library of Congress Cataloging-in-Publication Data
Names: Donoghue, Christopher, editor.
Title: The sociology of bullying : power, status, and aggression among adolescents / edited by Christopher Donoghue.
Description: New York : New York University Press, [2022] | Series: Critical perspectives on youth | Includes bibliographical references and index.
Identifiers: LCCN 2021039780 | ISBN 9781479803873 (hardback ; alk. paper) | ISBN 9781479803880 (paperback ; alk. paper) | ISBN 9781479803897 (ebook) | ISBN 9781479803903 (ebook other)
Subjects: LCSH: Bullying—Social aspects. | Aggressiveness in adolescence—Social aspects. | Control (Psychology) in adolescence—Social aspects. | Social status.
Classification: LCC BF637.B85 .S657 2022 | DDC 302.34/30835—dc23
LC record available at https://lccn.loc.gov/2021039780

New York University Press books are printed on acid-free paper, and their binding materials are chosen for strength and durability. We strive to use environmentally responsible suppliers and materials to the greatest extent possible in publishing our books.

Manufactured in the United States of America

10 9 8 7 6 5 4 3 2 1

Also available as an ebook

CONTENTS

Foreword   vii
  Robert Crosnoe

Introduction   1
  Christopher Donoghue

1. The Inflation of Bullying   19
  Randall Collins

2. The Taxonomy of Harm: A Response to Collins   25
  Robert Faris and John Faris

3. The Role of Status in Bullying: On Murray Milner's *Freaks, Geeks, and Cool Kids*   38
  Amy L. Best

4. Addressing Queer Youth and Bullying: Sociologically Informed Approaches   48
  Melissa J. Smith and Elizabethe Payne

5. Bullying as a Social Problem: Interactional Homophobia and Institutional Heteronormativity in Schools   76
  C. J. Pascoe

6. Mean Girls and Tough Guys: Gender, Sexuality, and the Individualization of Anti-Bullying Efforts   95
  Sarah A. Miller

7. Status Motivation, Network Stability, and Instrumental Cruelty   120
  Robert Faris and Liann Tucker

8. Conflict with Friends and Social Status Mobility in Middle School   139
  Laura Callejas

9. Social Differentness and Bullying: A Discussion of Race, Class, and Income   166
   Todd Migliaccio

10. Cultures of Peer Harassment or Support in Schools: An Interactionist Account of Student Culture   188
    Hana Shepherd

11. The Anti-Bullying Myth: Bullying and Aggression in an Inhabited Institution   220
    Brent Harger

12. Prevention and Intervention Programs for Bullying Perpetration and Victimization   247
    Denise Wilson, Kirsten L. Witherup, and Allison Ann Payne

13. Understanding Culture to Combat Bullying: A Mixed-Methods Approach   274
    Alicia Raia-Hawrylak

14. Full of Bull: Militarized Capitalism, Education, and Psychologists   293
    Yale R. Magrass and Charles Derber

15. Bullying from a Psychological Perspective: A Response to Magrass and Derber   297
    Ann H. Farrell and Tracy Vaillancourt

Acknowledgments   305
About the Contributors   307
About the Editor   315
Index   317

FOREWORD

ROBERT CROSNOE

The same week that I received the full draft of this edited volume on the sociology of bullying, I happened to spend part of a long drive listening to a podcast about the 1999 mass shooting at Columbine High School in Colorado. I am not sure why I decided on that "entertainment," given that I was so scarred by that massacre that I do not like to dwell on it too much even now so many years later, but I did. The podcast went through what is now a common journey of understanding, first covering the initial and long-standing explanation that the two boys resorted to such extreme violence because they had been victims of persistent bullying by the jocks and other popular students at the school and then discussing how that explanation gradually has been debunked over the years. All true. Yet, something the podcast hosts mentioned while doing this debunking gave me pause. As evidence that the two boys had not indeed been victims of persistent bullying, the hosts described how the boys themselves had often bullied other students, how they were neither low status nor high status in their high schools, and that much of the apparent bullying directed at them came from students with whom they were friends and who inhabited a similar social space as them in the high school. I agree that these pieces of information are true, but I—like many sociologists—disagree that such truths are evidence that the two boys had not been bullied at school.

Of course, kids can be bullied and bully, even at the same time. No, being bullied does not necessarily connote low social status. Yes, bullying can be perpetrated within seemingly close-knit social circles. *It's really complicated!* The stereotypes that we have about bullying are just that: stereotypes. They are both too broad and too shallow. As a result, sometimes they fit, but sometimes they do not. The only way to capture that complexity is to zoom in to look very closely at the people involved and then, with equal attention, zoom out to better see where they are and how the interactions between them are embedded in a larger sense of time and place. We might need to use multiple lenses to get all of that done, but we have to try.

For decades, the scientific literature on bullying and the public debates and policy agendas that literature informs have been very heavy on the zooming-in part. That is partly a reflection of how developmental psychologists have been such important thought leaders putting the risks and resilience of young people at center stage. More than scholars of pretty much any other scientific discipline, they have long kept us focused on what young people need, the challenges they face, and what they have to offer us. As such, the ways that we think about bullying are guided by how developmental psychologists study young people, which emphasizes individual thought and meaning, interpersonal interaction, and the proximate settings of daily life. This perspective dovetails with the cultural prism of individualism through which many Westerners—especially Americans—view social problems to increase its influence on public thought. To be clear, that psychological perspective is valuable, but it is only one perspective. The sociological perspective on display in this volume is about the zooming-out part, and more fully incorporating it into how we talk about bullying is necessary to move forward, in terms of both understanding the problem and doing something about it.

In this sense, this volume is not by sociologists for sociologists. It is by sociologists for a much broader array of readers who care about this issue and get that their knowledge of it should be both deep and broad to make a difference. We need to round out what they know.

The Dominant Story Line

This kid is a bully. This kid is a victim. When we talk about bullying, we tend to do so in such essentialist terms that label young people in a fixed way, giving them identities that follow them from day to day and place to place.

Historically, much of the scientific research on bullying encouraged this line of thinking. Bullying was seen as a psychopathology, a character trait of someone who had something wrong in the head or heart. Further research developed ideas about bullying and victimization that were less strictly tied to the individual person but were still very much confined to a small social space. Such interpersonal interpretations of bullying were more about relations between bully and victim and how the characteristics of both and the ties between them converged to encourage one to bully the other. Here is where important concepts like power come into play, with bullying arising out of power imbalances between people.

The interpersonal approach, the consideration of power, and many other ecological frameworks for studying bullying are good examples of zooming in, but there is still more room to go. They embed individual people in larger social systems (i.e., more than the dyad or small group), but what is often missing is the *large* social systems at work. Social structure, status hierarchy, culture. These things matter to how all people live their lives, relate to others, and think about themselves, so of course they matter to young people. Once we bring in such ideas, we can get a better feel for why young people do some of the things that they do that we really wish they would not.

Murry Milner's book *Freaks, Geeks, and Cool Kids*, expertly described by Amy Best in chapter 3, is a great starting point for anyone who wants to see the value of looking to the system to understand bullying. It crystallizes how many of the seemingly irrational behaviors of teenagers are actually quite rational given the system in which they live. Status is a valued good in their worlds, and it is something of a zero-sum game in which a gain by one is a loss by another. The intense competition for status in this zero-sum game, which itself is embedded in a context where any one person is merely a face in a very large crowd, breeds all sorts of behaviors. Some of those behaviors are prosocial and positive, which makes it easier for adults to understand them. Other behaviors are widely viewed by adults as harmful and destructive but, through the eyes of teenagers, are a potentially effective way of getting what they want. Those behaviors—even when distasteful to them—are a means to an end, and they often work. That type of data-driven calculus can be labeled with many different terms, but irrational it is not.

When I spent a long time conducting an ethnography of a large and diverse high school in Texas for my book *Fitting In, Standing Out*, I was able to see Milner's way of thinking at work in many ways. For example, binge drinking was a widespread activity at this high school, as it is in many high schools, and one that administrators and parents viewed primarily as dangerous and unhealthy. That view is certainly not incorrect, and most of the students accepted that it was true. If they knew it to be true, however, why did they still engage? Well, they tended to focus on different dimensions of drinking—how it gave status, how it helped them gain entrée to events and relationships, how it was a type of social glue within the in-crowd—that highlighted how it could also be viewed as their ticket to a happier high school existence. They could weigh the pros and weigh the cons, and, in that moment, the former outweighed the latter. Consequently, I came away with an understanding of binge drinking that was equal parts kids not thinking at all and kids thinking a lot.

Bullying is the same way. To see why people bully, do not just look inside them to see who they are. Look outside them to see what it gets them in the systems in which they live. To that, I would add one more wrinkle, which is that sometimes the not thinking part of the equation is not simply about the heightened tendency for adolescent brains to orient toward sensation seeking over cognitive regulation. Sometimes they do things without thinking—or thinking much—because they are being guided by the norms and values of social systems that they have internalized so deeply that they do not have to think to act on them. This volume is as good as it gets in explaining why bullying arises because social systems make young people think too much and also because social systems guide young people even when they do not recognize that it is happening.

The Power of the System

Sociologists, including many featured in this volume, have shown us how schools and neighborhoods act as their own unique social systems, with opportunity structures, status hierarchies, and cultures that regulate and incentivize behaviors in ways that promote bullying. As just two examples, the different but highly complementary work of Robert Faris and Liann Tucker (chapter 7) and Laura Callejas (chapter 8) has demonstrated that bullying is a key mechanism through which young people jockey for position. Indeed, bullying the right person at the right time is a key strategy for climbing the hierarchy that some—not all—young people try. It often brings rewards, and the promise of rewards keeps young people trying. Otherwise, it might fade away or at least be confined to psychopathology. With this strategic jockeying within a system, the same young people can bully and be bullied, sometimes on the same day, and young people who know each other and consider themselves friends may experience periods as bully and victim within their relationship over time.

This interplay of bullying, strategy, and reward is why sociologists argue that bullying should not be discussed as solely a characteristic of the person or even really as a behavioral attribute. It is situational, something that emerges from a specific set of circumstances that come and go and incentivize young people in different ways at different times.

When thinking about schools and neighborhoods as social systems that encourage the use of bullying as a not irrational social strategy for some youth, we also must follow the lead of the sociologists featured in this volume who argue that these systems are strongly influenced by the social currents in the broader society that organizes them. In the United States, for example, the capitalistic ethic of winning, heteronormative modes of thinking, and the norms of the gender binary that are persistent within larger cultural systems (e.g., media, law) filter down into school curricula, neighborhood relations, and other institutional and interpersonal processes of daily lives to shape what social status looks like to young people and how they think they need to act to gain status or avoid losing status. Chapters 4 (Smith and Payne), 5 (Pascoe), 14 (Magrass and Derber), and 6 (Miller) vividly illustrate the often insidious ways that ideas and practices filter down through the set of concentric circles of social systems in which individual people operate. Here is where we should return to the "not thinking" I mentioned above. Young people may consciously act on such internalized messages to get ahead and/or protect themselves, but sometimes they just act without too much consciousness. In both cases, bullying can result.

Using sociology to round out the way that we—as individual people, as a society—interpret and explain bullying is not simply about our knowledge and understanding. It is also about action. If we think that bullying is psychopathology or that it is about interpersonal power, we develop prevention and intervention efforts guided by that way of thinking. If bullying is about much more, our prevention and intervention efforts will never achieve the results we want because they are incomplete, narrow. To prevent or stop bullying, systems have to change—concrete systems encapsulated by schools and neighborhoods but also the broader and more abstract systems that help to determine what goes on in those concrete systems. The final chapters of this volume—by Migliaccio (9), Shepherd (10), Harger (11), and Raia-Hawrylak (13)—delve into the challenges of doing so but also reinforce the vital need to meet those challenges. What does the system incentivize and why? What do we do to change those incentives? Perhaps posing these questions is the real contribution of this volume, even more than the answers it provides to other kinds of questions.

Sociological Understanding as Public Understanding

In his first chapter of this volume, Randall Collins touches on an important lesson that I have learned studying young people, teaching them, and, now, parenting two of them. That lesson is that young people often know better than adults about the major phenomena that affect their lives. With bullying, young people really do understand some basic truths more than adults, which is why they are often dismissive of adults' lectures about bullying and/or efforts to reduce bullying. At the same time, building some common ground with young people around those basic truths gives adults an in to build on those basic truths with more systematic knowledge of the problem and, potentially, to take more effective action.

Every year that I have taught first-year students at the University of Texas, I have talked in my classes about bullying from a sociological perspective—featuring much of the scholarship and many of the scholars in this volume—and have been amazed time and again how much it resonates with college students' own experiences in the K–12 system. It speaks to them and what they knew to be true but perhaps had not yet been able to articulate. Why couldn't they articulate it? I think that one reason is that their parents and teachers never talked to them about bullying in a sociologically informed way. This volume is one way to change that.

Introduction

CHRISTOPHER DONOGHUE

We don't have any bullying in this school! These were the words of a principal from a private elementary school I once advised in a bullying consultation. His choice of words and his emphatic tone made it clear that this was a mantra he had expressed before and one in which he firmly believed. Surely he thought, if there were bullies in his school he would know about them. *Mean kids always stick out!* As the popular opinion goes, boy bullies are bigger than other kids and pick on the weak to convince others not to challenge them. Girl bullies, on the other hand, are the super pretty ones, preoccupied with their looks and lacking remorse when they spread rumors and exclude their weaker peers or slut-shame one another. Or maybe he thought there were not any misfits among his kids for the others to pick on. Since it was a highly religious school, he probably was not aware of many openly LGBTQ students, and if he was, current standards of decency would tell him that they were the ones who needed to be protected the most from other students. So luckily for him, his school had no bullying, and he would be praised simply for being forward thinking enough to have engaged in the consultation.

Since the 1970s, psychologists have dominated the vast wealth of research on adolescent bullying, and this work has occurred in front of a backdrop of grave concern in recent years over a rise in school shootings and suicides by young victims of bullying. The media have also contributed to the intensity of the response, particularly on cyberbullying among children, which has been depicted as a modern epidemic that celebrities and politicians alike have been striving to address with advocacy, outreach programs, documentaries, and internet campaigns. Anti-bullying programs, new school personnel, and rigid state laws have followed, and they have been accompanied with a booming new industry of therapists and psychiatrists who aim to properly treat both bullies and victims alike.

It is something of an enigma then that the first book on a sociology of bullying has been missing from our shelves for so long. Aggressive behavior among children is firmly in the realm of sociological interest, and sociologists have so much to offer this field, especially considering the many social forces and contextual realities that are at play in bullying situations. Sociologists are also keenly aware that aggressive children are imitating behaviors they are taught by adults, and this makes the antibullying movement troubling since there is so little interest in stopping adults from bullying. So the absence of sociological voices on the topic of bullying might make you wonder if they think that *Kids will be kids!* or *Bullying is just a rite of passage!*

As surprising as it sounds, however, the explanation might be that sociologists do not view bullying as abnormal behavior. In fact, many might define it as *normal behavior*, especially in total institutions like prisons, schools, and psychiatric departments of hospitals where the conditions are perfect for it. The inmates (or patients or students) in these spaces have some autonomy, but they are subject to many restrictions on their freedoms.[1] There are social rewards they can pursue (e.g., early release for inmates or academic honors for students), but they do not have the power to choose what they are. Oftentimes people subjected to these conditions create their own informal reward systems like popularity contests or memberships in desirable cliques, clubs, or gangs. This argument was laid out by Murray Milner in his 2004 book *Freaks, Geeks, and Cool Kids*, and as Amy Best explains in chapter 3, this work has greatly influenced the sociological study of aggressive adolescent behavior.

Now just because bullying might be normal, this does not mean all students experience it, nor does it mean it cannot be reduced. Estimates from the National School Crime and Victimization Survey show that about 20 percent of children between the ages of twelve and eighteen reported being bullied in 2015 and 2017.[2] But bullying statistics do not tell the whole story, especially since they mainly rely on self-reported victimization. Surveys about involvement in bullying also overlook the fact that children suffer from bullying at school and at home even when they are not directly being victimized. This is exemplified by the challenges faced by students with disabilities, LGBTQ students, and ethnic and racial minorities when they attend school in an atmosphere that is rife with biases such as ableism, heteronormativity, cisnormativity, and racism.

The authors in this book explore an array of sociological (and also criminological) approaches to bullying. If you are familiar with the existing adolescent bullying research, we anticipate you will find their perspectives to be different, and sometimes unexpectedly thought-provoking. One thing most of the chapters have in common is that they challenge the psychological paradigm that bullying is best understood as an individual phenomenon. Instead, these authors take a broader view that incorporates theory on social networks, school culture, symbolic interactionism, and macrosociological causes. Rather than individualizing bullying, they address it as a byproduct of social systems, biases, and status hierarchies. Other works in the volume focus on debates over the definition of bullying, the successes and failures of anti-bullying programs, and the benefits of triangulating research methods on bullying. Before getting into them, let us briefly review the departure that sociology takes from psychological research on bullying.

The Psychology of Bullying versus the Sociology of Bullying

The psychologist Dan Olweus is arguably the most well-known expert on bullying. According to his definition, bullying is a form of repeated intentional aggression against another person or group in a situation in which the aggressor has more power than the victim.[3] It may include physically aggressive behavior (as in pushing, punching, kicking, or pinching), verbal abuse (such as name-calling, slut-shaming, or using slurs or epithets), social bullying (exclusion, rumor telling, or avoidance), or cyberbullying in which the bullies use technology (phones, computers, or video game consoles) to aggress against others in virtual spaces, such as through texts, direct messaging, live chats, and social media. Bullying may also take the form of threats, intimidation, or damage to another's property.

The Olweus definition of bullying has stood the test of time in the field of psychology and in education policy and research, even though it has many critics. Some argue that intentionality is too hard to measure, that the power differential is often unclear, and that the narrow criteria just miss too many forms of aggression that obviously look like bullying.[4] Arguments have been made to include sexual harassment and other forms of generalized aggression that might not involve a power imbalance.[5] Adolescents also seem out of touch with the Olweus definition. Research shows that they do not use the same language to define bullying as school personnel do (e.g., "repeated acts" and "power imbalance") when given the chance to use their own words.[6] This book features fresh critiques of the psychological definition of bullying by Robert Faris and John Faris in chapter 2 and Melissa Smith and Elizabethe Payne in chapter 4.

These disagreements about the definition notwithstanding, psychological research has brought bullying to the forefront among issues in education, and it has led to a proliferation of anti-bullying campaigns, outreach, and laws. It is common now for children and parents to report that bullying is going on in school (or in the vicinity of school), and it is normal for schools to measure their school climate and levels of bullying with surveys. A myriad of health research has also emerged to demonstrate the harms of being a bully, a victim, and a bully-victim (those involved in both). These include anxiety, depression, lack of sleep, and various somatic illnesses such as stomachaches and headaches.[7] The research on these conditions has led to better practices for school counselors, psychologists, and social workers.

Historically, psychologists have relied upon an individual paradigm for understanding why bullying occurs among adolescents. This means they identify children as bullies, victims, and bully-victims, and they use mainly quantitative research to identify personality traits, demographic characteristics and individual experiences that are reliable predictors of involvement in bullying. For example, psychological research has shown that bullies are callous or overly prone to peer pressure.[8] Or they are responding to repeated provocations, acting out due to a lack of sleep, or failing to predict negative consequences of their actions.[9] These explanations suggest there are things about the bullies that lead them to abuse others, and we see this theme in popular culture as well, although the movies and TV shows that feature bullies are normally colored by stereotypes that often do not align with the psychological literature. In these depictions, bullies are seen as cowards pretending to be tough, kids who lack self-esteem, or victims of past abuse who are taking it out against others to get revenge or to make themselves feel better. These images are pervasive, children believe them, and they seem to confirm the common view that schools need to do a better job of finding and punishing the bullies.[10]

This individualistic view of bullying has left psychology vulnerable to the criticism that it does not take into account other social factors that are at play. Following the work of Bronfenbrenner, however, psychologists have addressed this claim by employing social ecological theory to examine the roles played by parents, teachers, administrators, and school communities in bullying.[11] Some sociologists like Todd Migliaccio, Hana Shepherd, and Brent Harger see potential in this approach. In chapters 9, 10, and 11, they look for ways that psychology and sociology can work together on bullying by blending social ecological theory with symbolic interactionism. They find that child and teacher interactions are integral to the development of ideas and norms about what bullying is, which behaviors are acceptable, and how bullying should be addressed in schools. Others such as Yale Magrass and Charles Derber in chapter 14 argue that psychology is still not up to the task of accounting for social power in bullying relationships. Ann Farrell and Tracy Vaillancourt refute this idea in their response to the chapter, demonstrating cases where power is built into the social ecological framework.

But is psychology the *only* appropriate starting point for understanding bullying? Are the anti-bullying programs that this research has inspired the best remedy for addressing bullying? The sociological essays in this volume suggest that the answer is no, or as Charles Derber and Yale Magrass argue, we cannot *Just Say No to Bullying!*[12] In their view, bullying is embedded in America's system of militarized capitalism. Bullying is something that Americans are taught to do at a young age in order to survive and to get ahead. From their point of view it is puzzling that we have decided to punish the bullies and treat them with psychiatric medication, since the hidden reality is that they are engaging in the behaviors that adults ultimately expect them to excel at later in life.

A key difference between the psychology of bullying and the sociology of bullying is that sociologists consider the act of bullying, and not the bullies or the victims themselves, to be the most appropriate unit of analysis. As C. J. Pascoe has argued, by introducing a nonpathological approach to bullying, sociologists aim to interrogate the impact of social forces on bullying among adolescents, such as inequality, heteronormativity, militarized capitalism, racism, cancel culture, power, and competition.[13] This is a key objective in this book as well. By advancing sociological perspectives on bullying, it is our goal to shift the national conversation from one that focuses on villainizing bullies and evoking sympathy for victims to one that encourages an inward look at the aspects of our culture that foster bullying behavior among children.

We see this kind of sociological approach in *The Bully Society* by Jessie Klein, who identifies bullying as the cause of many school shootings in the latter part of the twentieth century and the early part of the twenty-first.[14] Klein describes young people as status obsessed and apt to mimic the behaviors they see in adults as a way to gain praise and popularity. In a similar vein, social network theorists view bullying as a behavior that adolescents see as instrumental to social climbing.[15] It may be a surprise to hear that social network theorists find that children with relatively high social standing in schools actually exhibit some of the lowest levels of aggression toward others. In fact, some evidence shows that they are even more likely to become victims than others, and they sometimes suffer more from these abuses than other children.[16] These studies further indicate that the young people who use aggression to get ahead are often strategic about it, selecting victims based on perceptions of their own dominance or the level of popularity for the victim, and that it often works.[17] It may also be a surprise to hear that aggressors often victimize their own friends. We learn more about that in a study by Laura Callejas in chapter 8.

Most anti-bullying programs now employ a "whole-school" approach, which is largely based on social ecological theory, but in sociology symbolic interactionist theory is equally important to understanding the value of that strategy. Sociologists working on this research add a more nuanced account of social context and macro-level forces to the psychological model. In *Bullying as a Social Experience*, Todd Migliaccio and Juliana Raskauskas do this by opening up ways of understanding school communities that rely less upon the quality of relationships between individuals and more upon the power dynamics between them.[18] According to their modified ecological view, it is the understanding and negotiation of power in a school community that best defines the reasons why bullying occurs. So in contrast to the "whole-school" anti-bullying programs that discourage aggressive behavior by creating warmth, setting rules, or establishing an anti-bullying ethos, these sociologists aim to identify the cultural biases and inequalities that foster bullying in a school community and strive for greater inclusiveness within them. We learn more about the effectiveness of whole-school strategies in chapter 12, by Denise Wilson, Kirsten Witherup, and Allison Ann Payne.

Toward a Sociology of Bullying

To be clear, sociological research on power and aggression among adolescents is anything but new. So it makes sense to question whether sociologists should use the term "bullying" more often. Could this new field weaken our efforts to protect children by dividing our research into different camps? If some of us use the term "bullying" while others focus on power and aggression more generally, could we be limiting our ability to bring about change?

One answer to these questions is that the word "bullying" is very important to people right now, even if they cannot agree on what it means. Children and parents see bullying as a particular kind of aggression that can be cruel, humiliating, and unfair. They use the word to call attention to subtle forms of aggression that can be hurtful even if we do not see them. The invisibility of these gestures can be so complete that it is impossible to find them and reduce them, such as when children use coded gestures, vague social media posts, or oddly specific memes to hurt one another. Ignoring the term might make us seem tone-deaf, and it could put us at a loss in our efforts to help schools discourage them. But of course we are still handcuffed by the problem that bullying is so hard to define.

Maybe it seems like the exact definition of bullying is unimportant, but these definitions matter to parents and children, state legislators, and those tasked with enforcing anti-bullying laws. Consider the children who have had the bravery to voice complaints about getting bullied only to find out that the behavior does not meet their school's or state's definition of what is punishable by the local anti-bullying rules. These kinds of fears and frustrations are commonly experienced by children and parents.[19] The problem of defining bullying is also important since studies show that when children are offered a definition of bullying on a survey, or even when the word "bullying" appears on the questionnaire, they are less likely to say that it has happened to them.[20] Some think children may simply define an act as bullying as long as it is "mean" or only if the victim was sufficiently harmed.[21]

These considerations suggest that we do need a word for this kind of aggression, and it is our position that sociologists have an important perspective to bring to the topic. The authors in this volume have done this in a variety of ways. Some have taken a macro approach by examining the broad social forces that encourage bullying behavior among children. Others have explored the impact of heteronormativity and cisnormativity on schools and their anti-bullying efforts. Social network theory is used by some to understand how children use aggressive behavior as a means to achieve desirable ends. Anti-bullying programs and methods for studying bullying are reviewed in other chapters and critiqued from a sociological perspective. Some authors have sought to modify the traditional definition of bullying. Still others have refined the symbolic interactionist theories about how norms around bullying are established and enforced. In the next section I describe the organization of the book and highlight some of the parallels, and also the disagreements, between the chapters.

Organization of the Volume

The volume begins with an essay by Randall Collins, in which he argues that the recent explosion of media coverage on bullying implies that the problem is bigger now than it ever was, even though logic dictates otherwise. According to Collins, the term "bullying" has long been used to refer only to an abusive relationship between stronger (normally older) members of a group and weaker ones, the so-called network isolates. We see it in places like prisons, where the inmates have so little freedom and also scarce protections from their aggressors by the staff. Collins argues that as the media (and perhaps social scientists too) have dropped this restrictive definition and broadened the term, we have artificially created a popular perception that bullying is on the rise, and this may not be warranted. However, in a response to Collins, Robert Faris and John Faris argue in chapter 2 that the Olweus definition upon which Collins relies is greatly flawed. Faris and Faris instead call for a thin definition of bullying that depicts the act as a malicious and unnecessary form of cruelty. As we will see in other parts of the book, several other authors push the definition of bullying in different ways as well. For example, Smith and Payne in chapter 4 propose a new sociological definition that can be used in schools, and Callejas in chapter 8 argues for the inclusion of conflict among friends in the bullying criteria.

In chapter 3, Amy Best discusses the enduring significance of *Freaks, Geeks, and Cool Kids* by the recently departed Murray Milner. As Best explains, Milner's suggestion was that we focus our attention on the structure of status relations among adolescents. If we can understand the often invisible status hierarchies they develop, we can see the ways they use aggression instrumentally to climb them. Milner argues that, ironically, it is their lack of power that makes adolescents so determined to garner the respect of their peers. The extent of their obsession with status can be so extreme that they create caste-like systems that are so rigid that they deem some of their peers to be essentially untouchable, since association with them can lower their own status. The theory is important from a macrosociological point of view because Milner ties it to the enterprising nature of businesses that capitalize on adolescent consumer behavior by selling them the status symbols (e.g., fad clothing styles and high-end electronics) that they use to draw lines between themselves and others. It is also influential in social network research that has confirmed many of the hypotheses Milner set forth in the book but did not have the evidence to test.

The next two chapters deal with stigma and bias in education. Melissa Smith and Elizabethe Payne in chapter 4 make a strong case for injecting a sociology of bullying into school policy. Drawing upon their years of research and advocacy in the state of New York, they argue that bullying needs to be addressed not only with anti-bullying programs but also with structural changes to the heteronormative culture in schools. Existing anti-bullying programs are organized with a deficit framework for LGBTQ students, they argue, as this population is perceived to be vulnerable to attacks and in need of protection. But why do LGBTQ students begin with this disadvantage? The answer can be found in the heteronormative and cisnormative culture that oppresses them so completely in both the formal and the informal curricula at school. Thus, ending cruelty, harassment, and other forms of aggression against LGBTQ students requires a more complete cultural rejection of these biases, and this can occur only when teachers are more adeptly trained in inclusiveness and state policy makers work toward structural change in school climate.

In the following chapter, C. J. Pascoe compares two ethnographies that she performed a decade and a half apart in two different schools to demonstrate different manifestations of bias based on gender and sexuality. In her older work we see signs of what she calls interactional homophobia expressed outwardly in verbal and physical gestures. In this school it was normal for students to insult one another with slurs related to their sexuality that sounded homophobic (e.g., fag), even though, as Pascoe noted in *Dude, You're a Fag*,[22] they were really intended to demonstrate their own successes in living up to heteronormative standards of masculinity and to degrade others for failing at it. In Pascoe's later ethnography, we see a school that has so palpably sanctioned an institutionalized form of heteronormativity that it perceives the best way to address bullying against LGBTQ students is to just punish their aggressors rather than aim for a more inclusive culture. Wisely, the LGBTQ students remark that they would rather be accepted than protected.

Following this, in chapter 6 Sarah Miller analyzes the ways that two anti-bullying campaigns she observed reinforce harmful gender norms. In these programs, girls and boys were taught to stop bullying in ways that are surprisingly consistent with larger societal stereotypes about masculinity, femininity, and aggression. Girls were taught that they are their own worst enemies, as femininity, not gender inequality, puts girls at odds with one another. Stop harming one another and girls will be better off, they are taught, with no consideration paid to the structural forces that shape their conflicts or the role that boys often play in their victimization. Boys on the other hand were encouraged to stop aggressing like girls because relational aggression is not manly behavior and because the days are gone when they could have gotten away with it. Further, both boys and girls are taught that the age of social media and increased reporting of harassment means that they need to be ever vigilant in how they handle conflict at school, as their futures could be in jeopardy. In Miller's account, we see something Collins was keenly aware of in chapter 1, that if adults rigidly promote behaviors that are out of step with youth understandings of aggressive behaviors, they run the risk of appearing clueless. In fact, this is exactly what we see in some of the students' responses to the adult messaging in the study. Some of them saw right through the adult biases and felt even more oppressed and misunderstood.

In the two chapters that follow, social network theories are used to analyze bullying. In Milner's classic work on peer aggression, young people are thought to be status obsessed. It's the blend of limited power and growing autonomy that makes them desire status so much. But in chapter 7, Robert Faris and Liann Tucker ask, if they are so consumed with status, why don't more of them use aggression to achieve it? Evidence available even to the children themselves shows that bullying others can be effective in raising their standing. But surprisingly, the data in this chapter and elsewhere show that most adolescents are not strongly driven to become more popular, preferring instead to invest in a few close friendships.[23]

In chapter 8, Laura Callejas calls for consideration of interpersonal conflict between friends as a form of status-seeking behavior that may escalate to bullying, even when it does not include physical aggression. Engagement in conflict generally may arise more frequently than traditional bullying in schools given its more subtle nature, and conflict with friends specifically may be less risky than challenging those outside of one's friendship group. Just like the way that bullying a weaker peer can raise one's status in school, engaging in conflict with friends can bring status rewards as well. Like Faris and Tucker in the previous chapter, Callejas places a greater emphasis on the motivation for the conflict, rather than the status of the target. The results of her empirical tests show that interpersonal conflict between friends raises one's brokerage status or betweenness centrality, although only for boys, and in this way it can be successfully used to accomplish the same goals as aggressing against the weak.

In chapter 9, Todd Migliaccio uses the modified social ecological view of bullying to analyze race, class, and income as forms of differentness that are associated with bullying.[24] The modified social ecological view situates bullying behavior inside larger systems, and systems within systems, such as the school, the community, and culture. In this essay, Migliaccio pushes the analysis further by considering not only how ethnic and racial minorities might experience different levels of bullying in their communities, but also how divisiveness in national politics, such as that which was seen during the Trump era, can influence bullying based on race, ethnicity, and class. For example, Migliaccio argues that local debates over whether to adopt an antiracist teaching curriculum such as the 1619 Project or to support a curriculum based on patriotism, as in the former president's favored 1776 Commission, may have fostered feelings of disconnection between children of color and their schools.

In the next chapter, by Hana Shepherd, we see that this same process of social reproduction can work in reverse. In a theory that Shepherd calls the interactionist norm account of culture, an argument is made for the ability of adolescents to influence norms through their own behaviors. Shepherd's approach is different from Migliaccio's in that she focuses less on individual perceptions of meaning and more on how those perceptions—and the behaviors they engender—become shared by adolescents in school. In this way, a school culture can become conducive to high levels of bullying when aggressive behaviors are deemed acceptable and effective, but it can also discourage bullying when students outwardly reject it, and we see evidence of this in her research. In the earlier chapters of this volume, we hear explicit and implicit calls for adults and school personnel to enact a cultural shift. Here we see signs that children can also participate in a shift through their actions and endorsements of one another's behavior.

In chapter 11, by Brent Harger, we see these same two sources of socialization (institutional bias and actor behavior) depicted together as he uses inhabited institutionalism to examine how individual approaches to bullying are perpetuated and reproduced in two elementary schools. Much like the school principal discussed in the opening paragraph of this chapter, some of the adults Harger observed did not think bullying was a problem. In this study, students and adults defined acts as bullying when they fit their stereotypes and overlooked them when they did not. This allowed both students and adults to see their behaviors in more favorable ways, with aggressive students defining themselves as non-bullies and adults claiming the legitimacy of their anti-bullying efforts. Despite the presence of widespread aggressive interactions between students, then, to define bullying as an issue to be addressed at the level of school culture would have been inconsistent with the beliefs of many that there were very few "bullies" to address.

The next chapter considers the successes and failures of anti-bullying programs from a sociological and criminological perspective. In chapter 12, Wilson, Witherup, and Payne review the anti-bullying literature and find that whole-school approaches are the most successful at reducing bullying perpetration and victimization because they operate at multiple levels with multiple components. Individual outcomes in these programs result from the complex interplay between individuals and their environments, which are further influenced by developmental and contextual periods of time. Programs that fail to include peers, families, schools, and the broader community are unlikely to make real and lasting changes to the prevalence of bullying. While approaches such as the Olweus Bullying Prevention Program and restorative justice have been associated with positive outcomes, their effects are sometimes modest. Given such findings, important areas for future research that aim to improve and adapt programs based on the specific needs of all levels of the social ecological model are discussed. In other chapters in the volume we hear from authors who call for a greater departure from approaches that only support the individual paradigm of bullying and do not call for a greater culture change. This movement advocates for a more sociological engagement that takes the entire school culture into account.

In chapter 13, Alicia Raia-Hawrylak makes the unsettling observation that school climate and bullying survey data may look the same in two schools in the aggregate, despite the presence of very obvious differences in the levels of aggression that can be seen in the classrooms. Since the advent of anti-bullying laws in the United States, many schools have turned to schoolwide surveys to measure bullying victimization. But the questions raised above about how children define bullying and the extent to which they understand adult terms for it suggest that this lack of fit between quantitative data and real experiences is not all that surprising. Raia-Hawrylak explains the mismatch as a product of the classroom idiocultures, or localized understandings of bullying and what it means to be victimized, that students develop as they interact with one another at school. As other authors observe in this volume, school culture is important to understanding bullying, but here we see that smaller subcultures are relevant too, and they may defy our measurement efforts at the school level. Addressing this problem is complex and necessarily points to the need for more mixed-methods research.

In chapter 14, Yale Magrass and Charles Derber expound upon the argument in *Bully Nation*,[25] that bullying is an extension of militarized capitalism and that children who bully are paradoxically doing what they have been trained to do, which is get ahead by pushing others down. They also make the case that psychologists and school counselors are too eager to treat bullies with therapy and medication. According to the authors, nothing can "solve the problem" of bullying because no one really wants it to be solved; and without it, militaristic capitalism would collapse and the elite would lose their wealth and power. In a response to this piece in the next chapter, Ann Farrell and Tracy Vaillancourt refute the idea that psychologists view most bullies as disturbed and in need of professional treatment. They argue that more commonly psychologists see bullies as less prosocial or lacking in empathy. They also contend that psychologists have already moved well beyond the individual level in their framing of bullying, and this can be seen in the ways that social power is built into the social ecological perspective of bullying.

Setting a Goal for the Sociology of Bullying

The goal of this book is *not* to reflect upon what sociologists have learned about bullying or to make an argument that sociology is better for understanding bullying than psychology. Its objective is to *advance* the sociology of bullying as a relevant and important framework for understanding and defining the problem. The success of our efforts can be measured only over time. Will our colleagues in sociology pick up the baton and push this research forward? Will sociologists advocate for cultural change? Will they earn a seat at the consulting tables of schools and districts where the challenging work is done to create anti-bullying policies, or push for the creation of school sociologist positions? These are questions we would prefer to receive positive answers to, but we also hope to advance a sociology of bullying by inspiring our colleagues in psychology, education, counseling, and other fields to consider the sociological aspects of their work.

NOTES

1 Milner, 2004.
2 U.S. Department of Justice, 2015, 2017.
3 Olweus, 1978, 1993.

4   Carrera et al., 2011; Cascardi et al., 2014; Chan, 2009; Cheng et al., 2011; Cunningham et al., 2010; Mishna, 2004.
5   Donoghue and Raia-Hawrylak, 2016; Stein, 2002.
6   DeLara, 2012; Donoghue et al., 2015; Donoghue and Raia-Hawrylak, 2016; Harger, 2016; Monks and Smith, 2006; Vaillancourt et al., 2008.
7   Gini et al., 2014; Hymel and Swearer, 2015; Klomek et al., 2009; Kowalski and Limber, 2013; Krizan and Herlache, 2016; Løhre et al., 2011; Nielsen et al., 2015; Smokowski et al., 2014; Swearer et al., 2010; Turner et al., 2013.
8   Swearer and Hymel, 2015.
9   Crick and Dodge, 1994.
10 Thornberg, 2010, 2011.
11 Bronfenbrenner, 1979.
12 Derber and Magrass, 2017.
13 Pascoe, 2013.
14 Klein, 2013.
15 Faris and Felmlee, 2011.
16 Faris and Felmlee, 2014; Felmlee and Faris, 2016.
17 Faris, 2012; Faris and Ennett, 2012; Veenstra et al., 2007; Veenstra et al., 2010.
18 Migliaccio and Raskauskas, 2016.
19 Bird, 2020; Farzan, 2019.
20 U.S. Department of Justice, 2017.
21 Donoghue et al., 2015; Guerra et al., 2011.
22 Pascoe, 2011.
23 Faris and Felmlee, 2011.
24 Swearer and Hymel, 2015.
25 Derber and Magrass, 2017.

REFERENCES

Bird, Sophie. 2020. "Almost 25% of Parents in Kent Say Their Child's School Didn't Handle Bullying Situations to Their Satisfaction." *KentOnline*, July 6. www.kentonline.co.uk.

Bronfenbrenner, Urie. 1979. *The Ecology of Human Development: Experiments by Nature and Design*. Cambridge, MA: Harvard University Press.

Carrera, María Victoria, Renée DePalma, and María Lameiras. 2011. "Toward a More Comprehensive Understanding of Bullying in School Settings." *Educational Psychology Review* 23 (4): 479–499.

Cascardi, Michele, Cathy Brown, Melinda Iannarone, and Norma Cardona. 2014. "The Problem with Overly Broad Definitions of Bullying: Implications for the Schoolhouse, the Statehouse, and the Ivory Tower." *Journal of School Violence* 13 (3): 253–276.

Chan, John H. F. 2009. "Where Is the Imbalance?" *Journal of School Violence* 8 (2): 177–190.

Cheng, Ying-Yao, Li-Ming Chen, Hsiao-Chi Ho, and Chih-Ling Cheng. 2011. "Definitions of School Bullying in Taiwan: A Comparison of Multiple Perspectives." *School Psychology International* 32 (3): 227–243.

Coleman, James. 1961. *The Adolescent Society: The Social Life of the Teenager and Its Impact on Education*. Westport, CT: Greenwood.

Crick, Nicki R., and Kenneth A. Dodge. 1994. "A Review and Reformulation of Social Information-Processing Mechanisms in Children's Social Adjustment." *Psychological Bulletin* 115 (1): 74.

Crosnoe, Robert. 2011. *Fitting In, Standing Out: Navigating the Social Challenges of High School to Get an Education*. New York: Cambridge University Press, 2011.

Cunningham, Charles E., Lesley J. Cunningham, Jenna Ratcliffe, and Tracy Vaillancourt. 2010. "A Qualitative Analysis of the Bullying Prevention and Intervention Recommendations of Students in Grades 5 to 8." *Journal of School Violence* 9 (4): 321–338.

DeLara, Ellen W. 2012. "Why Adolescents Don't Disclose Incidents of Bullying and Harassment." *Journal of School Violence* 11 (4): 288–305.

Derber, Charles, and Yale R. Magrass. 2017. *Bully Nation: How the American Establishment Creates a Bullying Society*. Lawrence: University Press of Kansas.

Donoghue, Christopher, and Alicia Raia-Hawrylak. 2016. "Moving Beyond the Emphasis on Bullying: A Generalized Approach to Peer Aggression in High School." *Children & Schools* 38 (1): 30–39.

Donoghue, Christopher, Dina Rosen, Angela Almeida, and David Brandwein. 2015. "When Is Peer Aggression 'Bullying'? An Analysis of Elementary and Middle School Student Discourse on Bullying at School." *Qualitative Research in Education* 4 (1): 26–44.

Faris, Robert. 2012. "Aggression, Exclusivity, and Status Attainment in Interpersonal Networks." *Social Forces* 90 (4): 1207–1235.

Faris, Robert, and Susan Ennett. 2012. "Adolescent Aggression: The Role of Peer Group Status Motives, Peer Aggression, and Group Characteristics." *Social Networks* 34 (4): 371–378.

Faris, Robert, and Diane Felmlee. 2011. "Status Struggles: Network Centrality and Gender Segregation in Same- and Cross-Gender Aggression." *American Sociological Review* 76 (1): 48–73.

———. 2014. "Casualties of Social Combat: School Networks of Peer Victimization and Their Consequences." *American Sociological Review* 79 (2): 228–257.

Farzan, Antonia Noori. 2019. "A Teenager Said There Was a Rapist at Her School. She Was Suspended for Bullying." *Washington Post*, October 8. www.washingtonpost.com.

Felmlee, Diane, and Robert Faris. 2016. "Toxic Ties: Networks of Friendship, Dating, and Cyber Victimization." *Social Psychology Quarterly* 79 (3): 243–262.

Gini, Gianluca, Tiziana Pozzoli, Michela Lenzi, and Alessio Vieno. 2014. "Bullying Victimization at School and Headache: A Meta-analysis of Observational Studies." *Headache* 54 (6): 976–986.

Guerra, Nancy G., Kirk R. Williams, and Shelly Sadek. 2011. "Understanding Bullying and Victimization during Childhood and Adolescence: A Mixed Methods Study." *Child Development* 82 (1): 295–310.

Harger, Brent. 2016. "You Say Bully, I Say Bullied: School Culture and Definitions of Bullying in Two Elementary Schools." *Education and Youth Today* 20:93–121.

Hymel, Shelley, and Susan M. Swearer. 2015. "Four Decades of Research on School Bullying: An Introduction." *American Psychologist* 70 (4): 293.

Klein, Jessie. 2013. *The Bully Society: School Shootings and the Crisis of Bullying in America's Schools*. New York: New York University Press.

Klomek, Anat Brunstein, Andre Sourander, Solja Niemelä, Kirsti Kumpulainen, Jorma Piha, Tuula Tamminen, Fredrik Almqvist, and Madelyn S. Gould. 2009. "Childhood Bullying Behaviors as a Risk for Suicide Attempts and Completed Suicides: A Population-Based Birth Cohort Study." *Journal of the American Academy of Child & Adolescent Psychiatry* 48 (3): 254–261.

Kowalski, Robin M., and Susan P. Limber. 2013. "Psychological, Physical, and Academic Correlates of Cyberbullying and Traditional Bullying." *Journal of Adolescent Health* 53 (1): S13–S20.

Krizan, Zlatan, and Anne D. Herlache. 2016. "Sleep Disruption and Aggression: Implications for Violence and Its Prevention." *Psychology of Violence* 6 (4): 542.

Løhre, Audhild, Stian Lydersen, Bård Paulsen, Magne Mæhle, and Lars J. Vatten. 2011. "Peer Victimization as Reported by Children, Teachers, and Parents in Relation to Children's Health Symptoms." *BMC Public Health* 11 (1): 278–284.

Migliaccio, Todd, and Juliana Raskauskas. 2016. *Bullying as a Social Experience: Social Factors, Prevention and Intervention*. London: Taylor & Francis.

Milner, Murray, Jr. 2004. *Freaks, Geeks, and Cool Kids: American Teenagers, Schools, and the Culture of Consumption*. London: Taylor & Francis.

Mishna, Faye. 2004. "A Qualitative Study of Bullying from Multiple Perspectives." *Children & Schools* 26 (4): 234–247.

Monks, Claire P., and Peter K. Smith. 2006. "Definitions of Bullying: Age Differences in Understanding of the Term, and the Role of Experience." *British Journal of Developmental Psychology* 24 (4): 801–821.

Nielsen, Morten Birkeland, Tone Tangen, Thormod Idsoe, Stig Berge Matthiesen, and Nils Magerøy. 2015. "Post-traumatic Stress Disorder as a Consequence of Bullying at Work and at School: A Literature Review and Meta-analysis." *Aggression and Violent Behavior* 21:17–24.

Olweus, Dan. 1978. *Aggression in the Schools: Bullies and Whipping Boys*. Washington, DC: Hemisphere.

———. 1993. *Bullying at School: What We Know and What We Can Do*. London: Blackwell.

Parker, Stephen, Donna Eder, Professor Donna Eder, and Catherine Colleen Evans. 1995. *School Talk: Gender and Adolescent Culture*. New Brunswick, NJ: Rutgers University Press.

Pascoe, C. J. 2011. *Dude, You're a Fag: Masculinity and Sexuality in High School, with a New Preface*. Berkeley: University of California Press.

———. 2013. "Notes on a Sociology of Bullying: Young Men's Homophobia as Gender Socialization." *QED* 1 (1): 87–104.

Smokowski, Paul R., Caroline B. R. Evans, and Katie L. Cotter. 2014. "The Differential Impacts of Episodic, Chronic, and Cumulative Physical Bullying and Cyberbullying: The Effects of Victimization on the School Experiences, Social Support, and Mental Health of Rural Adolescents." *Violence and Victims* 29 (6): 1029–1046.

Stein, Nan. 2002. "Bullying as Sexual Harassment in Elementary Schools." *Jossey-Bass Reader on Gender Education* 2002:409–428.

Swearer, Susan M., Dorothy L. Espelage, Tracy Vaillancourt, and Shelley Hymel. 2010. "What Can Be Done about School Bullying? Linking Research to Educational Practice." *Educational Researcher* 39 (1): 38–47.

Swearer, Susan M., and Shelley Hymel. 2015. "Understanding the Psychology of Bullying: Moving toward a Social-Ecological Diathesis-Stress Model." *American Psychologist* 70 (4): 344–353.

Thornberg, Robert. 2010. "Schoolchildren's Social Representations on Bullying Causes." *Psychology in the Schools* 47 (4): 311–327.

———. 2011. "'She's Weird!'—The Social Construction of Bullying in School: A Review of Qualitative Research." *Children & Society* 25 (4): 258–267.

Turner, Michael G., M. Lyn Exum, Robert Brame, and Thomas J. Holt. 2013. "Bullying Victimization and Adolescent Mental Health: General and Typological Effects across Sex." *Journal of Criminal Justice* 41 (1): 53–59.

U.S. Department of Justice, Bureau of Justice Statistics. 2015. "School Crime Supplement (SCS) to the National Crime Victimization Survey (NCVS)." Washington, DC: U.S. Department of Justice.

———. 2017. "School Crime Supplement (SCS) to the National Crime Victimization Survey (NCVS)." Washington, DC: U.S. Department of Justice.

Vaillancourt, Tracy, Patricia McDougall, Shelley Hymel, Amanda Krygsman, Jessie Miller, Kelley Stiver, and Clinton Davis. 2008. "Bullying: Are Researchers and Children/Youth Talking about the Same Thing?" *International Journal of Behavioral Development* 32 (6): 486–495.

Veenstra, René, Siegwart Lindenberg, Anke Munniksma, and Jan Kornelis Dijkstra. 2010. "The Complex Relation between Bullying, Victimization, Acceptance, and Rejection: Giving Special Attention to Status, Affection, and Sex Differences." *Child Development* 81 (2): 480–486.

Veenstra, René, Siegwart Lindenberg, Bonne J. H. Zijlstra, Andrea F. De Winter, Frank C. Verhulst, and Johan Ormel. 2007. "The Dyadic Nature of Bullying and Victimization: Testing a Dual-Perspective Theory." *Child Development* 78 (6): 1843–1854.

1

The Inflation of Bullying

RANDALL COLLINS

Bullying was once a fairly well-defined phenomenon.[1] Recently the term has been expanded by journalists, by politicians, and in popular expression. What difference does it make what we call these events? The word is being used to cover differing types of conflict, which have different causal paths, and thus very different implications for what to do about them, and for the damage done.

Traditional bullying is picking on network isolates—victims who are lowest in the group status hierarchy, who lack friends and allies and lack the emotional energy to defend themselves. Bullying is a repetitive relationship, the same bullies persistently domineering and tormenting the same victims. The classic version was in British boarding schools, where older boys were allowed to make a younger boy into a servant, carrying their books, cleaning their rooms, and generally deferring and taking orders. Nineteenth-century school administrators regarded this system as a salutatory way for boys to learn discipline; but it often intensified into maliciousness, physical abuse, and commandeering the younger boy's possessions. Some boys became school bullies.[2] The system was called fagging, and the younger boys were called fags; this was the origin of the slang term for homosexuals, although that was not its original connotation.

Bullying is not a single event but an ongoing relationship, that is, a network tie with asymmetrical content: one side bullies the other, never vice versa. It has a specific network location: bullies are not the top of the status hierarchy but midlevel, not very popular themselves, but aggressors rather than victims. Bullying should not be confused with a dominance contest over who is the top-ranking male, which centers on the top contenders, and matches good fighters and leading personalities against each other. Bullying is exploitation by a particularly predatory type of individual from the middle against the bottom. In effect bullies make up for not very good social skills by picking on those who are even worse. Being a bully is not just anybody who fights; it is a specialized role in the status hierarchy, and not a very honorific one.

Classic bullying arises in total institutions like prisons, boarding schools, or camps. Key conditions are as follows: there is no escape from close contact with the same set of people; reputations are widely circulated; and the split between control staff and inmates creates a code of no snitching, which cuts off victims from protection by authorities. The totalness of institutions is a continuum; as the strength of these variables increases, we may expect bullying relationships to be more frequent.

Classic bullying should be distinguished from scapegoating, where everyone in the group gangs up on a single victim. Usually this is someone who is blamed for a community catastrophe or otherwise becomes the center of hostile attention. Scapegoating tends to be a single-shot event rather than an ongoing relationship. The scapegoat might be low-ranking, an isolate, a new arrival, or a cultural deviant; but scapegoats can also be selected from the elite. This happens in scandals, where the secondary scandal—threatening supporters of the scandalous individual with contagious blame if they don't join the condemnatory majority—can rapidly strip even eminent persons of support.

Scapegoating is not carried out by bullies seeking individual dominance but is genuinely a mass-participation ritual of community solidarity, self-righteous Durkheimian unity at its least attractive. Scapegoating tends to arise in tightly integrated communities—not the hierarchical ones characteristic of bullying; in complex societies, scapegoating requires a huge media frenzy to generate a comparable amount of focus and social pressure. It is misleading to refer to all kinds of personal conflict as bullying, even if it does happen in school or among young people. Bullying, as a repetitive, unequal relationship among individuals, where distinctive bullies target low-status isolates, has a very different structure and causality than two-sided fights. Among the latter are:

Individual honor contests: Two rivals square off against each other, whether with fists, blades, or guns, informally or under conventional rules like a duel. Honor contests are almost never top against the bottom, because there is no honor to be gained unless you show you can beat someone of considerable prowess, or at least stand in with them. This is a reason why bullies have mediocre status at best.

Intergroup fights: Horizontal struggles between rival gangs, ethnic groups, schools, or neighborhoods. These can be pretty nasty, in part because the antagonists tend to be mutually closed Durkheimian communities, so they have no moral compunctions against vicious tactics; on the verbal level, they are prone to derogatory stereotyping, including racial slurs. And because confrontational tension makes fighting difficult to carry out in real life, groups are most successful when they engage in ambushes, drive-bys, or ganging up on outnumbered members of an opposing group who happen to stray into vulnerable territory. Thus, actual incidents between gangs or ethnic groups may have something of the look of bullying, where a stronger group beats up on a weaker. News stories about a single incident cannot tell us whether it is bullying or not. Horizontal conflict is not a repetitive relationship of institutionalized inequality, but generally a sequence of alternating tactical advantages.

Another important difference is that intergroup violence chooses its targets as members of a group, not as low-status isolates. For this reason, intergroup violence is probably not as psychologically debilitating as being a bully victim and may even give emotional energy and solidarity. In contrast to bullying, which leaves victims with very negative self-images, intergroup violence often gives members meaningful self-narratives—one of the main attractions of belonging to a fighting group.[3]

Some intergroup fights combine with aspects of bullying, where a weaker group is repeatedly attacked by a stronger group. Instances include school-majority Black students attacking academically better-performing Asian minorities (e.g., in Philadelphia high schools in 2009–2010). But although one side is dominant in the violence, there is an element of horizontal conflict as well, as the two groups compete with different resources—violence versus academic capital.

Insult contests: Individuals bragging, boasting and making gestures about their alleged superiority to others. This can be done in a tone of entertainment and humor, or it can be hostile and malicious, attempting to establish emotional dominance; it can remain contained, or escalate in emotional tone and physical violence. Ethnographies of gangs and youth culture show a great deal of this. Although insults can be part of a bullying relationship, where they serve to maintain emotional dominance, or to provoke the victim into futile and humiliating outbursts, nevertheless such insults are not part of an unequal relationship. Moves in an insult contest are often reciprocal and may be compatible with equality and even a ritualistic form of play producing solidarity. An observer cannot simply classify all insults as bullying, without seeing what kind of relationship it is.

Malicious gossip: This is a form of insult, but instead of being in your face, allowing the possibility of direct response, negative gossip is indirect. Gossip is felt to be more unfair, because it is harder to counteract. Nevertheless, malicious gossip is not necessarily bullying. It does not always, or even generally, take the form of an attack on those at the bottom; often it is an attack on those at the top, and on leaders of rival groups. Nor need gossip originate from bullying specialists. Most importantly, malicious gossip is often two-sided, between factions mutually attacking each other.

Research on children's and adolescent's status systems shows that girls tend to engage in more verbal attacks than boys. This is sometimes referred to as bullying, but before deciding, we need to examine the structure of relationships. Outcomes can be quite different, depending on whether the target is isolated, or herself a well-integrated member of a clique. Girls' two-sided quarrels in the goldfish bowl of school or neighborhood may well be the equivalent of gang fighting for boys, manufacturing a sense of excitement and meaningful narratives for their lives. How you experience this depends on your network location.

Research Methodology Makes a Crucial Difference

There are widely disparate reports on the amount of bullying in schools. High estimates come from using survey questions that ask whether someone is subjected to being left out of activities, name-calling, rumors, teasing, sexual comments, threats, pushing, or hitting.[4] But we have no way of knowing from such answers whether these are two-sided fights, insult contests, or teasing games; or if they fit the bullying pattern of repeated, asymmetrical aggression between specialists in domineering isolated low-status victims. We can tell the dynamics of bullying—and other varieties of violence—only if we explicitly ask whether these aggressive actions are reciprocated; if they are repeated, and between whom; and what the network positions are of these individuals in the status hierarchy.

As it stands, there is no good evidence to suggest there is any more widespread bullying than in the past; conceivably real bullying could be lower, as schools have become more control-oriented. What seems certain is that the appearance of an epidemic of bullying has been created by inflating the definition, so that it now includes all kinds of horizontal fighting, and indeed any negative expressions at all among children.

Bottom Line

Many different kinds of conflicts can take place in closed communities like schools, both in direct confrontation and via old and new media. Bullying has the most severe results for its victims, chiefly because they are in isolated network positions. Other kinds of conflict may actually generate a good deal of solidarity and meaningfulness for participants, albeit at the cost of some physical casualties and organizational disruption.

But bullying can be recognized only if one knows the location of participants in their social networks. Teachers may not have a very good sense of the network and status structure that is the context for any particular event of name-calling, exclusion, or violence. It may seem that the best policy is simply to ban everything that is the slightest bit aggressive or negative. School administrators, who are even further from the action, are even less likely to know the social realities on the ground.

Kids themselves can generally tell the difference between the class bully being mean to an isolate and playful teasing among friends, honor contests, or group rivalries. Officials trying to impose discipline by blanket orders, prohibiting all less-than-ideal middle-class-politeness, may get a certain amount of surface compliance—if they invest enough resources in monitoring. But such authorities also convince the kids that adults are rigid doctrinaires, clueless about what is really going on. The result may be nothing worse than to reinforce the normal suspiciousness on the part of the youth underground against official authorities. More seriously, it may make some kids feel they are being unjustly punished for acts misunderstood by self-righteous adults, reinforcing a spiral of alienation and defiance that is a component of criminal careers.

The practical advice may not be easy to carry out, but it is this: learn the network structure of the group and judge all conflict in terms of its location.

NOTES

Editor's Note: For a response to this essay, see chapter 2 by Robert Faris and John Faris.
1 A longer version of this paper appeared in Collins, 2011.
2 Collins, 2008.
3 Jackson-Jacobs, 2009.
4 Bradshaw et al., 2007.

REFERENCES

Bradshaw, Catherine P., Anne L. Sawyer, and Lindsey M. O'Brennan. 2007. "Bullying and Peer Victimization at School: Perceptual Differences Between Students and School Staff." *School Psychology Review* 36 (3): 361–382.

Collins, Randall. 2008. *Violence: A Micro-sociological Theory*. Princeton, NJ: Princeton University Press.

Collins, Randall. 2011. "The Inflation of Bullying: From Fagging to Cyber-effervescent Scapegoating." *Sociological Eye*, July 7. http://sociological-eye.blogspot.com.

Jackson-Jacobs, Curtis. 2009. "Tough Crowd: An Ethnographic Study of the Social Organization of Fighting." PhD diss., University of California, Los Angeles.

2

The Taxonomy of Harm

A Response to Collins

ROBERT FARIS AND JOHN FARIS

Confronted with infinite variety, every taxonomist must decide which similarities are important and which differences are not. Early plant taxonomists, such as Shen Nung, emperor of China (ca. 3000 BCE) and the Greek Dioscorides (40–90 CE), grouped them according to their practical and medicinal uses, ignoring obvious physiological differences. For Aristotle, the presence of blood was the fundamental distinction, one that, with the exception of the crocodile icefish, corresponds with the structural properties of vertebrates still used in classification today; his tertiary categorization, however, grouped bats, birds, and bees together. Linnaeus's emphasis on sex organs did not differentiate between conifers and castor beans.

Though each of these early taxonomists increased the raw number of scientific distinctions made about flora and fauna, by modern standards they were all "lumpers," to use Darwin's term. Modern taxonomy, conversely, is dominated by "splitters," and not just in biology: beginning with its earliest predecessor in 1918, what became psychiatry's *Diagnostic and Statistical Manual* added at least eighty new mental disorders with each new edition until the comparatively modest increases of thirty-two and fifteen in the *DSM-IV* and *DSM-5*, respectively.[1] Carrying on the modern turn toward splitting, Randal Collins—whose own contributions to the sociology of conflict are enormous—offers a taxonomy of harm, including a honed version of Dan Olweus's scientific description of bullying, juxtaposed with a litany of other conflicts. Here, we offer an alternative conception and make a case for lumping along the way.

The Long Shadow of Olweus

Dan Olweus is one of the few scholars to have created an entire subfield of study, and it is his definition of bullying that Collins refers to above. Olweus's trailblazing research in the 1970s, culminating in the 1978 publication of *Bullies and Whipping Boys*, marks the beginning of bullying as a subfield, distinct from the established field of aggression. Not content to merely study bullying, Olweus also tried to prevent it, developing an intervention program that has been implemented widely in Europe and elsewhere. Today, Olweus's research has been cited at least forty thousand times, and bullying is a multidisciplinary subfield, spanning psychology, education, social work, and sociology, with several journals dedicated exclusively to the topic and nearly a hundred thousand academic articles on it.

Olweus was a giant, with shoulders broad enough for generations of scholars to stand upon. But he was not a god, and if the field he created is to progress it must move beyond his conceptualization of bullying, which is simultaneously too narrow, overly broad, and plagued by tautology. Its widespread embrace led the field to pathologize bullying and ignore its instrumental uses for too long. Today, its popularity is now met with dissatisfaction in nearly equal measure, but thus far dissent has failed to coalesce around a single alternative, leading two prominent scholars to conclude, in 2003, that "perhaps the most challenging aspect of bullying prevention programming is reaching a consensus on a definition of bullying."[2] A decade later, they were joined by other leading researchers in concluding that little conceptual progress had been made and there was still no adequate definition of bullying.[3] In my own work (RF), I sidestepped this definitional debate, resorting to terms like "aggression" and "victimization." But the word "bully" is too entrenched in the popular imagination to cede or jettison, with rhetorical power that none of its synonyms carries. It evokes visceral memories for those of us who have experienced it. So we must define it.

From the beginning, the chief conceptual problem with bullying has been distinguishing it from the more general concept of aggression. It is easy to observe that bullying is different from other conflicts and fights, but it is difficult to say exactly *how* it is different. Olweus's influence is such that every subsequent conceptualization has had to either embrace or at least engage with his original one: "aggressive behavior or (1) *intentional* harmdoing which is carried out (2) *repeatedly and over time* in an interpersonal relationship characterized by (3) *an imbalance of power*" (italics and numbering ours).[4]

All three of Olweus's criteria entail problems, and none are integral to youths' own definitions of bullying,[5] but perhaps most controversial is the requirement that bullying be repeated over time. While repetition may compound the harm done to victims, lasting damage can arise from single incidents as well.[6] Tyler Clementi's suicide, apparently instigated by the discovery that his roommate had filmed and tweeted about his romantic encounter with another man, is one of several widely publicized tragedies that did not conform to the accepted definition of bullying, despite inspiring multiple anti-bullying campaigns.[7] Considerations such as these led the Centers for Disease Control and Prevention to expand its definition of bullying to also include harmful behaviors with a "high likelihood" of being repeated.[8] Left unspecified, however, is how the likelihood of repetition is to be assessed.

By contrast, the requirements that bullying be intentional and involve a power imbalance have achieved some form of scholarly consensus, with Olweus and others insisting that they are *the* central characteristic of bullying.[9] But what conscious action could not be said, at least in retrospect, to have had some intention or goal underlying it? The prospect of ulterior motives means true ones are elusive, nor can they necessarily be inferred from outcomes: the group solidarity achieved by the scapegoating mob could be an incidental byproduct of finger pointing by individuals diverting attention away from their own shortcomings.[10] Power imbalances are similarly difficult to discern, even in the seemingly straightforward case of physical capacities for violence (otherwise there would be no betting on prize fights), as Collins brilliantly demonstrated in earlier work.[11]

Methodological problems aside, Olweus's definition of bullying is both too narrow and overly broad. Too narrow in that it excludes, with minimal theoretical or empirical justification, significant harms that may have been caused by a single incident or by an equal (or even a social inferior, as can occur in digital forums). Too broad insofar as *any* intentional harm qualifies as bullying, so long as it meets the other criteria. Consider the following hypothetical examples involving a popular student, Pat, and a socially marginal one, Kerry: *A)* Pat repeatedly breaks into Kerry's locker to steal money; *B)* Kerry breaks into Pat's locker, finds an embarrassing photo of Pat wearing Mickey Mouse ears, and posts it on Instagram for their whole school to see. By standard definitions,[12] *A* is bullying and *B* is not, even though many teenagers would find the latter scenario to be profoundly humiliating, while none would recognize the former as bullying.

If disagreements about definitions were merely semantic, they could be resolved through translation. But definitions are optical devices that guide what we look at and how we look at it, and rarely does a definition state outright that it is a microscope instead of a telescope. As such, they are capable of smuggling theories into scholarship; arguably that is what happened with Olweus's. Specifically, its requirements that bullying involve a power imbalance and be repeated over time focused its optical lens on antisocial and pathological behaviors, cropping from view instrumental, normalized cruelties—which are less likely to be repeated and more likely to be directed at rivals rather than subordinates. This is probably why it took more than two decades for scholars to discover that bullies are often in fact quite popular, and use a wider and more subtle array of tactics than previously believed.[13]

The Taxonomy of Harm and the Case for Lumping

It is that trend toward more expansive notions of what bullying is and who does it that Collins bucks by adopting Olweus's definition and further restricting it with the additional requirement that victims be socially isolated and perpetrators of middling status. This more restrictive conception of bullying necessitated a recategorization of adjacent forms of conflict (previously thought of as bullying), cumulating in a taxonomy.

Just as spines differentiate cats from crayfish, for Collins social location distinguishes these different types of conflict, and offers the comparative advantage of being somewhat observable (at least relative to motives or power). But it is not easily fixed: status hierarchies are far more fluid than would be expected. High-status individuals are in fact attractive targets of not just gossip, as Collins anticipates, but also other types of attacks,[14] including verbal harassment, ostracism, and even physical violence, all of which overlap significantly.[15] Victims sometimes turn the tables on bullies, symmetrizing what began as an asymmetric relationship. Retaliation is possible in real-life bullying, if not by the definition above. The "species" described in this taxonomy—dominance contests, scapegoating, honorific duels, intergroup fights, insult contests, malicious gossip—can all mutate and interbreed, propagating hybrids that arguably approximate bullying.

But even if we could pinpoint a conflict's location in the shifting sands of adolescent social structures, what purpose is served by using this to "split" harmful acts into a taxonomy? Collins's primary motivation is to forestall "concept creep," or the overuse and expansion of a term to the point of meaninglessness, the danger being that "bullying" winds up describing trivial conflicts and justifying hypersensitivity.[16] Yet for most of the categories described above, there is no evidence that they correspond to *systematic* differences in the severity of damage they cause—the basis of categorization in most criminal justice systems, which mete punishment largely according to the amount of harm done, considering questions of intent and motive only secondarily (sometimes not at all).[17] We have, for instance, little cause to anticipate that victims of boarding school bullies, prominent subjects of malicious gossip, and scapegoats for hostile crowds experience consistently different degrees of trauma.

To be clear, the conflicts Collins describes are not all the same—some are apples, others oranges. But they aren't fruit salad either. To extend what will become an unfortunate metaphor, the messy reality of adolescent conflicts might be better approximated by smoothies, with different flavors perhaps, but often the same aftertaste.[18]

A Thin Alternative

Collins's description of bullying is specific but also *thick*, to borrow Gould's term,[19] in the sense that his reconceptualization not only includes detailed criteria but also approximates a narrative, with a setting (total institutions), motives (compensation for poor social skills), and consequences (further isolation for victims). In contrast, Gould makes a case against narrow, thick concepts in favor of thin, broad ones, with just enough specificity to retain their core meaning.[20] To offer yet another analogy, murder in the first degree is defined as intentional and premeditated, but homicide is simply the killing of a human, regardless of intent, motive, or lack thereof. Thin concepts facilitate measurement, just as it is easier to record a homicide than it is to establish first-degree murder. More importantly, they invite empirical inquiry into the social relationships and motivations typical of bullying (or homicide) instead of building them into the definition. For example, defining bullying as asymmetric and motivated by inadequacy would have forestalled the discoveries that retaliation is relatively likely,[21] that perpetrators are typically high status,[22] or that the desire for popularity motivates much of it.[23]

There is a methodological advantage to adopting a thin, readily measurable definition of bullying, but there is an even greater moral imperative for embracing a broad one encompassing a wide range of incidents. No one will ever mount a national campaign to prevent scapegoating, gossip, or related humiliations, but those experiences should not be sidelined by restrictive definitions and their targets should benefit from prevention efforts. Best to cast a wide net.

However, broadening the concept by simply excising the repetition and power imbalance criteria would render it indistinguishable from general aggression. We must heed Collins's warning about concept creep, which can render a term hollow just as hyperinflation does currency. It must retain some core meaning, which is to be taken seriously. To us, its essence is cruelty, and all of the taxa described by Collins can propagate it.

Arguably, cruelty is integral to the concept of bullying, much more so than power differences, location, repetition, or even harm, which is not specific enough: it is the wantonness, the unnecessary malice, the extra twist of the knife that is degrading, humiliating, and deeply personal. One might object that cruelty is subjective, but unlike power and motive, it is at least readily observable. Indeed, the American justice system has developed a robust legal standard of cruelty for spouses and animals alike, and routinely adjudicates criminal and civil cases on that basis. It is not the infliction of pain alone but its seeming purposelessness that defines cruelty: pain inflicted in the name of some larger commitment embraced by its targets—such as might occur in the course of military training, hazing rituals, or other unpleasantries occurring during rites of passage—is not cruelty. Nor does it encompass all intentional, harmful actions that yield commensurate gains for their perpetrators, for many of them are self-explanatory: the mugging victim does not wonder why she was robbed, nor is she likely to take it especially personally, no matter how traumatized she is. Cruelty, by contrast, defies understanding, and rather than a means to an end, can seem like an end in itself, though often only superficially. But even when cruelty serves some longer-term goal like higher status, it remains gratuitous since there are superior means of achieving it (and, given its ephemeral nature, better goals to pursue).

Of course, equating *all* instances of cruelty to bullying errs by decontextualizing a fundamentally "local," circumscribed process. A cutting remark, never to be repeated, directed at a passing stranger at an airport or state fair has different implications than the same one-off remark about a schoolmate, for several reasons. First, prolonged exposure to their tormentors forces victims to continually revisit their trauma. Second, victims who routinely encounter their bullies risk continued abuse and are likely to live in fear of this possibility even if it never materializes. Finally, the social psychological consequences of bullying to a great degree depend on the audience, or potential audience, for them, and on how long that audience remains in the figurative theater formulating their impressions of those onstage and witnessing the damage to their reputations. Methodologically, it is also more feasible to assess the expectation of continued exposure to a perpetrator than the likelihood of repetition. We therefore conceive of bullying as *acts of cruelty or meanness, with no ostensible purpose beyond malice, occurring between people with reason to anticipate prolonged exposure to one another.*

Conclusion

By now, it is clear that bullying—by any definition—is not inherently pathological and antisocial. More often than not, it is normalized, routine, and instrumental. Yet the alternative conception offered here, centered as it is on the experience of the targets of cruelty, makes no claims about the underlying motivations for it, be they social climbing, jealousy, or psychological pathology. It does not smuggle any theories, or embed explanation. There are many potential reasons for cruelty, and they are better investigated as empirical questions rather than (un)stated assumptions.

Ultimately, this redefinition is unlikely to recategorize most of what we already thought of as bullying, except, ironically, for the hoary cliché about forcibly stolen lunch money on the playground. Most of what involved repeatedly harming defenseless schoolmates would also qualify as cruel. Much more importantly, this alternative encompasses the experience of Tyler Clementi, as well as the smaller, daily heartaches of the teen being ostracized for the first time, or whose attempt to retain honor through fisticuffs backfired spectacularly, or who was asked out as a joke, or who was the subject of a demeaning rumor, or who was shoved into a toilet. These cruelties may look a little different, but they are all of the same species.

NOTES

1. Kawa and Giordano, 2012.
2. Espelage and Swearer, 2003.
3. Hymel et al., 2013, cited in Volk et al., 2014.
4. Olweus, 1978.
5. Vaillancourt et al., 2008.
6. Ybarra et al., 2014; Arora, 1996.
7. Tyler Clementi Foundation, https://tylerclementi.org.
8. Centers for Disease Control and Prevention, 2019.
9. Olweus, 2010; Rodkin et al., 2015; Volk et al., 2014.
10. Small and Cook, 2021.
11. Collins, 2008a.
12. For an exception, see the Ontario Ministry of Education (2020) definition: "Bullying is defined as a form of repeated and aggressive behaviour directed at an individual or individuals that is intended to cause (or should be known to cause) fear and distress and/or harm to another person's body, feelings, self-esteem, or reputation."
13. Vaillancourt et al., 2003; Espelage and Holt, 2001; Farmer et al., 2003.
14. Faris and Felmlee, 2014.
15. Faris and Felmlee, 2011.
16. Haslam, 2016.
17. The Huli tribe of Papua New Guinea, for instance, use village courts (or "worry courts"), which often ignore intent, to adjudicate disputes; while living in the area, I (R. F.) learned of a clan forced to pay significant compensation to the family of a boy who fell to his death from a tree on their land, though it was no fault of their own.
18. One might anticipate that two-sided conflicts would stand out as oranges among these apples, and indeed they are different, but not in their potential for harm. Duels, insult contests, and fights may all begin between ostensible

equals—or, as Gould so elegantly theorized, between those whose relative rank is ambiguous—but the losers of these bouts may experience intolerable humiliation, sufficient to drive them to murder. Absent cultural scripts for face saving (e.g., losers of duels retained honor, provided they survived), the vanquished may suffer humiliating indignities and reputational damage equivalent to that of victims of bullying.

19 Gould, 2003.
20 Gould, 2003.
21 Faris et al., 2020.
22 Faris and Felmlee, 2011.
23 Faris and Ennett, 2012.

REFERENCES

Andrews, Naomi C. Z., Laura D. Hanish, and Carlos E. Santos. 2017. "Does an Aggressor's Target Choice Matter? Assessing Change in the Social Network Prestige of Aggressive Youth." *Aggressive Behavior* 43 (4): 364–374.

Arora, Cristina M. J. 1996. "Defining Bullying: Towards a Clearer General Understanding and More Effective Intervention Strategies." *School Psychology International* 17 (4): 317–329.

Bearman, Peter S., James Moody, and Katherine Stovel. 2004. "Chains of Affection: The Structure of Adolescent Romantic and Sexual Networks." *American Journal of Sociology* 110 (1): 44–91.

Bradshaw, Catherine P., Anne L. Sawyer, and Lindsey M. O'Brennan. 2007. "Bullying and Peer Victimization at School: Perceptual Differences between Students and School Staff." *School Psychology Review* 36 (3): 361–382.

Brixval, Carina S., Signe L. B. Rayce, Mette Rasmussen, Bjørn E. Holstein, and Pernille Due. 2011. "Overweight, Body Image and Bullying—An Epidemiological Study of 11- to 15-Years Olds." *European Journal of Public Health* 22 (1): 126–130.

Centers for Disease Control and Prevention. 2019. "Facts about Bullying." www.stopbullying.gov.

Chase, Ivan D. 1980. "Social Process and Hierarchy Formation in Small Groups: A Comparative Perspective." *American Sociological Review* 45:905–924.

Collins, Randall. 2008a. "Attacking the Weak: I. Domestic Abuse." In *Violence: A Micro-sociological Theory*, 134–155. Princeton, NJ: Princeton University Press.

———. 2008b. *Violence: A Micro-sociological Theory*. Princeton, NJ: Princeton University Press.

———. 2011. "The Inflation of Bullying: From Fagging to Cyber-effervescent Scapegoating." *Sociological Eye*, July 7. http://sociological-eye.blogspot.com.

Cook, Clayton R., Kirk R. Williams, Nancy G. Guerra, Tia E. Kim, and Shelly Sadek. 2010. "Predictors of Bullying and Victimization in Childhood and Adolescence: A Meta-analytic Investigation." *School Psychology Quarterly* 25 (2): 65–83.

Cornell, Dewey, and Susan P. Limber. 2015. "Law and Policy on the Concept of Bullying at School." *American Psychologist* 70 (4): 333–343.

Crick, Nicki R., and Kenneth A. Dodge. 1994. "A Review and Reformulation of Social Information Processing Mechanisms in Children's Social Adjustment." *Psychological Bulletin* 115:74–101.

Duffy, Amanda L., Sarah Penn, Drew Nesdale, and Melanie J. Zimmer-Gembeck. 2017. "Popularity: Does It Magnify Associations between Popularity Prioritization and the Bullying and Defending Behavior of Early Adolescent Boys and Girls?" *Social Development* 26 (2): 263–277.

Espelage, Dorothy L. 2014. "Ecological Theory: Preventing Youth Bullying, Aggression, and Victimization." *Theory into Practice* 53 (4): 257–264.

Espelage, Dorothy L., and Melissa K. Holt. 2001. "Bullying and Victimization during Early Adolescence: Peer Influences and Psychosocial Correlates." *Journal of Emotional Abuse* 2 (2–3): 123–142.

Espelage, Dorothy L., and Susan M. Swearer. 2003. "Research on School Bullying and Victimization: What Have We Learned and Where Do We Go from Here?" *School Psychology Review* 32 (3): 365–383.

Farmer, Thomas W., David B. Estell, Jennifer L. Bishop, Keri K. O'Neal, and Beverley D. Cairns. 2003. "Rejected Bullies or Popular Leaders? The Social Relations of Aggressive Subtypes of Rural African American Early Adolescents." *Developmental Psychology* 39 (6): 992–1004.

Faris, Robert, and Susan Ennett. 2012. "Adolescent Aggression: The Role of Peer Group Status Motives, Peer Aggression, and Group Characteristics." *Social Networks* 34 (4): 371–378.

Faris, Robert, and Diane Felmlee. 2011. "Status Struggles: Network Centrality and Gender Segregation in Same- and Cross-Gender Aggression." *American Sociological Review* 76 (1): 48–73.

———. 2014. "Casualties of Social Combat: School Networks of Peer Victimization and Their Consequences." *American Sociological Review* 79 (2): 228–257.

———. 2018. "Best Friends for Now: Friendship Network Stability and Adolescents' Life Course Goals." In *Social Networks and the Life Course: Integrating the Development of Human Lives and Social Relational Networks*, vol. 2, edited by D. F. Alwin, D. H. Felmlee, and D. A. Kreager, 185–203. Basel: Springer.

Faris, Robert, Diane Felmlee, and Cassie McMillan. 2020. "With Friends Like These: Aggression from Amity and Equivalence." *American Journal of Sociology* 126 (3): 673–713.

Fekkes, Minne, Frans We.M. Pijpers, A. Miranda Fredriks, Ton Vogels, and S. Pauline Verloove-Vanhorick. 2006. "Do Bullied Children Get Ill, or Do Ill Children Get Bullied? A Prospective Cohort Study on the Relationship between Bullying and Health-Related Symptoms." *Pediatrics* 117 (5): 1568–1574.

Goldbaum, Suzanne, Wendy M. Craig, Debra Pepler, and Jennifer Connolly. 2003. "Developmental Trajectories of Victimization: Identifying Risk and Protective Factors." *Journal of Applied School Psychology* 19 (2): 139–156.

Gould, Roger V. 2003. *Collision of Wills: How Ambiguity about Social Rank Breeds Conflict*. Chicago: University of Chicago Press.

Hartl, Amy C., Brett Laursen, Stéphane Cantin, and Frank Vitaro. 2020. "A Test of the Bistrategic Control Hypothesis of Adolescent Popularity." *Child Development* 91 (3): e635–e648.

Haslam, Nick. 2016. "Concept Creep: Psychology's Expanding Concepts of Harm and Pathology." *Psychological Inquiry* 27 (1): 1–17.

Hawley, Patricia H., and Anne Williford. 2015. "Articulating the Theory of Bullying Intervention Programs: Views from Social Psychology, Social Work, and Organizational Science." *Journal of Applied Developmental Psychology* 37:3–15.

Huitsing, Gijs, René Veenstra, Miia Sainio, and Christina Salmivalli. 2012. "'It Must Be Me' or 'It Could Be Them?' The Impact of the Social Network Position of Bullies and Victims on Victims' Adjustment." *Social Networks* 34 (4): 379–386.

Hymel, Shelley, Susan Swearer, Patricia McDougall, Dorothy Espelage, and Catherine Bradshaw. 2013. "Four Decades of Research on Bullying: What Have We Learned and How Can We Move the Field Forward?" Symposium, Society for Research in Child Development, Seattle.

Jackson-Jacobs, Curtis. 2009. "Tough Crowd: An Ethnographic Study of the Social Organization of Fighting." PhD diss., University of California, Los Angeles.

Janssen, Ian, Wendy M. Craig, William F. Boyce, and William Pickett. 2004. "Associations between Overweight and Obesity with Bullying Behaviors in School-Aged Children." *Pediatrics* 113 (5): 1187–1194.

Kawa, Shadia, and James Giordano. 2012. "A Brief Historicity of the Diagnostic and Statistical Manual of Mental Disorders: Issues and Implications for the Future of Psychiatric Canon and Practice." *Philosophy, Ethics, and Humanities in Medicine* 7 (2): 1–9.

Kendrick, Kristin, Göran Jutengren, and Håkan Stattin. 2012. "The Protective Role of Supportive Friends against Bullying Perpetration and Victimization." *Journal of Adolescence* 35 (4): 1069–1080.

Li, Yan, and Michelle F. Wright. 2014. "Adolescents' Social Status Goals: Relationships to Social Status Insecurity, Aggression, and Prosocial Behavior." *Journal of Youth and Adolescence* 43 (1): 146–160.

Malamut, Sarah T., Molly Dawes, and Hongling Xie. 2018. "Characteristics of Rumors and Rumor Victims in Early Adolescence: Rumor Content and Social Impact." *Social Development* 27 (3): 601–618.

Mishna, Faye. 2003. "Learning Disabilities and Bullying: Double Jeopardy." *Journal of Learning Disabilities* 36 (4): 336–347.

Monks, Claire P., Peter K. Smith, and John Swettenham. 2005. "The Psychological Correlates of Peer Victimization in Preschool: Social Cognitive Skills, Executive Function and Attachment Profiles." *Aggressive Behavior* 31: 571–588.

Moody, James, Wendy D. Brynildsen, D. Wayne Osgood, Mark E. Feinberg, and Scott Gest. 2011. "Popularity Trajectories and Substance Use in Early Adolescence." *Social Networks* 33 (2): 101–112.

Moon, Byongook, Hye-Won Hwang, and John D. McCluskey. 2011. "Causes of School Bullying: Empirical Test of a General Theory of Crime, Differential Association Theory, and General Strain Theory." *Crime & Delinquency* 57 (6): 849–877.

Ojala, Kris, and Drew Nesdale. 2004. "Bullying and Social Identity: The Effects of Group Norms and Distinctiveness Threat on Attitudes towards Bullying." *British Journal of Developmental Psychology* 22 (1): 19–35.

Ojanen, Tiina, and Findley-Van Nostrand. 2014. "Social Goals, Aggression, Peer Preference, and Popularity: Longitudinal Links during Middle School." *Developmental Psychology* 50 (8): 2134–2143.

Olweus, Dan. 1978. *Aggression in the Schools: Bullies and Whipping Boys*. Washington, DC: Hemisphere.

———. 1980. "Familial and Temperamental Determinants of Aggressive Behavior in Adolescent Boys: A Causal Analysis." *Developmental Psychology* 16 (6): 644–660.

———. 2010. "Understanding and Researching Bullying: Some Critical Issues." In *Handbook of Bullying in Schools: An International Perspective*, edited by Shane R. Jimerson, Susan M. Swearer, and Dorothy L. Espelage, 9–34. New York: Routledge.

Ontario Ministry of Education. 2020. "Bullying Awareness and Prevention Week." November 17. www.edu.gov.on.ca.

Parker, Jeffrey G., Christine M. Low, Alisha R. Walker, and Bridget K. Gamm. 2005. "Friendship Jealousy in Young Adolescents: Individual Differences and Links to Sex, Self-Esteem, Aggression, and Social Adjustment." *Developmental Psychology* 41 (1): 235–250.

Peets, Kätlin, and Ernest V. E. Hodges. 2014. "Is Popularity Associated with Aggression toward Socially Preferred or Marginalized Targets?" *Journal of Experimental Child Psychology* 124: 112–123.

Pellegrini, Anthony D. 2012. "Bullying, Victimization, and Sexual Harassment during the Transition to Middle School." *Educational Psychologist* 37: 151–163.

Pellegrini, Anthony D., and Maria Bartini. 2000. "A Longitudinal Study of Bullying, Victimization, and Peer Affiliation during the Transition from Primary School to Middle School." *American Educational Research Journal* 37 (3): 699–725.

Rodkin, Philip C., Dorothy L. Espelage, and Laura D. Hanish. 2015. "A Relational Framework for Understanding Bullying: Developmental Antecedents and Outcomes." *American Psychologist* 70 (4): 311–321.

Roland, Erling, and David Galloway. 2002. "Classroom Influences on Bullying." *Educational Research* 44: 299–312.

Salmivalli, Christina. 2010. "Bullying and the Peer Group: A Review." *Aggression and Violent Behavior* 15 (2): 112–120.

Salmivalli, Christina, and Kätlin Peets. 2008. "Bullies, Victims, and Bully–Victim Relationships." In *Handbook of Peer Interactions, Relationships, and Groups*, edited by William M. Bukowski, Brett Laursen, and Kenneth H. Rubin, 322–340. New York: Guilford.

Sijtsema, Jelle J., René Veenstra, Siegwart Lindenberg, and Christina Salmivalli. 2009. "Empirical Test of Bullies' Status Goals: Assessing Direct Goals, Aggression, and Prestige." *Aggressive Behavior* 35 (1): 57–67.

Small, Mario L., and Jenna M. Cook. 2021. "Using Interviews to Understand Why: Challenges and Strategies in the Study of Motivated Action." *Sociological Methods & Research*. doi:10.1177/0049124121995552.

Smith, Jeffrey A., and Robert Faris. 2015. "Movement without Mobility: Adolescent Status Hierarchies and the Contextual Limits of Cumulative Advantage." *Social Networks* 40: 139–153.

Tolsma, Jochem, Ioana van Deurzen, Tobias H. Stark, and René Veenstra. 2013. "Who Is Bullying Whom in Ethnically Diverse Primary Schools? Exploring Links between Bullying, Ethnicity, and Ethnic Diversity in Dutch Primary Schools." *Social Networks* 35 (1): 51–61.

Ttofi, Maria M., and David P. Farrington. 2008. "Bullying: Short-Term and Long-Term Effects, and the Importance of Defiance Theory in Explanation and Prevention." *Victims and Offenders* 3 (2–3): 289–312.

Vaillancourt, Tracy, Shelley Hymel, and Patricia McDougall. 2003. "Bullying Is Power: Implications for School-Based Intervention Strategies." *Journal of Applied School Psychology* 19 (2): 157–176.

Vaillancourt, Tracy, Patricia McDougall, Shelley Hymel, Amanda Krygsman, Jessie Miller, Kelley Stiver, and Clinton Davis. 2008. "Bullying: Are Researchers and Children/Youth Talking about the Same Thing?" *International Journal of Behavioral Development* 32 (6): 486–495.

Veenstra, René, Siegwart Lindenberg, Bonne J. H. Zijlstra, Andrea F. De Winter, Frank C. Verhulst, and Johan Ormel. 2007. "The Dyadic Nature of Bullying and Victimization: Testing a Dual-Perspective Theory." *Child Development* 78 (6): 1843–1854.

Volk, Anthony A., Andrew V. Dane, and Zopito A. Marini. 2014. "What Is bullying? A Theoretical Redefinition." *Developmental Review* 34 (4): 327–343.

Ybarra, Michele L., Dorothy L. Espelage, and Kimberly J. Mitchell. 2014. "Differentiating Youth Who Are Bullied from Other Victims of Peer-Aggression: The Importance of Differential Power and Repetition." *Journal of Adolescent Health* 55 (2): 293–300.

3

The Role of Status in Bullying

On Murray Milner's Freaks, Geeks, and Cool Kids

AMY L. BEST

Freaks, Geeks, and Cool Kids: American Teenagers, Schools, and the Culture of Consumption, by the recently deceased sociologist Murray Milner,[1] is an arguable classic. Milner answers the question of why teens can be capable of such cruelty and meanness toward each other. This question has long puzzled parents, teachers, and just about any other adult who has had a front-row seat to the theater of adolescent behavior.

Milner didn't set out to explain bullying when he started studying American teenagers. In truth, his intellectual interests could hardly be said to be about teens. Milner's aspirations were largely theoretical. His career as a scholar was primarily focused on building the type of conceptual scaffolding social scientists can use to empirically explain wide-ranging social phenomena. Milner's real fascination was with status, how status systems operate and the status relations emanating from these systems that guide our behavior. For Milner, the insular world of teens offers itself as an interesting case for studying status relations since status is a key resource in this bounded enclave.

In focusing his lens on status relations, Milner offers a new understanding of a familiar phenomenon, bullying. The book provides a useful conceptual roadmap helping us to see the organizational and behavioral contexts rife for aggressive behavior. Bullying has long been parcel to the collective life of adolescence. This we know. Films and TV have catalogued the sordid cruelties exacted upon the American teen by the American teen for decades. The bully and the bullied are an easily recognizable pair, endlessly recycled for a viewing audience. For the sociologist, most portrayals of bullying tend to be overly individualistic, sometimes appearing in the form of narrow psychological portraits, other times explained away with roughshod biological snapshots. As appealingly familiar each may be for a general audience, neither reckons with how fully bullying operates as a social phenomenon. Milner offers a corrective, explaining that bullying is a consequence of a complex status system by which teens vie for recognition, visibility, and rank by peers, derive membership in groups, and solidify group identity by excluding others.

Milner's formulation begins with a few key working assumptions. For one, adolescents hold little if any political or economic power, even as they gain greater autonomy. They are essentially disenfranchised and dependent. They can't vote, their participation in the labor market is consigned to its lowest paying sectors, most are ineligible to drive, and many live under the silencing cloak of local curfews, constrained by the close-fisted clutch of parents' purse strings. Teachers control grades, and students have little recourse against an unfair teacher. In the absence of any real power, status, which is largely a symbolic good, ascends in significance. For Milner "status is the only meaningful power available to them" (192), and in that context "social pressure to put people down is strong" (192). Gossip, smack talk, and other means by which small cruelties are conveyed are a direct consequence of the absence of other forms of power. Status's hold over what Milner terms "crowds and cliques" (status groups) is exacerbated by the fact that adolescents experience a high degree of age segregation. A day spent in school amounts to a day largely spent with peers. In this context, the peer group emerges as a primary reference group, and peer evaluation becomes singularly important. Left to their own devices, teens essentially construct their own status system.

What can we learn about the social organization of bullying by paying attention to the structure of status relations? For Milner, bullying is a result of structural location and the status conferred by it. "The isolation of the people at the bottom is largely a function of social location" (91), writes Milner. "If everybody 'reaches up' and you are on the bottom, there is no one below attempting to establish relationships with you" (91). "Those at the bottom are seen as not only lowly, but degraded. Accordingly, they are avoided and often harassed and victimized. Whatever the sources and mechanisms of rejection and isolation of the lowest strata, the result in high schools is a social world in which the lowest status students are deprived of many of the things available to other students" (91).

On some basic level we already know this. We watched it play out over and over in high school as we moved through lunch lines and hallways, carefully distancing ourselves from those unlucky souls consigned to the very bottom. Perhaps we even experienced it directly, keeping our head down, trying to avert scrutiny, buying our time until graduation. If Milner's theory holds, and many sociologists agree it does, then mapping the status hierarchy of a school is likely to reveal who are the bullied and also point us to its primary offenders. But that's not what is actually so important, nor so interesting about Milner's theory of status relations. Rather its value lies in its explanatory riches. Milner explains why bullying happens, how it happens, and under what conditions it emerges.

We know from the social science literature that bullying in teen worlds follows a pattern. It is most common between seventh and ninth grades and recedes in frequency in the final years of high school. Milner's conceptual model explains why. Seventh to ninth grade is a period when status and respect are relatively scarce, not easily conferred (95). This, Milner explains, creates a situation of competition, whereby individuals and groups compete to accumulate status. The problem, however, is status is finite. It is, in Milner's terms, *inexpansible*. As someone moves up the ladder, someone else must move down. Status, then, is a resource with clear limits. The inexpansibility of status "accentuates the likelihood of conflict because for someone to claim more honor usually requires reducing the honor of someone else" (208). This idea, that there is only so much status to go around, is a core component of Milner's theory of status relations. In this context, teens direct their wrath toward relative equals and not those on the lowest ladder rung because they are "competing for an inexpansible resource" (90). Bullying behavior arises in this context and explains why friends can turn on each other.

Unlike other types of power, status is a relational good. It must be bestowed. It cannot be claimed or taken, only gifted by others. It is *inalienable*. "It resides in other people's mind" (32), explains Milner. To state that status is inalienable is to suggest status cannot be easily transformed into something else. It doesn't convert into other forms of power, at least not in the short term. And it can't be substituted by other resources. For example, a high GPA or admission to an elite university cannot be immediately traded in for greater status. By extension, it is not easily transferrable from one person to the other.

In Milner's formulation, status, both inalienable and inexpansible, is derived from two primary sources: *conformity* to social norms and *associations*. Conforming to social norms of the group serves as a basis for status, and it also explains why group norms in high school tend be ever-changing. A complex tangle of increasingly obscure social norms and rituals makes it difficult for outsiders to break through, hence the challenge new students face. *Conformity* to group norms is a key status source. This creates pressure to protect accrued status by complicating the norms, making them more intricate, more elaborate so they become more difficult for those who aren't in the know to follow. That fashion trends, youth styles and slang, and other symbols of cool are ever changing and often prove elusive provides an example.

At the same time, rigid conformity to group norms can also foment a host of conflicts and problems, especially in settings marked by a high level of homogeneity. For teens whose social identities can be stigmatized or marginalized, like LGBTQ or gender-nonconforming youth, religious or ethnoracial minorities, settings where a high level of conformity is normative, life can be precarious and unsafe. The demands of gender or heteronormative conformity can incite in-group hostility toward the out-group, create a deep sense of alienation and existential angst for those on the margins, and intensify the likelihood of being targeted by bullies.

The second source of status is *associations*. Whom you eat lunch with, sit beside in class, party with on weekends express and determine status position. Milner explains that "high school status requires the careful management of social distance and intimacy" (90). Food, for instance, is an important symbol of friendships and group bonds. "Food not only symbolizes established intimacy and solidarity, but can also be a means to establish these" (69). That a high-ranking student is unwilling to share a coveted food item in the cafeteria with just anyone is because the intimacy of the connection and status is on full display. Teens' preoccupation with accruing status manifests in a rigid caste-like status system most visible at the lunchroom table. Elaborate and complicated rituals and norms ensure rigid group boundaries, dampening the possibility of association across status unequals, while also strengthening in-group ties. The more intimate the ritual, the greater the distance between status unequals.

Milner did not live long enough to see the seismic migration of social life to mediated online worlds, only its beginnings. Were Milner to apply his theory of status relations to the online world of Snapchat, TikTok, and Instagram, online platforms where teens cluster, he likely would note that status conferral and status displays are publicly communicated by the same logics as the offline, face-to-face interaction of brick-and-mortar schools. The online mediated space where teens can be found are bounded enclaves, and the rules of engagement are largely mediated by status concerns. Conformity and association are the primary mechanisms by which status is parsed and elaborate rituals of contact pattern exchanges between teens. Whether someone receive "likes," multiple heart emojis, or a more elaborate-worded affirmation depends upon the associational tie shared between the posting teen and the responding teen. A high-status girl is not likely to provide a lengthy response to a post by a lower-status girl. A 2015 *This American Life* episode, "Status Updates," hosted by Ira Glass, provides a wonderfully detailed exploration of status and the self in girls' online worlds, decoding the subtle and indirect ways status updates are both communicated and deciphered. Milner would likely also have noted two confounding factors that distinguish the status relations online from face-to-face, with consequences for understanding the insidious nature of online bullying. In online settings, bullying can operate anonymously, which is often more pernicious and more difficult to trace back to a single offending individual, making the bullying seem more diffuse and all pervading. Online interactions also tend to follow you home. The status struggles weighing a teen down at school are no longer left at the school door. Now, the 24-7 cycle of online information and updates in peer worlds can engulf a teen at home and leave few avenues for escape or tune out.

Online or not, membership symbols mark the boundaries between cliques and crowds. Shared activities and rituals operate as a basis of solidarity within groups and exacerbate the dividing lines between groups. Claims to space, central to group identity and membership, also operate as critical ground for conflicts between status groups, which explains why rival groups often vie for the same table in the lunchroom or the back of the bus, and lower-status students are quickly ousted from specific areas. These spaces are assigned a quasi-sacred status by clique members, and the presence of lower-status students threatens to pollute the space and by extension the group. Those with higher status tend to temper their interactions with those holding lesser status for this reason. Avoidance rituals communicate disassociation.

There are exceptions to this rule, of course. *Instrumental relations* tend to transcend or suspend status consideration. Consider teacher-assigned class projects, which can bring together a cross-section of individuals from different cliques, each with a different status ranking with little conflict arising. This is because instrumental relations are task oriented. They are limited to the task at hand, emotional bonds are absent, and the end goal is the glue that holds the group together. The group dissolves when the end goal is reached. The stakes are low in these encounters and the status order remains unshaken. School administrators intent on reducing the prevalence of bullying may find success in building more frequent instrumental ties among students. Field days, when students are assembled to compete as teams, tend to be appealing to school officials precisely because they build solidarity among the whole and diminish the preponderance of crowds and cliques, at least temporarily.

Expressive relations, in contrast, tend to be accompanied by high levels of intimacy. The more intimate the relation the less likelihood of contact between individuals from different status groups. Emotional bonds are the glue that holds the group together. "The more intimate an expressive relationship, the more associations are socially regulated" (64). In school contexts among teens "these are the kinds of associations that most affect and symbolize one's status" (64). Milner cautions that we should not hold our breath that somehow intimate expressive bonds will magically cease because we will them away. Those will endure and indeed should. They are a valuable source of support for students during the rocky period of adolescence. But school administrators should take note—instrumental relations reduce the salience of status and by extension the likelihood of bullying.

Milner is resolute that status relations may manifest in teen worlds but arise because of the organization of them by adults. This is a critical sociological point challenging our default explanation, which tends to fix responsibility to teens themselves, ignoring the role of organizational and institutional context and failing to recognize that individual behavior arises in context. As famed sociologist Erving Goffman once wrote, "Not, then, men and their moments, but rather moments and their men" (3).[2]

Cast as the great fixer, schools are rarely seen as problem creators. Yet for Milner, the salience of status is exacerbated by the organization of schools. Schools are structured to produce specific patterns of relations and behavior that make status more salient. Bullying is not a result of a school's failure, rather its success, Milner asserts. A school's size and structure shape the status configurations of students. Small, homogenous schools, what Milner terms "traditional schools," tend to have a clear, vertical hierarchy. The popular crowds' dominance is pretty absolute. The status system of traditional schools looks a lot like a ladder, with cliques positioned on descending rungs. Milner contrasts traditional schools with pluralistic schools, which are often more racially, ethnically, and class diverse. Whereas traditional schools have a ladder-like status hierarchy, pluralistic schools' status structure looks more like a lattice or a grid. This is because there is little consensus on rankings or the basis of status. Rankings occur and cliques form, but they are more divergent with multiple status systems in evidence. In both school formations, mobility upward is constrained. But bullying is less likely to flourish in pluralistic settings. Milner's work did not focus on questions of race and racial injustice, but we can take lessons from his theory of status relations to understand the racial organization of bullying. Racially motivated bullying for Milner would likely be explained in terms of a perception of status threat. We could predict that in settings where a status threat is perceived by whites, white supremacist rhetoric would intensify, for example.

Milner also identifies a direct link between teen status concerns and consumer society's expansion, pointing to the critical part of adolescent status systems to society beyond school. American teens are an important and sizable consumer market, after all. "The structure of the American secondary education—keeping teenagers in their own isolated world with little economic and political power or few non-school responsibilities—result in status preoccupation of teenagers. These status concerns, in turn, play a significant contributing role in the development and maintenance of consumer capitalism" (166). In this sense, Milner's broader interest in explaining the impact of noneconomic institutions on economic behavior drew him to understanding high school systems. The draw of status accumulation among peers drives teen consumption, according to Milner, operating as an economic engine, propping up consumer markets and propelling consumer society forward, which may explain the blind eye and slow response by so many adults to effectively address bullying.

In a Nutshell

Milner's *Freaks, Geeks, and Cool Kids* applies a general theory of status relations to American teens, shedding light on the conditions that create the likelihood for bullying. At the center of Milner's theory of status relations is recognition that institutional settings and activities within them influence how salient status will be. Within the organizational setting of school, status considerations proliferate and ranking abounds. This is in part because schools are age-segregated bounded enclaves and because teens have little other power to exercise. And while some variation by school type holds sway, school itself exacerbates a status-conscious social system. For Milner status systems by which individuals and groups vie for increased status ranking set the conditions for the bully to emerge.

Milner identifies four enduring features relevant to understanding the nature and form of status relations in American high schools: conformity, association, inalienability, and inexpansibility. Status is both inexpansive and inalienable. It can't be traded for something else, and it is finite. These two features of the status system are critical for understanding the social basis of bullying. They explain why teens develop such rigid, caste-like divisions in the first place. Milner also identifies the character and type of the relations that drive status concerns as he hones in on patterns of behavior characteristic of status groups and between status groups. Conformity to social norms and associations serves as a source of status. Status increases in importance in expressive relations and recedes in instrumental relations. This is because of the importance of role association in how status is given. These tools for understanding status as a complex social system offer significant analytical purchase for addressing the causes of bullying and envisioning interventions to reducing its likelihood.

A Parent's Coda

I became a sociologist before I became a parent. And while my sociology is informed by what I have come to learn as a parent to two teenagers, the toolkit of sociology has proved indispensable time and again, helping to hem my own needless worry and offer solutions when none appear forthcoming.

As a parent I have long embraced the idea that it's best to avoid "putting all your eggs in one basket." By this I mean young people should draw a sense of self from settings outside school. Their entire world should not be eclipsed by school. Milner's model explains exactly why we should heed that warning. If your school group turns on you, which they sometimes do, you have other groups to buoy you—be it a rec sports team, a synagogue or church group, a neighborhood pickup basketball group, or friends from a part-time job. I have also watched as the school district my children attend has adopted policy and practice to reduce status salience. This has meant dispensing with some time-honored (perhaps just tired) school traditions: no more academic ranking of students, no valedictorian, no salutatorian. If students want to participate in sports teams in middle school, they participate in rec teams organized at a low cost through the county parks and recreation system. I have watched as the school district has sought to reduce the inalienability of status by fostering a "multidimensional status system," with Science Olympiad, debate team, theater, band, cheer, and sports on (mostly) equal footing. Most district high schools are large and diverse; they look more like Milner's pluralistic schools than traditional schools. The outcome is multiple centers from which status flows.

As a sociologist, I know some of these interventions depend on being in a well-resourced school district, offering a stark reminder of the vastly unequal schools our children attend. In many school districts across the United States where resources are stretched thin, cultivating a multidimensional status system is an elusive goal. Compounding this problem are disparities in family resources. Parents' resources often determine the chance to be in non-school activities. But associational ties exist across income groups. Faith-based centers are viable alternates to school organizations, and mixed-age, volunteer-based neighborhood, community, and civic groups and organizations provide opportunities for teens to forge ties outside their age group within their communities. These alternate networks offer a similar buffer from rigid peer status groups.

I have also observed as other schools commit to reducing status and dampening conditions rife for bullying by increasing instrumental activities through comprehensive project-based learning, ensuring the formation of working groups with membership across cliques. The effect is greater group cohesion, ever-shifting associations, and a softening of the firmly etched boundaries that maintain cliques. The sum total effect: fewer bullies. As a parent, it's easy to get behind that.

NOTES
1 Milner, 2004.
2 Goffman, 1967.

REFERENCES

Goffman, Erving 1967. *Interaction Ritual: Essays on Face-to-Face Behavior*. New York: Pantheon.

Milner, Murray. 2004. *Freaks, Geeks, and Cook Kids: American Teenagers, Schools and the Culture of Consumption*. New York: Routledge.

4

Addressing Queer Youth and Bullying

Sociologically Informed Approaches

MELISSA J. SMITH AND ELIZABETHE PAYNE

For ten years, the co-authors of this chapter have been entangled in ideological battles about *bullying*. Mainstream conversations about bullying (the *dominant bullying discourse*) have been shaped by psychologized, individualized assumptions and belief systems related to youth, peer relations, and the causes of aggression. The questions most commonly asked about bullying include the following: What is the definition? What "counts" as bullying, and what does not? Who are the victims and why? Who are the aggressors and why? How can aggressors be motivated to change their behavior? What are best practices for interrupting and changing antisocial behavior? We have argued that these questions are behavior management questions, and what is needed instead are questions about the ideological roots of persistent, predictable patterns of peer targeting and violence. In other words, how do the mainstream value systems that shape life in institutions like schools normalize and perpetuate various forms of youth aggression—from teasing to peer group exclusion, verbal taunts, harassment, and physical assault? In the context of our scholarship on LGBTQ-inclusive schooling, we have argued that institutional privileging of heterosexuality and binary cisgender categories is an ideological thread that connects teacher education, local and state education policy, K–12 curriculum, and every facet of school life. When institutions are invested in the assumption that all students (and adults) will fit into distinct and heterosexual gender categories, queer stigma is codified. LGBTQ students have no chance of the same institutional recognition and status as heterosexual, cisgender peers, and all students learn the lesson that this kind of social stratification is acceptable and normal.

Regardless of the nuanced ways bullying debates may manifest in published scholarship and academic conferences, when it comes time to craft practical solutions to bullying problems the same tension prevails: Is bullying a problem of individual bad behavior and intolerance, or is it symptomatic of deeper social ills? In other words, do we only need policies and practices to address bullying as it occurs, or do we also need to identify and address cultural systems that stimulate and support bullying behaviors?

The answer to this last question is undoubtedly "both," but it is worth noting that the latter approach is rarely undertaken in on-the-ground efforts to address bullying problems. Our work is specifically focused on school life for LGBTQ students, and in this context intervention efforts are preoccupied with keeping LGBTQ victims away from intolerant aggressors. Scholars have consistently called for holistic examination and overhaul of educational institutions in order to address the pernicious effects of systemic heteronormativity. Such work involves explicit and direct work related to toxic masculinity, sexual harassment, and queer stigma—all of which are byproducts of heteronormativity. And yet this culture work is positioned as an add-on to behavior management priorities such as comprehensive codes of conduct, consistent reporting and investigation procedures, and clear guidelines for how to categorize and punish "bullying" and other forms of aggression. Focusing on these logistical and procedural concerns may help with day-to-day school management, but it also distracts the U.S. education system from reckoning with a difficult truth: the value system that produced the purposes and structure of the K–12 education system also privileges normative gender and normalizes gender-based targeting. We argue that disrupting this value system is not "add-on" work. It is *the* work.

In this chapter, we advocate for *sociology of bullying* as a pathway toward more effective and meaningful interventions. We believe that the ways in which "various behaviours and practices that encompass school violence are culturally perceived and understood will impact the strategies employed to prevent or counteract this violence."[1] We provide a synopsis of our scholarship on shifting bullying conversations away from the psychological and toward sociological frameworks.[2] We then articulate how our understanding of LGBTQ bullying informs our research and intervention work in two areas: professional development and state-level education policy. In both arenas, we argue that in order for schools to become safer for LGBTQ students, stakeholders must invest in developing a culture that recognizes and values gender and sexuality differences. To that end, we promote policy and create professional development content focused on increasing educators' knowledge about diversity, patterns and forms of peer-to-peer aggression, systems of privilege and marginalization, and equity-focused educational practice. We present data collected during the processes of implementing these interventions and conclude with proposals for advancing a vision of bullying intervention that prioritizes educational tools for dismantling cultural investments in drawing lines between "normal" and "different."

Changing the LGBTQ Bullying Conversation

The consequences of heteronormative school systems are dangerous and well documented. Scholars have examined the history of heteronormative socialization in schools;[3] hetero-gender normativity in policy,[4] curriculum,[5] and teaching practices;[6] and relationships between LGBTQ oppression and school dropout,[7] lower academic performance,[8] and health risks.[9] In total, education researchers have produced a detailed account of causes, effects, and manifestations of insidious gender and sexuality regulation in schools, and this body of research makes a case for addressing a systemic problem with systemic solutions.

Systemic, sociocultural strategies for LGBTQ-inclusive educational practice challenge status quo thinking about what it takes to improve schools. Mainstream discourse defines *LGBTQ youth problems* as *safety problems* and *LGBTQ youth* as *victims*. LGBTQ students' futures are most often imagined in terms of risk for bullying, suicide, or school dropout and not in terms of opportunities to pursue ambitious goals within and beyond school. Then, when education officials imagine helping LGBTQ youth, they use the correlating deficit framework to think through the students' needs and design interventions. Anti-bullying policies and practices are used to eliminate safety threats and help vulnerable students avoid tragic consequences. Effective, consistent responses to immediate safety threats are nonnegotiable, but it is only one component of creating school environments where queer youth can thrive. A sociocultural approach to LGBTQ-inclusive schools pursues the goal of opening up every opportunity for queer youth to be intellectual, athletic, and artistic; to make mistakes and recover from them; to be leaders; to build genuine friendships; to connect with trusted adults; to feel belonging in their school. This kind of work involves raising queer visibility and dismantling heteronormativity and cisnormativity in all schooling systems: curriculum, behavior management, extracurricular opportunities, social activities, athletics, facilities, policy, parent outreach, and beyond.

Our ongoing scholarship about LGBTQ bullying pursues three broad objectives.[10] First, we critique and deconstruct the hegemonic bullying discourse in order to identify the ways that mainstream thinking does not fully explain patterns of aggression. This critique involves exploring how and why the anti-bullying industry remains disengaged from reckoning with the relationships between peer-to-peer targeting and systems of oppression. Second, we explore the relationships between dominant bullying discourse and the policies and practices that have gained traction in U.S. schools over the past three decades. We argue that preoccupation with the interactions between individual bullies and victims has resulted in interventions that neither account for the range of aggression that happens within peer groups nor recognize that *bullying is social behavior with social benefits*. Third, we advocate for holistic approaches to school culture change that are in line with sociological understandings of what bullying is, why it happens, and why it is impervious to individualized interventions. In the rest of this chapter, we summarize the rationale for our claims about what bullying *is*; these arguments inform our decisions about policy advocacy and designing educator professional development experiences.

Bullying Is Social

It is widely assumed that bullying is antisocial behavior—behavior that sabotages successful engagement in the social scene of school or that indicates a child's failure to understand appropriate peer relationships. Imagery and narratives about bullies reflect specific beliefs about the personal qualities that bullies generally have in common: they have instability or violence in their homes, experience irrational anger, solve problems with violence, have low self-esteem, are prone to jealousy, and lack empathy. These characteristics are interpreted as personal shortcomings that increase the likelihood a child or adolescent will engage in acts of power over more vulnerable peers (the victims). It is presumed that without appropriate social skills or guidance from responsible adults they seek an unhealthy outlet to resolve their inner turmoil. Research and interventions follow this thinking: the problems that bullying scholars are trying to understand and educators are trying to solve have been defined "in terms of [the bullies'] individual or family pathology."[11]

Power is another fundamental factor in the dominant bullying discourse. Dan Olweus's definition of bullying is widely used in research, school climate instruments, and schoolwide intervention programs, including the Olweus Bullying Prevention Program. He says that aggressive behavior is *bullying* if it is intentional, is repeated, and exploits an imbalance of power between bully and victim.[12] Olweus is referring to an individualized, interpersonal form of power that manifests in behaviors such as physical, verbal, and online abuse, intimidation, and coercion; gatekeeping membership in friend groups; spreading rumors; and other behaviors that serve the goal of helping a bully feel power over the feelings, choices, and experiences of targeted peers. When this form of power is understood as the primary problem, the subsequent solutions are targeted at the goal of correcting bullies' antisocial uses of power, and these solutions can range from teaching bullies more appropriate social skills to assigning behavioral consequences for persistent or escalating infractions. Furthermore, this way of thinking about the relationship between *power* and *bullying* defines the individuals who impose power over others as social outcasts themselves or, at least, in violation of a school's norms and values. Bullies disturb the school atmosphere, and, the logic goes, correcting the antisocial power games will remedy the environment for everyone.

We argue that this individualized understanding of bullying does not encompass the social function of peer-to-peer aggression in school. Bullying is *social* behavior because acts of aggression are quite often aligned to hierarchical power dynamics that are normalized and supported within and beyond school environments, and there are social advantages to claiming higher status in social hierarchies. When youth use aggressive tactics to enforce the cultural rules about who is normal and who is different, they are also claiming a higher social position for themselves. Countless low-level aggressions are continuously serving this regulatory function in schools, and when acts of aggression are perceived to exceed the boundaries of "normal" or "harmless" peer policing (i.e., become "antisocial"), they are labeled *bullying*. Regardless of their severity, all forms of peer aggression contribute to the lessons children learn about "their place" in the political and social order—at school and beyond.[13] In particular, peer-to-peer aggression teaches lessons about the relationships between conforming to gender norms and forms of success including popularity, increased privileges granted by adults, and more open pathways to various forms of school success. As will be illustrated in the next section, all youth (and adults) participate in enforcing white heteropatriarchal boundaries between "normal" and "different," and this pattern of identity policing targets queer gender identities and expressions most severely.

Bullying Regulates (Gender) Differences

School is "a community of actors and actions, where possibilities for violence, for violation, for ridicule are always present."[14] In fact, some forms of violence or aggression are understood to be rites of passage and, therefore, are so normalized that adults barely notice. These "normative cruelties"[15] are interpreted as relatively harmless experiences that teach important lessons about navigating conflict and being resilient *unless* they take the form of a bully imposing power over a victim, which is recognizably dangerous antisocial behavior. Rather than categorize youth aggression as "bullying" or "not bullying" and making intervention decisions depending on those categories, we argue that all forms of aggression—verbal, cyber, relational, and physical; frequent, occasional, and isolated—need to be considered collectively. The entire system of peer-to-peer targeting is evidence of which social norms are being enforced among peers and how severely, how the community draws lines between "normal" and "different," and what kinds of difference attract the most severe social consequences.

The social function of many acts of peer-to-peer aggression is to target and punish social norm violations. From birth, youth begin to learn the lines between "normal" and "different" through their experiences living in a social world that is shaped by oppressive systems. Like other institutions, schools privilege white, heterosexual, gender-normative, middle-class norms, which are maintained through the everyday practices of schooling—including peer interactions. In other words, youth learn what identities, expressions, behaviors, and achievements are most valuable through "mundane and day-to-day"[16] school experiences like riding the school bus, walking to class, sitting through lessons, and eating lunch in the cafeteria. As they move through these daily routines, interacting with teachers and peers along the way, they observe and experience patterns of privilege and recognition, exclusion and discrimination. These patterns teach lessons about which forms of difference are stigmatized and deserve to be targeted and about how to negotiate norms in ways that, hopefully, earn social acceptance and status. Starting in early childhood, young people's concern for being "normal" or meeting social expectations is part of the important business of negotiating friendship groups, and much of this concern is about gender expectations.[17] As children transition to adolescence, their socialization rituals continue on a trajectory that is oriented toward heterosexual gender roles. As youth interact with each other, heteronormative gender expectations are reliably powerful tools for securing one's own social position and making judgments about someone else's.

In 2011, we asked high school students participating in several extracurricular programs in urban, suburban, and rural schools to write down and share with us the bad names that students call one another. There were 113 names that appeared more than once on the lists. Though our prompt to students did not include any mention of gender or sexuality, each of those bad names was some form of (often creative) slut-shaming, heteronormative critique of women's bodies, or anti-LGBTQ slur ("hoe bag," "Obeast," "fudgepacker," "lez," "he-she," etc.). These "bad names" circulate in schools as tools to harm students viewed as gender transgressors. "Bullying," as a concept, does not currently encompass the range of behaviors that regulate masculine and feminine expressions, nor does it account for the relationship between peer targeting and white heteropatriarchal gender rules. We use the concept *gender policing* to better describe the system of social interactions that enforce cultural expectations for "normal" masculine and feminine expression.[18] These cultural standards are dependent on "enduring heteronormative discourses that inscribe a linear relationship between sex, gender, and (hetero) sexuality."[19] In concrete terms: individuals whose sex, gender, and sexuality do not remain within cisnormative and heteronormative boundaries are subject to targeting. In addition to abusing the targeted individual, the social effect of this targeting is to send a message about what forms of identity expression will be allowed throughout the community. Researchers have consistently found that homophobic abuse and shaming girls' sexualities are prevalent and powerful tools for ruining another's social status, and yet they are also so normalized that adults hardly recognize when these things happen, let alone notice how damaging they are.[20] Homophobia works within friendship groups to police and secure acceptable forms of masculinity for boys (and men). It is about more than sexuality and the fear of or disdain for same-sex-attracted people—it is about gender and power and preservation of the status quo. Boys regulate their own and each other's behaviors through jokes, contests, and actions that repudiate traits and behaviors associated with femininity while asserting the superiority of normative masculine behaviors and attitudes.[21] Cultural expectations for girl behaviors are also rooted in heterosexual expectations and the gender binary: to be a "nice" girl means to be "caring, nurturing, sexually innocent/respectable."[22] These expectations are enforced within and across girl friendship groups often through sexual shaming. These everyday gender regulations and low-level forms of violence are the normalized aggressions that underlie the more visibly escalated forms of peer-to-peer violence institutionally labeled as bullying.

When gender transgressions are viewed as clear and egregious, peer aggression intensifies because the aim is to both bring the transgressor into line and signal the social consequences for norm violations to others. Therefore, "we call for a paradigm shift—one that positions the aggression targeting LGBTQ and gender nonconforming students within a broader system of gender regulation that is experienced by all people in all contexts."[23] Redefining the problem as *gender policing* "produce[s] new possibilities for sustainable reform efforts that target cultural manifestations of hegemonic gender, rather than only focus on eliminating overt bullying behaviors and developing tolerance between peers."[24]

In 2013, we proposed a new definition of bullying that addresses the issues described above but still provides enough familiarity to be useful to schools. We wanted to develop a definition that draws attention to the daily violence that often fades into the landscape of "normal" adolescent behavior, the relationship between these lower-level aggressions and the acts typically labeled as bullying in schools, the relationship between bullying behaviors and larger issues of oppression and marginalization, and to present gender as important to understanding bullying dynamics. We solicited feedback from other sociologists working on these issues and amended the definition accordingly.

> Bullying is overt verbal, physical, or technology-based ("cyber," text messaging, etc.) aggression that is persistently focused on targeted person(s) over time. This behavior is visible aggression that has escalated from a larger system of low-level or covert normalized aggression that polices the boundaries between "normal" and "different" in a specific social context. Targeted person(s) are victimized because they are perceived to be outside the boundaries of "normal" as culturally defined within a peer group. This aggression can be a tool for acquiring higher social status in a peer group because by targeting others as "different," the aggressor claims a higher position in the social hierarchy and reinforces the social "rules" of acceptability. Peer-to-peer aggression typically replicates structural inequality, and therefore patterns of targeting are likely to reflect systemic marginalization along lines of gender, sex, sexuality, race, (dis)ability, and class. Bullying frequently reinforces gender norms—ideas about "correct" and "normal" masculinity and femininity. Students who are viewed as having non-normative gender (and by extension, sexuality) are frequent targets. Not all aggressive behaviors between students can be termed "bullying"—some are the result of individual conflict or personality differences.[25]

By redefining bullying in this way, we hope to disrupt the cultural mythology of bullying as a taken-for-granted, coming-of-age experience in U.S. K–12 schools. This definition is meant to create emphasis on the oppressions that underlie "the problem" of peer-to-peer aggression, which will ultimately drive interventions that focus on shifting cultural norms and help to address the "specific ways that particular children, and not others, are continual targets of peer violence."[26]

Implications for LGBTQ-Inclusive Schools

Developing a deeper understanding of bullying is key to envisioning new possibilities for creating school environments where LGBTQ students can thrive. Because *bullying* and *LGBTQ students* are so intertwined in educational discourses, the taken-for-granted strategy for creating inclusive schools is to *stop homophobic bullies*. This is a victimization narrative, which means that LGBTQ youth are being interpreted in terms of the dangers and stigmas associated with being queer, and they can be categorized as a liability or disruption because they "attract" targeting with their difference. Adopting a sociological approach to bullying involves understanding school culture and LGBTQ students' positioning within that, and redefining LGBTQ youth from "victims" to full members of the school community.

We are critical of using anti-bullying programs to address violence against LGBTQ students because this practice exemplifies a pattern of education leaders applying technical "solutions" to complex social patterns. Anti-bullying programs generally include (1) data collection to define the scope of the bullying problem, (2) procedures to intervene when bullying is reported, (3) schoolwide education about what bullying is and is not, and (4) a reporting system that places responsibility on all members of the school community to report if they witness possible bullying activity.[27] If the number of bullying incidents decreases, the anti-bullying program is considered successful. However, this system depends on the bully/victim binary and the narrow, mainstream definition of bullying, which does not encompass the various forms of subtle or normalized peer aggression that polices gender and sexuality norms. This means that an LGBTQ student might never be persistently targeted by a single bully, but they are likely subject to many forms of gender policing every single day and may also be aggressively targeted by multiple peers. We need interventions that take aim at the root of gender policing: heteronormative culture.

Throughout our policy advocacy and professional development content, we argue that school change conversations need to define the "problem" to be addressed as an issue of *culture*. Culture is the system of values and beliefs that shape all facets of institutional life. The cultural "rules" determine who has access to social power and the benefits of that power, and those rules are used to categorize all students and adults into "normal" and "different" categories. If an institution's value system involves rejection of particular forms of difference—like gender differences—then people in those "difference" categories will experience pervasive stigma and rejection. To that end, we envision policy and professional development efforts that focus on equipping educators with the knowledge and resources to recognize how heteronormativity creates oppressive learning experiences for LGBTQ youth, and then take action to dismantle curricula, rituals, policies, and practices that uphold white, heterosexual, middle-class gender expectations. For the remainder of this chapter we describe how we have engaged in this work in two different areas: state education policy advocacy and professional development for K–12 educators.

Data Sources

Data excerpts shared here are from two streams of Queering Education Research Institute (QuERI) scholarship. The first is from our work on educator professional development including two ongoing studies, one on Dignity for All Students Act professional development for Dignity Act Coordinators, and the other on a new Reduction of Stigma in Schools (RSIS) model.[28] The Dignity Act professional development was piloted in 2019. RSIS is a research-based workshop on LGBTQ issues in education designed for practicing educators. We first delivered RSIS training in 2006 and offered it free to schools in New York until 2014. In 2019 we redesigned the model and are now using the workshop primarily as a research tool to gain a greater understanding of teacher engagement with the content. It was piloted in the winter of 2020. The data shared from both studies are from feedback forms at the end of the sessions. The second stream is research related to our public policy work. Those data are from two studies on the implementation of New York's Dignity for All Students Act, which is the state's school anti-bullying law. The first study explored the experiences of key members of the Dignity Act Task Force who advocated for clear and LGBTQ-inclusive regulations and implementation strategies. Participants shared their stories through interviews and in writing.[29] The second study is from a statewide exploration of Dignity Act implementation. The study includes two rounds of data collection, 2014–2015 and 2017–2018. Dignity Act Coordinators from around New York were interviewed by phone. Findings from this study were compiled as reports and shared with the New York State Education Department in late 2015 and again in 2018.

Professional Development

Professional development (PD) about K–12 LGBTQ concerns is often used as an intervention strategy to address LGBTQ bullying problems. The logic is that if school personnel are aware of safety threats and feel empathy for LGBTQ students, they will be more likely to take action against homophobic and transphobic bullying. The limited research about LGBTQ in-service education indicates that schools where the staff have been trained are perceived to be safer for LGBTQ students,[30] and educators who complete training express higher levels of awareness, empathy, and intention to do something about the safety of LGBTQ students.[31] From our perspective, PD that is motivated by anti-bullying intentions is unsatisfying because it defines LGBTQ youth in terms of their vulnerability, and educators are asked to do little more than provide basic safety. We argue that this approach underestimates the capabilities of both LGBTQ youth and their educators and misses the opportunity to engage school professionals in a more complex conversation about root causes of violence targeting gender and sexuality differences and proactive approaches to stopping gender-based abuse.

Our original design of the RSIS PD program in 2006 was an attempt to answer this question: What does PD look like when it is rooted in sociology and research on the school experiences of LGBTQ youth and families? We made a conscious choice not to rely too heavily on schools' legal obligations to protect LGBTQ youth or the shock value of statistics about health and safety risks. Instead, we aimed to illustrate how heteronormativity is at work in day-to-day school happenings and affects the lives of all people who spend their days in a school—and how these social patterns produce the high incidences of risk for LGBTQ youth. Using qualitative research about institutional heteronormativity in schools, we demonstrated how the assumption and celebration of heterosexuality and its signs and symbols is a primary organizational structure in school culture, which underlies the hostile experiences LGBTQ students have in school. Introducing heteronormativity supports teachers in understanding how LGBTQ youth come to be targets and why it is so difficult to stop the harassment in a system that glorifies heterosexuality and the binary sex/gender systems that drive the harassment.

When we originally designed RSIS, we knew that some workshop attendees would need to be convinced that LGBTQ students' experiences are relevant to their professional practice. We admit that statistics about bullying experiences, health risks, and other "risk" data can be powerful tools in such a situation, but we wanted to create a narrative with these data to demonstrate that LGBTQ identities are not inherently risky. *Risks are the consequences of social stigma in a heteronormative society.* A key section of the workshop, titled Stigma and Risk, reviewed the research about LGBTQ youth experiences both in and out of school. Using findings from qualitative research studies, we presented three sites of stigma as key in the experiences of LGBTQ youth—family, community, and school—and we demonstrated that these youth often have no emotional and physical respite within these three primary settings of their lived experience. The goal was to help educators understand that it is not their sexual and gender identities that put LGBTQ youth "at risk" but rather societal responses to their identities and expressions of those identities. By framing "the problem" in this way, we intended to pull educators' attention away from the victimization and risk discourses when they think and talk about LGBTQ kids (i.e., suicide risk or bullying) and shift their focus from queer identities as "the problem" to the larger issues of stigma and systemic discrimination. We frame schools as potentially positive sites for LGBTQ youth, and we discuss their role in creating more accepting communities—rather than reflecting existing (potentially negative) community attitudes.

In our first evaluation study on RSIS, we learned that PD participants latch onto content about safety, risk, and tolerance much more than we anticipated.[32] "Risk" data were discussed for only a few minutes in every presentation, and yet during follow-up interviews (six to twelve months post-training), the participants remembered the health, safety, and academic risks above all other PD content. Furthermore, they repeated status quo interpretations of school ally work that are reliant on safety- and tolerance-informed versions of diversity work.[33] In total, we have consistently found that educators are comfortable with—or at least have the language to talk about—forms of ally work that are related to bullying, harassment, or homophobic language intervention and tolerance-informed mindsets, such as "supporting all students, regardless of differences." Educators' impulse is to smooth over problems that emerge because of differences, not necessarily dig into the cultural roots of problems such as deep personal and institutional investments in gender normativity. One of our major goals of PD is to shift thinking away from "differences shouldn't matter" to "differences need to be recognized and valued."

In 2019 and 2020, we piloted two new PD workshops in which we address some of the gaps in the earlier RSIS training model and expand our PD work to address broader concerns related to implementation of the Dignity for All Students Act (DASA) in New York. One of our priorities for both models was to add content about the distinction between *school climate* and *school culture: culture* is the norms, values, practices, patterns of communication, language, laws, customs, and meanings shared by a group of people located in a given time and place;[34] and *climate* is "quality and character of school life"[35] that is the "surface manifestation of culture."[36] The purpose of this content is to develop attendees' foundational knowledge so they can then engage in *proactive* approaches to combat youth aggression. Proactive strategies involve identifying specific examples of oppressive ideology (i.e., heteronormativity) showing itself in a school's culture, and formulating plans for confronting and dismantling the oppressive value system. Our recommendations for proactive strategies revolve around an overall theme of disrupting bias and stereotypes by teaching about differences, power, and privilege. The more youth (and adults) know about different ways of experiencing the world and diverse contributions to history, literature, art, sciences, and other areas of culture, the less likely they will be to rely on stereotypes and oppressive belief systems in their interactions with people—including their peers.

When asked about their primary "takeaway" ideas, recent PD attendees have often responded that they would like to initiate conversations about climate and culture as part of efforts to cultivate proactive thinking in their schools' approaches to addressing bullying. One participant said they reached the end of the PD thinking about "holistic culture/climate" approaches to school change "versus just the incident management" approach. Another said, "We will be looking for ways to engage in more deep, meaningful and complex conversations about climate/culture vs . . . just process and procedure." Others took up our proposal that having direct and purposeful conversations about differences is a proactive, culture-focused strategy for interrupting patterns of bias and aggression. One participant wrote that they want to "pursue ways to diversify curriculum in an effort to educate in an embedded manner." Others wrote they learned that "talking about and teaching differences can combat bullying proactively" and "we can be proactive by teaching kids to challenge gender stereotypes." These preliminary data suggest that some PD participants are taking in our message that stopping bullying is about much more than effective incident intervention. It is about understanding the social tools that youth use to target one another, tracing those tools to institutional culture, and taking action to (try to) shift the values and beliefs that are being used to decide which peers are "different" and deserve to be targeted.

Another priority for both PD programs was to disrupt participants' taken-for-granted commitments to a traditional, psychologized *bullying* definition. To that end, we included content about peer-to-peer aggression that reflects our sociological bullying scholarship: (1) bullying serves the social function of regulating differences; (2) many forms of identity policing seem "normal" or harmless because they reflect dominant cultural values; (3) normalized gender policing is one component of a system of aggressions that put LGBTQ people at disproportionate risk for more severe targeting and harassment. Written reflections immediately after training indicate that participants recognize the importance and utility of thinking about bullying differently. Educators reported learning about "deeper social and cultural contexts of bullying." Multiple participants wrote that they are taking away new ways to think about the aggression they observe between students:

> I will watch more for the "policing of norms" so I can be pro active.
> I learned a good deal about some of the subtle aggressions that are all around us.

> We need to address low level issues before they build up to a bigger problem.
>
> "Peer policing" was a new term that will help tease out bullying vs conflict.
>
> That bullying is a social issue not an anti-social one!
>
> The association of bullying and harmful words being gender based was an eye-opening connection.
>
> I feel I have better tools to have conversations with students about the root of microaggressions and how society enforces heteronormativity.

These reflections suggest that our PD content rooted in sociological approaches to bullying is making some progress toward helping participants develop a new vocabulary for talking about peer-to-peer aggression with students and colleagues. These data indicate increased awareness about normalized forms of aggression that—along with more obvious forms of bullying—are reinforcing social norms and contributing to hostile school experiences for youth who are marked as "different." Future research will be necessary to determine if and how shifting understandings of "bullying" impact professional practice.

We are cautiously optimistic that our sociological approaches to PD are resonating with at least some of the participants. Ultimately, our goal is for PD participants to recognize that school culture and patterns of aggression, exclusion, and belonging are intertwined. When students say "I don't fit in," it means that their identities and values do not align with the school's and students' cultural values. Lines between "normal" and "Other" are embedded in culture—and serve as tools for placing self and others within various social hierarchies. Bullying is a social strategy used by youth (and adults) to police the lines between "normal" and "different." Therefore, in order to create safe and inclusive learning environments, *school culture* must be the focus of reform efforts.

State-Level Policy

Over the years, our aims in engaging anti-bullying state-level policy have included limiting the potential harm these laws can do when focused on punitive measures and shifting implementation strategies toward the experiences of students disproportionately targeted in acts of bullying. Anti-bullying laws across the United States vary widely in their legislative language and in their implementation policies. New York's Dignity for All Students Act (Dignity Act or DASA) is distinctive within the context of these laws. First, it includes "actual or perceived" sexual orientation, gender identity, and gender expression in the protected categories. Only twenty states include these protections in their student safety laws.[37] Second, the Dignity Act states an expectation that schools will take *proactive* approaches to "foster civility" and "prevent" both discrimination and harassment. Together, these elements provide a language for shifting implementation strategies away from the individualized bully/victim binary, at-risk discourses, and policies that focus on individual discipline and punishment.

We began working on the Dignity Act before it passed, providing legislators and advocacy groups with research-based arguments supporting the inclusion of gender identity and sexual orientation in the enumeration. Enumerated anti-bullying legislation and implementation policies list characteristics of students who have been historically targeted for bullying and discrimination in the school environment. Race, disability, religion, ethnicity, national origin, sex, gender, sexual orientation, and gender identity are all characteristics commonly included in enumerated laws. The phrase "actual or perceived" may be used before the list of enumerated categories to recognize that individuals can be targeted for characteristics and identities they claim or for characteristics perceived by aggressors to belong to the target. In 1996 the U.S. Supreme Court articulated support for enumeration as an "essential device used to make the duty not to discriminate concrete."[38]

Enumeration in state anti-bullying policies represents recognition that acts of bullying often repeatedly target groups of people who are perceived as "different" and that such discrimination is rooted in larger cultural biases and can thus challenge the mainstream bullying discourse where "social difference tends to not be implicated as a significant factor of bullying."[39] The presence of enumeration opens space for conversations on bias, stigma, discrimination, oppressions, and the role that bullying plays in perpetuating social hierarchies that reward conformity in gender and sexuality. This is a conversation that challenges the bully/victim binary and the assertion that bullies are antisocial individual actors. This is one access point to a more sociological approach to state-level policy. Even as state-level implementation strategies often fail to acknowledge the enumerated categories included in their anti-bullying legislation, the presence of the categories in law is a type of ongoing leverage that can be used to push for better implementation policy that addresses the social nature of bullying.[40]

After DASA passed in 2010, the authors served on the Dignity for All Students Act Task Force convened by the governor of New York. The purpose of the Task Force was to bring stakeholders together to develop recommendations and resources for implementation. A great deal of our time was spent during the first year educating Task Force members on the social nature of bullying and challenging their beliefs about intervention. In time, Task Force members representing powerful groups were able to shift their thinking and began strategizing with us on drafting policy recommendations focused on discrimination against those in the enumerated categories including LGBTQ students, addressing school culture, and limiting the potential increase of damaging school disciplinary practices. The Task Force and the State Education Department were at odds. A fellow member of the Task Force commented,

> I believe one of the biggest barriers to the full implementation of the Dignity for All Students Act is that the State Education Department never felt fully comfortable providing clear guidance to the school districts on how to address issues of sexual orientation and gender identity, particularly gender identity.... Why? I don't know, but I would presume the only reason why they never went the distance was because of their own political reasons. They may have been concerned with being too prescriptive in their approach and then being labeled as a hyper-progressive state bureaucracy that is imposing its own set of values and beliefs on heterogeneous school districts.

Ultimately, the State Education Department perceived the shift to a more social understanding of bullying and the related policies we proposed as "political" due to their focus on the experiences of students in the enumerated categories rather than a singular focus on intervention in individual incidents, punishment, and incident reporting.[41]

The State Education Department determined that our insistence that preservice teacher education be part of the implementation strategy went beyond the scope of law. We began to work with legislators who were already drafting a cyberbullying amendment to the law to add in a preservice teacher education component. That amendment passed in 2012. The determination of what this legislatively required teacher education component should entail has been an ongoing debate in the New York State Education Department since it passed. Currently there is a six-hour workshop required. We have continued to provide the state with research on the importance of increasing teacher knowledge on meeting the needs of diverse student populations as central to a proactive approach to the reduction of bullying.

We conducted two statewide studies (2014–2015, 2017–2018) and interviewed ninety-nine Dignity Act Coordinators about local implementation.[42] We found that educators' lack of preparation to address the enumerated categories—particularly but not exclusively gender identity and sexual orientation—and their lack of understanding of what "proactive" approaches to anti-bullying might entail were impeding implementation around the state. Most DASA-related training that educators received had been delivered by school district attorneys and focused on "legal stuff. It was how to report. Going over the process for how to do that" (Dignity Act Coordinator). No participants reported that their training provided substantial information on bullying behaviors or the experiences of students in the enumerated categories. When we asked about the bullying experiences of LGBTQ students in their schools and what steps they had taken under DASA to proactively address it, most participants were unable to name any steps, and many had difficulty responding in respectful language, particularly regarding transgender students. These responses from three participants were not atypical: "I do not believe we have a transgender here." "We did have a student dress as a female to the prom, and, you know, some people were upset about it. But, it is what it is and right from the get-go, I said, you know, 'DASA,' 'We gotta let him in.'" While educators in our research knew that sexual orientation and gender identity were included in the enumeration of the law, much like the State Education Department, they had not taken up that inclusion in their work to implement it.

> Interviewer: What do you think a supportive environment for a transgender student would look like?
> Dignity Act Coordinator: I have no idea.

Most participants acknowledged having insufficient knowledge about the enumerated categories and did not understand how to make them relevant to implementation. "Ya' know, we need to know, um, as far as understanding, you know, the different categories, and um, you know, the different needs of different kids. We could use training on that, around what different people need, and we didn't get that part. It was just defining terms [in their DASA training]." Over the course of our interviews, it also became clear that most educators did not understand what a proactive approach to anti-bullying might look like. Often, when asked about the proactive steps they had taken, the responses were reactive, naming quick responses to individual bullying incidents as "proactive." "They [administration] are very proactive—if anything comes up it's addressed. She [principal] tells teachers they have [said with emphasis] to address every comment, you're fat, gay, she tells all teachers they have [said with emphasis] to say something if a kid says anything offensive, that it's the law." Diligence to incident intervention was seen as a primary "proactive" strategy with no recognition that action taken after an incident has occurred is reactive, not proactive. One educator suggested self-defense was proactive: "We need to model and teach how to treat others as humans, but bullying always comes up. It always happens. So people need to learn how to defend themselves." This is also a reactive response, and individual students resorting to self-defense when repeatedly bullied can have tragic consequences. We believe that proactive approaches require understanding the ways students may be marginalized and then taking steps at an institutional level, as well as a classroom level, to improve. Such approaches must be taught through thorough professional development and preservice teacher preparation. Participants' inability to answer questions about proactive strategies and their misunderstanding about what it means to take a proactive approach to antidiscrimination or anti-bullying work are clear signs of the need for more precise guidance from the State Education Department and better preparation of educators to address school culture and climate.

We have presented our research to the State Education Department with the argument that DASA is not being implemented according to legislative intent because of neglect of the enumerated categories and districts' failure to approach reducing bullying proactively. We have argued, among other things, that new educators need to learn about bullying and the experiences of students in the enumerated categories while in their preservice programs. Placing this content in university coursework (versus the current six-hour workshop) creates opportunities for more in-depth study of antibias education. It provides time to engage future teachers in projects and assignments that challenge them to use their new knowledge to create antioppressive educational tools for disrupting bias, harassment, and violence in school environments and to reflect upon their own biases and prejudices. Studies indicate that teacher development is necessary for long-term school change and effective school change must be understood as a process that occurs over time.[43] These recommendations are under consideration with an expansion of the preservice requirement likely. LGBTQ topics are often omitted from preservice education courses or are pathologized (connected to HIV, suicide risk, etc.) if present, so we have also provided the state with an outline of LGBTQ content that should be included in the expanded requirement. If our recommendations are taken up, in time the education workforce of New York will all have participated in conversations on bullying, gender and sexuality, as well as race, ethnicity, language, religion, nationality, and other categories of difference prior to entering the classroom.

For schools to become more affirming places for sexual and gender minority youth, teacher preparation programs must both include study of the experiences of LGBTQ students and routinely "interrogate the underlying patterns of privilege and oppression"[44] supported by the histories and daily practices of schooling. We believe that ultimately teacher education programs need to integrate issues of gender and sexuality throughout their programs of study—with particular attention to how hegemonic gender norms manifest in the policies, practices, and curricula of K–12 education. These social norms are fundamental to how schools envision the "successful" student, reward achievement, practice classroom management, and execute countless other seemingly mundane institutional procedures. They subtly, continuously teach students the narrow expectations for whom boys and girls are supposed to "be" and implicitly condone the peer-to-peer gender policing that constitutes in-school bullying and harassment.[45] If teachers begin to develop critical tools for recognizing these norms and how they work in schools during preservice training, they will be better equipped to make pedagogical decisions in the interest of disrupting the systemic marginalization of LGBTQ students and creating school environments that value and affirm a broader range of identities. Helping teachers critically examine how schools participate in providing "permission to look at LGBT people with disdain"[46] or sending the "explicit message" that LGBTQ students "constitute acceptable targets" or "simply do not belong in school"[47] is an essential step in the overall project of empowering educators to envision affirming spaces for LGBTQ students and create proactive plans to reduce LGBTQ bullying.

Conclusion

We are deeply invested in closing the gaps between research and practice; therefore, our scholarly interrogation of the dominant bullying discourse is motivated *and* informed by our work with educators and policy leaders. Mainstream anti-bullying programs that individualize the problem or "fram[e] . . . the notion of bullying in a generic manner"[48] simply do not address the needs and experiences of LGBTQ students. Sociological approaches to bullying bring the *social* function of bullying to the surface: it preserves the status quo, privileges heterosexuality and gender conformity, and "reflects, reproduces, and prepares young people to accept inequalities embedded in larger social structures."[49] The professional development and policy work we have described in this chapter represents open-ended, ongoing efforts to translate a sociological approach to bullying into meaningful change in K–12 schools.

In the professional development work, this has involved directly confronting the hegemonic bullying discourse. *School culture* is presented as a frame for teaching participants about working proactively to stop bullying—cultural norms are the tools being used to draw boundaries between "normal" and "different," so institutional culture must be evaluated to determine what identities are being marginalized and devalued. Once this problem is named, work can begin to make cultural change through curriculum, communication practices, school rituals, discipline policies, and other elements of school life. Likewise, our policy work aims to use the tools of state education law and regulations to raise the stakes of creating school cultures that authentically include and value diverse identities. Enumeration creates a legal imperative to account for the needs of LGBTQ youth and other marginalized groups, and our implementation priorities have been focused on the long-term goal of filling schools with educators who know enough about institutional inequities and diversity to take up proactive, culture-focused work. We know that layered institutional structures are positioned to resist sociological approaches to school bullying, but our research to date indicates that—particularly when the interventions are directly communicated to educators—there is potential to shift mindsets about youth aggression in potentially transformative ways. Our future work will continue to challenge the dominant bullying discourse and pursue opportunities to support educators in learning about bullying and addressing school culture.

NOTES

1 Saltmarsh et al., 2012.
2 Payne and Smith, 2018.
3 Blount, 2000.
4 Loutzenheiser, 2015; Payne and Smith, 2019.
5 Blackburn et al., 2016; Sumara and Davis, 1999; Ullman and Ferfolja, 2015.
6 Bower and Klecka, 2009; Fredman et al., 2015; Korth, 2007; Vega et al., 2012.
7 Bidell, 2014.
8 Kosciw et al., 2013.
9 Johns et al., 2018; Johns et al., 2019.
10 Payne and Smith, 2012b, 2013, 2016, and 2018.
11 Bansel et al., 2009.
12 Olweus et al., 2019.
13 Lugg, 2006.
14 Bansel et al., 2009.
15 Ringrose and Renold, 2010.
16 Youdell, 2004.
17 Renold, 2000, 2006.
18 Payne and Smith, 2016.
19 Youdell, 2004.
20 Chambers et al., 2004; Eliasson et al., 2007; Ringrose and Renold, 2010; Thurlow, 2001; Pascoe, 2007.
21 Pascoe, 2013; Ringrose and Renold, 2010; Smith and Smith, 1998.
22 Ringrose and Renold, 2010.
23 Payne and Smith, 2016.
24 Payne and Smith, 2016.
25 Payne and Smith, 2013.

26 Walton, 2011.
27 Jacobson, 2013.
28 Payne and Smith, 2010, 2011, 2012b.
29 Payne and Smith, 2019.
30 Szalacha, 2004.
31 Greytak et al., 2013; Kull et al., 2017; Stargell et al., 2020; Szalacha, 2004.
32 Payne and Smith, 2010, 2011, 2012b.
33 Smith, 2015, 2018.
34 Sensoy and DiAngelo, 2017.
35 National School Climate Center, 2007.
36 Van Houtte, 2005.
37 Human Rights Campaign, 2019.
38 Centers for Disease Control and Prevention, 2018.
39 Walton, 2010.
40 Payne and Smith, 2019.
41 Payne and Smith, 2019.
42 Under the Dignity for All Students Act, each school building is required to have a Dignity Act Coordinator to oversee implementation. This duty is in addition to their teaching, counseling, or administrative responsibilities.
43 Payne and Smith, 2012b, 2013; Terry, 2010.
44 Schoorman and Bogotch, 2010.
45 Payne and Smith, 2013.
46 Hirschfeld, 2001.
47 Adelman and Woods, 2006.
48 Walton, 2010.
49 Pascoe, 2013.

REFERENCES

Adelman, Madelaine, and Kathryn Woods. 2006. "Identification without Intervention: Transforming the Anti-LGBTQ School Climate." *Journal of Poverty* 10 (2): 5–26.

Bansel, Peter, Bronwyn Davies, Cath Laws, and Sheridan Linnell. 2009. "Bullies, Bullying and Power in the Contexts of Schooling." *British Journal of Sociology of Education* 30 (1): 59–69.

Bidell, Markus P. 2014. "Is There an Emotional Cost of Completing High School? Ecological Factors and Psychological Distress among LGBT Homeless Youth." *Journal of Homosexuality* 61 (3): 366–381.

Blackburn, Mollie, Caroline Clark, and Wayne Martino. 2016. "Investigating LGBT-Themed Literature and Trans Informed Pedagogies in Classrooms." *Discourse* 37 (6): 801–806.

Blount, Jackie M. 2000. "Spinsters, Bachelors, and Other Gender Transgressors in School Employment, 1850–1990." *Review of Educational Research* 70 (1): 83–101.

Bower, Laura, and Cari Klecka. 2009. "(Re)considering Normal: Queering Social Norms for Parents and Teachers." *Teaching Education* 20 (4): 357–373.

Centers for Disease Control and Prevention. 2018. "Anti-bullying Policies and Enumeration: An Info Brief for Local Education Agencies." www.cdc.gov.

Chambers, Deborah, Estella Tincknell, and Joost Van Loon. 2004. "Peer Regulation of Teenage Sexual Identities." *Gender and Education* 16 (3): 397–415.

Eliasson, Miriam A., Kerstin Isaksson, and Lucie Laflamme. 2007. "Verbal Abuse in School: Constructions of Gender among 14-to 15-Year-Olds." *Gender and Education* 19 (5): 587–605.

Epstein, Debbie, and Richard Johnson. 1998. *Schooling Sexualities*. Buckingham, UK: Open University Press.

Fredman, Amy J., Nicole J. Schultz, and Mary F. Hoffman. 2015. "'You're Moving a Frickin' Big Ship': The Challenges of Addressing LGBTQ Topics in Public Schools." *Education and Urban Society* 47 (1): 56–85.

Greytak, Emily A., Joseph G. Kosciw, and Madelyn J. Boesen. 2013. "Educating the Educator: Creating Supportive School Personnel through Professional Development." *Journal of School Violence* 12 (1): 80–97.

Hirschfeld, Scott. 2001. "Moving Beyond the Safety Zone: A Staff Development Approach to Anti-heterosexist Education." *Fordham Urban Law Journal* 29: 611–640.

Human Rights Campaign. 2019. "State Maps of Laws and Policies: School Anti-bullying." www.hrc.org.

Jacobson, Ronald B. 2013. *Rethinking School Bullying: Dominance, Identity, and School Culture*. New York: Routledge.

Johns, Michelle M., Richard Lowry, Jack Andrzejewski, Lisa Barrios, Zewditu Demissie, Timothy McManus, et al. 2019. "Transgender Identity and Experiences of Violence Victimization, Substance Use, Suicide Risk, and Sexual Behaviors Among High School Students—19 States and Large Urban School Districts, 2017." *CDC Morbidity and Mortality Weekly Report* 68 (3): 67–71.

Johns, Michelle M., Richard Lowry, Catherine N. Raspberry, Richard Dunville, Leah Robin, Sanjana Pampati, et al. 2018. "Violence Victimization, Substance Use, and Suicide Risk among Sexual Minority High School Students—United States, 2015 to 2017." *CDC Morbidity and Mortality Weekly Report* 67 (43): 1211–1215.

Knotts, Greg. 2009. "Undoing Gender through Legislation and Schooling: The Case of AB 537 and AB 394 in California, USA." *International Review of Education* 55 (5–6): 597–614.

Korth, Barbara. 2007. "Gendered Interpretations Veiled with Discourses of the Individual." *Ethnography and Education* 2 (1): 57–73.

Kosciw, Joseph G., Neal A. Palmer, Ryan M. Kull, and Emily A. Greytak. 2013. "The Effect of Negative School Climate on Academic Outcomes for LGBT Youth and the Role of In-school Supports." *Journal of School Violence* 12 (1): 45–63.

Kull, Ryan M., Joseph G. Kosciw, and Emily A. Greytak. 2017. "Preparing School Counselors to Support LGBT Youth: The Roles of Graduate Education and Professional Development." *Professional School Counseling* 20 (1): 13–20.

Loutzenheiser, Lisa W. 2015. "'Who Are You Calling a Problem?' Addressing Transphobia and Homophobia through School Policy." *Critical Studies in Education* 56 (1): 99–115.
Lugg, Catherine A. 2003. "Sissies, Faggots, Lezzies, and Dykes: Gender, Sexual Orientation, and a New Politics of Education?" *Educational Administration Quarterly* 39 (1): 95–134.
———. 2006. "Thinking about Sodomy: Public Schools, Panopticons, and Queers." *Educational Policy* 20 (1): 35–58.
Mac an Ghaill, Mairtin. 1994. *The Making of Men: Masculinities, Sexualities and Schooling*. Buckingham, UK: Open University Press.
MacGillivray, Ian K. 2004. *Sexual Orientation and School Policy: A Practical Guide for Teachers, Administrators, and Community Activists*. Lanham, MD: Rowman & Littlefield.
National School Climate Center. 2007. "What Is School Climate." www.schoolclimate.org.
Olweus, Dan, Susan P. Limber, and Kyrre Breivik. 2019. "Addressing Specific Forms of Bullying: A Large-Scale Evaluation of the Olweus Bullying Prevention Program." *International Journal of Bullying Prevention* 1:70–84.
Pascoe, C. J. 2007. *Dude, You're a Fag: Masculinity and Sexuality in High School*. Berkeley: University of California Press.
———. 2013. "Notes on a Sociology of Bullying: Young Men's Homophobia as Gender Socialization." *QED* 1 (1): 87–104.
Payne, Elizabethe, and Melissa Smith. 2010. "Reduction of Stigma in Schools: An Evaluation of the First Three Years." *Issues in Teacher Education* 19 (2): 11–36.
———. 2011. "The Reduction of Stigma in Schools: A New Professional Development Model for Empowering Educators to Support LGBTQ Students." *Journal of LGBT Youth* 8 (2): 174–200.
———. 2012a. "Rethinking Safe School Approaches for LGBTQ Students: Changing the Questions We Ask." *Multicultural Perspectives* 14 (4): 187–193.
———. 2012b. "Safety, Celebration, and Risk: Educator Responses to LGBTQ Professional Development." *Teaching Education* 23 (3): 265–285.
———. 2013. "LGBTQ Kids, School Safety, and Missing the Big Picture: How the Dominant Bullying Discourse Prevents School Professionals from Thinking about Systemic Marginalization or . . . Why We Need to Rethink LGBTQ Bullying." *QED* 1 (1): 1–36.
———. 2016. "Gender Policing." In *Critical Concepts in Queer Studies and Education*, edited by Nelson M. Rodriguez, Wayne J. Martino, Jennifer C. Ingrey, and Edward Brokenbrough, 127–136. New York: Palgrave Macmillan.
———. 2018. "Violence Against LGBTQ Students: Punishing and Marginalizing Difference." In *The Wiley Handbook on Violence in Education: Forms, Factors, and Preventions*, edited by Harvey Shapiro, 393–415. Hoboken, NJ: Wiley-Blackwell.
———. 2019. "Insider Stories: Tensions, Resistances, and Missed Opportunities in State LGBT-Inclusive Anti-bullying Policy." *International Journal of Bullying Prevention* 1 (4): 231–245.

Renold, Emma. 2000. "'Coming Out': Gender, (Hetero)Sexuality and the Primary School." *Gender and Education* 12 (3): 309–326.

———. 2006. "'They Won't Let Us Play . . . Unless You're Going Out with One of Them': Girls, Boys and Butler's 'Heterosexual Matrix' in the Primary Years." *British Journal of Sociology of Education* 27 (4): 489–509.

Ringrose, Jessica, and Emma Renold. 2010. "Normative Cruelties and Gender Deviants: The Performative Effects of Bully Discourses for Girls and Boys in School." *British Educational Research Journal* 36 (4): 573–596.

Saltmarsh, Sue, Kerry Robinson, and Cristyn Davies. 2012. *Rethinking Schools: Theory, Gender, Context*. New York: Palgrave Macmillan.

Schoorman, Dilys, and Ira Bogotch. 2010. "Moving Beyond 'Diversity' to 'Social Justice': The Challenge to Re-conceptualize Multicultural Education." *Intercultural Education* 21 (1): 79–85.

Sensoy, Ozlem, and Robin DiAngelo. 2017. *Is Everyone Really Equal? An Introduction to Key Concepts in Social Justice Education*. New York: Teachers College Press.

Smith, George W., and Dorothy E. Smith. 1998. "The Ideology of 'Fag': The School Experience of Gay Students." *Sociological Quarterly* 39 (2): 309–335.

Smith, Melissa J. 2015. "It's a Balancing Act: The Good Teacher and Ally Identity." *Educational Studies* 51 (3): 223–243.

———. 2018. "'I Accept All Students': Tolerance Discourse and LGBTQ Ally Work in US Public Schools." *Equity & Excellence in Education* 51 (3–4): 301–315.

Stargell, Nicole A., Shenika J. Jones, Whitney P. Akers, and Maggie M. Parker. 2020. "Training School Teachers and Administrators to Support LGBTQ+ Students: A Quantitative Analysis of Change in Beliefs and Behaviors." *Journal of LGBT Issues in Counseling* 14 (2): 118–133.

Sumara, Dennis, and Brent Davis. 1999. "Interrupting heteronormativity: Toward a Queer Curriculum Theory." *Curriculum Inquiry* 29 (2): 191–208.

Szalacha, Laura A. 2004. "Educating Teachers on LGBTQ Issues: A Review of Research and Program Evaluations." *Journal of Gay & Lesbian Issues in Education* 1 (4): 67–79.

Terry, Troy M. 2010. "Blocking the Bullies: Has South Carolina's Safe School Climate Act Made Public Schools Safer?" *Clearing House* 83 (3): 96–100.

Thurlow, Crispin. 2001. "Naming the 'Outsider Within': Homophobic Pejoratives and the Verbal Abuse of Lesbian, Gay and Bisexual High-School Pupils." *Journal of Adolescence* 24 (1): 25–38.

Ullman, Jacqueline, and Tania Ferfolja. 2015. "Bureaucratic Constructions of Sexual Diversity: 'Sensitive,' 'Controversial' and Silencing." *Teaching Education* 26 (2): 145–159.

Van Houtte, Mieke. 2005. "Climate or Culture? A Plea for Conceptual Clarity in School Effectiveness Research." *School Effectiveness and School Improvement* 16 (1): 71–89.

Vega, Stephanie, Heather Glynn Crawford, and J-Lynn Van Pelt. 2012. "Safe Schools for LGBTQI Students: How Do Teachers View Their Role in Promoting Safe Schools?" *Equity & Excellence in Education* 45 (2): 250–260.

Walton, Gerald. 2010. "The Problem Trap: Implications of Policy Archaeology Methodology for Anti-bullying Policies." *Journal of Education Policy* 25 (2): 135–150.

———. 2011. "Spinning Our Wheels: Reconceptualizing Bullying Beyond Behaviour-Focused Approaches." *Discourse* 32 (1): 131–144.

Youdell, Deborah. 2004. "Wounds and Reinscriptions: Schools, Sexualities and Performative Subjects." *Discourse* 25 (4): 477–493.

5

Bullying as a Social Problem

Interactional Homophobia and Institutional Heteronormativity in Schools

C. J. PASCOE

Just the other morning, I listened to my favorite morning radio program as the hosts joked around about the day's news. One of them, Vinnie, shared a story about a local high school. The newspaper reported that at a football game the previous weekend, several football players had taunted a male cheerleader with homophobic epithets. "How times have changed!" Vinnie exclaimed. He recounted stories from his own childhood, a time when homophobic harassment certainly did not make front-page news. Rather, he described these types of taunts as acceptable parts of everyday life. Indeed, when he was in school he was just "happy to walk into a room" without friends throwing homophobic epithets at him. In exclaiming "how times have changed," Vinnie highlights a significant cultural shift, a shift in which homophobic bullying used to be treated as normative and unremarkable and is now, in many places, considered aberrant and reprehensible, worthy of a front-page story in a local paper and disciplinary action by a school.

Vinnie is on to something. Times have changed. I have seen it in my own work. Fifteen years ago, when I conducted research for my doctoral dissertation in River High School, a public working-class school in the extended suburbs of the San Francisco bay area, homophobic harassment was not only the norm but fairly unremarkable, serving as regular fodder on popular sitcoms like *Friends* (even as it prominently featured one of mainstream TV's first same-sex parents). Rarely did a day pass during that research when I did not hear a homophobic epithet or watch as, once again, boys made a feminine man the butt of a joke. With the exception of one instance that had more to do with the criminalization of young Black men in schools than with concern over gendered and sexualized harassment, I never saw a school administrator step in to deal with this sort of behavior, behavior that we would now widely recognize as bullying.

That was in the early 2000s. I'd like to contrast those findings with ones from research conducted in 2015, a decade and a half later in a working- and middle-class high school in suburban Oregon, American High School. Walking into the school I was immediately greeted with anti-bullying posters—some generated by the state, others by the school district, and some by the students themselves. Blue posters designed by "SafeOregon" were posted throughout the school. They read "Use SafeOregon to anonymously report bullying, violence, drugs or harm you see or hear about at school," followed by a web address, a text/phone contact, an email address, and the name of a downloadable app to facilitate students' reports. When I asked a wide variety of students from different social groups at the school about bullying at American High, they reported that it simply did not happen. From what I saw during my two years there, they were right. I saw very little homophobic or gender-based harassment in the hallways or other public areas of the school.

The phenomenon of bullying at these two schools seems dramatically different. At American High School, rather than walking into an auditory world of harassment and bullying, instead I entered a school making explicit statements against bullying and providing resources to combat it. This distinction could be chalked up to differences between the schools themselves as well as their geographic location. Surely that is part of the story, but the change is bigger than those distinctions. The differences between these two schools also represent a larger cultural shift characterized by declining levels of homophobia and an emergent discourse of bullying that was almost nonexistent when I was researching at River High School.

Measurements of homophobia levels in the United States have shown a definitive decline over the past thirty years.[1] Expressions of homophobia among North American college students have declined relatively steadily since the 1970s.[2] By 2016 support for gay marriage had reached an unprecedented level of 55 percent of Americans.[3] This is a dramatic and rapid rise from Pew's 2003 survey that indicated a level of support of 32 percent.[4] These changes in opinions about same-sex marriage and homosexuality in general are part of a larger cultural shift in terms of gender and sexual norms, especially among young men, a change that has been reflected in national, state, and local policies.[5] It is no longer acceptable to be seen as homophobic, in many social milieus. Part of being a good citizen now is espousing support for civil rights for gays and lesbians, even if that support is uneven, reflecting other forms of gendered, race, and class inequalities.

The phenomenon of "bullying" increasingly took center stage as a social problem during the time period between these two studies.[6] Likely fueled, at least in part, by a concern over so-called cyberbullying, politicians, scholars, educators, and youth workers focused on the issue of bullying as the pressing problem of the day for young people.[7] The White House began hosting summits and a website about bullying; celebrities started foundations to promote kindness and resiliency; influencers participated in campaigns aiming inspirational messages at GLBTQ youth dealing with homophobic bullying; states and municipalities passed anti-bullying legislation; schools and police forces increasingly linked bullying to concerns over mental health and school violence resulted in initiatives like SafeOregon. The language of bullying became, in many ways, the national language for dealing with inequality in childhood.[8]

This chapter explores these changes by analyzing the way gender- and sexuality-based bullying manifests at River High School and American High School. While River High and American High are not an ideal match (nor were they designed to be), they provide two useful cases with which to think through how a focus on "bullying" as the locus of harm can reproduce gendered and sexualized inequalities. I suggest that River High School is an example of "interactional homophobia," or a way that gendered and sexualized norms are reproduced through aggressive interactions between students that we now easily recognize as bullying one another. I argue that what we see at American High School is what we might call a case of "institutional heteronormativity," in which "interactional homophobia" is rendered unacceptable. However, even in the absence of particular forms of bullying, schooling processes convey normative messages about gender and sexuality. Analyzing these two cases illustrates that a focus on bullying locates the harm of homophobia in aggressive interactions between young people and not in the organization of the school itself. This focus on bullying as *the* problem obfuscates the way that schools as institutions convey messages about acceptably gendered and sexualized identities and practices.

Interactional Homophobia

When I began my research at River High School in the early 2000s, I was interested in answering this question: after three waves of feminist activism and significant cultural changes in norms surrounding girlhood and femininity, how do boys come to think of themselves as masculine in their transition into young adulthood? What I found as I entered the school was a world rife with homophobic harassment, something we would now recognize as bullying. Rarely could I walk down a hallway without hearing a boy yell "faggot" or perform an imitation of an unmasculine man. Scenes like the following were not uncommon: A teenage boy yelled to a group of younger students, "There's a faggot over there! There's a faggot over there! Come look!" and led the group of boys toward the student to whom he was referring, who was walking with exaggerated hip swings and hands dangling from the end of limp wrists.

During a year and a half of researching young people's understandings and practices of masculinity at a working-class high school, River High, in Northern California, I documented that boys came to think of themselves and others as acceptably masculine largely through the homophobic harassment of other boys and through heterosexual harassment of girls. In other words, I found that a large part of what constituted adolescent masculinity were practices that we would later call bullying. When looking at young men's understandings and enactments of masculinity, it becomes increasingly clear that behaviors that look an awful lot like homophobic bullying are a central part of their socialization process.

After being struck by the amount of homophobic harassment I was seeing, I began to ask young men at River High about it. In particular I asked them about the use of the word "fag," a word used by boys and directed at other boys. In talking to young men at River High about their use of the word, they repeatedly told me that "fag" is the ultimate insult for a boy. As Darnell stated, "Since you were little boys you've been told, 'hey, don't be a little faggot.'" Jeremy told me that this insult figuratively reduced a boy to nothing: "To call someone gay or a fag is like the lowest thing you can call someone. Because that's like saying that you're nothing." Many boys explained their frequent use of epithets like "queer," "gay," and "fag" by asserting that, as Keith put it, "guys are just homophobic."

However, several boys strongly suggested that descriptors like fag, queer, and gay had little to do with actual sexual practices or desires. As Darnell claimed, "It doesn't have anything to do with being gay." Adding to this sentiment, J. L. said, "Fag, seriously, it has nothing to do with sexual preference at all. You could just be calling somebody an idiot, you know?" As David explained, "Being gay is just a lifestyle. It's someone you choose to sleep with. You can still throw a football around and be gay." David's final statement clarifies the distinction between popular understandings of these insults and young people's actual use of them. That is, they have to do with men's same-sex eroticism, but at their core they are best understood as discursive strategies that discipline gender practices and identities. In asserting the primacy of gender to the definition of these seemingly homophobic insults, young men reflect what Riki Wilchins calls the "Eminem Exception."[9] Eminem explains that his use of the term "faggot" does not refer to sexual orientation; rather, he claims that it simply means that they are weak and unmanly. While it is not necessarily acceptable to be gay, if a man were gay *and* masculine—as in David's portrait of the football-throwing gay man—he does not deserve the insult.

The assertion that homophobic insults have little to do with one's sexuality is reflected in other studies of homophobic language. In a survey of 111 Canadian undergraduate men, *none* of them answered affirmatively to the question "if you were to call a straight man a 'fag' or 'faggot' would you seriously be suggesting that you really and truly believe the man is gay?"[10] Yet, only 21 percent of them stated that they would *not* use a homophobic epithet to refer to another man.[11] Much like the surveyed Canadian undergraduate men,[12] boys at River High indicated that homophobia is not specifically about sexuality.

The students at River High made clear that this homophobia is as much about failing at tasks of masculinity as it is about fear of actual gay men. As one young man succinctly wrote on Twitter, "a faggot isn't gay; its someone who acts like a woman." Among the teenagers at River High, homophobia becomes a catchall for anything that can be framed—even in an instant—as unmasculine. In other words, homophobic epithets such as "fag" have gendered and sexual meanings. The insult is levied against boys who are not masculine (even momentarily) and boys who identify or are identified by others as gay. This sets up a very complicated daily ordeal in which boys continually strive to avoid being subject to the epithet but are constantly vulnerable to it.

Because so many activities could render a boy vulnerable to these insults, perhaps it is little surprise that Ben asserted that one could be labeled for "anything, literally anything. Like you were trying to turn a wrench the wrong way, 'dude you're a fag.' Even if a piece of meat drops out of your sandwich, 'you fag!'" While this research shows that there are a particular set of behaviors that might provoke the slur, it is no wonder that Ben felt this way. In that statement, he reveals the intensity and extent of the policing boys endure to avoid the epithet. What renders a boy vulnerable to the epithet often depends on local definitions of masculinity. Being subject to homophobic harassment has as much to do with failing at masculine tasks of competence, heterosexual prowess, or revealing weakness as with a sexual identity. Boys have told me that seeming "too happy or something" or serenading one's girlfriend could render them vulnerable to homophobic epithets.

This sort of homophobia appears frequently in boys' joking relationships. Sociologists have pointed out that joking is central to men's relationships in general.[13] Boys often draw laughs through imitating effeminate men or men's same-sex desire. At River High, Emir frequently imitated effeminate men who presumably sexually desired other men to draw laughs from students in his introductory drama class. One day his teacher, disturbed by noise outside the classroom, turned to close the door, saying, "We'll shut this unless anyone really wants to watch sweaty boys playing basketball." Emir lisped, "I wanna watch the boys play!" The rest of the class laughed at his imitation—collectively repudiating a gendered and sexual performance of masculinity. No one in the class thought Emir was actually gay, as he purposefully mocked both same-sex sexual desire and an effeminate gender identity and performance. Rather, this sort of ritual reminded other youth that *masculine* men do not desire other men, nor do they lisp or behave in other feminine ways. It also reminded them that those men who do behave in these ways merit laughter and social derision.

Detailing these interactions at River High suggests that what looks like homophobic bullying has as much to do with demonstrating one's masculinity as with an actual fear of other gay men.[14] These insults are levied against boys who are not masculine, if only momentarily, *and* boys who identify (or are identified by others) as gay. Boys use these epithets more than girls do and take them much more seriously.[15] According to this line of research, homophobic bullying is a part of boys' gender socialization into normatively masculine behaviors, practices, attitudes, and dispositions.[16] To capture the gendered nature of these interactions, I came to refer to these young men's homophobic practices as a "fag discourse."[17] A "fag discourse" consists of jokes, taunts, imitations, and threats through which boys publicly signal their rejection of that which is considered unmasculine, usually through homophobic language.

One of the ways young men can escape this form of sexuality and gender-based bullying was, perhaps ironically, to deploy a different homophobic phrase, "no homo." Often framed as simple homophobic bullying (see, for instance, http://nohomophobes.com), the phrase "no homo" actually does complicated interactional work to allow young men to express sentiments that could trigger a round of the fag discourse. The expression "no homo" is shorthand for "I'm not a homosexual" and is perhaps a follow-up to the use of "pause," which conveyed similar sentiment. It emerged out of hip-hop culture in the 1990s to negate gender and sexual transgressions but has disseminated through wider culture since.[18] This phrase is often used when men are expressing affection toward one another or acting in a way that could be deemed unmasculine or weak[19] or when talking about their friends.[20]

A study of the use of the phrase "no homo" on Twitter shows it is used by male tweeters to accompany expressions of friendship, joy, love, and pleasure.[21] The phrase "no homo" thus carves out a space to express positive emotions about a wide variety of topics—from friendships to hot cocoa—while simultaneously preventing men from becoming victims of homophobic bullying for, as Ben asserted "anything, literally anything." While the phrase is not actually used to accompany "anything, literally anything," it is used to accompany expressions of friendship and affections.

About half the time the phrase is used, it accompanies liking things like movies, sports, celebrities, music, food, doing a particular activity, or even experiencing nature, as in the following examples:

JEFF: The Day After Tomorrow is still a tight movie #nohomo.
LANCE: I wouldn't mind if I had a voice like Trey Songz #nohomo.
HECTOR: My love for Kobe Bryant tho. . . . #NoHomo.

The other half of the time, the phrase is deployed by men expressing friendship with other men, either expressing the daily work of friendship or deep love and affection for other men:

FRANKIE: just DM me ur number bro I lost ur #. Nohomo.
COLIN: I miss you #nohomo.
GENE: Really appreciate this dude man not too many dudes can say
    they have Solid bros but god bless me with 1 love you bro nohomo.

In other words, using a homophobic epithet allows for seemingly unmasculine behavior and inoculates one against homophobic bullying from others, illustrating the complicated nature of homophobic epithets—that they can be used both to shore up normative masculinity but also to protect a person when he enacts behavior that may not be in line with these gendered expectations. Deploying "no homo" mitigates against the risk of the "fag discourse" often deployed in such instances. These uses of the phrase "no homo" illustrate the process of carving out spaces for pleasure and platonic intimacy to be expressed, while simultaneously doing the performative work that one needs to maintain a claim on normative masculinity. "No homo" anticipates the sort of interactional homophobia we see with the fag discourse.

Both the fag discourse and no homo represent a form of interactional homophobia. In other words, what looks like homophobic bullying, using homophobic epithets, is not simply about a dislike of gay people but is also a form of gendered norm enforcement. Understanding homophobic bullying as a part of boys' gender socialization process suggests that the current discourse about bullying needs some reworking. Framing young men's aggressive behavior solely as "bullying" can elide the complicated way in which interactional homophobia is a central part of a gender socialization process that supports and reproduces gender and sexual inequality. Locating the problem of homophobia in bullying results in responses to inequality that are largely individualistic and symbolic rather than structural and systemic. Doing so obfuscates the role that institutions play in passing along similar messages about gender and sexuality. Through pedagogical practices, disciplinary structures, school rituals, and civic engagement, schools convey messages about gender and sexuality, while placing blame for problematic messages on bullying and hate, rather than bureaucratic processes.

Institutional Heteronormativity

Bullying, homophobia, and gendered norms have changed over the past two decades, a shift that was clearly indicated when I began to conduct research at American High School, a working- and middle-class high school in suburban Oregon. Rather than hearing an endless barrage of homophobic epithets, instead I read anti-bullying messages that covered the school walls. One series of posters was titled "No Room for Hate" and was filled with student-generated messages like the following:

> Racism: If I hear people making racist jokes, then I can ask them to stop
> Homophobia: If I hear any homophobic comments, then I will ask why does it matter
> Playful Joking: If I see another person physically harassing someone else, then I will speak up and protect the victim
> Sexism: If I see/hear a sexist comment, then I will stop and say how would that feel if that was you?

Students at American High School regularly told me that unlike the well-resourced school down the road, where students are regularly "bullied out," bullying simply didn't happen at American. Rather, the ethic was one of care, kindness, and "open mindedness." It wasn't unusual to hear students describe American like this: "I think it's nicer. I think people are a little bit more open . . . I feel like there's a little bit less of a socio-economic caste system." Another student shared, "As far as high schools go, American is probably one of the more accepting that I've found." Based on what I saw during my two years of research at American, this claim rings true. This behavior at American High may be an example of the outcome of a national focus on bullying as a social problem. At American, gendered and sexualized norms were conveyed not primarily through interactional homophobia but through institutional practices, something I am calling institutional heteronormativity. The concept of institutional heteronormativity captures the way that homophobia is framed (as it is in the anti-bullying posters) as something that belongs to an individual in an aggressive interaction like bullying and not something that resides in institutional practices and rules. Using a case study of the Gay-Straight Alliance (GSA) at American High School, the following section documents the way institutions reproduced gendered and sexual inequalities by focusing on policies that place the responsibility for it on interactional homophobia.

On a cool January night, a local drag troupe called the House of the Ridiculous Absurd, about ten students from the GSA, and several teachers gathered to put on a drag show for family and friends. About seventy people were in the audience—judging by age, most of them appeared to be parents or family members and not fellow students. This was the first drag show ever put on at American High. The GSA advisor, Rose, said the students did all the work. They contacted the drag queens and conducted all the rehearsals. While she tried to refrain from providing advice, she did discourage them from advertising widely and advised them to only put posters up around the school because she did not want them "to draw the wrong kind of attention from the larger community."

Rose had "assumed they [school administrators] were going to say no" to the event and that the GSA "would be able to push and get some sort of compromise." She had primed the GSA members to be "aware that drag doesn't mean the same thing to somebody who is not in queer culture as it does to someone that is." Rose warned the GSA that "you are going to go in and these adults are going to think that you're asking to do a weird sex thing on campus. So you have to figure out how to make them understand that this isn't just a weird sex thing." But when Sarah, a well-spoken white sophomore with big glasses who identifies as asexual, presented the GSA's case to the "operations committee" (the committee at the school that approves such things), "She did such a great job. She came in. She couched everything in very academic language. She talked about, drag is an expression of gender performance, talking about how this is allowing people to explore identities, push limits on their identities or whatever." After her presentation, the operations committee approved the event.

The result was that over the course of two hours, students, professional drag queens, and teachers put on a charming and understated drag show. Because this was the first time most in the audience had attended a drag show, Queen Quixotic, the mother of the House of the Ridiculous Absurd explained to attendees what a drag show is, what gender is, how to behave at a drag show, and what a drag family is. Dressed in typical drag makeup, with long wavy black hair, a formal red sparkly dress, and an equally sparkly belt, topped by a stole, she said, "I love the sound of my own voice! Applaud for me one more time! . . . I grew up in San Diego and we would never have had anything like this." She explained that the queens worked with the students: "We worked, we turned, we practiced. I taught them how to walk in heels. I taught them how to do a drag queen wave" and said of the show, "It will be fierce!" She taught the audience how to show their appreciation in a drag show, instructing them to say "Yaass!" and "Work!" by repeating after her with a raised arm. Queen Quixotic explained drag by saying "many people think that drag is this," motioning to herself, "a cisgender man doing all this work. But that's not it. Drag is the performance of gender. It's the performance of our identity."

The show featured a variety of performances of teachers, students, and drag queens. The first was Storm, a student who says that their "pronouns depend on the day," wearing a short burgundy bob wig and an ill-fitting purple, shiny, floor-length gown over a black turtle neck in a full face of overstated drag makeup dancing intently to the song "Love You Like a Love Song." They received raucous applause from the audience as they executed small jumps in time to the music. This dance was followed by twelve other performances, ranging from traditional drag queens in shiny dresses, high heels, and sparkling jewelry to three students performing as the Schuyler sisters from the hit musical *Hamilton* singing to a cisgender male white teacher playing a ukulele and lip-synching.

The final teacher to perform was the only out trans teacher at the school, Max. As the opening notes of Billy Joel's "Only the Good Die Young" played, a piano and a stained glass window were revealed onstage. The only drag king of the show appeared dressed up as Billy Joel in jeans and a leather jacket playing the piano. Max appeared dressed in a white demure dress walking slowly with hands folded in prayer. Over the course of the song he transformed from this seemingly innocent female character focused on praying to a jubilantly dancing man wearing a black Transsexual Menace T-shirt and jeans. Transsexual Menace was a trans rights organization founded in 1993, the first direct action group of its kind. This act brought down the house with wild cheers and applause.

Queen Quixotic took the microphone to close the show, saying that she wanted a "safe future for our gender diverse siblings out there. Please never stop being yourself. Keep doing you! See these people here? They all support you!" The lights came up, and Lady Gaga's queer anthem "Born This Way" blared and the students rushed the stage, waving their arms in the air, waving jackets around, and dancing exuberantly. A mom said to her son as they walked out, "Are you inspired?" The students closed the night by taking pictures with each other and dancing with an exuberance usually seen at proms or football games. Rose said later that the students "were really proud of themselves."

On first glance, this drag show is a dramatic moment of inclusion in which a school created a space for the celebration of queer identities and culture, even if the school itself did not actively advertise or publicly endorse the event. But I want to unpack the drag show a little bit more, perhaps complicating it with what came next.

In the weeks following the drag show, Rose's concerns about community response were partially realized, in that some parents and "admins" were "not happy" about what happened at the drag show. The district's equity coordinator shared her concerns with Rose, who shared those concerns with students at a subsequent GSA meeting. The equity coordinator's comments were threefold. First, she was concerned that the trans students would be the target of public outrage and anger if there was pushback to the drag show. Second, she feared that the drag show would affect trans students who were not out, asking, what if "people ask to borrow a trans students wig"? Finally, Rose said that according to the equity representative, a show could be offensive to trans students because drag usually consists of cisgender folks dressing like the "opposite" (Rose accompanied this word with air quotes) sex.

The GSA students expressed criticism of this response. They repeatedly interrupted Rose with "what" and "huh" and other dissents as she relayed this information. Two students at one point broke out with "BUT I'M TRANS!," laughing in confusion at the equity coordinator's response. Indeed half of the regular attendees of GSA meetings did not identify as cisgender. Nia also highlighted how "powerful" it was for a cisgender white male teacher to dress in drag and sing to show support for queer students.

The district official's response to the drag show suggests that the school had a particular conception of whom trans students are and what their needs are, needs that are seemingly divorced from a legacy of play, celebration, and irreverence that characterizes queer culture, a culture that, in part, emerged out of needs that gave birth to the practice of drag balls in the United States, where many gender queer and trans folk—especially economically marginalized and racial ethnic minorities—found homes.

A trans student for the district exists as an imagined potential victim who must be protected from bullying. This conception is deeply related to the location of bullying as the place where homophobia and gender norms reside. That is, the biggest threat to a trans student is characterized as interactional aggression, not being a member of a school community that does not recognize or celebrate queer culture. While the district seeks to protect vulnerable students, it does so in a mode that locates harm in interactional aggression and not on institutional messages about gender and sexuality.

Queer students at American High did not generally report experiencing this sort of interactional aggression around issues of gender identity or presentation. They expressed occasional frustration about teachers not using the correct pronouns—such as when Marcel, a trans cheerleader, said that one of his teachers "kept misgendering" him because, as one of his teachers said, "I just know so many Marcels who are girls!" This was followed up with laughter and an affirmation that indeed the teachers were trying to do the right thing. The students in the GSA on one occasion had a discussion about giving their teachers grades to rank how "LGBTQIAA affirming" they were, and on the whole the group gave them As and Bs. In other words, even when students may have experienced less than ideal interactions around gender and sexuality, the general perception was that folks were trying to be respectful.

When talking about the challenges they faced, students in the GSA seemed to be less afraid of bullying, being closeted, or experiencing victimization than they were frustrated with school policy and infrastructure regarding sexuality and gender identity. In other words, the biggest challenges for students were not those imagined by school representatives—bullying and forcible outing. Rather, the students expressed concerns with formal and informal policies as well as physical infrastructure in the school. Their frustrations were directed not at other students per se but at systemic, institutional issues.

For example, GSA members spent several meetings reviewing the twenty-five-page district policy document for "Gender Nonconforming Students." The students put the document up on a doc cam and worked through its pages, correcting outdated language and pointing out problematic, if seemingly well-intentioned, policies. As the president of the GSA, Ave, said, it's "oddly dated for something that was written in 2016." Matt pointed out that it used "the phrase transgendered." Greta replied, "It's not a verb!," and they talked over each other recalling and demonstrating jokingly with their bodies how they enacted "transgenderedness." The GSA president dangled her arm awkwardly, swinging it back and forth to demonstrate how they enacted it saying, "we decided it was this." Everyone laughed. The GSA members also critiqued the part of the document where there was a claim that there was "little research" on young people and transition.

Ave asked, of the language used throughout, "What does gender nonconforming even mean?" Marcell answered, imitating a teacher using a mock formal stilted voice: "You are wearing a men's T-shirt today, are you going by them/they pronouns?" Others murmured in assent. Brett said, also imitating an adult, "You play sports, are you a man?" Wynn added, "it" "makes it sound like the sex assigned at birth is related to their gender." Greta chimed in, "Like, would they say a transboy is engaging in gender nonconforming behavior if he's doing 'boy' behavior?" Finally, Ave claimed, "They are confusing behavior with identity." The latter comment or variations of it was made multiple times. The students seemed adamant that behavior and identity were different and that identity could not be discerned from behavior and seemed frustrated that the district experts were not recognizing that in the guidelines.

The students expressed frustration at the continued use of "transboy" and "transgirl" throughout the text, suggesting that the guidelines themselves continually reified a gender dichotomy. Matt said, "In a weird way it invites [teachers] to ask about their genitals which they do not need to do." Marcell provided an example of conversations he had where he would say, "I'm a transboy," and then the response was, "Oh, so you're a girl / or you were a girl," saying he responded with "uh, no." Instead the students insisted that the wording in the policy should be of boys and girls, not transboys and transgirls.

Similarly the GSA members were frustrated with the fact that requirements for Pink Prom were different from those for the regular prom. The organization sponsoring the event required that attendees present permission slips that had been signed by parents to enter the prom. The prom is sponsored by multiple school districts and staffed by volunteers mostly from the local university. School-specific proms do not require permission slips. The GSA members expressed concern that requiring these types of forms would result in students being forcibly outed or prevented from attending in the first place. While there might be a legal reason behind this, it did not appear to justify the risk for the students. As Ave said, this happens "because people are homophobic and everything sucks."

Finally, GSA members expressed concern about the "bathroom problem." David and Marcell, both trans students, talked about how difficult it is to have only one gender-neutral bathroom, located at the very front of the school. David said, "I don't use it because there's only one stall." And that awkwardness ensued when he used the more conveniently located boys' bathroom: "The only time I used the boys' bathroom it was hilarious. Oh my god, they were in [there] hiding," laughing and making motions like they were trying to hide their eyes. Marcell said, "If I have to do my business during [cheerleading] practices I usually just go in the guys' bathroom." He described how the boys' bathroom in the gym is on the other side from the girls, and that during one practice he was coming out and another cheerleader asked suspiciously "where were you?" and he responded, using a sarcastic tone, "the bathroom."

The district was slated to build a few new buildings and had opened them up for a comment period. The GSA students had a focused discussion on comments to provide, saying "priorities are gender-neutral bathrooms." Their suggestions included:

- The bathrooms need more than one stall
- The bathrooms need to be accessible
- There needs to be more than one gender-neutral bathroom

David said, "People will freak out about multiple occupancy gender-neutral bathrooms." Another added, "It is very heteronormative!" as other students laughed and said "yes!" Brett said that they heard that a local middle school had a gender-neutral bathroom but that it was locked. Wynn lamented that "students have to get a key from a teacher, effectively outing them." Another said that a different local middle school had "an easily accessible bathroom. It was just in the middle of a hallway. It was nice." Finally, a student added, "They have to have somewhere to put pads and tampons!" Others chimed in "inside the stall" and "you can't do anything with period stuff in the guys' bathroom."

The queer students were making some very concrete structural requests of the school—to change and update their policies about gender, to make it easier for students of all genders to experience bodily integrity by taking care of their bodily needs, and to change rules governing participation in meaningful rituals that might expose sexual- and gender-minority students to increased risk. What they were not suggesting is that the school address bullying. Apart from some awkwardness from boys in the bathroom or girl cheerleaders, both of which the group laughed off, the students simply did not report much interactional aggression. What they were concerned with was the institutional setup regarding gender and sexuality, not interactional homophobia.

This perspective sheds light on which students are framed as potential victims—queer youth—and who and what those in charge think these students need protection from—being outed, being drag, or being the target of homophobic attacks from the larger community. The heteronormative practices of the institution itself obfuscate the actual needs of LGBTQ students, needs like menstrual products in gender-neutral and boys' bathrooms. Framing the problem as interactional homophobia elides students' institutional claims about equality. They are asking for a place to be able to take care of their bodily needs with the ease that other students can and for the school to update its guiding policies on trans and gender-nonconforming students to reflect their actual needs.

This increased focus on bullying positions these interactional moments as the location of inequality and not school infrastructure like normative rituals, rules, and lived environment. A focus on queer students' experiences at American High, however, suggests that sexual norms are built into the institution itself, not just passed through aggressive interactions between students.

Conclusion

So what do the stories of homophobia and heterosexuality at these two schools tell us about Vinnie's comment, that times sure have changed? Well, they indicate that times have changed, but precisely how they have changed is uneven and not always obvious. While narratives about the problem of bullying are now a culture-wide way to frame issues of aggression, by locating the problem of homophobia and heteronormativity in bullying, it is harder to see the way that norms of gender and sexuality are reproduced institutionally. Thinking back to Vinnie's comment, for instance, is instructive. Likely the football team at River High School is still all male. The cheerleading team is primarily filled with girls who cheer on the hardworking male football team. A heteronormative logic still organizes the school, in other words. Institutionally the school still structures gender and sexuality in particular and unequal ways.

Over the past two decades popular discourse and educational institutions have focused on reducing bullying as a way to combat multiple social ills such as youth depression, suicide, violence, and substance abuse. However, framing the problem as bullying renders gender and sexuality an individual problem of kindness or meanness, even in institutions like American High School that take a proactive anti-bullying stance. The result is that while we can easily recognize messages about gendered and sexualized norms at River High as located in homophobic bullying, even a school like American High School reproduces inequality by embedding it in the very culture of the school through the embrace of an apolitical doctrine of kindness and heteronormativity. But calling this homophobic bullying and locating the problem of homophobia there means that schools can neglect the way that particular norms about gender and sexuality are embedded in their institutions and rituals.

NOTES

1 Pew Research Center, 2016.
2 Altemeyer, 2001.
3 Lance, 2008; Pew Research Center, 2016.
4 Pew Research Center, 2003.

5   Bridges and Pascoe, 2014.
6   Pascoe, 2013.
7   Pascoe, 2013.
8   Pascoe, 2013.
9   Wilchins, 2003.
10 Brown and Alderson, 2010.
11 Brown and Alderson, 2010.
12 Brown and Alderson, 2010.
13 Kehily and Nayak, 1997.
14 Corbett, 1994.
15 Thurlow, 2001.
16 Corbett, 2001; Kimmel, 1994; Pascoe, 2011.
17 Pascoe, 2011.
18 Brown, 2011.
19 Ikard, 2013.
20 Way, 2012.
21 Pascoe and Diefendorf, 2019.

REFERENCES

Altemeyer, Bob. 2001. "Changes in Attitudes toward Homosexuals." *Journal of Homosexuality* 42 (2): 63–75.

Bridges, Tristan, and C. J. Pascoe. 2014. "Hybrid Masculinities: New Directions in the Sociology of Men and Masculinities." *Sociology Compass* 8 (3): 246–258.

Brown, Joshua R. 2011. "No Homo." *Journal of Homosexuality* 58 (3): 299–314.

Brown, Tyler L., and Kevin G. Alderson. 2010. "Sexual Identity and Heterosexual Male Students' Usage of Homosexual Insults: An Exploratory Study." *Canadian Journal of Human Sexuality* 19 (1/2): 27–42.

Corbett, Jenny. 1994. "A Proud Label: Exploring the Relationship between Disability Politics and Gay Pride." *Disability & Society* 9 (3): 343–357.

Corbett, Ken. 2011. "Faggot = Loser." *Studies in Gender and Sexuality* 2 (1): 3–28.

Ikard, David. 2013. "Boys to Men: Getting Personal about Black Manhood, Sexuality, and Empowerment." *Palimpsest* 2 (1): 59–73.

Kehily, Mary Jane, and Anoop Nayak. 1997. "'Lads and Laughter': Humour and the Production of Heterosexual Hierarchies." *Gender and Education* 9 (1): 69–87.

Kimmel, Michael S. 1994. "Masculinity as Homophobia: Fear, Shame and Silence in the Construction of Gender Identity." In *The Masculinities Reader*, edited by Stephen M. Whitehead and Frank Barrett, 266–287. Thousand Oaks, CA: Sage.

Kimmel, Michael S., and Matthew Mahler. 2003. "Adolescent Masculinity, Homophobia, and Violence Random School Shootings, 1982–2001." *American Behavioral Scientist* 46 (10): 1439–1458.

Lance, Larry M. 2008. "Social Inequality on the College Campus: A Consideration of Homosexuality." *College Student Journal* 42 (3): 789–794.

Pascoe, C. J. 2011. *Dude, You're a Fag: Masculinity and Sexuality in High School*. 2nd ed. Berkeley: University of California Press.

———. 2013. "Notes on a Sociology of Bullying: Young Men's Homophobia as Gender Socialization." *QED* 1 (1): 87–104.

Pascoe, C. J., and Sarah Diefendorf. 2019. "No Homo: Gendered Dimensions of Homophobic Epithets Online." *Sex Roles* 80 (3–4): 123–136.

Pew Research Center. 2003. "Republicans Unified, Democrats Split on Gay Marriage." November 18. http://assets.pewresearch.org.

———. 2016. "Changing Attitudes on Gay Marriage." May 14. www.pewforum.org.

Thurlow, Crispin. 2001. "Naming the 'Outsider Within': Homophobic Pejoratives and the Verbal Abuse of Lesbian, Gay and Bisexual High-School Pupils." *Journal of Adolescence* 24 (1): 25–38.

Way, Niobe. 2012. "Close Friendships among Adolescent Boys." *Thymos* 6 (1–2): 116–136.

Wilchins, Riki. 2003. "Do You Believe in Fairies?" *The Advocate*, February 4, 72.

6

Mean Girls and Tough Guys

Gender, Sexuality, and the Individualization of Anti-Bullying Efforts

SARAH A. MILLER

In the fall of 2015, posters line Township High School's hallways promoting the upcoming anti-bullying assembly, Operation Nice.[1] Below the hot-pink byline, "a movement bringing awareness of the effects of meanness within girl world," is a cartoon depiction of a bewildered redhead surrounded by gossiping girls, their conversation simulated in talk bubbles: "what is she wearing?," "back stabber," "so fat," "trashy," "don't trust her," "anorexic," "no one likes you," "fake," "so ugly," "poor." Apparently, in girl world, girls are not so nice.

"That tracks," Amber, a blonde, low-income, bisexual sophomore, tells me, nonchalantly gesturing to one of the posters as we walk to the cafeteria. "I guess I'd say that I've been bullied by girls. A lot." Over the two school years I got to know her while conducting ethnography at Township, Amber's adolescence was filled with so-called mean girl aggression. The abuses ranged from rumors about her sexuality to systematic avoidance and the spread of a topless photo she had taken for an ex. Amber was always reticent to report these experiences to the school administration. However, when she learned that multiple anti-bullying assemblies were headed to school that fall, she had hope that they would help.

She was quickly disappointed. During Operation Nice, young women were given few solutions as they were taught about the "harsh realities of girl-on-girl crime." In this assembly, students were taught to ignore the inequitable contexts that shape their conflicts, and instead focus on "spreading kindness." At the next anti-bullying training, Project Cyber Safety, young women were taught that if they participate in sexting, they will automatically be known as "sluts" because "boys will be boys" and most of the school will end up seeing them. As one trainer told the audience, "What you put online is like walking through cement.... Sexting is a mistake you can never take back." Visibly upset as she left this second assembly, Amber told me that she was ashamed that her peers might be remembering her topless photo, which had recently circulated on their phones, and also about the freshly reinforced permanence of her sexual reputation. She was also distraught by the overarching message: rather than focusing on bullying, the focus was on girls' own "mistakes."

Amber is one of many teens I met at Township whose marginality was reinforced by well-intended anti-bullying efforts. A version of what Max Greenberg calls "the curricularization of youth social problems,"[2] anti-bullying programming is now commonplace in many U.S. K–12 schools.[3] While scholars have found that these programs rely heavily on discourses of individualism,[4] we currently know less about their gendered and sexual content. This chapter focuses on what anti-bullying efforts look like as local practices, exploring the messages they are sending young people, beyond surface-level directives of kindness and conflict prevention. Through an analysis of two case studies, Project Cyber Safety and Operation Nice, including their marketing strategies, the content of their assemblies, and observations of young people's experiences of them, I illustrate how bullying prevention's hidden curriculum reinforces the role of gender inequality in youth conflict.

Anti-bullying and Inequality

Compared to the proliferation of scholarship on bullying practices, less research has focused on the rapidly expanding policies and initiatives that schools employ for bullying prevention. The majority of studies that do explore anti-bullying largely focus on assessing efficacy, primarily through the examination of pre- and post-initiative evaluations and quantitative school climate survey results, as well as shifts in attitudes and decreases in bullying and victimization measures.[5] This research largely does not include a critical examination of the messages disseminated through these programs or their impact on school communities as wholes rather than on aggregated individuals.

However, a growing body of literature exploring anti-bullying rhetoric in texts, legislation, and the media documents how this discourse consistently ignores the role of structural inequality in bullying practices.[6] This "individualization" of bullying emphasizes familial and/or personal pathology,[7] rehabilitation, and reform, reinforcing a good/bad binary between bullies and their victims.[8] The focus on bullying and bullying prevention as individual choices teens make often obscures the cultural and social contexts that limit and structure the choices teens *have* to make.[9] Further, the research of both Meyer[10] and Abels[11] on a variety of commonly used anti-bullying texts finds that they decouple bullying from gender- and sexuality-based power relations and ignore the prevalence of heteronormativity and homophobia in bullying practices.

Prevention programming's inattention to the inequitable contexts that shape bullying runs counter to contemporary bullying research. As many scholars have shown us, bullying is about inequality: through bullying, teens negotiate status,[12] police social norms related to gender, sexuality, race, class, and ability,[13] and make meaning out of the varying social norms present in their local communities.[14] This is especially the case in relationship to gender and sexuality. For example, research has documented how many of the homophobic and sexist ideologies espoused through bullying content generate meanings about gender and sexuality central to teens' gendering processes and the policing of gender norms.[15] In other words, bullying is a key site where heteronormativity and patriarchy are reinforced between youth. However, just as the textual analyses of a variety of anti-bullying programs indicate,[16] Township's anti-bullying programming also ignores the relationship between bullying and inequality and instead emphasizes teens' individual responsibility for preventing conflict. Further, as the two case studies illustrate below, some campaigns reinforce traditional gender norms, while obfuscating the role that gender and sexual inequalities play in generating many bullying encounters.

A central framing used within Township's anti-bullying programming is the trope of the "mean girl." Based on an array of knowledge produced in the early 2000s on girls' conflicts, which diverged from earlier years of feminist research claiming that women are the more nurturing, relationship-oriented gender,[17] the "mean girl" archetype emphasizes that girls are aggressive toward other girls in indirect ways. Girls purportedly participate in a "hidden culture of indirection"[18] that produces the cattiness, backstabbing, and in-group/out-group cliquing that are often represented as fundamental to girl culture. This modern dilemma of girlhood has proven consumable to a wide audience, launching a variety of articles and books in the popular press,[19] including multiple national best sellers,[20] as well as a series of talk show specials, television programs, and feature films. A culturally valued expression of misogyny, this discourse is not easily detached from the figure of "the mean girl," simultaneously disparaging young women's conflict strategies while blaming them for their "inherent" incapacities to get along.[21]

In response to increasing attention on aggressive privileged girls, and particularly in the wake of a series of high-profile "bullycides" that led to the criminalization of some bullying practices,[22] many steps have been taken within schools in recent years to make all girls less "mean." In addition to traditional anti-bullying programs that include segments on gendered bullying practices, a series of girl-focused intervention programs are now widely available on the anti-bullying market. However, these interventions have the potential to affect girls unevenly, mitigating "meanness" among privileged girls, while increasing penalties for low-income girls of color, as relationally aggressive incidents that used to go unnoticed are now more likely to result in police involvement.[23]

The "mean girl" archetype represents white, middle-class femininity norms that limit certain girls' expression of anger, frustration, and fear. Many authors argue that girls' aggression is not independent from inequality.[24] Girls participate in horizontal aggression in response to gender oppression, as a relatively safe and acceptable way to expel their frustrations—particularly in white, middle-class communities.[25] However, this discourse also consistently involves explicit, yet uninterrogated attention to class-privileged, heterosexual, cisgender, white girlhood—the girlhood represented in popular culture and politics as innocent and in need of protection throughout U.S. history.[26] This representation has historically been made meaningful at the expense of low-income girls and girls of color who are often depicted as more aggressive and more in need of institutional reform.[27] Further, lesbian, bisexual, queer, and transgender girls, many of whom are also low income and/or youth of color, are often excluded from this discourse, even though their gender identities and sexualities are often policed through bullying,[28] as well as larger forms of social control and violence.[29]

Notably, there is not a corresponding "mean boys" discourse in anti-bullying programming, an absence that is also reflected in educator practices. In the midst of this cultural emphasis on preventing "mean girl" behavior, boys' participation in and experiences of relational aggression are often invisible[30] to educators and to youth themselves. For instance, in Mishna et al.'s study[31] of Canadian elementary, middle, and high schoolers, boys' relationally aggressive practices were ignored while girls' were "spotlighted" as early as fourth grade, as girls were disproportionately blamed for bullying and cyberbullying. At the same time, boys' participation in direct physical aggression has been coded by educators and youth as a practice of "intelligible masculinity,"[32] normalized and encoded into traditional masculine gender roles.[33]

Compared to discourses on relational aggression among girls, boys are often expected to be violent in order to solve conflict. Diane Reay's study[34] on primary schoolchildren's gendered cultures illustrates how boys' violence is both sanctioned and, in some cases, demanded, as a form of "heroic masculinity." While being coded as a bully is an undesirable label among boys, if boys are threatened, participating in physically aggressive practices is often the only acceptable, normatively masculine behavior they feel that they can employ. However, as Jessica Ringrose and E. J. Renold[35] argue, because this normalized masculine violence is not accounted for within anti-bullying discourses, they offer boys minimal practical or symbolic resources to engage when navigating conflict. Instead, these discourses reflect and reinforce the institutionalized gendered hierarchies within schools, normalizing certain versions of gendered aggression and not others.

This chapter explores two anti-bullying campaigns situated within this larger social history. Operation Nice and Project Cyber Safety frame girls' and boys' social worlds as "separate cultures," giving youth explicitly gendered messages on how to handle conflict. Boys are taught to not "act like pussies" by participating in relational aggression and instead "act like men" by dealing with their conflicts through physical means. At the same time, girls' "meanness" is both emphasized and individualized, while boys' often integral role in girls' experiences of bullying is ignored. Girls are taught to be nice, sexually chaste, and empathetic, while they are simultaneously instructed to both tolerate and protect themselves from boys' and men's bad behavior. Finally, both campaigns emphasize an idealized white, heterosexual, cisgender, and class-privileged girlhood deserving of both protection and reform, while obscuring the increased structural and social challenges LGBTQ youth, low-income youth, and youth of color face when navigating conflict. Read together, I argue that Operation Nice and Project Cyber Safety reinforce inequalities through the messages they impart to young people about gender and sexuality.

Methods

This chapter is based on data collected through two school years of intensive fieldwork at Township, a small, rural high school in the Northeast. The study included observations, content analysis of bullying protocols and reports, 127 in-depth interviews of school officials and teens, and digital ethnography. I spent an average of four days per week observing a variety of classrooms, the cafeteria, staff meetings, and after-school events. The bulk of my interviews were with youth, each lasting approximately an hour. I spoke with a hundred fourteen- to nineteen-year-olds, including teens from across the social hierarchy and class backgrounds. The sample was closely divided between boys and girls and included two students who identified as transgender, nineteen students of color, and twenty-seven students who identified their sexual orientations as other than heterosexual or questioning. Students offered their own terms for their sexual identities, which ranged from lesbian to gay, heterosexual, bisexual, pansexual, "unsure," "fluid," "whatever—but not straight," and "all the flavors of the rainbow," among others. Finally, I observed seventy-five students' posts on social media sites that teens gave me permission to follow, including Facebook, Twitter, Tumblr, and Instagram. In order to ensure anonymity, names and other forms of identifying information have been altered, including the names of the participants, the school, and the anti-bullying campaigns discussed in this chapter.

Spreading Kindness Like Confetti

Operation Nice is a traveling national campaign involving a mandatory girls-only assembly as well as an optional ongoing club aimed at preventing what the founders call "girl-on-girl crime." Though any teen who identifies as a girl is potentially welcome, the programming does not address gender diversity and instead focuses exclusively on the experiences of cisgender, heterosexual "females." This emphasis on a binary understanding of gender is reflected in their advertising. Including hot-pink promotional materials and inspirational directives on pastel backdrops, such as "sprinkle kindness like confetti," "be a nice human being," and "girls are magic," the campaign is branded by normative femininity. Their motto is: "We've all been the victim, unfortunately we're also the cause. Help us change." This message—that girls are prone to and responsible for meanness—was sent to the entire student body, received clearly by boys as they were not the recipients of a required assembly or classroom instruction where they were schooled on their problematic, uniquely "male" relational practices.

Upon entering the auditorium one fall morning, girls are each handed a button with the saying "you can sit with us" and an individual Kleenex package (an Operation Nice sponsor) complete with cheerful pastel quotes exclaiming "happy tears are the best tears" and "hard times call for a soft touch." Before even sitting down, these objects emphasize the expectation of girls' inherent emotionality and responsibility to be nice to each other. Taylor and Grace, two slim, striking white women in their twenties, carefully address the auditorium in soft voices: "Hello, hello girls, how you doing?" Gradually the girls focus their attention on the stage. Taylor begins by describing why they created Operation Nice, explaining that their inspiration was not only their own experiences with "girl-against-girl crime" but also "growing up in world where girls can often have such a hard time being nice to one another." Grace continues, "We wanted to go out and find out how this happens and how we can unite through this universal experience that we as girls share, and create change together."

The central message that relational aggression is a universal experience that girls are also individually responsible for is hit home early on with an activity. Taylor asks the audience for a show of hands, replaying a version of a memorable scene from the film *Mean Girls*: "How many of you in this room have been negatively affected by something another female has said or done to you?" Nearly everyone raises their hands. They follow up with a second question, asking for another show of hands for those who have "ever done or said something that has negatively affected another female." About half of girls raise their hands for this one, many looking around, laughing. Grace continues, smiling, "We do this to show you that we are all in this together. We're not standing up here pointing our fingers at anyone, except at ourselves. Because we all realize that we've not only all been affected by the things said and done to us, but we're also recognizing that every single one of us plays a role."

They then introduce their film, which charts their travels across the United States "to gain a nationwide perspective on how this affects females across the country." As the lights dim, the documentary begins with a sequence of news announcers discussing relational aggression and Operation Nice: "It's a tough subject one that can have dire consequences." "These young women are fighting the hate, spreading kindness across the country." Two women walk across the screen, exchanging hostile glances. Taylor's voice narrates over somber background music: "Remember that look? Us girls, we know that look. . . . We know because we've gotten that look, and we've given that look. But girl against girl crime isn't just about that look, it's the gossip we tell, the rumors we spread, the friends we betray, the words we call each other: bitch, fat, slut, ugly. It's girl world. It can be harsh. It can be cruel." The film continues like this for over an hour. Interspersed between media coverage clips of bullycides, girl fighting, and TV specials featuring Taylor and Grace telling bully victims that they are "beautiful" and "worth it" is footage of interviews with teen girls about their experiences with "girl-on-girl crime."

The narrators often make the point that relational aggression is universal, narrating to the audience, "We haven't met a single girl who hasn't been affected by this." At one moment, an empirically empty statistic displays across the screen: "One hundred percent of girls experience female bullying at some point in their school experience. Source: our road trip." Yet, most of the girls featured are white, heterosexual, cisgender, and class-privileged. Along the way, Taylor and Grace stop at a series of their friends' childhood homes to conduct focus groups. In each case, while the girls and their mothers recount a familiar formula of backstabbing and jealousy over their friends' superior beauty and resultant ease at attracting boys, leading to regret, tears, and apologies, the home they are comfortably seated in displays the owner's vast wealth.

Luxurious furniture, grand pianos, porcelain figurines, and chandeliers surround them.

There are moments when Taylor and Grace do talk to low-income girls and girls of color. They pause in Washington to talk to Kathy, a poor, white, single teen mom struggling to get by and living on her own after being abandoned by a father who abused her. Taylor is visibly devastated by Kathy's story, crying while noting, "I don't think I've ever sat down with someone who's had so many traumatic experiences in their life." Yet her take away for the audience was not that Kathy needed affordable child care, a decent-paying job, educational opportunities, or protection from familial violence. Instead, Taylor laments that what Kathy really needed was a friend. The few Black girls included in the film have their voices narrated with subtitles—a practice that was employed only for their interviews. There are also cartoon girls of various races and ethnicities who provide a visual over additional girls' voices. However, though the campaign stopped in "sixty cities in twenty-eight states," only one school featured a classroom that was not predominantly white. And while lesbian, bisexual, and transgender girls are bullied at significantly higher rates than their heterosexual and cisgender peers,[36] neither they nor their experiences are represented in this film at all. In other words, the universality of "girl-on-girl crime" was largely represented as the province of the privileged.

The notion that girls are meaner than boys is also a common theme. This message is narrated extensively by adult men who are given a surprising amount of air time, often making fun of girls' conflicts, while obfuscating any discussion of boys' and men's aggression. As teacher Jim Collins explains, "Between girls, it's like an ancient roman war. On good days they're all cute and writing hearts on each other's papers—on bad days it's, you know, a blood bath." Multiple scenes animated by humorous music echo this sentiment while trivializing girls' conflicts. Without getting into *why* girls might be in competition or how that competition relates to gender inequality, psychologist Mark D'Asta explains the difference between boys and girls: "They're two different cultures. What's paramount in adolescence for girls is defining selves in their relationship to others—and depending on how needy girls are at this time, based on their earlier experiences, greater emphasis is placed on relationships." He does not go on to explain boys' unique developmental processes nor explicate how these "two cultures" are actually different. Instead, Taylor and Grace build on this interview, lamenting the lack of "sisterhood" girls have compared to the universal "brotherhood" boys seem to experience with their friends.

The crux of this documentary—and of the assembly as a whole—is that girls alone are responsible for their meanness. While a series of experts do touch briefly on the role of inequality in girls' conflicts, describing the pressures of media sexualization and impossible beauty standards, girls are ultimately taught to ignore those factors and recognize that the onus of change is ultimately on their shoulders. This last point is driven home at the conclusion of the film, where an image of a blackboard collects a series of words. Taylor's voice narrates as they are written out in cartoon chalk, "you can blame the media, society, parents, gender roles, technology, school systems." Then, the words are erased by a cartoon eraser as Taylor's voice continues: "It's not about that. Although they do play a huge role, pointing the finger at those things makes this a complicated mess without a solution." When the room is left with an empty chalkboard, she finishes: "The solution is simple—it's us."

As the assembly ends, students file out of the auditorium and head to lunch. Their mixed reactions are telling. Faith immediately hands me her "you can sit with us" button, asking "would you take this? I don't want it." At this table of sophomores, the girls are disturbed by the messages they just received. Mahala tells the group, "I felt like the way it portrayed teenage girls, it was just like we're cruel, vicious animals.... it was a little unsettling." Kelsey adds, "it's not cool that there's no focus on boys. Boys supposedly don't have problems with each other. Only us. And there's no focus on bullying or even friendships between guys and girls." Faith, clearly irritated, says, "yeah, it's not gender, it's not culture, it's not media," she makes whish, whish signs with her hands, insinuating these ideas being erased, as they were on the film's chalkboard. "Nope. It's us ladies. We're the problem." Caleb, the only boy in the group, asks, "Well aren't you? I mean we just got to dick around while all of you all had to learn how to not be bitches."

This statement, meant in jest, encapsulates the differing gendered experiences of Township's approach to anti-bullying, policing girls' problematic relational practices while ignoring boys'. In an interview a few weeks afterward, fourteen-year-old Emma expands on this insight, as she describes her discomfort with Operation Nice's key messages:

> You can't just decide like, "I am—like a white, educated, college woman and I know everything about the world and I'm going to tell every single girl across the country that you are not capable of resolving your own conflicts and having your own relationships." It's like, I don't know. Like—it's not like I have a lot of experience in the world, but I know I can make good relationships with people. . . . And like we had to sit through this—while guys are completely validated in their relationships, they're allowed to fight, they're allowed to be assholes to girls, they're allowed to do whatever.

As Emma points out, the emphasis on "mean girls" absolves boys of their contributions to girls' conflicts as well as their own participation in conflict with girls. It also distracts from the larger realities that girls often have to deal with, including the pervasive threat of normalized sexual violence[37] and the social downfall from slut-shaming and sexual rumor spreading from which boys often participate in and benefit.[38]

Further, while Operation Nice offers girls a chance to apologize to each other and to pledge to do better, the campaign largely doesn't address or offer girls the opportunity to talk about the content of their conflicts, nor the constraints that shape their relationships and desires. Instead, Township teens were offered an additional training that only reinforces these constraints under the guise of cyberbullying prevention.

Project Cyber Safety

One week after Operation Nice, teens were ushered into Township's auditorium for another assembly. Composed of gender-segregated trainings, Project Cyber Safety was organized by law enforcement and contained a variety of messages about gendered sexuality under the auspices of cyberbullying prevention. The training began with a focus on digital footprints, laying out a foundational message that what teens post online permanently shapes their reputation. However, this message was nuanced differently for boys and girls.

In the boys' training, the emphasis was on preventing young men from losing access to opportunities. Officer George Whelan begins with an attempt to identify with the boys in the room: "Believe it or not, when we were in high school we did some pretty stupid things, some fun things, some risky things. But when we did those things it was different for us because there were no computers, no phones, no iPads." Officer Ed Jones adds, "That's not the world you guys are living in. What we want is for you to not get in trouble." According to these officers, "trouble" came from digital images that captured them having "too much fun." For example, they show a cartoon clip of a boy whose scholarship aspirations are thwarted because of the spread of a series of pictures of him drunk at a party. Afterward, they tell the boys that they know they're going to party, just "don't be stupid" about what they post online. According to Officer Jones, "Everything counts when it's online. It's all going on your permanent record."

This message was decidedly different for the girls, with excess emphasis placed on their sexual propriety. Officer Carol Jackson begins this same segment by discussing reputations and suggests that teens make choices about who to associate with, based on them. "Reputations are how people think of you and what you've done. . . . Some girls have a reputation for being rude or slutty, right? Reputation is really, really important to us. It's our self-image to the world. It's what people think of us. You hear a name, and you immediately think of things about a person." Officer Jackson presents this segment as though the young women in the audience don't already have to navigate reputations and their outcomes. Rather than asking girls to think critically about the underlying reasons why girls' reputations have so much social purchase, she instead reifies them and emphasizes their negative impacts.

She then opens up a conversation about the many ways that reputations can shape a young woman's life chances. She asks the girls for some examples. Tiffany, a senior, offers, "Posting inappropriate pictures." Officer Jackson nods: "Absolutely. We can say it. Slutty pictures. You guys are ladies, right? What's the bad reputation for a lady? Being slutty, right? And photographs that give that impression, even if you don't mean it, are gonna have that effect. Slutty pictures have a permanent effect. Your reputation, it's really hard to change it. I want you think beyond what you post."

I look around the room at the faces of the young women I've gotten to know. On Instagram, Twitter, and Facebook, their pictures often reveal different sides of the girls seated in the auditorium that morning. Many carefully cultivate images that present themselves in ways that others might find attractive. The more revealing the photo, the more affirmation they often receive in the form of likes, hearts, thumbs-ups, and comments. This affirmation is certainly reflected in the culture that surrounds them. It is not at all surprising that some of them want to appear sexy online. However, as Officer Jackson makes abundantly clear, when you're an adolescent girl, your presentation of self is often judged on the fine line of the slut continuum. Girls are aware of this line and are policed on it regularly,[39] often through bullying practices[40] like Amber and many other girls in this room already experienced. This training only added to the already deeply entrenched constraints on girls' sexualities in schooling,[41] emphasizing that this line exists, and further, that if a girl ends up on the wrong side of it, the effects are permanent.

This message is carried into the next Project Cyber Safety unit, which features an anti-cyberbullying public service announcement. In the video, a group of girls sit at a kitchen table doing homework, a mother washing dishes in the background. One girl says directly to another, "Megan. You're a tramp." At this moment, during both the boys' and girls' trainings, the entire room bursts out in laughter. The camera pans back to Megan's face, clearly hurt by this insult. The girl continues berating Megan: "Ryan Fitch told me you guys made out. And that your breath smells like garbage, and that he almost puked. Everybody knows. He said you're the most desperate girl he knows, besides your mom. How many boyfriends does she have anyway, lots?" The camera fades to black and the PSA tag line says, "If you wouldn't say it in person, why say it online? Delete cyberbullying. Don't forward it."

The lights in the room come back up as the students try to curb their amusement, the PSA reiterating to them how little these adults understand about their experiences of bullying. Once the laughter dies down in the girls' training, Officer Jackson does not address how Megan's attack was mobilized through the cruel treatment by Ryan Fitch, a boy that she presumably trusted. Instead she asks, "See the pain on her face? It's so hurtful. Just because you're saying it on a tablet, on a screen it doesn't mean it doesn't hurt. I want you to think twice before you say something mean online, like calling someone a slut." Though important, this appeal does not question the concept of a slut, which Officer Jackson had just reified herself in the segment on digital reputations. Instead, this appeal is focused simply on not causing another girl shame.

While girls learn about the pain and validity of slut-shaming through this unit, the boys learn that cyberbullying is a feminine behavior. Officer Whelan moves on from the "Megan you're a tramp" PSA in the boys' training to emphasize how cyberbullying isn't manly, not like the kind of bullying boys took part in when he was a teen: "When we were growing up—if you wanted to be a bully, you had to be man enough to get up in my face. If you want to give me shit, you gotta get in my face to do that. Now you don't have to do that—you can do it over text messaging. You can make yourself feel like you're a real tough guy by saying all this bad stuff about other people and not even have to get up in their face. Well really how tough does that make you? Not really." Officer Jones adds to Officer Whelan's feminization of cyberbullying, telling the room slowly and gravely, "I'll tell you this straight up guys, if you need to go online and say that shit about other people to make yourself feel like a man. You are a long way away from being a man. In fact, you're going in the other direction."

This appeal reiterates multiple messages. Rather than instructing boys not to bully, these officers use this anti-bullying training to teach the boys to bully with brute force and not act like "sissies" by cyberbullying each other like girls do. Emphasizing a hierarchy of conflict forms, "manly" physical bullying is given more respect, while boys who cyberbully are emasculated. This message instructs boys that girls' conflicts are inferior to their own—and further, that girls' conflicts have nothing to do with them.

Importantly, Officer Jones does encourage the boys to think critically about the impact of cyberbullying on girls. However, he does so in a way that reinforces the well-worn trope of "locker room talk"[42] that reinforces their objectification: "I know that it happens about girls, right?" He mimics what a teen boy might say, "Oh—here's a picture of so and so—she's hot—I saw her at the swimming pool this summer in this bikini. She's smokin'. Let's tap that! We've all been there right?" Some boys laugh along with Officer Jones, seemingly attempting to "bro down" about objectifying girls, resorting to sexually violent language.

He continues, "Okay. But what if it's your sister in somebody else's picture? What kind of crap is she gonna get in when she shows up in the school in the fall? How many guys have already looked at that picture, seen a copy of it, maybe even put it in their spank bank, okay? Let's be real." Other young men shift uncomfortably in their seats. Paul, a white, working-class, gay senior yells out, "Oh my god, let's not!" Ignoring him, Jones drives home the point, "Do you want your sister in anybody else's spank bank? Don't send that stuff out there."

Officer Whelan steps in, offering an example of how a sister's nude image might end up in a random friend's camera roll and used for masturbatory purposes: "Look at it from this perspective guys. You're dating some girl she's really hot. You get her to sext with you, and send you some awesome picture of her, nice rack, what have you—awesome. And she then tells you 'you're not doing it for me anymore. I'm breaking up with you.' You're gonna be pissed off right? What are you gonna do with that picture?" The boys are silent. Officer Whelan continues, "In all honesty, you're gonna be like, 'okay bitch. You're gonna treat me like that, this is what I'm gonna do.'" He then mimics forwarding a picture on an imaginary phone in his palm, declaring, "and that's how they get shared." In this anti-bullying segment, these officers draw on misogynistic discourse circulating in the larger culture[43] to normalize both the idea that it is okay for boys to collectively talk about girls in degrading ways and the notion that this form of aggressive behavior is something boys will be compelled to do if a girl breaks up with them.

Officer Jones takes the floor again, attempting to intervene in Officer Whelan's example. "There's a couple of problems with this. One, this is bullying. And more importantly, it's a crime. You don't want your reputation to be 'oh—that's the guy I went to high school with but then he got arrested for producing and sharing child pornography,' because that's what it is. For anyone who's under eighteen, having naked pictures of somebody under eighteen on your phone or laptop—that's a crime. And you could go to jail." Both officers continue to give further examples of how boys end up with child pornography charges for keeping girls' nude pictures on their phones and emphasize that they should always delete them.

It is noteworthy that the takeaway message of this segment was ultimately not about preventing a very insidious form of sexual bullying—one that a series of Township young women, like Amber, had been subjected to by some of the young men sitting in this very room. The message was also not to stop asking girls for nude pictures or to protect their pictures once boys received them. The notion that teen boys will ask for nudes was taken as an unavoidable fact. Instead, the main message these officers impart is to simply not get caught with nude pictures so that Township boys do not receive criminal records.

Meanwhile, in this same segment of the girls' training, girls are taught not to trust boys or adult men. Officer Jones tells the girls, "At some point, you're gonna meet someone and you're gonna think, this is my forever man. You're gonna think it's my soul mate. And their gonna say, 'prove it to me, send me a picture. Take your shirt off, take your bra off, let me see those cute panties.'" Note, there are already multiple messages disseminated here about gendered (hetero)sexuality: that boys need for girls to "prove" their commitment to them, that girls would sext only if they believed it was with their "forever man," and even then, only if their "forever man" coerced them into doing it.

Officer Jones takes this warning to the next level, dismissing the notion that any boy can be trusted or that any teenage romance has the capacity to last: "I don't want to be a heart breaker, but that first person that you know you're in love with and you think it's gonna be forever, but it's not. I can tell you, it's not. But you know what *is* gonna be out there forever? That picture of your breasts. And what do you think they're gonna do with it? You break up with them, they break up with you, feelings are hurt, they're gonna take that picture and they're gonna plaster it everywhere—okay? Everywhere."

He goes on to describe all the different hands a young woman's photo might land in, including those of "some creepy dude in Canada" who is going to find her image and use it for extortion. "That's what sextortion is: I know who you are, I know where you live, I'll be waiting for you in the bushes. The reality is this is incredibly dangerous and the activity that they force you to do, it gets worse and worse. It's not just take your bra off, it's take that object and put it in a certain place, on video. That's what sextortion is. It's what happens when you send willing pictures out to boys you think you trust. Don't do it in the first place and this won't happen to you." This warning, which places the onus of sexual violence prevention on girls' shoulders, is underscored by yet another video of a white girl who is exposed by a boyfriend and ends up getting propositioned by other boys, teachers, neighbors, and seedy adult strangers. The video is narrated by a young woman's voice, "Once you post a photo online, you can't take it back. Anyone can see it. Remember, think before you post."

The girls, many of whom mentioned during interviews that they regularly sext with their significant others, are clearly uneasy, as they are now being told that they are already vulnerable to anyone seeing their naked body. Kelsey leans over at this point and whispers to me and her friend Jessa, "75 percent of girls in this room have sent a naked picture to someone—and you trust them, but what do you do about it?" Jessa, nods her head, adding about Township boys, "they *always* ask for nudes." Others are frustrated. I talk with seventeen-year-old Galen later that day who laments, "Adults completely miss the fact that sexting's completely normal. It happens to everyone at some point, you know what I mean? Like every single person. I think they just don't get it because they didn't go through it. . . . Like having sex is different now. So what are we supposed to do?"

While throughout Project Cyber Safety adults acknowledged that teens get bullied and that boys are often driven by (hetero)sexual desires, they ignored the reality that girls have sexual lives and desires as well. Girls' sexualities, also always framed as heterosexual, were addressed only through slut-shaming, through sexual bullying, or as objects of desire or predation. Further, adults' overarching presumption that sexting is not already a common practice among youth only reinforced the message that teens *should*, in fact, judge girls (notably, not boys) if they sext and get exposed. Ultimately, teens learn that girls are slutty, foolish, and tempting serious danger if they take part in a normalized sexual practice that is increasingly expected of them.

Conclusion

Read together, Operation Nice and Project Cyber Safety reinforce gender inequalities through the messages they impart to young people about gendered sexuality. They frame girls' and boys' conflicts as "separate cultures," ignoring the interaction between genders in many teen conflicts as well as the realities of many boys' experiences of bullying.

The narratives offered to teens are always individualized, obscuring the roles of adults and institutions in producing many of the constraints that teens navigate. These initiatives ignore the competing roles of race and class in teens' bullying experiences while offering a heteronormative framing of adolescent life, erasing the experiences of LGBTQ teens entirely. They emphasize girls' vulnerabilities to each other, to boys, and to society, while also trivializing their conflicts. At the same time, they position girls, not boys, as interpersonally challenged and responsible for creating a kind and compassionate school culture.

In Operation Nice, girls are schooled on the universality of "girl-on-girl crime," based not on empirical evidence but on two privileged young women's perceptions. Their unacknowledged emphasis on white, heterosexual, upper-middle-class, cisgender girlhood both ignores and obscures the bullying that nondominant teens regularly navigate. Though the documentary does pay lip service to the underlying societal precursors of aggression, it explicitly tells girls to ignore those factors—by literally erasing them—and to instead focus inward. Finally, the dual emphasis on girls' inherent meanness and the directive of being nice serves only to further discipline girls, depriving young women of their often very real, very justified anger at the outcomes of a patriarchal system designed to pit them against each other and put them in their place, again and again.[44]

In Project Cyber Safety, boys and girls receive a potpourri of competing gendered sexual messages. Teens learn that boys are inherently irresponsible, while girls are inherently attention seeking and ultimately vulnerable to teen boys' and adult men's advances. Boys' sexual desires are assumed, validated, and given boundaries. Meanwhile, girls' sexual desires are both obscured and penalized harshly—with cyberbullying, abuse, sextortion, and the threat of a permanently tarnished reputation. Further, girls learn that they are personally responsible for preventing these penalties: by not acting or presenting themselves as "slutty," by not engaging in online sexual activity that is both normative and expected in their peer groups, by not trusting that boys they meet online are whom they say they are, and also by not trusting boys they know and love. While Project Cyber Safety was designed to mitigate bullying, the approach replicated a series of related messages about girls' sexual morality already circulating at Township, further emphasizing the value of slut-shaming in girls' lives and the need to regulate their own actions and representations online.

Finally, while girls learn that they should prevent cyber conflicts by being nice, boys learn that girls handle conflict in inferior ways. In true irony, boys are taught—in school, by police officers, during an *anti-bullying training*—to physically fight their conflicts out and that if they cyberbully each other the way girls do, they're not "real men." Neither girls nor boys learn anything regarding what these conflicts are about or how the many pressures and penalties that adults delineated during this training deeply shape them.

While these initiatives are only two examples of the many programs available through the bullying prevention market, they offer a cautionary tale that warrants the need to think critically about the tools the anti-bullying era is offering today's youth. Here, boys' options for gender expression are bound by "preventative" messages that encourage the linkage of masculinity both to physical violence and to the objectification of girls and women. Meanwhile, girls are limited by gendered directives on the value of niceness met with anti-bullying lessons that equate their social value with their sexual actions. Anti-bullying initiatives are clearly not enough to contend with the extensive ways that gender and sexuality are policed in adolescence. Rather than teaching youth to "spread kindness like confetti," teens might be better served if adults more directly and systemically address the gender/sexual minefield youth have to negotiate routinely throughout their school days. Producing dichotomous models of girls who are "kind" and boys who "fight like men" does little to remedy these challenges. Our concern for teens must expand beyond the surface of their conflicts and instead attend to the much deeper, more divisive inequities that shape teenagers' lives and relationships. At the very least, our attempts to prevent bullying shouldn't reproduce them.

NOTES

1 All names are pseudonyms.
2 Greenberg, 2019.
3 Stuart-Cassel et al., 2011.
4 Meyer, 2016.
5 Evans et al., 2014; Jiménez-Barbero et al., 2016; Merrell et al., 2008; Polanin et al., 2012.

6   Foreman, 2015; Green et al., 2015; Meyer, 2016; Paceley and Flynn, 2012; Smith et al., 2012; Thornberg, 2011; Wayne, 2013; Weaver et al., 2013.
7   Bansel et al., 2009.
8   Formby, 2015; Ringrose and Renold, 2010; Walton, 2005b.
9   Pascoe, 2013; Payne and Smith, 2013; Ringrose, 2006; Ringrose and Renold, 2010; Walton, 2005a.
10 Meyer, 2016.
11 Abels, 2017.
12 Faris and Felmlee, 2011, 2014.
13 Bazelon, 2013; Klein, 2012; Messerschmidt, 2012; Meyer, 2009; Pascoe, 2013; Payne, 2012.
14 Miller, 2016.
15 Duncan, 1999; Messerschmidt, 2012; Pascoe, 2013, 2007; Payne and Smith, 2013; Rivers and Duncan, 2013.
16 Abels, 2017; Meyer, 2016.
17 Gilligan, 1982; Taylor et al., 1995.
18 Simmons, 2012.
19 Garbarino, 2006; Meadows, 2002, 2003; Prothrow-Stith and Spivak, 2005.
20 Simmons, 2012; Wiseman, 2009.
21 Brown, 2003; Chesney-Lind and Irwin, 2008.
22 Bazelon, 2013; Marcus, 2010; McNeil, 2010.
23 Chesney-Lind and Irwin, 2008; Chesney-Lind et al., 2007.
24 Brown, 2003; Chesney-Lind and Irwin, 2008; Chesney-Lind and Jones, 2010; Hadley, 2003.
25 Ness, 2010.
26 Davis, 1981; Levine, 2002; McCreery, 2008; Smith-Rosenberg, 1985.
27 Chesney-Lind and Irwin, 2008; Ness, 2010.
28 Miller, 2016; Norris and Orchowski, 2020; Payne, 2012.
29 Meyer, 2012; Schilt and Westbrook, 2009; Russell and Horn, 2016.
30 Mishna et al., 2018.
31 Mishna et al., 2018.
32 Ringrose and Renold, 2010.
33 Nayak and Kehily, 1996.
34 Reay, 2002.
35 Ringrose and Renold, 2010.
36 Basile et al., 2020; Norris and Orchowski, 2020.
37 Hlavka, 2014.
38 Miller, 2016; Payne, 2012.
39 Armstrong et al., 2014; Fjaer et al., 2015; Garcia, 2009; Wilkins and Miller, 2017; Wilkins, 2008.
40 Miller, 2016; Payne, 2012.
41 Bay-Cheng, 2003; Fine, 1988; Fine and McClelland, 2006; Garcia, 2012.
42 Simeone and Jeglic, 2019.

43 Cameron, 2020.
44 See also Brown, 2003.

REFERENCES

Abels, Margot. 2017. "The Kindness Cure: A Critical Inquiry into Discourses of Bullying, School-Based Prevention Education and the Reproduction of Gender Inequality." PhD diss., Northeastern University.

Armstrong, Elizabeth A., Laura T. Hamilton, Elizabeth M. Armstrong, and J. Lotus Seeley. 2014. "Good Girls: Gender, Social Class and Slut Discourse on Campus." *Social Psychology Quarterly* 77 (2): 100–122.

Bansel, Peter, Bronwyn Davies, Cath Laws, and Sheridan Linnell. 2009. "Bullies, Bullying and Power in the Contexts of Schooling." *British Journal of Sociology of Education* 30 (1): 59–69.

Basile, Kathleen, Heather Clayton, Sarah DeGue, et al. 2020. "Interpersonal Violence Victimization Among High School Students Youth Risk Behavior Survey, United States, 2019." MMWR Surveillance Summaries. Atlanta: U.S. Department of Health and Human Services, Centers for Disease Control and Prevention. www.cdc.gov.

Bay-Cheng, Laina. 2003. "The Trouble of Teen Sex: The Construction of Adolescent Sexuality through School-Based Sexuality Education." *Sex Education* 3 (1): 61–74.

Bazelon, Emily. 2013. *Sticks and Stones: Defeating the Culture of Bullying and Rediscovering the Power of Character and Empathy.* New York: Random House.

Brown, Lyn Mikel. 2003. *Girlfighting: Betrayal and Rejection among Girls.* New York: New York University Press.

Cameron, Deborah. 2020. "Banter, Male Bonding, and the Language of Donald Trump." In *Language in the Trump Era: Scandals and Emergencies,* ed. Janet McIntosh and Norma Mendoza-Denton, 158–167. Cambridge: Cambridge University Press.

Chesney-Lind, Meda, and Katherine Irwin. 2008. *Beyond Bad Girls: Gender, Violence, and Hype.* New York: Routledge.

Chesney-Lind, Meda, and Nikki Jones, eds. 2010. *Fighting for Girls: New Perspectives on Gender and Violence.* Albany: State University of New York Press.

Chesney-Lind, Meda, Merry Morash, and Katherine Irwin. 2007. "Policing Girlhood? Relational Aggression and Violence Prevention." *Youth Violence and Juvenile Justice* 5 (3): 328–345.

Damaske, Sarah. 2011. *For the Family? How Class and Gender Shape Women's Work.* New York: Oxford University Press.

Davis, Angela Y. 1981. *Women, Race & Class.* New York: Random House.

Duncan, Neil. 1999. *Sexual Bullying: Gender, Conflict and Pupil Culture in Secondary Schools.* London: Routledge.

Evans, Caroline B. R., Mark W. Fraser, and Katie L. Cotter. 2014. "The Effectiveness of School-Based Bullying Prevention Programs: A Systematic Review." *Aggression and Violent Behavior* 19 (5): 532–544.

Faris, Robert, and Diane Felmlee. 2011. "Status Struggles Network Centrality and Gender Segregation in Same- and Cross-Gender Aggression." *American Sociological Review* 76 (1): 48–73.

———. 2014. "Casualties of Social Combat School Networks of Peer Victimization and Their Consequences." *American Sociological Review* 79 (2): 228–257.

Fine, Michelle. 1988. "Sexuality, Schooling, and Adolescent Females: The Missing Discourse of Desire." *Harvard Educational Review* 58 (1): 29–53.

Fine, Michelle, and Sara McClelland. 2006. "Sexuality Education and Desire: Still Missing after All These Years." *Harvard Educational Review* 76 (3): 297–338.

Fjaer, Eivind Grip, Willy Pedersen, and Sveinung Sandberg. 2015. "'I'm Not One of Those Girls': Boundary-Work and the Sexual Double Standard in a Liberal Hookup Context." *Gender & Society* 29 (6): 960–981.

Foreman, Victoria. 2015. "Constructing the Victim in the Bullying Narrative: How Bullying Discourses Affirm Rather Than Challenge Discriminatory Notions of Gender and Sexuality." *Crime, Media, Culture* 11 (2): 157–176.

Formby, Eleanor. 2015. "Limitations of Focusing on Homophobic, Biphobic and Transphobic 'Bullying' to Understand and Address LGBT Young People's Experiences within and beyond School." *Sex Education: Sexuality, Society and Learning* 15 (July): 626–640.

Garbarino, James. 2006. *See Jane Hit: Why Girls Are Growing More Violent and What Can Be Done about It*. New York: Penguin.

Garcia, Lorena. 2009. "'Now Why Do You Want to Know about That?' Heteronormativity, Sexism, and Racism in the Sexual (Mis)education of Latina Youth." *Gender & Society* 23 (4): 520–541.

———. 2012. *Respect Yourself, Protect Yourself: Latina Girls and Sexual Identity*. New York: New York University Press.

Gilligan, Carol. 1982. *In a Different Voice: Psychological Theory and Women's Development*. Cambridge, MA: Harvard University Press.

Green, Michael, Ania Bobrowicz, and Chee Siang Ang. 2015. "The Lesbian, Gay, Bisexual and Transgender Community Online: Discussions of Bullying and Self-Disclosure in YouTube Videos." *Behaviour & Information Technology* 34 (7): 704–712.

Greenberg, Max. 2019. *Twelve Weeks to Change a Life: At Risk Youth in a Fractured State*. Berkeley: University of California Press.

Hadley, Martha. 2003. "Relational, Indirect, Adaptive, or Just Mean: Recent Work on Aggression in Adolescent Girls." *Studies in Gender and Sexuality* 4 (4): 367–394.

Hlavka, Heather R. 2014. "Normalizing Sexual Violence: Young Women Account for Harassment and Abuse." *Gender & Society* 28 (3): 337–358.

Jiménez-Barbero, Jose Antonio, José Ruiz Hernández, Laura Llor-Zaragoza, María Pérez-García, and Bartolomé Llor-Esteban. 2016. "Effectiveness of Anti-bullying School Programs: A Meta-analysis." *Children and Youth Services Review* 61 (1): 165–175.

Klein, Jessie. 2012. *The Bully Society: School Shootings and the Crisis of Bullying in America's Schools*. New York: New York University Press.

Lareau, Annette. 2003. *Unequal Childhoods: Class, Race, and Family Life*. Berkeley: University of California Press.

Levine, Judith. 2002. *Harmful to Minors: The Perils of Protecting Children from Sex*. New York: Thunder's Mouth Press.

Marcus, Ruth. 2010. "Should We Be Criminalizing Bullies?" *Washington Post*, April 7.

McCreery, Patrick. 2008. "Save Our Children / Let Us Marry: Gay Activists Appropriate the Rhetoric of Child Protectionism." *Radical History Review* 100 (Winter): 186–207.

McNeil, Leslie. 2010. "Suicide in South Hadley Bullied to Death?" *People*, February 22. https://people.com.

Meadows, Susannah. 2002. "Meet the Gamma Girls." *Newsweek*, June 3, 44–51.

———. 2003. "Girl Fight: Savagery in the Chicago Suburbs." *Newsweek*, May 18. www.newsweek.com.

Merrell, Kenneth W., Barbara A. Gueldner, Scott W. Ross, and Duane M. Isava. 2008. "How Effective Are School Bullying Intervention Programs? A Meta-analysis of Intervention Research." *School Psychology Quarterly* 23 (1): 26–42.

Messerschmidt, James W. 2012. *Gender, Heterosexuality, and Youth Violence: The Struggle for Recognition*. Lanham, MD: Rowman & Littlefield.

Meyer, Doug. 2012. "An Intersectional Analysis of Lesbian, Gay, Bisexual, and Transgender (LGBT) People's Evaluations of Anti-queer Violence." *Gender & Society* 26 (6): 849–873.

———. 2016. "The Gentle Neoliberalism of Modern Anti-bullying Texts: Surveillance, Intervention, and Bystanders in Contemporary Bullying Discourse." *Sexuality Research and Social Policy* 13 (4): 356–370.

Meyer, Elizabeth J. 2009. *Gender, Bullying, and Harassment: Strategies to End Sexism and Homophobia in Schools*. New York: Teachers College Press.

Miller, Sarah. 2016. "'How You Bully a Girl': Sexual Drama and the Negotiation of Gendered Sexuality in High School." *Gender & Society* 30 (5): 721–744.

Mishna, Faye, Kaitlin J. Schwan, Arija Birze, Melissa Van Wert, Ashley Lacombe-Duncan, Lauren McInroy, and Shalhevet Attar-Schwartz. 2018. "Gendered and Sexualized Bullying and Cyber Bullying: Spotlighting Girls and Making Boys Invisible." *Youth & Society* 52 (3): 403–426.

Nayak, Anoop, and Mary Kehily. 1996. "Playing It Straight: Masculinities, Homophobias and Schooling." *Journal of Gender Studies* 5 (2): 211–230.

Ness, Cindy D. 2010. *Why Girls Fight: Female Youth Violence in the Inner City*. New York: New York University Press.

Norris, Alyssa, and Lindsay Orchowski. 2020. "Peer Victimization of Sexual Minority and Transgender Youth: A Cross-Sectional Study of High School Students." *Psychology of Violence* 10 (2): 201–211.

Paceley, Megan S., and Karen Flynn. 2012. "Media Representations of Bullying toward Queer Youth: Gender, Race, and Age Discrepancies." *Journal of LGBT Youth* 9 (4): 340–356.

Pascoe, C. J. 2007. *Dude, You're a Fag: Masculinity and Sexuality in High School*. Berkeley: University of California Press.

———. 2013. "Notes on a Sociology of Bullying: Young Men's Homophobia as Gender Socialization." *QED* 1 (1): 87–104.

Payne, Elizabethe. 2012. "Slut." *Huffington Post*, October 12. www.huffingtonpost.com.

Payne, Elizabethe, and Melissa Smith. 2013. "LGBTQ Kids, School Safety, and Missing the Big Picture: How the Dominant Bullying Discourse Prevents School Professionals from Thinking about Systemic Marginalization or . . . Why We Need to Rethink LGBTQ Bullying." *QED* 1 (1): 1–36.

Polanin, Joshua, Dorothy Espelage, and Therese Pigott. 2012. "A Meta-analysis of School-Based Bullying Prevention Programs' Effects on Bystander Intervention Behavior." *School Psychology Review* 41 (1): 47–65.

Prothrow-Stith, Deborah, and Howard R. Spivak. 2005. *Sugar and Spice and No Longer Nice: How We Can Stop Girls' Violence*. San Francisco: Jossey-Bass.

Reay, Diane. 2002. "Shaun's Story: Troubling Discourses of White Working-Class Masculinities." *Gender and Education* 14 (3): 221–234.

Ringrose, Jessica. 2006. "The New Universal Mean Girl: Examining the Discursive Construction and Social Regulation of a New Feminine Pathology." *Feminism & Psychology* 16 (4): 405–424.

Ringrose, Jessica, and E. J. Renold. 2010. "Normative Cruelties and Gender Deviants: The Performative Effects of Bully Discourses for Girls and Boys in School." *British Educational Research Journal* 36 (4): 573–596.

Rivers, Ian, and Neil Duncan. 2013. *Bullying: Experiences and Discourses of Sexuality and Gender*. New York: Routledge.

Russell, Stephen T., and Stacey S. Horn, eds. 2016. *Sexual Orientation, Gender Identity, and Schooling: The Nexus of Research, Practice, and Policy*. New York: Oxford University Press.

Schilt, Kristen, and Laurel Westbrook. 2009. "Doing Gender, Doing Heteronormativity: 'Gender Normals,' Transgender People, and the Social Maintenance of Heterosexuality." *Gender & Society* 23:440–464.

Simeone, Stephanie, and Elizabeth Jeglic. 2019. "Is Locker Room Talk Really Just Talk? An Analysis of Normative Sexual Talk and Behavior." *Deviant Behavior* 40 (12): 1587–1595.

Simmons, Rachel 2012. *Odd Girl Out: The Hidden Culture of Aggression in Girls*. Rev. ed. Boston: Mariner Books.

Smith, Peter K., Allison Kupferberg, Joaquin A. Mora-Merchan, Muthanna Samara, Sue Bosley, and Rob Osborn. 2012. "A Content Analysis of School Anti-bullying Policies: A Follow-Up after Six Years." *Educational Psychology in Practice* 28 (1): 47–70.

Smith-Rosenberg, Carroll. 1985. *Disorderly Conduct: Visions of Gender in Victorian America*. New York: Oxford University Press.

Stuart-Cassel, Victoria, Ariana Bell, and J. Fred Springer. 2011. "Analysis of State Bullying Laws and Policies." Folsom, CA: U.S. Department of Education. www2.ed.gov.

Taylor, Jill McLean, Carol Gilligan, and Amy M. Sullivan. 1995. *Between Voice and Silence: Women and Girls, Race and Relationship*. Cambridge, Mass.: Harvard University Press.

Thornberg, Robert. 2011. "'She's Weird!'—The Social Construction of Bullying in School: A Review of Qualitative Research." *Children & Society* 25 (4): 258–267.

Walton, Gerald. 2005a. "Bullying Widespread: A Critical Analysis of Research and Public Discourse on Bullying." *Journal of School Violence* 4 (1): 91–118.

———. 2005b. "The Notion of Bullying through the Lens of Foucault and Critical Theory." *Journal of Educational Thought (JET) / Revue de La Pensée Éducative* 39 (1): 55–73.

Wayne, Rachel. 2013. "The Social Construction of Childhood Bullying through U.S. News Media." *Journal of Contemporary Anthropology* 4 (1): 37–49.

Weaver, Lori M., James R. Brown, Daniel B. Weddle, and Matthew C. Aalsma. 2013. "A Content Analysis of Protective Factors within States' Antibullying Laws." *Journal of School Violence* 12 (2): 156–173.

Wilkins, Amy C. 2008. *Wannabes, Goths, and Christians: The Boundaries of Sex, Style, and Status*. Chicago: University of Chicago Press.

Wilkins, Amy C., and Sarah A. Miller. 2017. "'Secure Girls': Class, Sexuality and Self-Esteem." *Sexualities* 20 (7): 815–834.

Wiseman, Rosalind. 2009. *Queen Bees and Wannabes: Helping Your Daughter Survive Cliques, Gossip, Boyfriends, and the New Realities of Girl World*. Rev. ed. New York: Three Rivers Press.

7

Status Motivation, Network Stability, and Instrumental Cruelty

ROBERT FARIS AND LIANN TUCKER

There is by now strong evidence that much (and perhaps most) bullying is instrumental in nature, intended for the purpose of social climbing. Bullying and related forms of cruelty can be seen as both a display of power and a means of attaining it. Rooted in the competition for social status, bullying is a tool used by the socially ambitious to ascend their school social hierarchies. Yet the theory of instrumental aggression gives rise to a paradox: *if bullying can bring social rewards, why are there not more bullies?* After all, even by the broadest definition, only a minority of students are engaged in bullying at any time.[1] We resolve this paradox with an empirical analysis of personal values and network structure, using a large panel study of adolescent social networks to document two countervailing cycles whereby values affect networks in ways that subsequently reinforce those same values.

Theories of Bullying, Instrumental and Otherwise

Early research on bullying tended to emphasize its psychological antecedents, such as empathy deficits, low self-esteem, and internalizing problems.[2] Research on the precursors of victimization, meanwhile, has long pointed to physical, social, and psychological vulnerabilities[3] such as depression and anxiety,[4] acne and related skin disorders,[5] obesity,[6] poor body image,[7] disability,[8] LGBTQ identities,[9] and social isolation or low-quality friendships.[10] None of these psychological or physical characteristics are traditionally associated with high status during adolescence. Yet as scholars turned their attention to the peer context, they quickly discovered that bullies are often in fact quite popular and generally well liked, and many have strong, rather than maladapted, social skills.[11]

If bullying and peer status were linked, it was not immediately clear if status fueled cruelty, with popular youth abusing their power over subordinates, or bullying boosted status, or both, and theories of bullying at that time, often imported from other fields in psychology, sociology, and criminology, did not offer clear direction on this. The theories tended to ignore the association between status and aggression altogether, focusing instead[12] on weak or insecure attachments to parents and caregivers,[13] pathological cultural traditions specific to some organizations,[14] defiant reactions to behavioral sanctions,[15] or in-group versus out-group conflicts.[16] Recent application of standard criminological theories, including strain theory, differential association, and self-control theory, to bullying received relatively minimal empirical support.[17] Bronfenbrenner's ecological theory provides a particularly useful framework for understanding interacting risk factors, such as behavioral modeling and exposure to violence, operating in overlapping peer, family, school, and neighborhood contexts.[18] Few if any theories could explain its connection to popularity or offer guidance as to who was likely to bully whom, and why.

The simplest explanation for the link between popularity and bullying is that the latter is an instrumental action intended to achieve the former. More formally, *in enduring social contexts lacking formally organized hierarchies, socially ambitious people are likely to cruelly antagonize each other in order to gain or maintain social status.* The first scope condition—that contexts be enduring—is important because those whose encounters are (expected to be) fleeting are unlikely to invest energy in climbing an ultimately ephemeral social ladder, and the second because formal role structures invest prestige and power in some at the expense of others, preempting the status contests before they begin. Cruelty may occur in such contexts, but it is probably motivated by other concerns.

Schools—at least ones that are not so large that many students could be strangers to each other—certainly meet both of these criteria. But while it is common to think of bullying as an exclusively adolescent phenomenon, we believe the greatest differences between adults and adolescents are not intrinsic to the life course but rather functions of the contexts in which they find themselves. Teenagers are caged, spending most of their waking hours confined in crowded settings lacking formal role structures and established hierarchies, and so they must sort out roles and statuses for themselves. Adults rarely find themselves in contexts that are like schools, instead spending most of their time either situated into organized roles via various institutions (the family) and formal organizations (the workplace) or as free-ranging actors whose unstructured encounters with others tend to be fleeting, diffuse (in the sense that they lack a stable audience for the interaction), and avoidable. In short, when adults are stuck together, they tend to have organized role relationships. When adults do find themselves confined within settings without (or with minimal) formal role relations, as they are in houses or on islands in reality TV, or more commonly in prisons, book clubs, retirement communities, parent-teacher associations, and academic departments, they sometimes find themselves behaving like high schoolers. So while here we apply the theory to adolescents in middle and high schools, it can be generalized to other cases as well.

A theory of instrumental bullying implies several testable hypotheses. First, and fundamentally, it should be specifically *status-motivated* behavior. Even if we are unable to observe directly the precise intentions behind specific acts of cruelty, instrumental cruelty implies a positive association between the desire for status and bullying, one that has been supported by empirical research.[19] Second, we should anticipate instrumental aggression to escalate following an increase in social status, which is accompanied by both greater capacity to do harm (through enhanced influence on others) and an increase in potential rivals, which now include those left behind as well as those whose ranks they have joined. In addition to cross-sectional associations, large, longitudinal studies have shown that gains in social status are associated with subsequent increases in aggressive behavior.[20] Yet just because bullies are popular does not mean they are instrumental—they could be sadists instead. If aggression is instrumental, then desistance should occur once status goals have been reached, which is what seems to happen.[21]

To the extent that it is instrumental, bullying should be directed at rivals of relatively high status. Bullying vulnerable schoolmates could be a way of enforcing (or defining) group norms, but it is unlikely to boost popularity.[22] To the contrary, it is more impressive to challenge the strong than to abuse the weak, so ambitious bullies must target prominent social rivals rather than wallflowers. Indeed, empirical research finds that victimization rates tend to increase, not decrease, as adolescents gain social status[23] or act aggressively themselves.[24]

Furthermore, the logic of social rivalry dictates that adversaries are not just powerful but proximate. If relationships are the currency of social status, then competition, and potentially aggression, is particularly likely at short social distances (e.g., within friendship groups). Additionally, upward mobility necessitates leaving old friends behind as new ones take their places, generating animosity in the process. Recent research confirms that cruelty and aggression are significantly more likely to occur between friends and between other structurally equivalent students, with especially distressing consequences for their victims.[25]

Finally, and crucially, aggression can in fact improve social status. Sophomore bullies were more likely to join elite social circles (as reflected in yearbook designations) by their senior year—provided that their victims were high status, socially close (e.g., friends, or at least within the same friendship group), or aggressive themselves.[26] Moreover, their victims were effectively banished from elite social circles.[27] Other research confirms that the status benefits of aggression depend on "punching up," finding that targeting high-status, rather than low-status, victims is associated with greater status gains.[28] Cumulatively, these results offer robust support for the existence of instrumental aggression, whereby aspiring social climbers tear down their popular rivals to boost their own prospects, desisting only once they ascend the peak of their school's social pyramid.

Structure and Motivation

Despite its empirical support, this theory introduces a paradox: if "social combat" allows aggressors to enhance their prestige and expand their influence while marginalizing their vanquished rivals, *then why is it not more common, and why does it not increase in prevalence?* Differences in measurement techniques can affect bullying prevalence rates, but regardless of the measure used, bullies and their victims invariably compose a small minority of any student body. Moreover, much of the bullying and aggression that does occur is directed toward the already vulnerable and does not fit the profile of instrumental aggression. Thus, its effectiveness notwithstanding, only a fraction of students would appear to be engaged in social combat at any given time. Moreover, this fraction shrinks over the course of adolescence, as has been widely documented.[29]

Part of the explanation no doubt lies in the fact that some of them have superior means at their disposal. If one wants to be popular in an American high school, bullying schoolmates is no doubt less efficient, and riskier, than being athletic, good-looking, or rich. But only a lucky few are able to fill those lanes to the top, and yet the many students they leave behind generally do not use aggression as a way to catch up. One might also imagine adolescent status hierarchies are highly crystallized, with few opportunities for mobility due to the weight of Matthew effects and other mechanisms of cumulative advantage. Yet these hierarchies are in fact highly turbulent, with abundant examples of rising fortunes to inspire the tactical use of aggression.[30] Yet most abstain.

We offer two propositions as an explanation. First, only a minority of students care deeply about status, with almost none putting it ahead of close friendships. Instead of eyeing the next rung on the social ladder, most teens prioritize the intimacy, support, and loyalty of existing friendships over the prestige of more popular ones.[31] With this in mind, using aggression to achieve status is risky in two ways: it may not work, and it may terminate existing friendships. While friendship termination is a normal part of development as adolescents develop new interests and values,[32] it can still result in distress due to the loss and stress,[33] distress that is only partly mitigated by newfound friendships.[34] The benefits of stable and close friendships include prosociality,[35] lower levels of loneliness,[36] and lower levels of aggression and victimization,[37] while unstable friendships put students at risk for worse academic performance and overall well-being.[38]

Second, motivations—for close friendships or for status—reinforce the stability (or turnover) in friendships, which in turn further bolsters those same values. Specifically, we anticipate two reinforcing cycles, one where adolescents who prioritize having close friends retain more of them over time, which subsequently strengthens the importance of close friendships, and a second where adolescents who prioritize status tend to change friends, further intensifying their thirst for popularity. But because most adolescents prioritize close friendships over popularity, they retain more friends over time, further invest in those same friendships, and ultimately devalue popularity and eschew the cruelties that can achieve it.

Data and Methods

We test these propositions using data from the Context study, a large NIH-funded panel study of over seven thousand adolescents from three counties in North Carolina from 2003 to 2007. At wave 1, all sixth, seventh, and eighth graders attending public schools in those counties were eligible to participate, and eligibility was extended to new students who joined the original cohorts in subsequent waves. Trained data collectors administered in-school paper surveys every six months, with the exception of wave 7, which was collected one year after wave 6. One county school district withdrew from the study after wave 5, for unrelated reasons. Response rates were high, between 89 percent (wave 1) and 73 percent (wave 7), and 7,174 students participated in at least one wave.

We estimate a maximum likelihood (with missing values) cross-lagged linear model with four endogenous variables, observed at waves 1, 3, and 5 (hereafter referred to as T1–T3), so each observation occurred in the spring of a school year, with one year between observations. The endogenous variables include status valuation, close friend valuation, friendship network centrality, and retained friends. Status valuation is measured using a question asking respondents how important "being popular" is to them, with four response categories (very, somewhat, not very, not at all). Close friend valuation is measured using a question asking respondents how important "having a close group of friends" is to them, with the same four response categories. The remaining two endogenous variables are calculated from the friendship networks, generated by asking respondents to name up to five of their best friends. Network centrality is measured using three-step in-reach, which is the percentage of the school network that can reach ego on incoming paths of length three or less.[39] Retained friends is simply the number of friend nominations that remained the same from the prior time point. We control for gender (with female as the reference), race/ethnicity (white, African American, Latinx, and other), and cohort (eighth, ninth, and tenth grades at T3).

Results

The sample is 51 percent white and 36 percent African American and is evenly divided by gender and grade in school (Table 7.1). At T1, the average student could be reached (on incoming ties) by 11 percent of their schoolmates; this figure drops to 8 percent by T2, when more of them have entered large high schools.

As anticipated, the desire for popularity is not as widespread as common wisdom or cinematic portrayals might suggest, as less than one-third of students reported that being popular is very important to them (Table 7.2). At T1, 62 percent of respondents said it is either very (32 percent) or somewhat (30 percent) important to be popular, compared to 95 percent who felt that having close friends is very (81 percent) or somewhat (14 percent) important. Also as anticipated, only a tiny fraction (3 percent or fewer) of students care more about popularity than about close friendships.

Interestingly, the importance of both status and friendships appeared to decline over time and at T3 had fallen to 90 percent and 50 percent of students reporting that close friends and popularity, respectively, are at least somewhat important. We explore trends in these priorities by combining the two lowest categories ("not at all" and "not very") and the two highest categories ("very" and "somewhat") for each variable and then cross-tabulating them over time. If there are value-reinforcing cycles, then, given the initial distribution of priorities, we should expect the importance of close friends to increase over time and the importance of popularity to decline. We find that this is the case: the proportion of students who value both popularity and close friendships declines over time, falling from over 60 percent to under 50 percent at T3 (Figure 7.1), while the percentage who cared only about close friendships increased, as did the percentage who cared about neither.

We test for reinforcing cycles using a cross-lagged linear model focusing on the relationships between these two values and friendship stability. Specifically, we include importance of popularity and importance of close friends as exogenous variables at T1, and endogenous variables at

TABLE 7.1. Descriptive Statistics

	Mean	SD	Min	Max
Importance of close friends T1	2.75	0.58	0	3
Importance of close friends T2	2.67	0.71	0	3
Importance of close friends T3	2.60	0.78	0	3
Importance of popularity T1	1.79	1.05	0	3
Importance of popularity T2	1.60	1.11	0	3
Importance of popularity T3	1.49	1.11	0	3
Centrality T1	0.11	0.10	0	0.71
Centrality T2	0.08	0.09	0	0.90625
Retained friends T1–T2	0.58	0.94	0	5
Retained friends T2–T3	0.48	0.89	0	5
Girl	0.49	0.50	0	1
Boy	0.51	0.50	0	1
African American	0.36	0.48	0	1
White	0.51	0.50	0	1
Latinx (nonwhite)	0.04	0.20	0	1
Other race/ethnicity	0.08	0.25	0	1
8th grade	0.34	0.47	0	1
9th grade	0.33	0.47	0	1
10th grade	0.33	0.47	0	1

Note: $N = 7{,}174$.

TABLE 7.2. Importance of Close Friends and Being Popular

	Importance of close friends			Importance of being popular		
	T1	T2	T3	T1	T2	T3
Not at all important	0.01	0.03	0.04	0.15	0.22	0.24
Not very important	0.04	0.05	0.06	0.23	0.23	0.27
Somewhat important	0.14	0.14	0.16	0.30	0.27	0.24
Very important	0.81	0.78	0.74	0.32	0.27	0.25
	T1	T2	T3			
Values close friends more than popularity	0.60	0.62	0.63			
Values both equally	0.37	0.35	0.34			
Values popularity more than close friends	0.03	0.02	0.03			

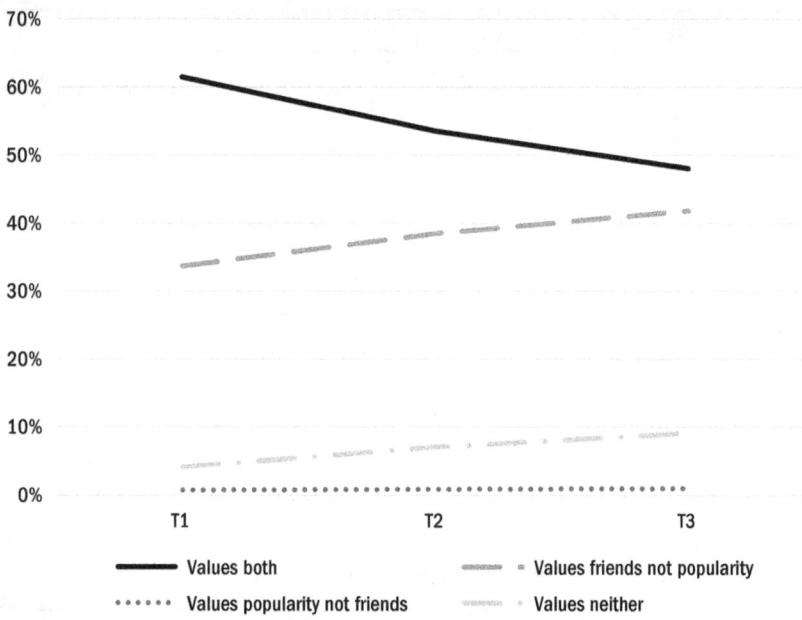

Figure 7.1. Proportion Valuing Popularity and Close Friends over Time

T2 and T3. We include retained friends at two stages, from T1 to T2 and from T2 to T3. Finally, because these processes are likely to affect and be affected by actual social status, we include network centrality (three-step in-reach) exogenously at T1 and endogenously at T2. We constrain to equality the paths that are repeated (e.g., the paths from importance of popularity T1 → retained friends T1–T2, and from importance of popularity T2 → retained friends T2–T3 are constrained to be equal). The path diagram, omitting repeated paths and exogenous controls (for gender, race, and grade), is shown in Figure 7.2.

Results are consistent with the existence of two countervailing cycles, one where adolescents who value close friendships retain more friends over time, which further strengthens the importance of friendship, and a second, where youth who value status subsequently gain status and retain fewer friends, both of which subsequently intensify their desire for status. Specifically, importance of popularity at T1 is associated with a significant increase ($\beta = 0.027$, $p < .05$) in centrality at T2 and with a significant decrease ($\beta = -0.044$, $p < .001$) in the number of friends retained between T1 and T2 (Table 7.3). Retaining fewer friends in turn is associated with increased importance of popularity ($\beta = -0.026$, $p < .01$). In contrast, students who strongly value having a close group of friends are subsequently likely to retain more friends ($\beta = 0.062$, $p < .001$), and retaining more friends is in turn associated with subsequent increases in the importance of close friendships ($\beta = 0.036$, $p < .001$).

In a bit of irony, the positive direct effect of importance of popularity on centrality is undercut by its negative effect on retained friendships (which is associated with increased centrality), rendering its total effect on centrality statistically marginal (Table 7.4). Meanwhile, status valuation, which does not itself have a significant direct effect on centrality, actually has a statistically significant and slightly larger positive total effect on centrality than status valuation by virtue of its strong effect on retained friends. As with Aesop's dog who, seeing his own reflection, dropped his meat in a jealous attempt to snatch the other dog's meal, the gains made by social climbers are foiled by their own actions, while those who do not seek status wind up attaining it inadvertently.

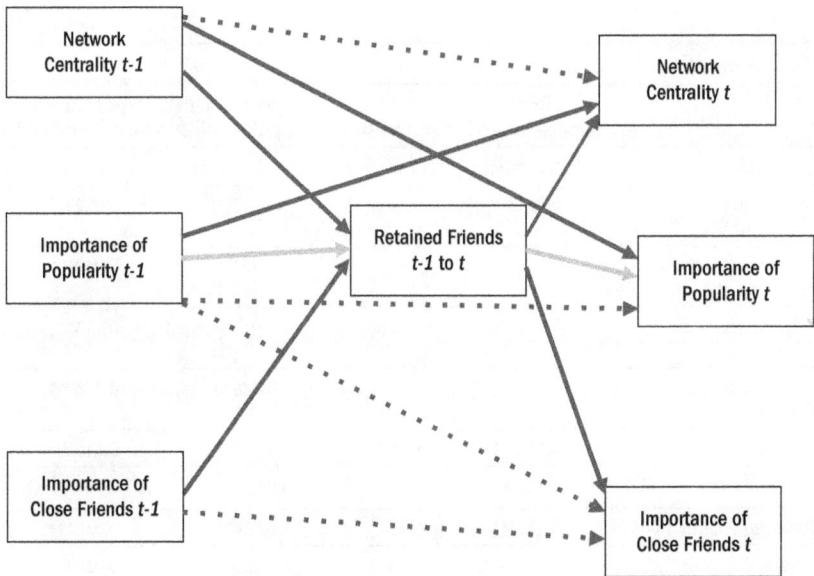

Figure 7.2. Cross-Lagged Linear Model Path Diagram

TABLE 7.3. Cross-Lagged Linear Model of Retained Friends, Status Valuation, Close Friend Valuation, and Centrality

Prior (T − 1) level of:	Retained friends at T Coeff.	SE	Centrality at T Coeff.	SE	Importance of popularity at T Coeff.	SE	Importance of close friends at T Coeff.	SE
Importance of popularity	−0.044***	0.009	0.027*	0.013	0.471***	0.012	0.042***	0.012
Importance of close friends	0.062***	0.010	0.020	0.013	0.025	0.013	0.352***	0.014
Centrality	0.127***	0.008	0.442***	0.011	0.061***	0.009	0.005	0.009
Retained friends	0.422***	0.009	0.121***	0.011	−0.026**	0.008	0.036***	0.008
Likelihood test vs. saturated (42)	309.87***							
RMSEA	0.028							
CFI	0.972							
TLI	0.944							

Note: Model includes controls for gender, race (white, African American, Latino, or other race), and cohort (8th, 9th, or 10th at T). All coefficients standardized. CFI = comparative fit index; RMSEA = root mean square error of approximation; TLI = Tucker–Lewis index.
*$p < .05$. **$p < .01$. ***$p < .001$.

TABLE 7.4. Standardized Total Effects on Tertiary Outcomes

Total effect of:	Retained friends T2–T3 Total effect	Centrality T2 Total effect	Importance of popularity T3 Total effect	Importance of close friends T3 Total effect
Importance of popularity T1	−0.031***	0.022†	0.213***	0.032***
Importance of popularity T2	−0.044***		0.472***	0.040***
Importance of close friends T1	0.042***	0.026*	0.017†	0.113***
Importance of close friends T2	0.062***		0.024†	0.354***
Centrality T1	0.115***	0.408***	0.055***	0.013
Centrality T2	0.127***		0.057***	0.009
Retained friends T1–T2	0.441***	0.121***	−0.016*	0.030***
Retained friends T2–T3			−0.026**	0.036***

†$p < .10$. *$p < .05$. **$p < .01$. ***$p < .001$.

Conclusion

This analysis resolves one paradox of instrumental aggression, namely that relatively few adolescents utilize it, despite its effectiveness for boosting status. The reason, we argue, is that, in contrast to common wisdom and media portrayals, comparatively few adolescents care deeply about being popular. Almost none care more about popularity than about maintaining close friendships. Moreover, the desire for status appears to wane as adolescents age. This would appear to be explained by the two countervailing cycles discovered in this analysis, one reinforcing the importance of status while destabilizing friendships, the other reinforcing the importance of close friendships while buttressing friendship networks. Considering that more students fall into the latter cycle, it should come as no surprise that somewhat fewer students care about status over time. Nonetheless, bullying and related forms of cruelty remain all too common, affecting millions of youth annually.

Unfortunately, most bullying prevention programs do not work, at least not under randomized controlled trials, and some even make matters worse.[40] Most of those that do reduce bullying do so modestly, with effect sizes of statistical but not practical significance. The ineffectuality of prevention programs is no doubt explained by the social rewards that can accompany aggression. Further evidence of this can be found the results of KiVa, one of the few programs to achieve meaningful reductions in bullying. Randomized trials find that KiVa cuts the rate of bullying nearly in half compared to control schools, but one group appears to be effectively immune to the program: popular bullies.[41] It should come as no surprise that those who benefit from aggression resist programs intended to eliminate it. Rather than futilely attempting to persuade them to desist, prevention efforts might be better served by addressing ends rather than means, by fostering stronger, more stable friendships, which would in turn redirect adolescents' priorities away from popularity contests and toward close friendships.

As evidenced by adolescent sexual networks and mores, structures imply norms and vice versa.[42] But structures are not static. Observed over time, one set of values may build stable, crystallized structures, while another churns away at them, with destructive consequences.

Fortunately there appear to be more of the former than the latter. Yet it is easier to tear down than to build, so the builders will need help.

NOTES

1. Of course, not all youth possess the assets and competencies required to effectively bully peers (Vaillancourt et al., 2003; Vaillancourt et al., 2008), but most have the capacity to bully *someone* and yet abstain.
2. Swearer et al., 2001; see Cook et al., 2010, for a meta-analysis.
3. Veenstra et al., 2007; Tolsma et al., 2013.
4. Fekkes et al., 2006.
5. Magin, 2013.
6. Janssen et al., 2004.
7. Brixval et al., 2011.
8. Mishna, 2003.
9. Friedman et al., 2011; Felmlee and Faris, 2016.
10. Pellegrini and Bartini, 2000; Faris and Felmlee, 2014; Kendrick et al., 2012.
11. Vaillancourt et al., 2003; Espelage and Holt, 2001; Farmer et al., 2003.
12. Crick and Dodge, 1994.
13. Monks et al., 2005.
14. Roland and Galloway, 2002.
15. Ttofi and Farrington, 2008.
16. Ojala and Nesdale, 2004.
17. Moon et al., 2011.
18. Espelage, 2014.
19. Salmivalli and Peets, 2008; Pellegrini, 2002; Li and Wright, 2014; Ojanen and Nostrand, 2014; Sijtsema et al., 2009; Faris and Ennett, 2012; see also Duffy et al., 2017.
20. Faris and Felmlee, 2011.
21. See Faris and Felmlee, 2011. This result contrasts with experimental research showing that high status erodes empathy (Galinsky et al., 2006); if aggressive behavior is driven by empathy deficits, we should then expect escalation at the top of the hierarchy, not desistance.
22. Pascoe, 2005.
23. Faris and Felmlee, 2014; Andrews et al., 2017; Malamut et al., 2018.
24. Goldbaum et al., 2003.
25. Faris et al., 2020.
26. Faris, 2012.
27. Faris, 2012.
28. Andrews et al., 2017; Peets and Hodges, 2014.
29. Olweus, 1992; Smith et al., 1999; Scheithauer et al., 2006.
30. Moody et al., 2011; Smith and Faris, 2015.
31. Berndt, 2002; Mortimer and Call, 2001; Selman, 1981.
32. Erwin, 1993.
33. Cairns et al., 1995; Rudolph et al., 2000.

34 Bowker et al., 2006.
35 Berndt, 1989; Berndt et al., 1999.
36 Parker and Seal, 1996.
37 Ellis and Zarbatany, 2007; Bowker et al., 2006.
38 Shepherd and Reich, 2020.
39 We use three-step in-reach to ensure that respondents' own friendship nominations, which are core to the retained friends measure, are not at all included in the measure of centrality.
40 Merrell et al., 2008; Smith et al., 2004; Ttofi and Farrington, 2011; Polanin et al., 2012.
41 Garandeau et al., 2014.
42 Bearman et al., 2004.

REFERENCES

Andrews, Naomi C. Z., Laura D. Hanish, and Carlos E. Santos. 2017. "Does an Aggressor's Target Choice Matter? Assessing Change in the Social Network Prestige of Aggressive Youth." *Aggressive Behavior* 43 (4): 364–374.

Arora, Cristina M. J. 1996. "Defining Bullying: Towards a Clearer General Understanding and More Effective Intervention Strategies." *School Psychology International* 17 (4): 317–329.

Bearman, Peter S., James Moody, and Katherine Stovel. 2004. "Chains of Affection: The Structure of Adolescent Romantic and Sexual Networks." *American Journal of Sociology* 110 (1): 44–91.

Berndt, Thomas J. 1989. "Obtaining Support from Friends during Childhood and Adolescence." In *Children's Social Networks and Social Supports*, edited by Deborah Belle, 308–331. New York: John Wiley.

———. 2002. "Friendship Quality and Social Development." *Current Directions in Psychological Science* 11 (1): 7–10.

Berndt, Thomas J., Jacquelyn A. Hawkins, and Ziyi Jiao. 1999. "Influences of Friends and Friendships on Adjustment to Junior High School." *Merrill-Palmer Quarterly* 45 (1): 13–41.

Bowker, Julie C. Wojslawowicz, Kenneth H. Rubin, Kim B. Burgess, Cathryn Booth-LaForce, and Linda Rose-Krasnor. 2006. "Behavioral Characteristics Associated with Stable and Fluid Best Friendship Patterns in Middle Childhood." *Merrill-Palmer Quarterly* 52 (4): 671–693.

Brixval, Carina S., Signe L. B. Rayce, Mette Rasmussen, Bjørn E. Holstein, and Pernille Due. 2011. "Overweight, Body Image and Bullying—An Epidemiological Study of 11- to 15-Years Olds." *European Journal of Public Health* 22 (1): 126–130.

Cairns, Robert B., Man-Chi Leung, Lisa Buchanan, and Beverley D. Cairns. 1995. "Friendships and Social Networks in Childhood and Adolescence: Fluidity, Reliability, and Interrelations." *Child Development* 66 (5): 1330–1345.

Centers for Disease Control and Prevention. 2019. "Facts about Bullying," www.stopbullying.gov.

Chase, Ivan D. 1980. "Social Process and Hierarchy Formation in Small Groups: A Comparative Perspective." *American Sociological Review* 45:905–924.

Cook, Clayton R., Kirk R. Williams, Nancy G. Guerra, Tia E. Kim, and Shelly Sadek. 2010. "Predictors of Bullying and Victimization in Childhood and Adolescence: A Meta-analytic Investigation." *School Psychology Quarterly* 25 (2): 65–83.

Cornell, Dewey, and Susan P. Limber. 2015. "Law and Policy on the Concept of Bullying at School." *American Psychologist* 70 (4): 333–343.

Crick, Nicki R., and Kenneth A. Dodge. 1994. "A Review and Reformulation of Social Information Processing Mechanisms in Children's Social Adjustment." *Psychological Bulletin* 115:74–101.

Duffy, Amanda L., Sarah Penn, Drew Nesdale, and Melanie J. Zimmer-Gembeck. 2017. "Popularity: Does It Magnify Associations between Popularity Prioritization and the Bullying and Defending Behavior of Early Adolescent Boys and Girls?" *Social Development* 26 (2): 263–277.

Ellis, Wendy E., and Lynne Zarbatany. 2007. "Explaining Friendship Formation and Friendship Stability: The Role of Children's and Friends' Aggression and Victimization." *Merrill-Palmer Quarterly* 53 (1): 79–104.

Erwin, Phil. 1993. *Friendship and Peer Relations in Children*. New York: John Wiley.

Espelage, Dorothy L. 2014. "Ecological Theory: Preventing Youth Bullying, Aggression, and Victimization." *Theory into Practice* 53 (4): 257–264.

Espelage, Dorothy L., and Melissa K. Holt. 2001. "Bullying and Victimization during Early Adolescence: Peer Influences and Psychosocial Correlates." *Journal of Emotional Abuse* 2 (2–3): 123–142.

Espelage, Dorothy L., and Susan M. Swearer. 2003. "Research on School Bullying and Victimization: What Have We Learned and Where Do We Go from Here?" *School Psychology Review* 32 (3): 365–383.

Faris, Robert. 2012. "Aggression, Exclusivity, and Status Attainment in Interpersonal Networks." *Social Forces* 90 (4): 1207–1235.

Faris, Robert, and Susan Ennett. 2012. "Adolescent Aggression: The Role of Peer Group Status Motives, Peer Aggression, and Group Characteristics." *Social Networks* 34 (4): 371–378.

Faris, Robert, and Diane Felmlee. 2011. "Status Struggles: Network Centrality and Gender Segregation in Same- and Cross-Gender Aggression." *American Sociological Review* 76 (1): 48–73.

———. 2014. "Casualties of Social Combat: School Networks of Peer Victimization and Their Consequences." *American Sociological Review* 79 (2): 228–257.

———. 2018. "Best Friends for Now: Friendship Network Stability and Adolescents' Life Course Goals." In *Social Networks and the Life Course: Integrating the Development of Human Lives and Social Relational Networks*, vol. 2, edited by D. F. Alwin, D. H. Felmlee, and D. A. Kreager, 185–203. Basel: Springer.

Faris, Robert, Diane Felmlee, and Cassie McMillan. 2020. "With Friends Like These: Aggression from Amity and Equivalence." *American Journal of Sociology* 126 (3): 673–713.

Farmer, Thomas W., David B. Estell, Jennifer L. Bishop, Keri K. O'Neal, and Beverley D. Cairns. 2003. "Rejected Bullies or Popular Leaders? The Social Relations of Aggressive Subtypes of Rural African American Early Adolescents." *Developmental Psychology* 39 (6): 992–1004.

Fekkes, Minne, Frans We.M. Pijpers, A. Miranda Fredriks, Ton Vogels, and S. Pauline Verloove-Vanhorick. 2006. "Do Bullied Children Get Ill, or Do Ill Children Get Bullied? A Prospective Cohort Study on the Relationship between Bullying and Health-Related Symptoms." *Pediatrics* 117 (5): 1568–1574.

Felmlee, Diane, and Robert Faris. 2016. "Toxic Ties: A Network of Friendship, Dating, and Cyber Victimization." *Social Psychology Quarterly* 79 (3): 243–262.

Friedman, Mark S., Michael P. Marshal, Thomas E. Guadamuz, Chongyi Wei, Carolyn F. Wong, Elizabeth M. Saewyc, and Ron Stall. 2011. "A Meta-Analysis of Disparities in Childhood Sexual Abuse, Parental Physical Abuse, and Peer Victimization among Sexual Minority and Sexual Nonminority Individuals." *American Journal of Public Health* 101 (8): 1481–1494.

Galinsky, Adam D., Joe C. Magee, M. Ena Inesi, and Deborah H. Gruenfeld. 2006. "Power and Perspectives Not Taken." *Psychological Science* 17 (12): 1068–1074.

Garandeau, Claire F., Ihno A. Lee, and Christina Salmivalli. 2012. "Differential Effects of the KiVa Anti-bullying Program on Popular and Unpopular Bullies." *Journal of Applied Developmental Psychology* 35 (1): 44–50.

———. 2014. "Differential Effects of the KiVa Anti-bullying Program on Popular and Unpopular Bullies." Journal of Applied Developmental Psychology 35 (1): 44–50.

Goldbaum, Suzanne, Wendy M. Craig, Debra Pepler, and Jennifer Connolly. 2003. "Developmental Trajectories of Victimization: Identifying Risk and Protective Factors." *Journal of Applied School Psychology* 19 (2): 139–156.

Gould, Roger V. 2003. *Collision of Wills: How Ambiguity about Social Rank Breeds Conflict*. Chicago: University of Chicago Press.

Hawley, Patricia H., and Anne Williford. 2015. "Articulating the Theory of Bullying Intervention Programs: Views from Social Psychology, Social Work, and Organizational Science." *Journal of Applied Developmental Psychology* 37:3–15.

Huitsing, Gijs, René Veenstra, Miia Sainio, and Christina Salmivalli. 2012. "'It Must Be Me' or 'It Could Be Them?' The Impact of the Social Network Position of Bullies and Victims on Victims' Adjustment." *Social Networks* 34 (4): 379–386.

Hymel, Shelley, Susan Swearer, Patricia McDougall, Dorothy Espelage, and Catherine Bradshaw. 2013. "Four Decades of Research on Bullying: What Have We Learned and How Can We Move the Field Forward?" Symposium, Society for Research in Child Development, Seattle.

Janssen, Ian, Wendy M. Craig, William F. Boyce, and William Pickett. 2004. "Associations between Overweight and Obesity with Bullying Behaviors in School-Aged Children." *Pediatrics* 113 (5): 1187–1194.

Kendrick, Kristin, Göran Jutengren, and Håkan Stattin. 2012. "The Protective Role of Supportive Friends against Bullying Perpetration and Victimization." *Journal of Adolescence* 35 (4): 1069–1080.

Li, Yan, and Michelle F. Wright. 2014. "Adolescents' Social Status Goals: Relationships to Social Status Insecurity, Aggression, and Prosocial Behavior." *Journal of Youth and Adolescence* 43 (1): 146–160.

Magin, Parker. 2013. "Appearance-Related Bullying and Skin Disorders." *Clinics in Dermatology* 31 (1): 66–71.

Malamut, Sarah T., Molly Dawes, and Hongling Xie. 2018. "Characteristics of Rumors and Rumor Victims in Early Adolescence: Rumor Content and Social Impact." *Social Development* 27 (3): 601–618.

Merrell, Kenneth W., Barbara A. Gueldner, Scott W. Ross, and Duane M. Isava. 2008. "How Effective Are School Bullying Intervention Programs? A Meta-analysis of Intervention Research." *School Psychology Quarterly* 23 (1): 26–42.

Mishna, Faye. 2003. "Learning Disabilities and Bullying: Double Jeopardy." *Journal of Learning Disabilities* 36 (4): 336–347.

Monks, Claire P., Peter K. Smith, and John Swettenham. 2005. "The Psychological Correlates of Peer Victimization in Preschool: Social Cognitive Skills, Executive Function and Attachment Profiles." *Aggressive Behavior* 31: 571–588.

Moody, James, Wendy D. Brynildsen, D. Wayne Osgood, Mark E. Feinberg, and Scott Gest. 2011. "Popularity Trajectories and Substance Use in Early Adolescence." *Social Networks* 33 (2): 101–112.

Moon, Byongook, Hye-Won Hwang, and John D. McCluskey. 2011. "Causes of School Bullying: Empirical Test of a General Theory of Crime, Differential Association Theory, and General Strain Theory." *Crime & Delinquency* 57 (6): 849–877.

Mortimer, Jeylan T., and Kathleen T. Call. 2001. *Arenas of Comfort in Adolescence: A Study of Adjustment in Context*. New York: Psychology Press.

Ojala, Kris, and Drew Nesdale. 2004. "Bullying and Social Identity: The Effects of Group Norms and Distinctiveness Threat on Attitudes towards Bullying." *British Journal of Developmental Psychology* 22 (1): 19–35.

Ojanen, Tiina, and Findley-Van Nostrand. 2014. "Social Goals, Aggression, Peer Preference, and Popularity: Longitudinal Links during Middle School." *Developmental Psychology* 50 (8): 2134–2143.

Olweus, Dan. 1978. *Aggression in the Schools: Bullies and Whipping Boys*. Washington, DC: Hemisphere.

———. 1980. "Familial and Temperamental Determinants of Aggressive Behavior in Adolescent Boys: A Causal Analysis." *Developmental Psychology* 16 (6): 644–660.

———. 1991. "Bully/Victim Problems among Schoolchildren: Basic Facts and Effects of a School Based Intervention Program." *Development and Treatment of Childhood Aggression* 17: 411–448.

———. 2010. "Understanding and Researching Bullying: Some Critical Issues." In *Handbook of Bullying in Schools: An International Perspective*, edited by Shane R. Jimerson, Susan M. Swearer, and Dorothy L. Espelage, 9–34. New York: Routledge.

Parker, Jeffrey B., and John A. Krommes. 2013. "Zonal Flow as Pattern Formation." *Physics of Plasmas* 20 (10): 100703.

Parker, Jeffrey G., Christine M. Low, Alisha R. Walker, and Bridget K. Gamm. 2005. "Friendship Jealousy in Young Adolescents: Individual Differences and Links to Sex, Self-Esteem, Aggression, and Social Adjustment." *Developmental Psychology* 41 (1): 235–250.

Parker, Jeffrey G., and John Seal. 1996. "Forming, Losing, Renewing, and Replacing Friendships: Applying Temporal Parameters to the Assessment of Children's Friendship Experiences." *Child Development* 67 (5): 2248–2268.

Pascoe, C. J. 2005. "'Dude, You're a Fag': Adolescent Masculinity and the Fag Discourse." *Sexualities* 8 (3): 329–346.

Peets, Kätlin, and Ernest V. E. Hodges. 2014. "Is Popularity Associated with Aggression toward Socially Preferred or Marginalized Targets?" *Journal of Experimental Child Psychology* 124:112–123.

Pellegrini, Anthony D. 2012. "Bullying, Victimization, and Sexual Harassment during the Transition to Middle School." *Educational Psychologist* 37: 151–163.

Pellegrini, Anthony D., and Maria Bartini. 2000. "A Longitudinal Study of Bullying, Victimization, and Peer Affiliation during the Transition from Primary School to Middle School." *American Educational Research Journal* 37 (3): 699–725.

Polanin, Joshua R., Dorothy L. Espelage, and Therese D. Pigott. 2012. "A Meta-analysis of School-Based Bullying Prevention Programs' Effects on Bystander Intervention Behavior." *School Psychology Review* 41 (1): 47–65.

Rodkin, Philip C., Dorothy L. Espelage, and Laura D. Hanish. 2015. "A Relational Framework for Understanding Bullying: Developmental Antecedents and Outcomes." *American Psychologist* 70 (4): 311–321.

Roland, Erling, and David Galloway. 2002. "Classroom Influences on Bullying." *Educational Research* 44:299–312.

Rudolph, Karen D., Constance Hammen, Dorli Burge, Nangel Lindberg, David Herzberg, and Shannon E. Daley. 2000. "Toward an Interpersonal Life-Stress Model of Depression: The Developmental Context of Stress Generation." *Development and Psychopathology* 12 (2): 215–234.

Salmivalli, Christina. 2010. "Bullying and the Peer Group: A Review." *Aggression and Violent Behavior* 15 (2): 112–120.

Salmivalli, Christina, and Kätlin Peets. 2008. "Bullies, Victims, and Bully–Victim Relationships." In *Handbook of Peer Interactions, Relationships, and Groups*, edited by William M. Bukowski, Brett Laursen, and Kenneth H. Rubin, 322–340. New York: Guilford.

Scheithauer, Herbert, Tobias Hayer, Franz Petermann, and Gert Jugert. 2006. "Physical, Verbal, and Relational Forms of Bullying Among German Students: Age Trends, Gender Differences, and Correlates." *Aggressive Behavior* 32 (3): 261–275.

Selman, Robert L. 1981. "The Development of Interpersonal Competence: The Role of Understanding in Conduct." *Developmental Review* 1 (4): 401–422.

Shepherd, Hana, and Adam Reich. 2020. "The Toll of Turnover: Network Instability, Well-Being, and Academic Effort in 56 Middle Schools." *Sociological Science* 7:663–691.

Sijtsema, Jelle J., René Veenstra, Siegwart Lindenberg, and Christina Salmivalli. 2009. "Empirical Test of Bullies' Status Goals: Assessing Direct Goals, Aggression, and Prestige." *Aggressive Behavior* 35 (1): 57–67.

Smith, J. David, Barry H. Schneider, Peter K. Smith, and Katerina Ananiadou. 2004. "The Effectiveness of Whole-School Antibullying Programs: A Synthesis of Evaluation Research." *School Psychology Review* 33 (4): 547–560.

Smith, Jeffrey A., and Robert Faris. 2015. "Movement without Mobility: Adolescent Status Hierarchies and the Contextual Limits of Cumulative Advantage." *Social Networks* 40: 139–153.

Smith, Peter K., Kirsten C. Madsen, and Janet C. Moody. 1999. "What Causes the Age Decline in Reports of Being Bullied at School? Towards a Developmental Analysis of Risks of Being Bullied." *Educational Research* 41 (3): 267–285.

Swearer, Susan M., Samuel Y. Song, Paulette Tam Cary, John W. Eagle, and William T. Mickelson. 2001. "Psychosocial Correlates in Bullying and Victimization: The Relationship between Depression, Anxiety, and Bully/Victim Status." *Journal of Emotional Abuse* 2 (2–3): 95–121.

Tolsma, Jochem, Ioana van Deurzen, Tobias H. Stark, and René Veenstra. 2013. "Who Is Bullying Whom in Ethnically Diverse Primary Schools? Exploring Links between Bullying, Ethnicity, and Ethnic Diversity in Dutch Primary Schools." *Social Networks* 35 (1): 51–61.

Ttofi, Maria M., and David P. Farrington. 2008. "Bullying: Short-Term and Long-Term Effects, and the Importance of Defiance Theory in Explanation and Prevention." *Victims and Offenders* 3 (2–3): 289–312.

———. 2011. "Effectiveness of School-Based Programs to Reduce Bullying: A Systematic and Meta-Analytic Review." *Journal of Experimental Criminology* 7 (1): 27–56.

Vaillancourt, Tracy, Shelley Hymel, and Patricia McDougall. 2003. "Bullying Is Power: Implications for School-Based Intervention Strategies." *Journal of Applied School Psychology* 19 (2): 157–176.

Vaillancourt, Tracy, Patricia McDougall, Shelley Hymel, Amanda Krygsman, Jessie Miller, Kelley Stiver, and Clinton Davis. 2008. "Bullying: Are Researchers and Children/Youth Talking about the Same Thing?" *International Journal of Behavioral Development* 32 (6): 486–495.

Veenstra, René, Siegwart Lindenberg, Bonne J. H. Zijlstra, Andrea F. De Winter, Frank C. Verhulst, and Johan Ormel. 2007. "The Dyadic Nature of Bullying and Victimization: Testing a Dual-Perspective Theory." *Child Development* 78 (6): 1843–1854.

Volk, Anthony A., Andrew V. Dane, and Zopito A. Marini. 2014. "What Is Bullying? A Theoretical Redefinition." *Developmental Review* 34 (4): 327–343.

Ybarra, Michele L., Dorothy L. Espelage, and Kimberly J. Mitchell. 2014. "Differentiating Youth Who Are Bullied from Other Victims of Peer-Aggression: The Importance of Differential Power and Repetition." *Journal of Adolescent Health* 55 (2): 293–300.

8

Conflict with Friends and Social Status Mobility in Middle School

LAURA CALLEJAS

Bullying has been defined and operationalized in a number of different ways.[1] In his classical work, Olweus defined bullying as intentional aggressive behavior that is carried out repeatedly over time and characterized by an imbalance of power such that the aggressor has more power than his or her victim.[2] While some researchers still rely on this definition of bullying in their work, others have assessed the prevalence of aggressive behaviors in schools more broadly. In this chapter, I call for further consideration of the role of interpersonal conflict between students and the impact of conflicts between those with similar levels of power and status, like friends. By paying closer attention to interpersonal conflict, we can more broadly gauge instances of disagreements that, if not resolved, can escalate to serious antisocial behaviors, including bullying. Understanding student interpersonal conflict is particularly important recently due to the shift to remote and hybrid learning environments due to the ongoing COVID-19 pandemic and the heightened political divisiveness during the 2020 presidential election.

Interpersonal conflict is a state of disagreement that arises when individuals have incompatible or opposing behaviors and views, which may or may not be manifested in acts of aggression.[3] According to sociologist Roger Gould, interpersonal conflict and social status have an intrinsic relationship.[4] Social status is the prestige accorded to individuals because of the positions they occupy in social hierarchies.[5] Since higher social status is associated with both material and nonmaterial rewards, such as respect and social approval, people frequently compete to achieve or maintain higher-status positions.[6] This competition can become a source of interpersonal conflict.

While conflict results from disagreement between individuals about relative dominance within the relationship, it can also serve as an opportunity to challenge existing dominance arrangements.[7] Not surprisingly, conflicts are common in schools because they are "fiercely competitive" settings where youth constantly challenge others for status.[8] Because students know that behaving aggressively can get them in trouble with school personnel, I suspect that conflict, given its more subtle nature, is more pervasive than aggression in schools. Despite this, much of the empirical literature in the field focuses on aggression specifically.

Generally, scholars have found that involvement in aggression is associated with students' social status.[9] Specifically, aggression is negatively associated with some status measures, like social preference (a measure of being well-liked), but positively associated with others, like peer-perceived popularity.[10] Further, some find that aggression can be instrumental to social climbing, particularly when students target high-status youth,[11] aggressive youth, or those in similar status positions, like friends.[12]

Psychologists, who produce a substantial proportion of the research on bullying, argue that aggression may be a response to frustration, humiliation, or mental pathologies. Others suggest that students act out aggressively because they lack the social skills necessary to resolve conflicts.[13] However, if youth care about status, and aggression can lead to status rewards, then it follows that some youth may strategically engage in antisocial behaviors as a means to gain status. Studies in the field would benefit from more seriously considering the importance of social status for adolescents and how the desire to attain status impacts behavior. Other scholars have called for careful reconsideration of the traditional criteria of bullying. Some suggest that expanding the definition of bullying to consider different forms of aggressive behaviors, regardless of intention of harm or whether they are reoccurring, maps on more clearly with students' lived experiences in schools.[14] And while the traditional definition of bullying requires a relationship characterized by an imbalance of power,[15] this excludes the experiences of students who have conflict with, and may subsequently be victimized by, those close in status, like friends.

Conflict among friends is bound to occur given that friends spend a lot of time together, and therefore there are many opportunities for disagreements to arise.[16] Further, Gould suggests that conflict is common among friends because there is more ambiguity in terms of status positions.[17] When it is not clear who in a relationship should be dominant, there is more room to challenge each other for status. Scholars have also found that friendships may increase the likelihood of being the victim of future incidents of electronic aggression.[18]

Given the negative impacts of aggression on student outcomes, and because conflict is not always necessarily problematic, it is not surprising that much of the literature in schools has focused on aggression specifically. However, because instances of conflict, if not resolved, can lead to aggression, bullying research would benefit from more seriously considering the role of interpersonal conflict between students. When we consider interpersonal conflict, we can assess the impact of subtle and likely more prevalent moments of disagreement on students' behaviors, including potential involvement in aggression and bullying. Further, research in the field would benefit from examining the impact of conflicts between those with similar levels of power and status, like friends.

In this chapter, I advance the literature by relying on theory from Gould to inform tests of the relationship between conflict with friends, versus non-friends, and status mobility in middle schools. Since youth become increasingly concerned with status as they reach adolescence,[19] schools are interesting sites not only because students spend a lot of time there but also because schools are characterized by informal status hierarchies that allow students to sort out status for themselves.[20] This makes it easier for students to make moves up and down the hierarchy than in settings with more formal hierarchies where status positions are clearly determined and harder to challenge. Middle schools are particularly important for this work since negative and antisocial behaviors tend to peak during this time[21] and since adolescents tend to view aggression more positively as they progress through middle school.[22]

I rely on data from a randomized field experiment conducted over the 2012–2013 school year in fifty-six middle schools in the state of New Jersey. I use change-score regression models to explore the effect of having conflict with friends on status mobility throughout the school year. Social status is measured using a network metric: betweenness centrality, or what I am referring to as *brokerage status*, which captures the number of times a student connects to others in the network via the shortest path (going through as few other people in the network as possible). Conflict with friends is measured using a network metric that captures overlap in "spend time with" nominations (a proxy for friendship) and conflict nominations to and from schoolmates.

Given research that demonstrates that the nature and structure of friendships differs for adolescent boys and girls[23] and that boys and girls engage in different forms of aggressive behaviors,[24] I examine the relationship between conflict with friends and status for boys and girls separately. My intention is not to test for gender differences by comparing the groups directly, but rather to examine how conflict with friends matters for these two groups of students. Findings reveal that conflict with friends, relative to conflict with non-friends, is positively associated with social status throughout the school year for boys.

Background

Previous studies suggest that among adolescents, aggression toward peers may be perceived and used as a strategic resource for acquiring social status through establishing dominance over others. Faris and Felmlee argue that aggression is likely perceived by students to be instrumental for gaining status, and thus social status may motivate the use of aggression.[25] Others have found that among adolescents, the strategic and proactive use of aggression is associated with popularity.[26] This body of research further suggests that youth make strategic decisions about whom they target for dominance displays. For instance, youth who are aggressive can gain status if they challenge highly liked students that they, the aggressors, personally dislike.[27]

Friendships ties in particular are important to consider when looking at the relationship between conflict and status during adolescence. In the following sections, I outline literature and theory from Gould regarding friendship ties, conflict, and status.[28]

Friendships Ties, Conflict, and Social Status

Friendship formation is common in schools for a couple of reasons. First, propinquity, or small differences in physical distance, increases the probability of social associations.[29] Friendships form in settings where individuals spend a lot of time together since they offer ample opportunities for interactions and for forging deep connections.[30] For this reason, friendship ties are common in settings like schools since students routinely interact with the same set of individuals. Second, during adolescence, youth start to distance themselves from parents and other adults and begin forming friendship ties with those outside of their immediate family.[31] Adolescents attribute greater importance to friends and spend more time socializing with friends compared to children and adults.[32]

Having friends in school has its benefits. In addition to companionship, having at least one friend can partially help youth avoid harassment from others.[33] However, conflict and aggression are also fairly common and even accepted at times among close friends.[34] In their study, Felmlee and Faris found that slightly more than 20 percent of all cyber aggression ties occur among friends and 25 percent occur among friends of friends. Further, friendships increase the likelihood of future incidents of electronic aggression among adolescents.[35]

Felmlee and Faris also suggest that aggression may be common among friends in part because friends interact frequently and thus there are more opportunities for misunderstandings to occur.[36] Similarly, friends know intimate information about each other, which they can use in harmful ways during disagreements. Further, friends are usually in direct competition for the attention and esteem of the same set of individuals since they often belong to the same teams and clubs and participate in similar activities in and outside of school.[37] This competition to gain or maintain status can lead to instances of aggression.[38]

The desire to achieve or maintain high levels of status also plays a role in how friendship ties are formed and maintained. Friendships usually form among individuals who share similar traits and characteristics.[39] For instance, there is evidence that youth select as friends others who are similar in terms of status.[40] An individual's status rank in turn is influenced by the status of those whom he or she hangs out with. Given the importance of status for adolescents, it is not surprising that youth with high levels of status are especially careful and selective about their friendship choices since befriending unpopular youth may lead to loss of status.[41]

Similarities in status ranks between friends also make it easier for interpersonal conflict to arise. In the following section, I outline Gould's theories regarding the role of status ambiguity in social relations and propose my own ideas about how conflict with friends impacts status mobility in middle schools.

Gould: Status Ambiguity and Interpersonal Conflict

According to Gould, conflict is a feature of many social relations, and particularly those in which individuals are similarly situated in terms of status rank.[42] Status ambiguity in social relations "breeds" conflict because when it is not clear who in a relationship should outrank whom, it is easier to challenge others for dominance.[43] So we might expect more conflict to arise between friends than we would between a boss and an employee, or between a parent and a child, because among friends, status positions are similar and therefore more ambiguous.

Gould further suggests that when conflicts occur among friends, they do not necessarily destroy the relationship but rather reflect moments when individuals challenge one another to gain more control.[44] The other person can either accept the new terms without opposition and assume a lower-status position, or object to the behaviors in order to maintain "stable dominance."[45] Although Gould does not explore how conflict with friends affects status mobility specifically, I suggest that if challenging a friend and countering a challenge from a friend are ways of shifting the terms of the relationship, then conflict with friends may impact status mobility in schools.

Since friends tend to occupy similar status positions, when students challenge a friend for dominance they are likely challenging within their own status group. Conversely, when students challenge those they are not friends with, they may or may not be challenging those similar in status. Challenging schoolmates outside of one's status group may lead to loss of social status if this act is deemed socially inappropriate by others. For instance, if a low-status youth challenges a status elite, it may reflect a lack of understanding of social norms on the challenger's behalf and may even lead to ridicule. Therefore, challenging a friend for dominance is likely less risky and deemed more appropriate than challenging non-friends and as a result may be more instrumental to status gains.

There is some empirical evidence to suggest that students who challenge friends can gain status. For instance, Faris found that among a sample of high school students, status is enhanced when adolescents are aggressive toward those who are socially close in their networks, like friends.[46] As previously mentioned, conflict is common among friends in part because friends compete for the respect and esteem of the same set of individuals.[47] Given this, and the fact that it is likely more appropriate to challenge those who are similarly situated in terms of status, like friends, I propose,

Hypothesis 1: Having conflict with friends, relative to having conflict with non-friends, will be associated with an increase in brokerage status throughout the school year.

A student's ability to broker ties (and subsequently gain brokerage status) may be impacted by his or her ability to behave in ways that are deemed appropriate and in accordance with social norms. Students who have conflict with friends demonstrate that they understand the rules by challenging within their own status rank. Because they behave in socially appropriate ways, these students may become desirable actors whom others want to be connected to. This in turn helps them occupy unique central positions in their school's network. On the other hand, students who challenge non-friends (and risk challenging outside of their status league) may have a harder time occupying central positions in their networks because others may choose not to associate with them given their lack of understanding or willingness to play by the rules.

How Gender Matters in Friendships

While boys and girls value similar things in friendships, such as trust, studies demonstrate that the structure of friendships may differ for adolescent boys and girls.[48] Compared to boys, girls tend to have smaller friendship networks with only one or a few close friends. Not surprisingly, girls tend to develop more intimate relationships that are characterized by self-disclosure.[49] For instance, they are more likely than boys to share and discuss personal and confidential information with their friends.[50] Girls also demonstrate a higher level of responsiveness and reciprocity in their communications with friends,[51] and they are more likely than boys to seek support from friends.[52]

On the other hand, boys are more likely to have large networks of friends and to organize around shared activities, like sports.[53] They are less inclined to talk about intimate matters[54] and are more prone to displays of masculinity, competition, and risk taking.[55] Boys are also more likely than girls to communicate with each other in assertive ways that emphasize dominance and power.[56] The emphasis on dominance in social relations among boys may be why physical forms of aggression are more prominent among boys and why relational forms of aggression that are less physical and more discrete (e.g., spreading rumors) are more common among girls.[57] It may also explain why boys are more likely than girls to seek out friends who are similarly aggressive[58] and why their friendships are characterized by higher levels of conflict than girls'.[59]

Ultimately, while girls emphasize the importance of "connection-oriented goals" in friendships, boys emphasize the importance of "dominance goals."[60] Given that dominance and competition are especially salient in boys' friendships, and conflict among friends is a way to challenge dominance arrangements, as Gould suggests, conflict with friends may be a stronger predictor of upward status mobility for boys compared to girls.[61] Although girls do compete for status, and empirical evidence suggests that conflict with schoolmates is a positive predictor of status mobility for girls,[62] when it comes to friendships, girls may be expected to act in more cooperative and prosocial ways. Therefore, I propose,

Hypothesis 2: Having conflict with friends, relative to having conflict with non-friends, will be associated with a greater increase in brokerage status throughout the school year for boys compared to girls.

Data and Analytic Technique

I address the question of how conflict with those students one chooses to hang out with, a proxy for friendship, influences brokerage status mobility throughout the school year. I use data from a yearlong field experiment with over 21,000 students in fifty-six middle schools in New Jersey.[63] The experiment tested whether the behavior of salient students could influence other students' perceptions of social norms of conflict and shift overall levels of conflict at the school.

Students in all the schools completed a survey at the beginning of the school year, in the fall of 2012, and at the end of the school year, in late spring 2013 ($N = 21{,}124$). Each survey included a network nomination section, a personal background and activities section, a section on perceptions of the norms of conflict-related behaviors, and an attitudes and experiences section. I do not focus on the causal effects of the intervention on social status mobility because the experiment was not designed to alter social status. Results do not differ when I control for being a treatment student (participating directly in the intervention program), so treatment controls are excluded from the analytical models below.

In order to examine the influence of conflict with friends on social status mobility throughout the school year, I use regression change score models, which allow researchers to examine the effects of events in two-wave panel data.[64] All models include school-level fixed effects and control for conflict and status at the beginning of the year. In order to explore the influence of gender, I examine the relationship between conflict with friends and status for girls and boys separately.

Since my intention is to compare students who have conflict with friends to students who have conflict with those they are not friends with, I limit my sample to students who have at least one conflict tie with a schoolmate at both time points in the year ($N = 12{,}322$). After accounting for missing data on one or more of the variables in the models, the final sample consists of 10,842 students: 5,660 girls and 5,182 boys.

Measures

Status Variable

I assess brokerage status using students' betweenness centrality scores. Betweenness centrality captures the number of times an individual connects others in the network via the shortest path or by going through as few other people as possible. Students with high betweenness centrality serve as bridges connecting others in the network.[65] Given their ability to brokerage ties, students with high brokerage status are likely highly visible members in their schools and thus well-known among their peers. I use change in status between the two waves of data as my dependent variable. Because residuals from the models predicting brokerage status are not normally distributed, I take the square root of these centrality scores (before calculating change) to normalize the residuals. I control for status at the start of the year in each model.

Conflict with Friends and Non-friends Variables

At both waves of the survey, students reported which other students at the school they "had conflict with," whether face-to-face, through texts, or online as well as whom they chose to spend time with (in person, both in and outside of school) in the past few weeks, which I use as a proxy for friendship. Using both reports of conflict students have with schoolmates and reports of whom students chose to spend time with at both waves, I created a series of dummy variables to indicate whether students had conflict with friends and/or non-friends over time. Specifically, the variables capture whether students have conflict with at least one friend at the beginning of the school year only, conflict with at least one friend at the end of the school year only, conflict with at least one friend at the beginning and end of the school year, and conflict with non-friends at both waves (treated as the reference category in the models below).

Since the sample is limited to students who have at least one conflict tie at both waves, the reference category includes students who had conflict only with non-friends at the beginning and end of the year (and no conflicts with friends at both waves). Additionally, because I use both waves of data, the categories of conflict only at the beginning of the year or only at the end of the year capture changes in friendship conflict relations from the beginning to the end of the year. These variables help to assess whether changes in friendship conflict relations throughout the school year matter, irrespective of the number of conflicts students can have.

Since challenging friends is a way to achieve "stable dominance"[66] and conflict with friends may be seen as more appropriate than challenging non-friends (given similarities in status ranks among friends), conflict with friends specifically may be instrumental to status gains. If that is the case, the distinction between challenging a friend versus a non-friend may be particularly important. Further, going from having conflict with non-friends at the beginning of the year, to having conflict with at least one friend at the end of the year (compared to only having conflict with non-friends at both waves) may suggest that students learn whom they should challenge in status competitions (as opposed to students who only challenge non-friends who are likely outside of their status league; I elaborate on this point in the results section below). Therefore, the dummy variables here examine whether these shifts between having conflict with friends and non-friends at different points in the year matter for status.

Although students were not explicitly asked to nominate others they consider friends, the "choose to spend time with" measure used here captures who individuals pay attention to and are exposed to in their group through actively choosing to spend time with them. This taps into the concept of friendship while avoiding the common measurement issue that occurs when students are asked to nominate friends, which is that the definition of friendship is subjective and can differ from student to student.[67]

All models control for the influence of total number of conflict nominations at the beginning of the school year.

Other Variables

I control for several variables that may serve as markers or determinants of status in middle school.

AGE APPEARANCE. At both waves, students reported their relative age appearance by answering the following question: "People say that I look . . . younger than/about the same age as/older than . . . most students in my grade."

ACTIVITIES AND DATING. Using a series of questions that students checked off to indicate participation and left blank to indicate lack of participation, at both survey waves, students reported whether they participated in sports, music club, and theater club. They also reported whether they did lots of homework, dated other students at the school, and used Facebook, Twitter, or Instagram. For each of these control variables, I created four sets of dummy variables to capture: no participation in either wave (reference categories), participation in both waves, participation in wave 1 but not wave 2, and participation in wave 2 but not in wave 1.

WAVE 1 VARIABLES. Additional control variables, available at wave 1 only, were included in the models. I consider whether students say they have friends who come over every week and whether students have friends who say their house is nice (proxy for income). For each of these variables students could indicate "yes" or "no."

I also control for whether students have positive or negative experiences at the start of the school year. "Positive experiences" are captured by combining answers to a series of yes/no questions that ask students whether in the fall, students have been nice to them, have posted good things about them (online or though text), have told them they look nice, and have spoken up for them (values range 0–4). "Negative experiences" are captured using a series of yes/no questions that ask students whether others have excluded them, have messed with them, have gossiped or spread rumors about them, have made fun of how they look, posted bad things about them (online or though text), threatened, hit, or pushed them, insulted their race or ethnicity, or said they are gay (values range 0–9). Students also responded to a series of questions (coded 1 if "yes" and 0 if "no") that capture whether they feel like they belong in school and whether they think they "have to be mean to survive."

Finally, disciplinary data provided by some of the schools are used to assess the number of incidents in which students were involved in physical and nonphysical altercations. I measure "physical altercation" by combining answers to several yes/no questions regarding whether students showed physical aggression toward other students (violence, pushing, kicking) or had inappropriate contact with other students (such as spitting) (range: 0–6). I measure "nonphysical altercation" by combining answers to several yes/no questions that assess if students used inappropriate language toward other students (written or verbal), had a verbal altercation with another student (made threats, spread rumors, or made biased comments), harassed peers online, incited violence / planned to fight, or made offensive gestures to other students (range: 0–5).

The following control variables were accounted for but later removed from the tables of results below because they were not significant in the regression models: student race/ethnicity, do lots of homework, do music, use Twitter, use Facebook, house is nice, negative experience, positive experience, and physical altercations.

Results

Table 8.1 shows basic descriptive statistics for the variables in the model for boys and girls. At the end of the school year girls and boys have higher levels of brokerage status than at the beginning of the year. Turning to the main conflict variables, most students indicate not having conflict with friends (77 percent of girls and 78 percent of boys). Approximately 10 percent of students have conflict with at least one friend at the beginning of the school year, about 8 percent have conflict with a friend at the end of the school year, and about 5 percent have conflict with a friend at the beginning and end of the school year. For more information on other variables in the model, see Table 8.1.

Students Who Have Conflict with Friends versus Conflict with Non-friends

In Table 8.2 I show results from a series of independent *t*-tests comparing average conflict and status levels for two major groups of students in the sample: (1) students who have conflict with friends and (2) students who have conflict with non-friends. When I compare these two groups of students (all of whom have conflict with at least one other schoolmate), I find that at the beginning and at end of the school year, the group of students who have conflict with friends have a significantly higher average number of conflict ties when compared to the group of students who have conflict with non-friends. This is true for boys and girls. When comparing status levels of these two groups, findings suggest that at the beginning and end of the school year, boys who have conflict with friends have significantly higher brokerage status when compared to boys who have conflict only with non-friends. The same is not true for girls.

These findings suggest the need to pay more attention to students who have conflict with friends. These students not only are generally higher in status than those who do not challenge their friends but also engage in more conflict overall.

TABLE 8.1. Descriptive Statistics for All Variables in the Models

	Girls (N = 5,660)				Boys (N = 5,182)			
	Mean	SD	Min	Max	Mean	SD	Min	Max
Status variable								
Brokerage status W1	0.00731	(0.01)	0	0.10	0.00733	(0.01)	0	0.10
Brokerage status W2	0.00733	(0.01)	0	0.11	0.00749	(0.01)	0	0.11
Brokerage status change score	0.00002	(0.04)	−0.18	0.20	0.00015	(0.04)	−0.21	0.20
Conflict variables								
Conflict with friends W1 and W2	0.052	(0.22)	0	1	0.047	(0.21)	0	1
Conflict with friends W1	0.104	(0.30)	0	1	0.100	(0.30)	0	1
Conflict with friends W2	0.078	(0.27)	0	1	0.077	(0.27)	0	1
Conflict with friends neither wave	0.766	(0.42)	0	1	0.776	(0.42)	0	1
Number of conflict ties W1	3.887	(2.81)	1	35	3.979	(3.25)	1	38
Control variables waves 1 and 2								
Appear older W1 and W2	0.187	(0.39)	0	1	0.130	(0.34)	0	1
Appear older W1	0.162	(0.37)	0	1	0.156	(0.36)	0	1
Appear older W2	0.224	(0.42)	0	1	0.199	(0.40)	0	1
Appear older neither wave	0.427	(0.49)	0	1	0.514	(0.50)	0	1
Plays sports W1 and W2	0.187	(0.39)	0	1	0.263	(0.44)	0	1
Plays sports W1	0.080	(0.27)	0	1	0.102	(0.30)	0	1
Plays sports W2	0.100	(0.30)	0	1	0.129	(0.33)	0	1
Plays sports neither wave	0.632	(0.48)	0	1	0.507	(0.50)	0	1
Dating W1 and W2	0.170	(0.38)	0	1	0.201	(0.40)	0	1
Dating W1	0.077	(0.27)	0	1	0.078	(0.27)	0	1
Dating W2	0.121	(0.33)	0	1	0.138	(0.34)	0	1
Dating neither wave	0.632	(0.48)	0	1	0.583	(0.49)	0	1
Does theater W1 and W2	0.118	(0.32)	0	1	0.027	(0.16)	0	1
Does theater W1	0.073	(0.26)	0	1	0.022	(0.15)	0	1
Does theater W2	0.048	(0.21)	0	1	0.023	(0.15)	0	1
Does theater neither wave	0.760	(0.43)	0	1	0.928	(0.26)	0	1
Instagram W1 and W2	0.542	(0.50)	0	1	0.320	(0.47)	0	1
Instagram W1	0.018	(0.13)	0	1	0.020	(0.14)	0	1
Instagram W2	0.236	(0.42)	0	1	0.295	(0.46)	0	1
Instagram neither wave	0.205	(0.40)	0	1	0.365	(0.48)	0	1
Control variables wave 1 only								
Friends come over weekly	0.562	(0.50)	0	1	0.566	(0.50)	0	1
Nonphysical altercations	0.015	(0.15)	0	3	0.045	(0.26)	0	5

Conflict with Friends and Social Status Mobility: Girls

Model 1 in Table 8.3 shows results predicting brokerage status mobility for girls. After controlling for a host of important variables, having conflict with friends at different points in the school year (at wave 1 only, at wave 2 only, or at wave 1 and wave 2) does not have a significant effect on social status mobility. These findings hold regardless of the reference group used to assess conflict with friends.

TABLE 8.2. *T*-test Comparing Average Conflict Ties and Average Status for Boys and Girls

Students who have:	Wave 1—Average conflict ties							
	Girls				Boys			
	N	Mean	SE		N	Mean	SE	
Conflict with non-friends	4,777	3.663	(0.04)	***	4,420	3.715	(0.05)	***
Conflict with friends	883	5.103	(0.09)		762	5.507	(0.11)	
	Wave 1—Average status score							
	Girls				Boys			
	N	Mean	SE		N	Mean	SE	
Conflict with non-friends	4,777	0.0073	(0.00)		4,420	0.0072	(0.00)	***
Conflict with friends	883	0.0076	(0.00)		762	0.0084	(0.00)	
	Wave 2—Average conflict ties							
	Girls				Boys			
	N	Mean	SE		N	Mean	SE	
Conflict with non-friends	4,920	4.425	(0.05)	***	4,540	4.344	(0.06)	***
Conflict with friends	740	5.632	(0.12)		642	5.868	(0.13)	
	Wave 2—Average status score							
	Girls				Boys			
	N	Mean	SE		N	Mean	SE	
Conflict with non-friends	4,920	0.0073	(0.00)		4,540	0.0074	(0.00)	**
Conflict with friends	740	0.0075	(0.00)		642	0.0085	(0.00)	

**p < .01. ***p < .001, one-tailed.

TABLE 8.3. Change Score Models Predicting Brokerage Status Mobility

	Model 1—Girls			Model 2—Boys		
	B	SE	Sig.	B	SE	Sig.
Main variables						
Conflict with friends W1 and W2	−0.0002	(0.002)		−0.0002	(0.002)	
Conflict with friends W1	−0.0011	(0.001)		0.0002	(0.002)	
Conflict with friends W2	−0.0002	(0.002)		0.0060	(0.002)	***
Number of conflict ties W1	−0.0003	(0.000)	*	−0.0002	(0.000)	
Brokerage status W1	−2.856	(0.065)	***	−2.780	(0.070)	***
Control variables waves 1 and 2						
Appear older W1 and W2	0.001	(0.001)		0.003	(0.002)	*
Appear older W1	0.001	(0.001)		0.003	(0.001)	*
Appear older W2	0.001	(0.001)		0.003	(0.001)	*
Plays sports W1 and W2	0.002	(0.001)		0.003	(0.001)	**
Plays sports W1	0.000	(0.002)		−0.005	(0.002)	**
Plays sports W2	0.001	(0.002)		0.001	(0.002)	
Dating W1 and W2	0.006	(0.001)	***	0.003	(0.001)	*
Dating W1	0.000	(0.002)		−0.003	(0.002)	*
Dating W2	0.008	(0.001)	***	0.004	(0.002)	**
Does theater W1 and W2	0.003	(0.001)	*	0.002	(0.003)	
Does theater W1	0.002	(0.002)		−0.004	(0.003)	
Does theater W2	0.002	(0.002)		0.007	(0.003)	*
Instagram W1 and W2	0.001	(0.001)		0.005	(0.001)	***
Instagram W1	0.002	(0.004)		−0.004	(0.004)	
Instagram W2	0.001	(0.001)		0.002	(0.001)	
Control variables wave 1 only						
Friends come over weekly	0.000	(0.001)		0.002	(0.001)	*
Nonphysical altercations	0.001	(0.003)		0.005	(0.002)	**
Constant	0.114	(0.003)	***	0.008	(0.003)	**
N	5,660			5,182		
R^2	.262			.250		

Note: The following control variables were removed because they were not significant in either model: do lots of homework, do music, use Twitter, use Facebook, house is nice, negative experience, positive experience, and physical altercation.
*$p < .05$. **$p < .01$. ***$p < .001$, one-tailed.

Status at the beginning of the school year is a negative predictor of status mobility. It may be the case that having more status at the beginning of the year is associated with a loss of status over time because there is less room to advance in the social hierarchy when students begin the year in higher-status positions. Number of conflict ties at the beginning of the year is also a significant and negative predictor of status mobility for girls.

Other control variables have a positive and significant effect on status mobility. More specifically, dating at the beginning and the end of the school year as well as dating just at the end of the school year are associated with increases in brokerage status. Similarly, participating in theater at the beginning and end of the school year is a positive predictor of status. These findings suggest that the more socially involved students are, the greater the likelihood they will forge connections with others and become well-known, which can then lead to increases in brokerage status.

Conflict with Friends and Social Status Mobility: Boys

Results from Model 2 in Table 8.3 suggest that boys who start the year having conflict with non-friends and then have conflict with at least one friend at the end of the school year gain brokerage status relative to boys who have conflict only with non-friends throughout the school year. This result holds regardless of the reference group used to assess conflict with friends and before and after controlling for a host of important variables. Specifically, boys who start the year having conflict with non-friends and then end up having conflict with at least one friend by the end of the year experience a .006 increase in brokerage status ($p < .001$).

Similar to results for girls, status at the beginning of the school year is a significant and negative predictor of status mobility for boys. Playing sports and dating at just the beginning of the school year are also negatively associated with status mobility. However, playing sports at the beginning and end of the school year and dating at just the end of the school year are positive predictors of brokerage status. It may be that boys are expected to engage in these behaviors throughout the school year, or at the very least, to catch up as the school year unfolds. As a result, those who date and play sports at the start of the year but do not continue doing so lose status over time.

Boys who look older than their age and use Instagram throughout the entire school year as well as those who participate in theater at the end of the year (relative to those that do not look older and do not engage in these activities at either wave) also gain social status. Having friends who come over every week is also instrumental to status gains. As previously mentioned, the more socially involved students are, on- and offline, the more well-known they are and the more they are able to form connections with other students. This in turn can lead to higher levels of brokerage status.

Finally, involvement in nonphysical altercations is a positive predictor of status for boys, though not for girls. This finding is interesting in light of the research that suggests that boys are more likely to engage in physical, versus nonphysical, forms of aggression with peers. However, it is consistent with other studies that suggest that subtle forms of aggression, compared to more physical forms of aggression, are instrumental to status in schools.[68]

Though not shown here, when the number of conflict ties students have with friends was used as a predictor of status mobility, it was not substantively or statistically significant. This suggests that the distinction between having conflict with a friend or multiple friends and having conflict with non-friends may be more important than the actual number of conflict ties that may overlap with friendship ties.

It is plausible that at the beginning of the year, students do not yet understand who in the social hierarchy is an appropriate target for status competitions. Status hierarchies and friendship groups may still be forming at this point. However, by the end of the year, students may realize that challenging friends as opposed to non-friends is more appropriate since in these social relations students are likely challenging status equals. Challenging appropriate targets in turn may be conducive to status gains since it is less risky than challenging someone outside of one's status league. This suggests that students may be conscious of their own and others' status positions and adapt in ways that allow them to challenge appropriate targets.

There is some evidence that individuals are conscious of their positions in status hierarchies and make informed decisions about the amount of time and attention they give to others based on where they stand.[69] Specifically, giving someone more time and attention (including negative attention) than they give to you signals to others that you occupy a lower-status position in the relationship. Because individuals typically desire reciprocation of attention, especially in friendships, they will "calibrate" their behaviors and withdraw some attention in order to maintain more equal status positions.[70]

For these reasons, students may be aware of each other's positions in the status hierarchy and use this information to determine whom they should and should not challenge. Whether they believe that challenging friends in particular is more conducive to status gains cannot be assessed with these data but should be further explored. Doing so would provide researchers with a better understanding of students' motivations for engaging in potentially antisocial behaviors with friends and a sense of their subjective experience of this process.

Conclusion

The focus on aggression and bullying behaviors in schools is warranted given the harmful effects of such behaviors on youths' well-being. Research continuously shows that students who are bullied report higher levels of anxiety, depression, and thoughts of suicide and lower levels of self-esteem; bullying is also associated with increased alcohol and drug use and involvement in violence and crime, particularly for boys.[71] Given this, and because conflict is not always necessarily problematic (i.e., students can resolve their conflicts or simply not act on them), it is not surprising that the literature has focused on aggression. However, because instances of conflict have the potential to lead to aggression if not resolved, bullying research would benefit from better understanding the role of interpersonal conflict in student interactions.

In this chapter, I call for further consideration of the role of interpersonal conflict and the impact of conflicts between friends on status mobility. By considering the impact of interpersonal conflict more broadly, we can assess the impact of subtle and likely more prevalent moments of disagreement on students' behaviors, including potential subsequent involvement in aggression and bullying behaviors. Given that conflict among friends is relatively common, the field would also benefit from examining the impact of conflicts between those with similar levels of power and status, like friends.

Conflict, broadly defined here to include aggression, can be instrumental to status gains. Considering the impact of friendships in this relationship is important for several reasons. First, friendships are shaped by status in meaningful ways (i.e., students purposely select friends who are similar in status).[72] Second, conflicts are common among friends in part because, as Gould suggests, status ambiguity among status equals, like friends, makes it easier for individuals to challenge each other for status.[73] Last, characteristics of friendship groups differ by gender in ways that may shape students' ability to gain status through participation in conflict with friends.

In this chapter, I examined how conflict with friends matters for brokerage status mobility among students who indicate having at least one conflict tie with a schoolmate. Findings suggest that students who have conflict with friends are not only generally higher in status than those who do not challenge friends but also more likely to engage in more conflict with schoolmates overall. Regression analyses further revealed that developing a conflictual relationship with a friend or friends is instrumental to status, relative to challenging non-friends throughout the year, but only for boys. Going from having conflict with non-friends to having conflict with friends may be instrumental to status because students adapt in ways that allow them to challenge those close in status, which is less risky and therefore more conducive to status gains.

Given that boys have larger friendship networks that are characterized as less nurturing and intimate,[74] and given the emphasis on dominance in boys' interactions with each other,[75] conflict with friends may be an appropriate means to status only for boys. Although girls compete for the esteem of peers and can gain status when they challenge schoolmates,[76] when it comes to friendships they may be expected to behave in more prosocial ways and may feel more pressure to resolve conflicts in order to avoid losing a close friend. Future studies would benefit from exploring whether boys purposely challenge friends as a means to achieve status because they think it will lead to status gains.

Regardless of their intentions, these findings point to the importance of considering friendships when assessing peer conflicts and status competitions in school settings. More often than not, adults might expect that students who choose to spend time together are interacting in positive and prosocial ways, but that may not always be the case. If conflicts between friends are not resolved they may escalate and result in aggression. Friendship ties can even increase the likelihood of experiencing future incidents of cyber aggression.[77] Therefore, rather than assume that friends do not have conflicts or that they can sort out their conflicts effectively, school personnel need to be mindful and strategic in focusing on friendship groups when implementing conflict-reduction strategies.

School-based interventions also need to be mindful of status motivations when addressing conflicts between students. For instance, teaching students conflict resolution skills is a good first step, but it may not be enough if students believe that they can gain status by engaging in conflict. For some, the opportunity to gain status may be more enticing than resolving conflicts. Even if students do not purposely engage in conflict to compete for status, the fact that conflict is positively associated with status suggests the need to keep status at the forefront when developing and implementing interventions.

School personnel would also benefit from better understanding what status means to students in their schools and what processes or behaviors students see as instrumental to status. This can be done through focus groups with student leaders or through assignments or questionnaires that allow students to expand on their definitions of status and mechanism for increasing it. If conflict is perceived by students to be a means to achieving status, and because adolescents in particular care about status, it might be beneficial to shift the culture in the school so that students who compete for status do so in less harmful ways.

Although beyond the scope of this chapter, it would also be important to explore the relationship between conflict and status with more expansive gender categories in ways that also allow for a better understanding of the experiences of LGBTQ youth given the higher rates of victimization these youth experience.[78] Moreover, while student race/ethnicity did not have a significant effect on status attainment in this study, research should continue to explore how race/ethnicity at the individual and/or schoolwide level might matter for youths' experiences with conflict in schools. It would be important to examine potential disparities in access to, and implementation of, schoolwide conflict resolution strategies and resources. Understanding these impacts is especially important given exacerbated inequities in schools brought on by the ongoing COVID-19 pandemic and continued racial and social justice issues.

The shift to remote and hybrid learning environments because of the pandemic has also given way to more virtual interactions among students, which has important implications for the study of conflict and aggression. Since many students are learning from home or are socially distanced while in the school building, instances of physical aggression may be low; however, nonphysical aggression and instances of interpersonal conflict may be just as prevalent, if not more so, than they were before the start of the pandemic. In addition to the aforementioned challenges, heightened political divisiveness during the 2020 presidential election showcased the importance of civil discourse and schools' roles in helping students understand and meditate conflicts that may arise during these times. Overall, the events of 2020 reaffirm the importance of understanding interpersonal conflict and of helping youth mediate and resolve conflicts effectively.

NOTES

1 Espelage and Swearer, 2003; Hong and Espelage, 2012.
2 Olweus, 1993.
3 Laursen and Pursell, 2009.
4 Gould, 2003.
5 Gould, 2002.
6 Gould, 2002; Merton, 1968; Ridgeway and Correll, 2004.
7 Gould, 2003.
8 Gould, 2003.
9 Faris, 2012; Faris and Felmlee, 2011; Prinstein and Cillessen, 2003; Shin, 2017.
10 Prinstein and Cillessen, 2003; Shin, 2017.
11 Andrews et al., 2017.
12 Faris, 2012.
13 Jimerson et al., 2006.
14 Carrera et al., 2011; Donoghue and Raia-Hawrylak, 2016; Vaillancourt et al., 2008.
15 Olweus, 1993.
16 Felmlee and Faris, 2016.
17 Gould, 2003.
18 Felmlee and Faris, 2016.
19 Li and Wright, 2014.
20 Faris, 2012.
21 Collins, 2009; Unnever and Cornell, 2003.
22 Pellegrini and Long, 2010.
23 Haynie et al., 2014.
24 Pellegrini and Archer, 2005; Prinstein and Cillessen, 2003; Shin, 2017.
25 Faris and Felmlee, 2011.

26 Prinstein and Cillessen, 2003.
27 Peets and Hodges, 2014.
28 Gould, 2003.
29 Blau, 1977; Festinger, 1950.
30 Blau, 1977; Felmlee and Faris, 2016.
31 Felmlee and Faris, 2016.
32 Giordano et al., 2003.
33 Mouttapa et al., 2004.
34 Gardella et al., 2020.
35 Felmlee and Faris, 2016.
36 Felmlee and Faris, 2016.
37 Felmlee and Faris, 2016.
38 Faris and Felmlee, 2011; Felmlee and Faris, 2016.
39 McPherson et al., 2001.
40 Dijkstra et al., 2013.
41 Dijkstra et al., 2013.
42 Gould, 2003.
43 Gould, 2003.
44 Gould, 2003.
45 Gould, 2002.
46 Faris, 2012.
47 Felmlee and Faris, 2016.
48 Haynie et al., 2014.
49 Rose and Rudolph, 2006; Shin, 2017.
50 Rose and Rudolph, 2006; Waldrop and Halverson, 1975.
51 Dishion et al., 2004.
52 Rose and Rudolph, 2006; Shin, 2017.
53 Benenson, 1990; Waldrop and Halverson, 1975.
54 Rose and Rudolph, 2006.
55 Agnew, 2009.
56 Shin, 2017.
57 Pellegrini and Archer, 2005; Prinstein and Cillessen, 2003; Shin, 2017.
58 Dijkstra et al., 2013.
59 Hawley et al., 2007.
60 Rose and Rudolph, 2006.
61 Gould, 2003.
62 Callejas and Shepherd, 2020.
63 Paluck et al., 2016.
64 Allison, 1994; Johnson, 2005.
65 Faris and Felmlee, 2011.
66 Gould, 2002.
67 Bearman and Parigi, 2004.
68 Prinstein and Cillessen, 2003.

69   Gould, 2002.
70   Gould, 2002.
71   National Academies of Sciences, Engineering and Medicine, 2016.
72   Dijkstra et al., 2013.
73   Gould, 2003.
74   Shin, 2017.
75   Agnew, 2009.
76   Callejas and Shepherd, 2020.
77   Felmlee and Faris, 2016.
78   Centers for Disease Control and Prevention, 2018.

REFERENCES

Agnew, Robert. 2009. *Juvenile Delinquency: Causes and Control*. 3rd ed. New York: Oxford University Press.

Allison, Paul. 1994. "Using Panel Data to Estimate the Effects of Events." *Sociological Methods & Research* 23 (2): 174–199.

Andrews, Naomi C. Z., Laura D. Hanish, and Carlos E. Santos. 2017. "Does an Aggressor's Target Choice Matter? Assessing Change in the Social Network Prestige of Aggressive Youth." *Aggressive Behavior* 43:364-374.

Bearman, Peter, and Paolo Parigi. 2004. "Cloning Headless Frogs and Other Important Matters: Conversation Topics and Network Structure." *Social Forces* 82:535–557.

Benenson, Joyce F. 1990. "Gender Differences in Social Networks." *Journal of Early Adolescence* 10:472–495.

Blau, Peter M. 1977. "A Macrosociological Theory of Social Structure." *American Journal of Sociology* 83 (1): 26–54.

Callejas, Laura M., and Hana Shepherd. 2020. "Conflict as a Social Status Mobility Mechanism in Schools: A Network Approach." *Social Psychology Quarterly* 83:319–341.

Carrera, María V., Renée DePalma, and María Lameiras. 2011. "Toward a More Comprehensive Understanding of Bullying In School Settings." *Educational Psychology Review* 23:479–499.

Centers for Disease Control and Prevention. 2018. "Youth Risk Behavior Survey Data Summary & Trends Report 2007–2017." www.cdc.gov.

Collins, Randall. 2009. *Violence: A Micro-sociological Theory*. Princeton, NJ: Princeton University Press.

Dijkstra, Jan Kornelis, Antonius H. N. Cillessen, and Casey Borch. 2013. "Popularity and Adolescent Friendship Networks: Selection and Influence Dynamics." *Developmental Psychology* 49 (7): 1242–1252.

Dishion, Thomas, Sara Nelson, Charlotte Winter, and Bernadette Bullock. 2004. "Adolescent Friendship as a Dynamic System: Entropy and Deviance in the Etiology and Course of Male Antisocial Behavior." *Journal of Abnormal Child Psychology* 32:651–663.

Donoghue, Christopher, and Alicia Raia-Hawrylak. 2016. "Moving beyond the Emphasis on Bullying: A Generalized Approach to Peer Aggression in High School." *Children and Schools* 38 (1): 30–39.

Espelage, Dorothy L., and Susan M. Swearer. 2003. "Research on School Bullying and Victimization: What Have We Learned and Where Do We Go from Here?" *School Psychology Review* 32 (3): 365–383.

Faris, Robert. 2012. "Aggression, Exclusivity, and Status Attainment in Interpersonal Networks." *Social Forces* 90 (4): 1207–1235.

Faris, Robert, and Diane Felmlee. 2011. "Status Struggles: Network Centrality and Gender Segregation in Same-and Cross-Gender Aggression." *American Sociological Review* 76 (1): 48–73.

Felmlee, Diane, and Robert Faris. 2016. "Toxic Ties: Networks of Friendship, Dating, and Cyber Victimization." *Social Psychology Quarterly* 79 (3): 243–262.

Festinger, Leon. 1950. "Informal Social Communication." *Psychological Review* 57 (5): 271–282.

Gardella, Joseph H., Benjamin W. Fisher, Abbie R. Teurbe-Tolon, Brien Ketner, and Maury Nation. 2020. "Students' Reasons for Why They Were Targeted for Bullying." *International Journal of Bullying Prevention* 2:114–128.

Giordano, Peggy C., Stephen A. Cernkovich, and Donna D. Holland. 2003. "Changes in Friendship Relations over the Life Course: Implications for Desistance from Crime." *Criminology* 41:293–328.

Gould, Roger V. 2002. "The Origins of Status Hierarchies: A Formal Theory and Empirical Test." *American Journal of Sociology* 107 (5): 1143–1178.

———. 2003. *Collision of Wills: How Ambiguity about Social Rank Breeds Conflict.* Chicago: University of Chicago Press.

Hawley, Patricia H., Todd D. Little, and Noel A. Card. 2007. "The Allure of a Mean Friend: Relationship Quality and Processes of Aggressive Adolescents with Prosocial Skills." *International Journal of Behavioral Development* 31 (2): 170–180.

Haynie, Dana L., Nathan J. Doogan, and Brian Soller. 2014. "Gender, Friendship Networks, and Delinquency: A Dynamic Network Approach." *Criminology* 52 (4): 688–722.

Hong, Jun Song, and Dorothy L. Espelage. 2012. "A Review of Research on Bullying and Peer Victimization in School: An Ecological System Analysis." *Aggressive and Violent Behavior* 17 (4): 311–322.

Jimerson, Shane R., Gale M. Morrison, Sarah W. Pletcher, and Michael J. Furlong. 2006. "Youth Engaged in Antisocial and Aggressive Behaviors: Who Are They?" In *Handbook of School Violence and School Safety: From Research to Practice*, edited by Shane R. Jimerson and Michael Furlong, 3–19. Mahwah, NJ: Lawrence Erlbaum.

Johnson, David. 2005. "Two-Wave Panel Analysis: Comparing Statistical Methods for Studying the Effects of Transitions." *Journal of Marriage and Family* 67 (4): 1061–1075.

Laursen, Brett, and Gwen Pursell. 2009. "Conflict in Peer Relationships." In *Social, Emotional, and Personality Development in Context: Handbook of Peer Interactions,*

Relationships, and Groups, edited by Kenneth H. Rubin, William M. Bukowski, and Brett Laursen, 267–286. New York: Guilford.

Li, Yan, and Michelle F. Wright. 2014. "Adolescents' Social Status Goals: Relationships to Social Status, Insecurity, and Prosocial Behavior." *Journal of Youth and Adolescence* 43:146–160.

McPherson, Miller, Lynn Smith-Lovin, and James M. Cook. 2001. "Birds of a Feather: Homophily in Social Networks." *Annual Review of Sociology* 27:415–44.

Merton, Robert K. 1968. "The Matthew Effect in Science." *Science* 159:56–63.

Mouttapa, Michele, Thomas Valente, Peggy Gallaher, and Louise A. Rohrback. 2004. "Social Network Predictors of Bullying and Victimization." *Adolescence* 39 (154): 315–335.

National Academies of Sciences, Engineering and Medicine. 2016. "Preventing Bullying through Science, Policy, and Practice." Washington, DC: National Academies Press.

Olweus, Dan. 1993. *Bullying at School: What We Know and What We Can Do*. Cambridge, MA: Blackwell.

Paluck, Elizabeth Levy, Hana Shepherd, and Peter M. Aronow. 2016. "Changing Climates of Conflict: A Social Network Experiment in 56 Schools." *Proceedings of the National Academy of Sciences* 113:566–571.

Peets, Kätlin, and Ernest V. E. Hodges. 2014. "Is Popularity Associated with Aggression toward Socially Preferred or Marginalized Targets?" *Journal of Experimental Child Psychology* 124:112–123.

Pellegrini, Anthony D., and Jon Archer. 2005. "Sex Differences in Competitive and Aggressive Behavior: A View from Sexual Selection Theory." In *Origins of the Social Mind: Evolutionary Psychology and Child Development*, edited by Bruce J. Ellis and David F. Bjorklund, 219–244. New York: Guilford.

Pellegrini, Anthony D., and Jeffrey Long. 2010. "A Longitudinal Study of Bullying, Dominance, and Victimization during the Transition from Primary School through Secondary School." *British Journal of Developmental Psychology* 20:259–280.

Prinstein, Mitchell J., and Antonius N. H. Cillessen. 2003. "Forms and Functions of Adolescent Peer Aggression Associated with High Levels of Peer Status." *Merrill-Palmer Quarterly* 49 (3): 310–342.

Ridgeway, Cecilia L., and Shelley J. Correll. 2004. "Unpacking the Gender System: A Theoretical Perspective on Gender Beliefs and Social Relations." *Gender & Society* 18 (4): 510–531.

Rose, Amanda J., and Karen D. Rudolph. 2006. "A Review of Sex Differences in Peer Relationship Processes: Potential Trade-Offs for the Emotional and Behavioral Development of Girls and Boys." *Psychological Bulletin* 132 (1): 98–131.

Shin, Huiyoung. 2017. "Friendship Dynamics of Adolescent Aggression, Prosocial Behavior, and Social Status: The Moderating Role of Gender." *Journal of Youth and Adolescence* 46:2305–2320.

Unnever, James, and Dewey Cornell. 2003. "The Culture of Bullying in Middle School." *Journal of School Violence* 2 (2): 5–27.

Vaillancourt, Tracy, Patricia McDougall, Shelley Hymel, Amanda Krygsman, Jessie Miller, Kelly Stiver, and Clinton Davis. 2008. "Bullying: Are Researchers and Children/Youth Talking about the Same Thing?" *International Journal of Behavioral Development* 32:486–495.

Waldrop, Mary F., and Charles F. Halverson. 1975. "Intensive and Extensive Peer Behavior: Longitudinal and Cross-Sectional Analyses." *Child Development* 46 (1): 19–26.

9

Social Differentness and Bullying

A Discussion of Race, Class, and Income

TODD MIGLIACCIO

Bullying has been shown to be an international social issue[1] negatively impacting all involved: victims, bystanders, bullies, teachers, parents, and so on. The U.S. Department of Education considers it one of the primary factors that limits student success, impacting students' personal health, academic success, social development, and relationships, in both the present and future. While numerous studies have identified the importance of demographic characteristics such as gender and sexuality, many fail to engage these factors as multifaceted issues. This chapter uses the social ecological perspective to consider the impact of race, class, and income on bullying experiences, highlighting the existence of social differentness in bullying.[2]

Social Ecological Perspective

The social ecological perspective, a systems theory, postulates that the rates of bullying are influenced by both macro and micro factors, which are nested within one another. A modified version of the theory highlights that it is not a unidirectional relationship (see Figure 9.1)[3] among the factors. Instead, both macro and micro factors influence one another, as is also noted in chapter 10 by Shepherd in her description of the development of school culture through student interactions. All social factors interact with one another to maintain or potentially change a school bullying culture. This also means that the different levels interact to determine the experiences of all stakeholders within a bullying dynamic. From this perspective, social-identity-based variables should be perceived not as factors separate from the larger culture, but rather as

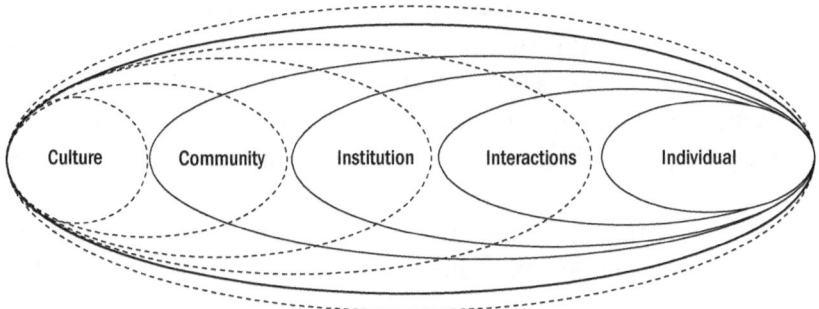

Figure 9.1. Modified Sociological Ecological Diagram

integrated concepts that derive from and validate the larger community that defines the existence of a bullying culture. Social factors serve as justifications and avenues through which bullying is displayed, or not. Who is bullied derives not from specified factors solely associated with the individual but is, in part, based on the culture in which bullying occurs, along with being performances of socially defined identities. Focusing on research on preconceived social categories that contribute to bullying maintains an emphasis on normative dichotomies.[4] When research focuses too much on highlighting the importance of key factors of the individuals involved, we fail to adequately understand the social dynamics at work within a culture. Doing so overlooks the crux of the issue about why bullying occurs: social differentness. Students are targeted for bullying because they exude characteristics via behaviors that the larger community has deemed less powerful or less acceptable. It is not that a student is working-class, an Asian American, or a person with a disability, but rather that a student is working-class in a community that is defined around class issues and inequality.

It is, however, more than just social difference as defined by the larger community and/or culture that is important.[5] It is that these characteristics define access to resources as well as power in the community, and ultimately the school.[6] Social factors are conduits for the pursuit of dominance and power via bullying,[7] the prominent driving force for bullying.[8] Individuals, in the hunt for control, often focus on factors that will most easily be associated with and offer them greater access to power. A victim of bullying is targeted not simply for their race or ethnicity but rather because the larger culture has deemed those factors as socially relevant to power dynamics, and the aggressor has identified they hold power in this context over the victim. Bullies then engage in behaviors that assert this perceived dominance over another, which validates the importance of these factors in the culture. There is a feedback loop in which social interactions construct and maintain community values.

Fully evaluating the social construction of difference, not just at the individual level but in conjunction with community inequity and discrimination along with interaction and/or performances of those involved, is important because findings about the statistical importance of social demographics are used to establish policies and interventions for bullying. Furthermore, aggressions enacted upon individuals who have been defined as marginal by the larger community legitimize the social hierarchy surrounding the identities. To truly understand and respond to bullying, "the interplay between culture and agency is crucial."[9] The focus must be on the social construction of difference at all levels of the system and how they interact to produce meaning for what defines power and status within a school, which are enacted upon students through interactions, determined by their "social differentness."

Race and Ethnicity

Any negative impact on the education of underrepresented students is important for the impact of bullying compounds the already negative experiences of students of color within the education system.[10] The analysis of which racial/ethnic groups experience higher or lower levels of bullying, however, is confounding. For example, two different studies concluded that Latinos were less likely to be involved with bullying in comparison to African Americans[11] and whites,[12] while other studies have concluded that African American students are less likely to be bullied than white or Latino students.[13] In comparison, in an analysis conducted by the author, African Americans and whites were the groups most likely to experience bullying, with Latinx most likely to be the aggressors.[14] In contrast, a different study found that Latinos were most likely to experience racially biased aggression.[15] And still another study concluded the most common group that is bullied are Native Americans.[16] A more recent study found that whites were more likely than

Hispanics or African Americans to be victimized.[17] Finally, Konold et al. found that while African American students were more likely to identify a negative school climate, there was no difference in the level of bullying across racial/ethnic groups as well as how school climate impacts bullying rates among groups.[18] Beyond victimization, research has identified that African Americans are no more likely to be bullies than any other racial group,[19] while a different study concluded that Blacks are the most likely group to bully.[20] While all of these findings are legitimate, they obfuscate the discussion concerning the experiences of specific racial and/or ethnic groups and bullying.

When evaluating generalized groups, studies have also resulted in oppositional conclusions, with one claiming that underrepresented students are more likely to be bullied[21] and another concluding nonwhite minority students are less likely to be bullied.[22] Still other researchers have claimed that race is not a factor in determining victimization rates.[23] Hoffman and Daigle found in an evaluation of the impact of race/ethnicity on bullying that including multiple key, control factors in the analysis, the impact of racial/ethnic group identity became limited.[24] Furthermore, race/ethnicity had no impact on willingness to disclose experience to parents and did not correlate with parental response and the subsequent impact on depression of victims.[25] One study identified that ethnic minorities are more likely to be bullies,[26] while a study by the Southern Poverty Law Center found an increase in attacks on ethnic minorities, largely by white students.[27] To further complicate these issues, studies have found when evaluating multiple factors, in comparison to race, that other factors may be more influential when evaluating bullying rates. Peskin et al. claimed that gender plays a much greater role in bullying than race.[28] Jackman et al. concluded that sexual-minority students had higher rates than heterosexual students, regardless of racial groups.[29] Peguero and Williams noted that SES mediated the relationship between race/ethnicity and bullying rates.[30] And Hoffman and Daigle identified that having disabilities was the prominent factor in determining bullying for all racial/ethnic groups.[31]

This is not to claim that race and/or ethnicity are not important in bullying analysis, for they consistently influence behaviors in schools. Gusler and Kiang[32] found that while race/ethnicity had no impact on bullying experiences, racial/ethnic minority students who experienced bullying were likely to identify race as being a contributing factor.[33] Students who feel bullied because of a specific factor, such as race, feel disconnected from school, which increases absenteeism and limits success in academia.[34] It has also been found that intervention programs differentially impact racial/ethnic groups in comparison to whites, even to the point of not changing bullying rates for some groups.[35] Furthermore, La Salle et al. concluded that race/ethnicity mediated the impact of school culture on suicidal ideation, increasing it for some groups.[36] Studies have found that students of color suffer at higher rates from health deficiencies, both physical and mental, as well as experience negative educational outcomes, as a result of bullying.[37]

Focusing on racial groups to evaluate bullying is limiting, as racial/ethnic groups are often characterized by preestablished categories that more often do not reflect the diversity of identities of students within a school. In an analysis of a large school district, the open-ended question about race/ethnicity resulted in twenty-two claimed racial/ethnic identities throughout the district.[38] Such a diverse range limits the ability to statistically evaluate the relationship between race/ethnicity and bullying. Often research collapses identities into smaller, culturally defined groups, which fails to acknowledge the existence of extensive identities and ultimately cultures in a school or district. Such an analysis measures a socially prescribed measure of bullying that would essentially be inaccurate to the experiences of each group. For example, of the twenty-two identities in the noted study, six could be characterized explicitly as Asian, ranging from the general moniker "Asian" to "Filipino" and "Indian," all of which are considered Asian and yet offer distinctly different social experiences. This does not include the multiethnic identities, at least one of which included an Asian identity (five more identities). Categorizing all of these groups who are affiliated with Asia or Asian background as "Asian" fails to account for the diversity of historical[39] and cultural experiences of these groups.[40] The diverse experiences, cultures, and histories alter bullying experiences of students,[41] and thus our understanding about how race and/or ethnicity contributes to bullying experiences.

A number of studies have noted that the impact of race/ethnicity on bullying is determined less by which societal group one is affiliated with and more by which group is a minority within the school.[42] Bullying of minority groups is compounded by the fact that bystander attitudes toward bullying are influenced by the size of the support group of the bullied individual.[43] Returning to the study that identified the existence of twenty-two potential identities, the study found Latinos to be the group most likely to be the aggressor, which corresponds with the statistical breakdown, as they composed over 65 percent of the student population.[44] Power differences among students that contribute to the likelihood of bullying are related to superior numbers.[45] It has been found that there has been an increase in race-based bullying since 2016, with students of color in predominantly white schools identifying higher rates of victimization.[46] Furthermore, in schools that were predominantly nonwhite, there was not an increase, but white students reported being bullied more than nonwhite students.

Being in the statistical minority in a school characterizes students as socially distinct, which influences racial bullying.[47] It is the expressed power of the majority group over the statistically identified minority group that largely promotes race as a significant factor (this does not consider the racism-driven attacks).[48] In line with this, racial bullying is less likely to occur in racially balanced diverse schools and classrooms.[49] In fact, having greater diversity throughout a school has been shown not only to reduce feelings of vulnerability of any racial or ethnic group but also to impact the perception of how teachers treated different racial groups, that is, more equitably.[50] This is supported by the finding that interventions that are impactful are those that emphasize greater cultural sensitivity and tolerance of diversity.[51] Focusing consistently on social acceptance limits the power through highlighting "differentness" of students, in particular, ethnic minorities.

Race-based bullying is not solely about numbers though, as racial discord persists throughout schools,[52] and engagement in racial bullying is influenced by the value placed upon race and racial dominance in the surrounding community.[53] In a country that has institutionalized white supremacist practices and ideology,[54] racial bullying is a constant threat to students of color,[55] who are more likely than white students to perceive schools as unsafe.[56] In fact, white supremacy is integrated into all aspects of school curriculum, including standard anti-bullying programs.[57] As a result, anti-bullying programs have little to no impact on Black students.[58] Individuals are not bullied simply because they are affiliated with a minority group but rather because the community and larger culture in which a school resides is racially charged. "Bullying is not a 'natural' adolescent behavior, but is conditioned by the surrounding social environment."[59]

Class and Income

Researchers have consistently noted that class is a prominent factor in bullying that limits student opportunities,[60] which regularly interacts with and even moderates the effect of race/ethnicity.[61] Socioeconomic status has been identified as translating into cultural status within a school,[62] isolating working-class students and elevating upper- and middle-class students. The importance of class in defining social status is influenced by the materialistic values of a society,[63] and more specifically, the surrounding community.[64] Hite and Hite noted that children can become aware of materialism and its importance in a society as early as two years old.[65] It can influence a student's self-worth,[66] educational goals,[67] and peer judgment.[68] Evaluation based on materialism, however, is not solely a unidirectional experience. Banerjee and Dittmar found that students who were rejected or perceived rejection increased their focus on materialism in an effort to fit in, showing that bullying in more materialistic cultures can potentially lead to a greater emphasis by a victim on materialistic values.[69]

Emphasis on materialistic success is not explicitly about actual class standing but about a performance of it. "Differences in financial backgrounds, even if sometimes minor, are exacerbated by the way students present themselves."[70] Bullying among poorer students is determined by others' perception of their social differences,[71] which is mediated by the importance of materialism in the community.[72] To offset any perceived or actual bullying, students and their parents try to offset potential class difference through material purchases.[73] This may be why some studies have concluded that actual SES does not influence bullying[74] because student SES is not driving the categorization of students but instead is determined by perceived class based on material possessions.

Some argue that the effect of social class is often masked by other factors.[75] For example, children within lower tiers of socioeconomic status tend to have fewer friends,[76] and children with fewer friends are more likely to experience victimization.[77] Similarly, Tippett and Wolke concluded in their meta-analysis of SES and bullying, "Accordingly, it might be that factors associated with low SES, such as how children are parented, get on with their siblings, or observe domestic violence, were better suited to predicting victim and bully-victim roles than socioeconomic level."[78] Ultimately, "household income could thus be too indirect to capture adolescents' experienced material and economic conditions."[79]

While household income may not be a clear indicator, larger societal determinants of SES "differentness" could be. In an extensive study of thirty-five countries, it was found that class is a significant factor, extending from the interactional level up to the societal.[80] The researchers concluded that children of the lower classes were at greater risk of being victimized, finding that economic inequality at schools increased the likelihood of experiencing bullying. Furthermore, for every level of difference between the wealthiest and the poorest in a school, there was a 13 percent increased likelihood of bullying at the same school. Economic disparity did not stop here, as greater inequity throughout a country increased the likelihood of students in the country experiencing bullying by as much as 34 percent. Essentially, poor students who attend schools that have higher levels of economic inequality, which are located in countries that display greater income disparity among their inhabitants, are at an increased likelihood of being bullied than any other student.[81] Furthermore, acceptance of such inequality also promotes negative treatment of those who are at the economic lower end, as well as their acceptance of victimization.

The larger community and cultural determinants that define the value of materialism influence the effect class has on bullying. Still, the impact of class on bullying is mediated by other factors, in particular the ability to perform "higher" class, clarifying the social construction of class as a factor. Ultimately, it is the presentation and truly the perception of "differentness," coupled with the cultural importance of the factor that defines the likelihood and level of class-based bullying that may occur.

Bullying in the Trump Era

Societal perspective can also change during different eras, depending on the emphasis on race and ethnicity by the larger society. For example,

Huang and Cornell[82] concluded that the increasing rate of race-based bullying since 2016 was largely a result of the sociopolitical climate. The Southern Poverty Law Center identified it as the "Trump Effect," citing specific quotations from election rhetoric used during bullying incidences.[83] Donald Trump's rhetoric during his time in office proffered institutionalized justification for hate speech and discrimination, including the criminalization of immigrants.[84] During this period of time, the number of hate-based groups doubled, along with a tripling of anti-Muslim groups.[85] There was also a subsequent 258 percent increase in white supremacist propaganda during the first year of Trump's presidency,[86] and a spike in hate crimes,[87] which were the highest rates that we had seen in over ten years.[88] I introduce these numbers not to engage in a debate concerning the dogma of the former president but more to clarify that divisive speech influences cultural and community perspectives and the subsequent actions around and in schools. In particular, the rhetoric facilitated greater feelings of vulnerability for students of color, while simultaneously amplifying for everyone a standpoint that immigrants and people of color are threats.[89] Ultimately, constructing specific groups as a peril to the status quo, that is, power structures, increases the likelihood of aggression and bullying toward the perceived threat.[90]

During Trump's time in office, there was also an increase of racial and ethnic bullying throughout the United States.[91] This included white students who were targeted when attending predominantly nonwhite institutions.[92] Durkin argues that nonwhite students were likely more aggressive toward white students when they outnumbered them in response to the negative idiom and, more important, the power inequity in the larger society. As discussed throughout this chapter, bullying rates, however, are not solely influenced by the larger societal culture, but are shaped also by the immediate surrounding community.[93] Huang and Cornell[94] found higher rates of race- or ethnicity-based bullying in communities that tended to promote negative ethnic and/or racial commentary. Similarly, prejudicial attitudes about immigrants that were supported in a community increased anti-immigration bullying.[95]

While macro cultures impact the experiences for students in schools, school climate can manipulate the culture in such a way as to counteract external issues.[96] Schools that promoted diversity, in their staff[97] and in their curriculum,[98] tended to have lower rates of bullying. Ali[99] identified that what is in the curriculum reflects the values of the school culture. More specifically, pedagogy that highlighted Black Lives Matter connected students of color to school by making course material more accessible and relevant to their lives.[100] Such inclusive efforts have been shown to not only increase student engagement and learning but also foster greater trust among underrepresented students in the classroom.[101] Equity-focused curriculum promotes the voice of students of color that increase their engagement and learning,[102] which increases comprehension, civic responsibility, and agency of all students, including white students.[103] Beyond the curriculum, an emphasis on diversity in the physical environment can also reflect the values of the school.[104] Murals created in school that mirror the students and their community bond students to schools,[105] which can positively alter their perception about education.[106] Integrating equity throughout a school, including staff, curriculum, and physical environment, increases student feelings of safety and connectivity, while also reducing bullying.[107] Students not only are able to engage more academically when the material is relevant to their experiences[108] but also become more connected to a community and, more importantly, gain a voice.[109] Similar to how external groups impact LGBTQ student experiences when bullying occurs, Black Lives Matter offers a group and a community that could offset the negative impact of bullying.

In contrast, schools that refrained from promoting education on racism and diversity limited inclusion for all students.[110] For example, many schools refused to integrate antiracism curriculum, such as the 1619 Project. The repudiation was influenced, in part, by Trump's commentary about the project and, more importantly, his administration's promotion of the 1776 Commission to infuse more patriotism in school curricula. Schools that sponsor perspectives that sustain the status quo and look to perpetuate divisions are more likely to maintain unsafe environments for students of color.[111] Even in instances when teachers attempted to draw on Black Lives Matter educational curriculum,[112] there was a backlash from community members,[113] who actively marginalized those teachers, labeling them as "problematic."[114] Many teachers choose then to refrain from integrating innovative practices, such as inclusive curriculum, when they do not feel supported by their schools.[115] Sustaining such practices highlights the importance of the dominant ideology concerning race, which further disconnects students of color from schools, while simultaneously promoting racial, ethnic, and/or anti-immigrant bullying.

While social differentness is relevant and important to evaluating and understanding bullying, we should not ignore the contextual issues that direct the degree and focus of the bullying. Trump's rhetoric promoted white supremacist ideology that enhanced racial, ethnic, and immigrant bullying in schools. The impact of the rhetoric, which derived from the larger societal ideology, interacted with the community and school cultures to influence rates and experiences of bullying. Ultimately, the focus on individual identity factors "mirrors broader social structures" of inequality and discrimination.[116] These broader ideologies that reflect hierarchical structures in a society are influenced by macro factors, such as institutionalized racism, community response (e.g., the rise of Black Lives Matter), and the larger contextual issues, which, in this case, was the active rhetoric of a nation's leader to augment a white supremacist system. These together influence the level and experiences of bullying within a school. This means that a surrounding community can contribute to mediating bullying, including racial and ethnic bullying and its impact on students.[117] Any analysis of race and/or ethnicity related to bullying needs to consider the "social differentness" of the students, which is influenced by the importance placed on race as expressed through the rhetoric in the country, larger community, and school climate and the statistical makeup of the specific identities within each school.

Conclusion

"Social differentness" cannot be explicitly applied to any specified group, yet it is a driving force for why students are targeted. Race, ethnicity, and class are all important factors that influence bullying within a school as they create division and power differentials among students. Drawing on the modified social ecological model, cultural expectations and values demarcate what characteristics define potential power divisions within school interactions. While larger societal hierarchies tend to reflect a heterosexual, male-centered, cisgender, able-bodied, middle-/upper-class, white lens, the importance of each is contextual and governed by the surrounding community and statistical makeup of the student population as well as societal issues. For example, in predominantly white schools in the South, race-based bullying increased following the 2016 election.[118] Students, drawing on explicit and divisive rhetoric of the culture and community, distinguish which identities and/or characterizations through which to assert power.

While community values define and characterize pathways to power, determination of "social differentness" exists through evaluations of performances by students; that is, they are based on perceptions, not "real" or even "chosen" identities of the targets. Returning to the modified social ecological model, the interaction among students is influenced by the societal and community levels. Essentially, those students associated with identities that are socially determined positions of power look to assert dominance over those who appear to be part of a marginalized group. Whether defining the socially ostracized status or attempting to negate a marginalized status, behaviors are key facets of the bullying experience; these performances not only determine who is (and is not) in power, but also simultaneously reflect and confirm the cultural expectations that define power. Bullying is not only a performance of dominance over individuals who have been designated as "different" but also a validation of the larger cultural determinants and values. It is a feedback loop based on the actions of those engaged in bullying that maintains the societal and school determinants of cultural values and hierarchies. The interface between the larger culture and community values and the social performance of identities within interactions regulate "social differentness" and power.

Without consideration of the cultural and community values, the makeup of the school and the interaction dynamics, it is more difficult to accurately evaluate, respond to, and prevent bullying within schools. Research findings that focus on social characteristics are limited in their application when they do not consider and then respond to the culture in which bullying exists, that is, the specific school and surrounding community.[119] "Social differentness" conceptualizes that differential of the social experiences of bullying.

NOTES

This chapter would not have been written without the support of my former colleague, Dr. Juliana Raskauskas, who passed away in January 2016. She believed that the ideas in this chapter were important to share and pushed me to work on it prior to her passing.

1. Migliaccio and Raskauskas, 2015.
2. Parts of this chapter originally appeared in Migliaccio and Raskauskas, 2015.
3. See Migliaccio and Raskauskas, 2015, for full discussion.
4. Forsberg and Thornberg, 2016.
5. Hamarus and Kaikkonen, 2008.
6. Forsberg and Thornberg, 2016.
7. Schumann et al., 2014.
8. For a full discussion, see Morales et al., 2016.
9. Forsberg and Thornberg, 2016, 15.
10. Priest et al., 2014.
11. Peskin et al., 2006.
12. Hanish and Guerra, 2000.
13. Spriggs et al., 2007; Storch et al., 2003.
14. Migliaccio and Raskauskas, 2015.
15. Jones et al., 2018.
16. Carlyle and Steinman, 2007.
17. Hoffman and Daigle, 2019.
18. Konold et al., 2017.
19. Goldweber et al., 2013.
20. Lovegrove et al., 2012.
21. Bauer et al., 2007; Dake et al., 2003.
22. Spriggs et al., 2007; DeVoe et al., 2004.
23. Fitzpatrick et al., 2010; Hepburn et al., 2012; Mouttapa et al., 2004.
24. Hoffman and Daigle, 2019.
25. Fernandez et al., 2018.
26. Xu et al., 2020.
27. Southern Poverty Law Center, 2012.
28. Peskin et al., 2006.
29. Jackman et al., 2020.
30. Peguero and Williams, 2013.
31. Hoffman and Daigle, 2019.
32. Gusler and Kiang, 2019.
33. Lai and Kao, 2018.
34. Priest et al., 2014.
35. Bauer et al., 2007.
36. La Salle et al., 2017.
37. Cooper and Sánchez, 2016; Priest et al., 2014; Xu et al., 2020.
38. Migliaccio and Raskauskas, 2015.
39. Espiritu, 1997.
40. Zhou and Bankston, 2020.
41. Koo et al., 2012.
42. Goldweber et al., 2013; Graham and Juvonen, 2002.

43 O'Brien, 2007.
44 Migliaccio and Raskauskas, 2015.
45 Horton, 2011; Rigby, 2008.
46 Huang and Cornell, 2019.
47 Lahelma, 2004; Englander, 2007; Horton, 2011; Thornberg, 2011.
48 For further discussion about this, see Migliaccio and Raskauskas, 2015.
49 Juvonen et al., 2006.
50 Juvonen et al., 2018.
51 Hoffman and Daigle, 2019; Spriggs et al., 2007.
52 Seaton et al., 2013.
53 Goldweber et al., 2013; LaVeist et al., 2011; Horton, 2011; O'Brien, 2007.
54 Kendi, 2019.
55 Hong et al., 2021.
56 Shelley et al., 2021.
57 Thomas, 2019.
58 Piquero, 2015; You et al., 2014.
59 Due et al., 2009, 912.
60 Chaux and Castellanos, 2015; Due et al., 2003; Fu et al., 2012; Jansen et al., 2011; Jansen et al., 2012; Moore et al., 2019; Borck, 2020; Hollingworth, 2020; Moore-Berg and Karpinski, 2019.
61 Koenig and Eagly, 2014; Peguero and Williams, 2013.
62 Dumais, 2002; Schor, 2004.
63 Schor, 2004.
64 Hoffman and Daigle, 2019.
65 Hite and Hite, 1995.
66 Richins, 2004.
67 Ku et al., 2014.
68 Banerjee and Dittmar, 2008.
69 Banerjee and Dittmar, 2008.
70 Klein, 2012, 64.
71 Fernqvist, 2013; Thornberg, 2011.
72 Hoffman and Daigle, 2019.
73 Kornrich and Furstenberg, 2013; Ridge, 2011.
74 Hjalmarsson, 2018; Han et al., 2017.
75 Hanish and Guerra, 2000; Jansen et al., 2012; Patterson et al., 1990.
76 Sletten, 2010.
77 Juvonen and Graham, 2014.
78 Tippett and Wolke, 2014, e56.
79 Hjalmarsson, 2018, 90.
80 Due et al., 2009.
81 Due et al., 2009.
82 Huang and Cornell, 2019.

83 Southern Poverty Law Center, 2016.
84 Nguyen and Kebede, 2017.
85 Potok, 2017.
86 Anti-Defamation League, 2018.
87 Petulla et al., 2017.
88 Hauslohner, 2018.
89 Hoefer, 2019.
90 Edmondson and Zeman, 2011; Durkin et al., 2012.
91 Mishna et al., 2020.
92 Durkin et al., 2012.
93 Saarento et al., 2015.
94 Huang and Cornell, 2019.
95 Caravita et al., 2020.
96 MacSuga-Gage et al., 2018.
97 Piquero, 2015.
98 Hong et al., 2021; Crozier and Davies, 2008.
99 Ali, 2018.
100 Polleck and Spence-Davis, 2020.
101 Filbin, 2021.
102 Kinloch et al., 2020.
103 Boyd and Miller, 2020; Kelly, 2020.
104 Christenson, 2017.
105 Turk, 2012.
106 Lopez and Hall, 2007.
107 Shelley et al., 2021.
108 Filbin, 2021; Kinloch et al., 2020; Polleck and Spence-Davis, 2020.
109 Polleck and Spence-Davis, 2020.
110 Gillborn, 2007.
111 Shelley et al., 2021.
112 Black Lives Matter, 2016.
113 Kingkade, 2020.
114 Myers and Bhopal, 2017.
115 Migliaccio, 2015.
116 Mishna et al., 2020.
117 Jones et al., 2018; Xu et al., 2020.
118 Southern Poverty Law Center, 2016.
119 Olweus, 1993.

REFERENCES

Anti-Defamation League. 2018. "ADL Finds Alarming Increase in White Supremacist Propaganda on College Campuses across U.S." www.adl.org.

Ali, Sunni. 2018. "How Race and Racism Empower a School's Curriculum." *Journal of Research Initiatives* 4 (1): 1–11.

Banerjee, Robin, and Helga Dittmar. 2008. "Individual Differences in Children's Materialism: The Role of Peer Relations." *Personality and Social Psychology Bulletin* 34 (1): 17–31.

Bauer, Nerissa, Paula Lozano, and Frederick Rivara. 2007. "The Effectiveness of the Olweus Bullying Prevention Program in Public Middle Schools: A Controlled Trial." *Journal of Adolescent Health* 40:266–274.

Black Lives Matter. 2016. "BLM at School." www.blacklivesmatteratschool.com.

Borck, C. Ray. 2020. "'I Belong Here': Culturally Sustaining Pedagogical Praxes from an Alternative High School in Brooklyn." *Urban Review* 52 (2): 376–391.

Boyd, Ashley S., and Jacinda Miller. 2020. "Let's Give Them Something to Talk (and Act!) About: Privilege, Racism, and Oppression in the Middle School Classroom." *Voices from the Middle* 27 (3): 15–19.

Caravita, Simona C. S., Sara Stefanelli, Angela Mazzone, Livia Cadei, Robert Thornberg, and Barbara Ambrosini. 2020. "When the Bullied Peer Is Native-Born vs. Immigrant: A Mixed-Method Study with a Sample of Native-Born and Immigrant Adolescents." *Scandinavian Journal of Psychology* 61 (1): 97–107.

Carlyle, Kellie E., and Kenneth J. Steinman. 2007. "Demographic Differences in the Prevalence, Co-occurrence, and Correlates of Adolescent Bullying at School." *Journal of School Health* 77 (9): 623–629.

Chaux, Enrique, and Melisa Castellanos. 2015. "Money and Age in Schools: Bullying and Power Imbalances." *Aggressive Behavior* 41 (3): 280–293.

Chaux, Enrique, Andrés Molano, and Paola Podlesky. 2009. "Socio-economic, Sociopolitical and Socio-emotional Variables Explaining School Bullying: A Countrywide Multilevel Analysis." *Aggressive Behavior* 35 (6): 520–529.

Christenson, Matt. 2017. "It's Time to Lead a Mural Project." Art of Education University, July 7. https://theartofeducation.edu.

Cooper, Adina C., and Bernadette Sánchez. 2016. "The Roles of Racial Discrimination, Cultural Mistrust, and Gender in Latina/o Youth's School Attitudes and Academic Achievement." *Journal of Research on Adolescence* 26 (4): 1036–1047.

Crozier, Gill, and Jane Davies. 2008. "'The Trouble Is They Don't Mix': Self-Segregation or Enforced Exclusion?" *Race Ethnicity and Education* 11 (3): 285–301.

Dake, Joseph A., James H. Price, Susan K. Telljohann, and Jeanne B. Funk. 2003. "Teacher Perceptions and Practices Regarding School Bullying Prevention." *Journal of School Health* 73 (9): 347–349.

DeVoe, Jill, Katharin Peter, Philip Kaufman, Amanda Miller, Margaret Noonan, Thomas Synder, and Katrina Baum. 2004. "Indicators of School Crime and Safety: 2004." *Education Statistics Quarterly* 6: 51–53.

Due, Pernille, John Lynch, Bjø Holstein, and Jens Modvig. 2003. "Socioeconomic Health Inequalities among a Nationally Representative Sample of Danish Adolescents: The Role of Different Types of Social Relations." *Journal of Epidemiology & Community Health* 57 (9): 692–698.

Due, Pernille, Juan Merlo, Yossi Harel-Fisch, Mogens Trab Damsgaard, Bjø E. Holstein, Jørn Hetland, Candace Currie, Saoirse Nic Gabhainn, Margarida Gaspar De Matos, and John Lynch. 2009. "Socioeconomic Inequality in Exposure to Bullying during Adolescence: A Comparative, Cross-Sectional, Multilevel Study in 35 Countries." *American Journal of Public Health* 99 (5): 907–912.

Dumais, Susan A. 2002. "Cultural Capital, Gender, and School Success: The Role of Habitus." *Sociology of Education* 75 (1): 44–68.

Durkin, Kevin, Simon Hunter, Kate A. Levin, Dermot Bergin, Derek Heim, and Christine Howe. 2012. "Discriminatory Peer Aggression among Children as a Function of Minority Status and Group Proportion in School Context." *European Journal of Social Psychology* 42 (2): 243–251.

Edmondson, Lynne, and Laura Dreuth Zeman. 2011. "Making School Bully Laws Matter." *Reclaiming Children & Youth* 20:33–38.

Englander, Elizabeth. 2007. "Is Bullying a Junior Hate Crime? Implications for Interventions." *American Behavioral Scientist* 51 (2): 205–212.

Espiritu, Yen. 1997. "All Men Are Not Created Equal: Asian Men in US History." In *Men's Lives*, edited by Michael Kimmel and Michael Messner, 35–44. Boston: Allyn & Bacon.

Fernandez, Alejandra, Alexandra Loukas, and Keryn E. Pasch. 2018. "Examining the Bidirectional Associations between Adolescents' Disclosure, Parents' Solicitation, and Adjustment Problems among Non-Hispanic White and Hispanic Early Adolescents." *Journal of Youth and Adolescence* 47 (12): 2569–2583.

Fernqvist, Stina. 2013. "Joining in on Different Terms—Dealing with Poverty in School and among 'Peers.'" *Young* 21:155–171.

Filbin, Deborah N. 2021. "Discovering How Black Lives Matter: Embracing Student Voice in the Art Room." *Art Education* 74 (1): 19–25.

Fitzpatrick, Kevin M., Akilah Dulin, and Bettina Piko. 2010. "Bullying and Depressive Symptomatology among Low-Income, African-American Youth." *Journal of Youth and Adolescence* 39 (6): 634–645.

Forsberg, Camilla, and Robert Thornberg. 2016. "The Social Ordering of Belonging: Children's Perspectives on Bullying." *International Journal of Educational Research* 78:13–23.

Fu, Qiang, Kenneth Land, and Vicki Lamb. 2012. "Bullying Victimization, Socioeconomic Status and Behavioral Characteristics of 12th Graders in the United States, 1989 to 2009: Repetitive Trends and Persistent Risk Differentials." *Child Indicators Research* (6): 1–21.

Gillborn, David. 2007. "Education Policy as an Act of White Supremacy: Whiteness, Critical Race Theory and Education Reform." *Journal of Education Policy* 20 (4): 485–505.

Goldweber, Asha, Tracy Waasdorp, and Catherine Bradshaw. 2013. "Examining Associations between Race, Urbanicity, and Patterns of Bullying Involvement." *Journal of Youth and Adolescence* 42 (2): 206–219.

Graham, Sandra, and Jaana Juvonen. 2002. "Ethnicity, Peer Harassment, and Adjustment in Middle School: An Exploratory Study." *Journal of Early Adolescence* 22 (2): 173–199.

Gusler, Stephanie, and Lisa Kiang. 2019. "Childhood Peer Victimization Experiences and Adult Psychological Adjustment: Examining Race/Ethnicity and Race-Related Attributions." *Journal of Social and Personal Relationships* 36 (1): 337–358.

Hamarus, Paivi, and Pauli Kaikkonen. 2008. "School Bullying as a Creator of Pupil Peer Pressure." *Educational Research* 50 (4): 333–345.

Han, Ziqiang, Guirong Zhang, and Haibo Zhang. 2017. "School Bullying in Urban China: Prevalence and Correlation with School Climate." *International Journal of Environmental Research and Public Health* 14:1116–1129.

Hanish, Laura D., and Nancy G. Guerra. 2000. "The Roles of Ethnicity and School Context in Predicting Children's Victimization by Peers." *American Journal of Community Psychology* 28 (2): 201–223.

Hauslohner, Abigail. 2018. "Hate Crimes Jump for Fourth Straight Year in Largest US Cities, Study Shows." *Washington Post*, May 11.

Hepburn, Lisa, Deborah Azrael, Beth Molnar, and Matthew Miller. 2012. "Bullying and Suicidal Behaviors among Urban High School Youth." *Journal of Adolescent Health* 51: 93–95.

Hite, Cynthia, and Robert Hite. 1995. "Reliance on Brand by Young Children." *Journal of the Market Research Society* 37:185–192.

Hjalmarsson, Simon. 2018. "Poor Kids? Economic Resources and Adverse Peer Relations in a Nationally Representative Sample of Swedish Adolescents." *Journal of Youth and Adolescence* 47 (1): 88–104.

Hoefer, Richard. 2019. "Dangers of Social Justice Advocacy." *Social Work* 64 (1): 87–90.

Hoffman, Chrystina, and Leah Daigle. 2019. "Racial and Ethnic Differences in the Risk Factors Associated with Bully Victimization." *Journal of Ethnicity in Criminal Justice* 17 (1): 16–41.

Hollingworth, Sumi. 2020. "Social Mixing in Urban Schools: Class, Race and Exchange-Value Friendships." *Sociological Review* 68 (3): 557–573.

Hong, Jun Sung, Simon C. Hunter, Jinwon Kim, Alex R. Piquero, and Chelsey Narvey. 2021. "Racial Differences in the Applicability of Bronfenbrenner's Ecological Model for Adolescent Bullying Involvement." *Deviant Behavior* 42 (3): 404–424.

Horton, Paul. 2011. "School Bullying and Social and Moral Orders." *Children & Society* 25 (4): 268–277.

Huang, Francis, and Dewey Cornell. 2019. "School Teasing and Bullying after the Presidential Election." *Educational Researcher* 48:69–83.

Jackman, Kasey, Elizabeth J. Kreuze, Billy A. Caceres, and Rebecca Schnall. 2020. "Bullying and Peer Victimization of Minority Youth: Intersections of Sexual Identity and Race/Ethnicity." *Journal of School Health* 90 (5): 368–377.

Jansen, Danielle E. M. C., René Veenstra, Johan Ormel, Frank C. Verhulst, and Sijmen A. Reijneveld. 2011. "Early Risk Factors for Being a Bully, Victim, or Bully/Victim in Late Elementary and Early Secondary Education: The Longitudinal TRAILS Study." *BMC Public Health* 11 (Suppl. 4): 440–446.

Jansen, Pauline W., Marina Verlinden, Anke Dommisse-van Berkel, Cathelijne Mieloo, Jan van der Ende, René Veenstra, Frank C. Verhulst, Wilma Jansen, and Henning

Tiemeier. 2012. "Prevalence of Bullying and Victimization among Children in Early Elementary School: Do Family and School Neighbourhood Socioeconomic Status Matter?" *BMC Public Health* 12 (1): 1–18.

Jones, Lisa M., Kimberly J. Mitchell, Heather A. Turner, and Michele L. Ybarra. 2018. "Characteristics of Bias-Based Harassment Incidents Reported by a National Sample of U.S. Adolescents." *Journal of Adolescence* 65:50–60.

Juvonen, Jaana, and Sandra Graham. 2014. "Bullying in Schools: The Power of Bullies and the Plight of Victims." *Annual Review of Psychology* 65 (1): 159–185.

Juvonen, Jaana, Kara Kogachi, and Sandra Graham. 2018. "When and How Do Students Benefit from Ethnic Diversity in Middle School?" *Child Development* 89 (4): 1268–1282.

Juvonen, Jaana, Adrienne Nishina, and Sandra Graham. 2006. "Ethnic Diversity and Perceptions of Safety in Urban Middle Schools." *Psychological Science* 17 (5): 393–400.

Kelly, Carol. 2020. "Tough Talking: Teaching White Students about Race and Responsibility." *Voices from the Middle* 27 (4): 31–34.

Kendi, Ibram X. 2019. *How to Be an Antiracist*. New York: One World.

Kingkade, Tyler. 2020. "How One Teacher's Black Lives Matter Lesson Divided a Small Wisconsin Town." *NBC News*, October 24www.nbcnews.com.

Kinloch, Valerie, Carlotta Penn, and Tanja Burkhard. 2020. "Black Lives Matter: Storying, Identities, and Counternarratives." *Journal of Literacy Research* 52 (4): 382–405.

Klein, Jessie. 2012. *The Bully Society*. New York: New York University Press.

Knight, Wanda. 2013. "Moving Beyond Preparing Just Art Teachers to Preparing Just Art Teachers: Teacher Education for Equity and Social Justice." In *Stand(ing) up, for a Change: Voices of Arts Educators*, edited by Kevin Tavin and Christine Ballengee Morris, 28–36. Alexandria, VA: National Art Education Association.

Koenig, Anne M., and Alice H. Eagly. 2014. "Evidence for the Social Role Theory of Stereotype Content: Observations of Groups' Roles Shape Stereotypes." *Journal of Personality & Social Psychology* 107 (3): 371–392.

Konold, Timothy, Dewey Cornell, Kathan Shukla, and Francis Huang. 2017. "Racial/Ethnic Differences in Perceptions of School Climate and Its Association with Student Engagement and Peer Aggression." *Journal of Youth and Adolescence* 46 (6): 1289–1303.

Koo, Dixie J., Anthony A. Peguero, and Zahra Shekarkhar. 2012. "The 'Model Minority' Victim: Immigration, Gender, and Asian American Vulnerabilities to Violence at School." *Journal of Ethnicity in Criminal Justice* 10 (2): 129–147.

Kornrich, Sabino, and Frank Furstenberg. 2013. "Investing in Children: Changes in Parental Spending on Children, 1972–2007." *Demography* 50 (1): 1–23.

Ku, Lisbeth, Helga Dittrnar, and Robin Banerjee. 2014. "To Have or to Learn? The Effects of Materialism on British and Chinese Children's Learning." *Journal of Personality & Social Psychology* 106 (5): 803–821.

Lahelma, Elina. 2004. "Tolerance and Understanding? Students and Teachers Reflect on Differences at School." *Educational Research & Evaluation* 10 (1): 3–19.

Lai, Tianjian, and Grace Kao. 2018. "Hit, Robbed, and Put Down (but Not Bullied): Underreporting of Bullying by Minority and Male Students." *Journal of Youth and Adolescence* 47 (3): 619–635.

La Salle, Tamika P., Cixin Wang, Leandra Parris, and Jacqueline A. Brown. 2017. "Associations between School Climate, Suicidal Thoughts, and Behaviors and Ethnicity among Middle School Students." *Psychology in the Schools* 54 (10): 1294–1301.

LaVeist, Thomas, Keisha Pollack, Roland Thorpe, Ruth Fesahazion, and Darrell Gaskin. 2011. "Place, Not Race: Disparities Dissipate in Southwest Baltimore When Blacks and Whites Live under Similar Conditions." *Health Affairs* 30 (10): 1880–1887.

Lopez, Alejandro, and McClellan Hall. 2007. "Letting in the Sun: Native Youth Transform Their School with Murals." *Journal of Strength-Based Interventions* 16 (3): 1–7.

Lovegrove, Peter J., Kimberly L. Henry, and Michael D. Slater. 2012. "Examination of the Predictors of Latent Class Typologies of Bullying Involvement among Middle School Students." *Journal of School Violence* 11 (1): 75–93.

MacSuga-Gage, Ashley S., Robin P. Ennis, Shanna E. Hirsch, and Lauren Evanovich. 2018. "Understanding and Trumping Behavioral Concerns in the Classroom." *Preventing School Failure* 62 (4): 239–249.

Migliaccio, Todd. 2015. "Teacher Understanding and Perception of Bullying: Managing a Teacher Identity." *Sociological Spectrum* 35:84–108.

Migliaccio, Todd, and Juliana Raskauskas. 2015. *Bullying as a Social Experience: Social Factors, Prevention and Intervention*. Surrey, UK: Ashgate.

Mishna, Faye, Jane E. Sanders, Sandra McNeil, Gwendolyn Fearing, and Katerina Kalenteridis. 2020. "'If Somebody Is Different': A Critical Analysis of Parent, Teacher and Student Perspectives on Bullying and Cyberbullying." *Children & Youth Services Review* 118:105366.

Moore, Hadass, Ron Avi Astor, and Rami Benbenishty. 2019. "A Statewide Study of School-Based Victimization, Discriminatory Bullying, and Weapon Victimization by Student Homelessness Status." *Social Work Research* 43 (3): 181–194.

Moore-Berg, Samantha L., and Andrew Karpinski. 2019. "An Intersectional Approach to Understanding How Race and Social Class Affect Intergroup Processes." *Social and Personality Psychology Compass* 13:e12426.

Morales, J. Francisco, Santiago Yubero, and Elisa Larrañaga. 2016. "Gender and Bullying: Application of a Three-Factor Model of Gender Stereotyping." *Sex Roles* 74 (3–4): 169–180.

Mouttapa, Michele, Tom Valente, Peggy Gallaher, Louise Ann Rohrbach, and Jennifer B. Unger. 2004. "Social Network Predictors of Bullying and Victimization." *Adolescence* 39 (154): 315–335.

Myers, Martin, and Kalwant Bhopal. 2017. "Racism and Bullying in Rural Primary Schools: Protecting White Identities Post Macpherson." *British Journal of Sociology of Education* 38 (2): 125–143.

Nguyen, Chi, and Maraki Kebede. 2017. "Immigrant Students win the Trump Era: What We Know and Do Not Know." *Educational Policy* 31 (6): 716–742.

O'Brien, Catherine. 2007. "Peer Devaluation in British Secondary Schools: Young People's Comparisons of Group-Based and Individual-Based Bullying." *Educational Research* 49 (3): 297–324.

Olweus, Dan. 1993. *Bullying at School*. Cambridge, MA: Blackwell.

Patterson, Charlotte J., Janis B. Kupersmidt, and Nancy A. Vaden. 1990. "Income Level, Gender, Ethnicity, and Household Composition as Predictors of Children's School-Based Competence." *Child Development* 61 (2): 485–494.

Peguero, Anthony A., and Lisa M. Williams. 2013. "Racial and Ethnic Stereotypes and Bullying Victimization." *Youth & Society* 45 (4): 545–564.

Peskin, Melissa Fleschler, Susan R. Tortolero, and Christine M. Markham. 2006. "Bullying and Victimization among Black and Hispanic Adolescents." *Adolescence* 41 (163): 467–484.

Petulla, Sam, Tammy Kupperman, and Jessica Schneider. 2017. "The Number of Hate Crimes Rose in 2016." *CNN*, November 13.

Piquero, Alex R. 2015. "Understanding Race/Ethnicity Differences in Offending across the Life Course: Gaps and Opportunities." *Journal of Developmental and Life Course Criminology* 1 (1): 1–10.

Polleck, Jody, and Tashema Spence-Davis. 2020. "Centering #Blacklivesmatter to Confront Injustice, Inspire Advocacy, and Develop Literacies." *English Journal* 109 (4): 87–94.

Potok, Mark. 2017. "The Year in Hate and Extremism." *Intelligence Report*, February 15.

Priest, Naomi, Ryan Perry, Angeline Ferdinand, Yin Paradies, and Margaret Kelaher. 2014. "Experiences of Racism, Racial/Ethnic Attitudes, Motivated Fairness and Mental Health Outcomes among Primary and Secondary School Students." *Journal of Youth and Adolescence* 43:1672–1687.

Richins, Marsha. 2004. "The Material Values Scale: Measurement Properties and Development of a Short Form." *Journal of Consumer Research* 31:209–219.

Ridge, Tess. 2011. "The Everyday Costs of Poverty in Childhood: A Review of Qualitative Research Exploring the Lives and Experiences of Low-Income Children in the UK." *Children & Society* 25 (1): 73–84.

Rigby, Ken. 2008. *Children and Bullying*. Malden, MA: Blackwell.

Rodriguez-Navarro, Henar, Alfonso García-Monge, and Maria del Carmen Rubio-Campos. 2014. "The Process of Integration of Newcomers at School: Students and Gender Networking during School Recess." *International Journal of Qualitative Studies in Education* 27 (3): 349–363.

Saarento, Silja, Claire F. Garandeau, and Christina Salmivalli. 2015. "Classroom- and School-Level Contributions to Bullying and Victimization: A Review." *Journal of Community & Applied Social Psychology* 25 (3): 204–218.

Schor, Juliet. 2004. *Born to Buy: The Commercialized Child and the New Consumer Culture*. New York: Scribner.

Schumann, Lyndall, Wendy Craig, and Andrei Rosu. 2014. "Power Differentials in Bullying: Individuals in a Community Context." *Journal of Interpersonal Violence* 29 (5): 846–865.

Seaton, Eleanor, Enrique Neblett, Daphne Cole, and Mitchell Prinstein. 2013. "Perceived Discrimination and Peer Victimization among African American and Latino Youth." *Journal of Youth and Adolescence* 42 (3): 342–350.
Shelley, Walter W., Justin T. Pickett, Christina Mancini, Robyn Diehl McDougle, Grant Rissler, and Hayley Cleary. 2021. "Race, Bullying, and Public Perceptions of School and University Safety." *Journal of Interpersonal Violence* 36 (1/2): NP824–NP849.
Sletten, Mira. 2010. "Long-Term Benefits of Social Ties to Peers—Even among Adolescents with 'Risky' Friendships?" *Journal of Youth Studies* 5:561–585.
Southern Poverty Law Center. 2012. "Religious Right Group Attacks 'Mix It Up' Program Intended to Lessen Bullying." *Church & State* 65 (11).
Spriggs, Aubrey, Ronald Iannotti, Tonja Nansel, and Denise Haynie. 2007. "Adolescent Bullying Involvement and Perceived Family, Peer and School Relations: Commonalities and Differences across Race/Ethnicity." *Journal of Adolescent Health* 41:283–293.
Storch, Eric A., Matthew K. Nock, Carrie Masia-Warner, and Mitchell E. Barlas. 2003. "Peer Victimization and Social-Psychological Adjustment in Hispanic and African-American Children." *Journal of Child & Family Studies* 12 (4): 439–452.
Thomas, Rhianna. 2019. "Identifying Your Skin Is Too Dark as a Put-Down: Enacting Whiteness as Hidden Curriculum through a Bullying Prevention Programme." *Curriculum Inquiry* 49 (5): 573–592.
Thornberg, Robert. 2011. "'She's Weird!'—The Social Construction of Bullying in School: A Review of Qualitative Research." *Children & Society* 25 (4): 258–267.
Tippett, Neil N., and Dieter Wolke. 2014. "Socioeconomic Status and Bullying: A Meta-analysis." *American Journal of Public Health* 104 (6): e48–e59.
Turk, Janelle. 2012. "Collaboration, Inclusion and Empowerment: A Life Skills Mural." *Art Education* 65 (6): 50–53.
Xu, Mariah, Natalia Macrynikola, Muhammad Waseem, and Regina Miranda. 2020. "Racial and Ethnic Differences in Bullying: Review and Implications for Intervention." *Aggression & Violent Behavior* 50:101340.
You, Sukkyung, Euikyung Kim, and Mirim Kim. 2014. "An Ecological Approach to Bullying in Korean Adolescents." *Journal of Pacific Rim Psychology* 8 (1): 1–10.
Zhou, Min, and Carl Bankston. 2020. "The Model Minority Stereotype and the National Identity Question: The Challenges Facing Asian Immigrants and Their Children." *Ethnic and Racial Studies* 43 (1): 233–253.

10

Cultures of Peer Harassment or Support in Schools

An Interactionist Account of Student Culture

HANA SHEPHERD

In recent years, school administrators and scholars have paid particular attention to the importance of school cultures in supporting students, promoting academic achievement, and reducing bullying and other forms of peer harassment.[1] This focus assumes that much of what we need to understand about bullying is rooted in social groups and collectives; bullying is not merely about individual bad actors and their victims, but is about what students are allowed to do by adults, and what they might be rewarded or sanctioned for from their peers. Much of this attention has focused on the role of top-down communication about culture from administrators and teachers.[2] Foundational work on bullying by Olweus emphasizes the role of adults in creating a social environment of support and firm, nonpunitive rules regarding treatment of other students.[3]

Another key dimension of school culture, however, is what students themselves produce through interacting with each other. Student-driven cultures can either support or undermine peer harassment in schools, and they may be more influential in shaping students' behaviors than adult-driven culture. Widespread and persistent patterns of peer harassment can emerge in schools, as when students commonly post disparaging comments about their classmates on social media, rally their friends to confront a student who has been spreading rumors, thus escalating the conflict, or pick on students with disabilities or those who identify as LGBTQ+. Students at these schools develop a language around these behaviors, like "starting drama." These behaviors may continue despite school rules and other efforts, both from school staff and from students, to stop them. Meanwhile, in other schools, composed of largely similar types of students and subject to similar types of rules and regulations, students may regularly sanction those who post negative comments on social media or who pick on students with disabilities, developing terms for the perpetrators like "haters" or creating fashion or public messaging in the school to communicate messages supporting students who identify as LGBTQ+.

This chapter examines these student-driven cultures relevant to peer harassment, how these cultures develop, and how they can change. I first review common ways of thinking about and measuring culture in the bullying literature, and articulate an account of group culture grounded in the focus within sociology of culture on shared meaning.[4] I argue for the value of a dynamic, interactionist approach—what I refer to as an interactionist norm account of culture—to understanding student cultures in schools. I use empirical evidence from fifty-six middle schools to illustrate a set of measures of student culture and demonstrate what thinking about these measures together can do to illuminate student culture. Finally, I briefly review recent intervention programs that take this type of view of student culture.

My focus on student-driven cultures is not to undervalue the role of formal school rules and disciplinary systems, or guidance and norms from teachers, administrators, and parents, in shaping student cultures of peer harassment. As other scholars have described, student harassment behaviors occur within an ecology: the context of the school, the community, and broader systems of meaning of what are acceptable behaviors.[5] This account of student-driven culture does not explicitly theorize how student dynamics interact with these other factors, nor does it preclude a role of these other factors in shaping overall patterns of behavior and meanings about behaviors. I focus on theorizing student-driven culture in large part because of the lack of focus on this aspect of the ecological system of peer harassment.

Throughout the chapter, I use the term "peer harassment" instead of "bullying" because peer harassment is a broader concept that captures a range of negative peer-directed behaviors, while the concept of bullying has legal and lay connotations that are narrow.[6] Most importantly, these connotations do not correspond to how students themselves think about negative peer-directed behaviors.

What We Mean When We Talk about Culture

Two paradigms dominate existing work linking culture to bullying: a focus on a broad conception of school climate, including the beliefs of different types of actors, school rules and organizational practices around education and safety, interpersonal relationships, and other features of schools, and a largely undertheorized conception of student culture of bullying.[7] Work on the latter cultural approach to bullying and peer harassment among students conceives of culture mainly in terms of a set of siloed concepts: student beliefs about peer harassment behaviors, student behaviors that stem from those beliefs that support or perpetuate peer harassment, values, and social norms.[8]

For example, Unnever and Cornell argue for understanding school climates conductive to bullying as characterized by a "normative set of shared beliefs that support or encourage bullying behavior."[9] They assess culture among about 2,400 students in six middle schools in Virginia using questions about how often students see others (students and adults) trying to intervene in cases of bullying; students' own feelings when they see others being bullied; and students' own behavioral intentions regarding bullying other students. Unnever and Cornell did not take variation across schools as an object of inquiry itself (indeed, they found little variation across these six schools).[10] Other researchers address students' beliefs as part of the larger context of the school climate that includes the beliefs of teachers, school officials, and parents.[11]

Normative beliefs are clearly an important aspect of peer culture, but there remains a lack of consensus regarding what constitutes normative beliefs and how they should be measured. Additionally, little work attempts to directly measure the extent to which students in a school share those beliefs beyond examining mean values of students' attitudes about bullying.

Another important line of work examines the role of peer influence and social norms in shaping bullying and peer harassment.[12] This work focuses in particular on the social feedback, often neutral or positive, that young people receive for bullying behaviors. Though few explicitly endorse peer harassment, students' public behavior often suggests active or passive support for harassment. For example, observers might smile or laugh in response to bullying incidents or publicly side with an aggressor "in part to protect their social status, reputation, and physical safety."[13] This can create perceptions of norms in groups that support and reinforce peer harassment.

The majority of existing work on school culture has been limited empirically by a lack of focus on school variation in favor of examining individual beliefs without a comprehensive assessment of the social context of students in a school, and theoretically limited by an underdeveloped conception of culture. Amid an abundance of both theoretical and empirical work on what constitutes culture, how it is transmitted, and how it shapes action in the world, I focus here on group culture— the particular behaviors, beliefs, systems of meaning, and ways of interacting—that develops within social groups.[14] This is akin to Fine's concept of an idioculture, or "a system of knowledge, beliefs, behaviors, and customs shared by members of an interacting group to which members can refer and employ as the basis of further interaction."[15] By focusing on student-driven culture, I emphasize in particular the development and sharing of meanings about peer-harassment-related behaviors among students. As I elaborate below, an interactionist norm account emphasizes the way that groups of people who regularly interact with each other establish meanings for particular behaviors within the group, and how those meanings persist or change over time.

An Interactionist Account of Cultures of Peer Harassment or Support

As Fine and Tavory articulate, interactionism assumes that (1) people act on meanings in communities that themselves depend on shared meanings, and (2) meanings depend on continuing, ongoing interactions between individuals.[16] Here, I bring together interactionism and work on social norms in groups: I argue for the value of thinking about the development and change in shared meanings *about* common and acceptable behaviors in a group—commonly referred to as social norms. Social norms are analytically important for understanding group cultures because they influence behavior.[17] Instead of accounting for the culture of a school as a byproduct of neighborhood context or as an overarching, undifferentiated macro variable,[18] this approach (which aligns with Migliaccio's account of social ecology in chapter 9) focuses on how culture is driven by patterns of interaction among group members (in this case, students) and social inferences about what is widely accepted as appropriate behavior within the group.

As shown in Figure 10.1, the interactionist norm account of culture acknowledges that the organizational rules and broader context influence how school-level patterns of behavior emerge. But the focus in this theory is on how individual-level interactions between students create schoolwide patterns of behavior, as students develop perceptions of what is widespread and desirable behavior among other students within their school—perceived norms—using information from the behavior and language of other students. These perceptions of social norms are produced through interactions and patterns of interaction that are consistent and repeated between group members (C and C_1 in the figure). One way to represent these patterns of interaction between group members is using social network measures. When these perceptions become shared among students, a process that can be facilitated or impeded by the structure of patterned interactions (the social network) (B in the figure), then behaviors consistent with those perceptions become widely practiced within the school (C in the figure). A student who perceives a behavior to be widespread and desirable will be more likely to engage or reward others for engaging in this behavior and less likely to punish others engaging in it. When perceptions of behavior are widely shared, behaviors may become entrenched such that they last over time and new students learn to engage in them. The interactionist norm account of culture is necessarily dynamic: as patterns of interaction change, so too does exposure to behaviors and information, which can change both the perception of social norms (C) and the extent to which those perceptions are shared within the group (B).

In an interactionist norm account of culture, school-level behavioral patterns can emerge or change when students perceive that other students behave in similar ways. If a student or a small number of students perceive the norm of the school to be a particular way, for example, that it is unacceptable to call students "gay" in a derogatory way, they will act accordingly. However, if their perception is a minority one, they will come across disconfirming information: other students behaving in ways that violate their perception of the norm by using the term "gay"

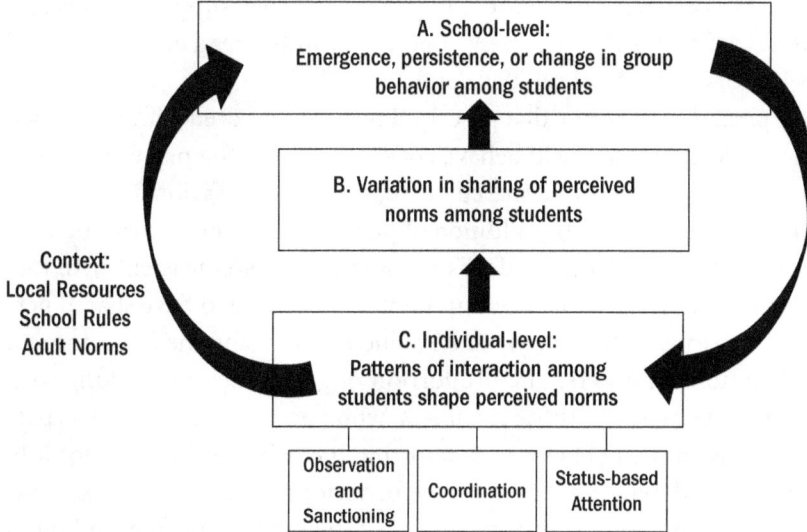

Figure 10.1. Illustration of Proposed Interactionist Norm Account

as an insult, or other students responding negatively to them if they do not condone or participate in calling others "gay" in a derogatory way. The lack of coordination or sharing of perceived norms may manifest in subtle or overt ways when students with different perceptions interact, and these interactions will provide information regarding what is practiced and accepted within the school, leading to updating of those perceptions. Depending on who holds what perceptions, that updating may or may not be mutual: both sides may adjust their perceptions, or one side might adjust their perceptions while the other side fails to do so. High-status students may be less likely to adjust their perceptions when interacting with a lower-status student, whereas lower-status students may be particularly likely to adjust their perceptions when interacting with a high-status student. If, however, two individuals or two groups of students share a perception of the norm, that, for example, it is unacceptable to call other students "gay" in a derogatory way, then when they interact, their behaviors should reaffirm their shared perception of the group norm. In turn, they will continue to behave in ways consistent with that perception, or at least fail to regulate or challenge consistent behavior. Their behavior will signal to others in the school what is acceptable behavior, and provide further support for certain perceived norms. Under these conditions, widespread and entrenched behaviors in a school can develop.

I posit that the more that perceived norms are shared within a school, the more individuals will behave consistently with the perceived norm, further generating more shared perceptions and behavior. This process may be linear, where the addition of people who come to share perceptions of a particular norm leads to more behavior consistent with that norm, or it may require a certain number of people to have shared perceived norms (a threshold) to be sufficient to shape the behavior and perceptions of others. The proportion of group members, along with the relative status of those members, who need to be perceived as participating in the behavior or supporting the behavior in order for it to be sustained may vary based on the behavior in question. For example, in scholarship on the historical case of the practice of footbinding in China, a behavior that required coordination between group members (i.e., it required parents of girls to perform the footbinding and the parents of boys to want to have their sons marry girls with bound feet in order to *stop* the cycle of footbinding), the parents of girls needed only to perceive a relatively small subset of the group to be willing to marry their sons to girls *without* bound feet, in order for them to consider the possibility of not binding their daughters' feet.[19] Perceiving a norm among a relatively small percentage of the group may be enough, then, to change a behavior that requires coordination among those group members. Perceived norms about some behaviors need not be perfectly shared to create persistent patterns of behavior, while others may require more widespread sharedness.

How Repeated Interactions Shape Perceived Norms

Patterns of interaction, the local network of relationships between students, can drive the formation of perceived norms. Behaviors may be unevenly distributed in a group; some individuals may participate in a behavior much more than others. Because of the uneven distribution of behaviors, some group members may perceive behaviors to occur with more frequency than others based on what and whom they are exposed to in the group. At the individual level, patterns of interactions between group members shape what and whom group members are exposed to and thus what perceptions they form.[20] Because of similarities and differences in these patterns of interactions, group members may develop perceived norms that are similar to or distinct from others in the group.

Given that different group members may fail to share similar perceptions of the norms of the group, what leads some group members to perceive a norm when others do not? Group members may have differential levels of access and exposure to the behaviors and reactions of others, and this access and exposure is structured by patterned interactions. We gain information about the behaviors of others in our group, and group members' reactions to those behaviors through interaction, though we may have differential levels of access and exposure to the behaviors and reactions of others. For example, in a school, students who have few friendships, and mainly have friendships with other students who also have few friends, are less likely to hear about many of the conflicts between other students. Thus, a crucial element in norm perception is an individual's chronic interactions with other group members (their social network ties), which both reflect past patterns of interactions and channel future interactions. These chronic interactions influence an individual's perception of how widespread and how widely endorsed a behavior is by shaping to whom an individual is exposed, the type of exposure, and the amount of exposure.[21] Thus, individuals' social network ties, both how many they have and to whom, provide them with a set of social cues that shape their perceptions of norms.

Patterns of interaction among group members across time drive the process of normative perception; we gain information about the behaviors of others in our group and group members' reactions to those behaviors through interaction. Interaction with others provides individuals with three types of cues about behavior relevant to norm inference, and these cues will differ based on individuals' particular pattern of interactions: (1) *How frequent is the behavior?* How many people engage in this behavior? (2) *Which group members participate in the behavior?* Do very public, socially salient individuals do the behavior more than others? Do high- or low-status individuals participate in the behavior more frequently? Do individuals who occupy particular roles in the group behave in certain ways? Do individuals who are socially closer to the perceiver perform the behavior more than do individuals who are socially more distant from the perceiver? (3) *How do other group members receive the behavior?* Is the behavior rewarded, sanctioned, or treated neutrally? How does this reception vary among group members?

An interactionist norm account of peer culture leads us to measure and assess culture in ways quite distinct from the types of measures and approaches in the current literature about cultures or climates of peer harassment. I now turn to an illustration of the type of empirical evidence that can help researchers and practitioners better assess cultures of peer harassment.

Empirical Variation in Cultures of Peer Harassment or Support

I use a unique dataset collected as part of an intervention program in fifty-six middle schools in New Jersey to describe empirical variation in student cultures of harassment and to illustrate how researchers might draw on an interactionist norm account of culture. I propose a broader set of quantitative measures of peer harassment culture, argue for the value of considering the relationships between them, and illustrate how a focus on school-level comparisons can help describe student-driven culture. These data are unique in a number of ways and allow me to develop metrics of student-driven culture that have not been taken into account in previous studies.

Data for this analysis come from a yearlong, randomized field experiment conducted over the 2012–2013 school year.[22] As I detail below, half of the schools were randomly assigned to receive our intervention program. Here, when examining change over the course of the school year, I note which schools were in the treatment condition and which were in the control condition because the sources of cultural change between those two types of schools were different due to the intervention. As part of the design and evaluation of the intervention, students in the fifty-six public middle schools completed a survey at the beginning of the school year, in the fall of 2012, and at the end of the school year, in the late spring of 2013 (N = 21,110 observed in both waves of the survey; 24,191 observed in at least one wave). Having information over the course of the school year allows me to illustrate features of change that correspond to a dynamic account of group culture. The extent of variation in the data is valuable for illustrating a range in how schools might be arrayed along various measures of peer harassment culture.

I identify the schools only according to numbers from 1 to 60 that we used during the course of the study in order to protect the anonymity of the schools. The numbers do not correspond to any traits of the schools. The schools represented in this dataset are similar but not identical to the population of public middle schools in New Jersey overall.

The characteristics of the schools vary greatly from one another: they range in size from 113 to 885 students; from 2 to 94 percent white students; from 46 to 57 percent female; from 0.1 to 85 percent of students receiving free or reduced-price lunch; from 7 to 88 percent of students who speak a language other than English at home; from 3 to 32 percent of students who live with only with their mother; from 17 to 68 percent of students who play sports at school; from 24 to 64 percent of students who report using the social media platform Instagram. Below, I describe the relationship between types of student culture and two school characteristics—size and socioeconomic status (SES)—but I cannot make claims about the role of the latter in shaping the former.

Measures

I use data on students' perceptions of the *descriptive norms* around peer harassment or support at their school (what they report seeing others do), *prescriptive norms* (how widespread they report beliefs about what is acceptable or desirable behavior to be among other students), their *personal experiences* of peer harassment and support, and their self-reported involvement in *conflict with peers*.

NORMS. To assess students' perceptions of peer harassment-related norms, students were asked, "How many students at this school think . . ." followed by one of ten phrases: "it's good to stay out of conflict with other students"; "it's funny, it is not a big deal, when people mess with, trash talk, or pick on other people at this school"; "it's okay to speak up for a student when other people are being mean to them"; "it's not funny, it is a big deal, to call someone gay"; "it's good to be friendly and nice with all students at this school, no matter who"; "it's funny, it is not a big deal, to post something mean about someone online"; "it's okay to use jokes to insult someone else's race or ethnicity"; "it's not good to threaten, hit, or push someone as a joke or for real"; "it's not okay when people gossip and start rumors about others at this school"; "it's not okay to tell an adult at school about student conflicts." Students reported answers on a 6-point scale (almost nobody, a few people, about 25 percent, about 50 percent, about 75 percent, almost everybody). The scale was accompanied by a visual depiction of a group of figures with the approximate number of the group shaded in for each response category.[23]

DESCRIPTIVE NORMS. Students answered questions regarding how frequently they saw other students do each of the ten behaviors assessed in the perceived norms measures. For example, students responded to these prompts: "At my school, I see other students ... staying out of conflict"; "messing with, trash talking or picking on someone"; "speaking up for a student when other people are being mean to them"; and "calling others gay." Students reported answers on a 5-point scale (never, 1–2 times/month, about 1 time/week, 2–3 times/week, and every day). These were also combined (with the positive items reverse coded) and divided by 10 to create an average measure (from 0 to 4) for descriptive norms for each individual at each of the two waves.

NEGATIVE PEER EXPERIENCES. At both survey waves, students reported on their specific experiences with peers at the school. Students reported their own negative experiences by indicating whether students at the school had done any of the following: "excluded me"; "messed with or picked on me"; "started rumors or gossiped about me"; "made fun of how I look"; "threatened, hit, or pushed me, as a joke or for real"; "insulted my race or ethnicity, not as a joke"; "said I am gay"; "posted online or texted something mean about me." These eight negative events were summed to create an index of negative experiences.[24]

OWN BEHAVIOR AND ATTITUDES. To gauge students' evaluations of their own participation in conflict at their school, at both waves of the survey, students were asked a binary question about whether they agreed with the statement, "I have a lot of conflict with other students at this school." This measure was related to the number of conflict nominations a student reported or received from other students; students who reported having a lot of conflict with others at wave 1 had significantly more overall conflict nominations than those who did not (4.82 vs. 2.43).

We also asked students to assess whether they agreed with the statement "Sometimes you have to be mean to others as a way to survive at this school" (a binary measure). This served as an individual attitude item about peer harassment.

NETWORK NOMINATIONS. Using a roster design, at both waves of the survey, students reported whom they had "decided to spend time with (in school, out of school, or online)" from their school in the past few weeks. Nominations were capped at ten. The phrasing was designed to elicit a behavioral measure of social connections.

Empirical Approach

I use the rich data and substantial variation between schools to provide descriptions of different cultures of peer harassment or support among the schools in this dataset. Drawing on the theoretical approach to group culture that I outline above, I assess culture along five dimensions: perceived peer harassment norms, student experiences of peer harassment, the relationship between norms and experiences, the behavior of high-status students, and change over time between types of students. These dimensions correspond to five sets of measures of school culture: (1) the mean values, extent of sharing (variance), and change over time in descriptive and prescriptive norms related to peer conduct; (2) the mean values, extent of sharing (variance), and change over time of students' own experiences of peer harassment or support; (3) the alignment (correlations) between norm perceptions and student experiences; (4) the self-reported conflict and harassment attitudes among high-status students; and (5) the difference in and change between norm perceptions among new students and older students. For each measure, I describe the relationship between it and an interactionist norm approach to peer harassment culture.

I use these data in a descriptive way and present only the correlations between measures. Observational correlations are necessarily limited in their analytical value, but I am more interested in their descriptive value here. I contend that examining these measures and the way schools vary across these measures can help us generate theory about student culture and provide the basis for future empirical work. I use a comparison between two ostensibly similar schools to make this point.

Measures of School Cultures

Descriptive and Prescriptive Social Norms

Students' perceptions of the frequency (descriptive) and acceptability (prescriptive) of social norms are the basis of *meanings* about behavior in the group. We can ask about the nature and extent of student norm perceptions within a school (mean values) and about the degree to which these perceptions are shared among students (variation).

I begin with an examination of the mean values in the indices for prescriptive and descriptive norms of peer harassment at the first wave of the survey, as represented in Figure 10.2. In this figure, the average of students' descriptive norms index values (how frequently students report seeing certain behaviors) for a school appear on the x-axis and the average of students' prescriptive norms index values (perceptions of what percentage of students believe a behavior to be acceptable) for a school appear on the y-axis. Higher values for both indices indicate perceptions of more frequent peer harassment behaviors among students and support for those behaviors among students. Across these schools, there is a close relationship between perceptions of the frequency of peer harassment and support for peer harassment ($r = .87$). This plot shows substantial distribution of schools across the range of values of the norms indices; school 55 represents the lowest norms about peer harassment among students, and school 45 represents the highest norms about peer harassment.

Mean values do not tell us how distributed these beliefs are among students in a school; Figure 10.3 provides this information using the standard deviation of norm perceptions among students in each school.

From this plot, we can see that a school may have relatively high agreement about such norm perceptions (for example, school 37), or relatively low agreement, where students' perceptions vary more (for example, school 38 or school 27). For each of these three schools, the

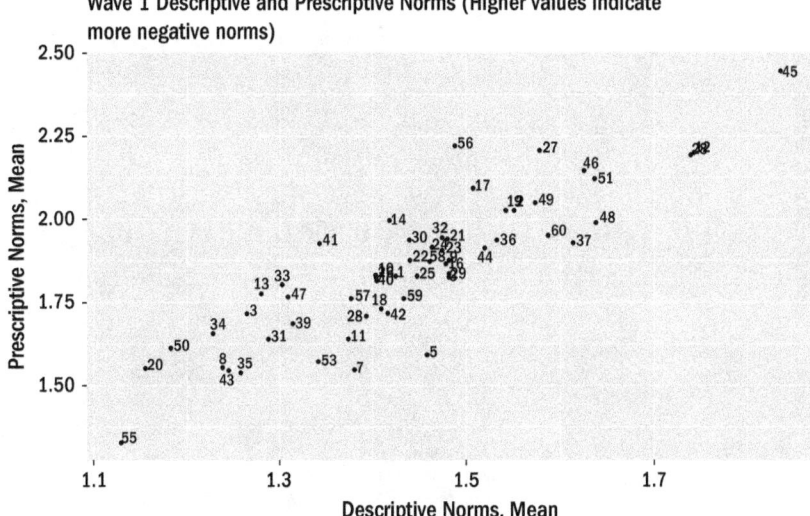

Figure 10.2. Mean Values of Norm Perceptions by School

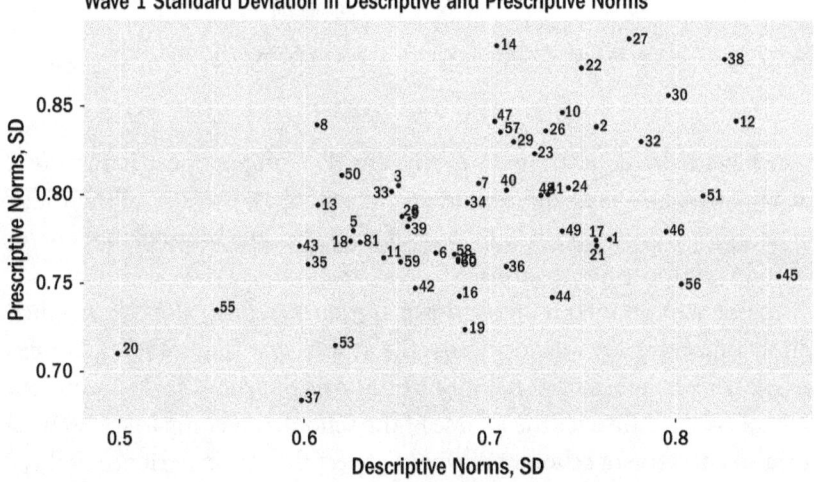

Figure 10.3. Variation in Norm Perceptions among Students in Schools

mean values of norm perceptions are high, indicating perceptions of peer harassment norms (see Figure 10.2), but we would expect the lived experience of these school cultures to differ since there is relative agreement among students in school 37 about the norms and relatively lack of agreement among students in school 27 or 38. Students in school 37

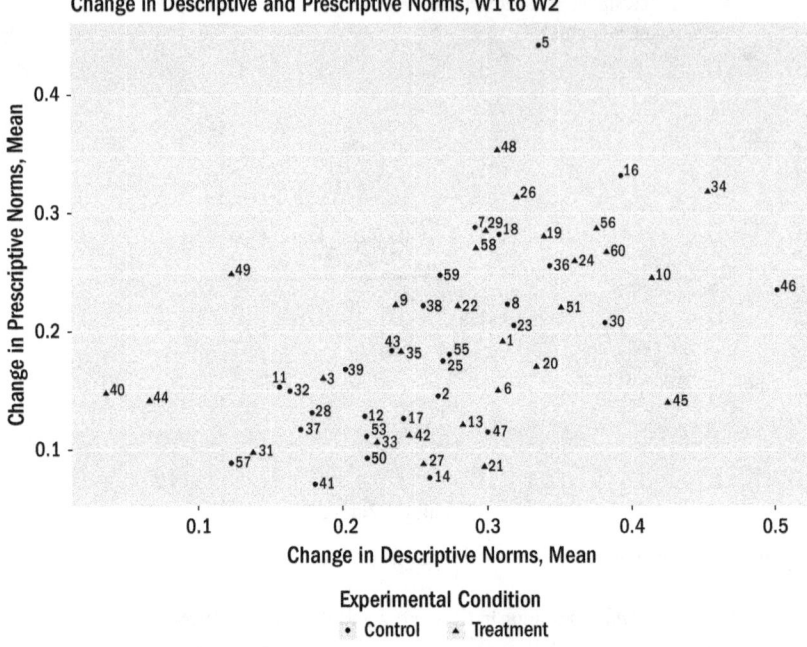

Figure 10.4. Change in Social Norms over the School Year by School

may have more coordinated perceptions that support peer harassment behaviors, while as a whole, students in school 27, because of their lack of shared perceptions, may be less likely to behave in ways that correspond with those perceptions.

In line with an interactionist norm approach, we can also ask in which direction norms are moving across the school year (Figure 10.4). For example, mean values of perceptions of norms in school 31—a treatment school—vary little over the course of the school year compared to school 34, also a treatment school. We would expect that the experience of these two school cultures for students to vary importantly. Researchers might pursue what interactional processes lead to change or a lack of change.

Personal Experiences of Peer Harassment

In addition to perceptions of peer harassment norms within a school, we can also examine patterns of peer harassment behavior, assessed through students' reports of their own experiences during the school year. We cannot tell, of course, whether these reports indicate greater amounts of peer harassment in these schools or a heightened perception among students that other students are harassing them. Both are informative about student culture.

Figure 10.5 provides the mean values and standard deviations of students' reports of the number of their negative peer experiences in the fall of the school year. Higher mean values indicate that students report more negative peer experiences; high standard deviations indicate that there is more variation around this mean value, with some students experiencing many negative peer events and other students experiencing few. There is a strong positive relationship between mean values and standard deviation for the number of negative experiences ($r = .92$), indicating that in schools where students report more negative peer experiences on average, those experiences are more unevenly distributed among students than in schools where students report fewer negative peer experiences. This seems to be a general feature of cultures of peer harassment; the negative social environment affects some students more than others.

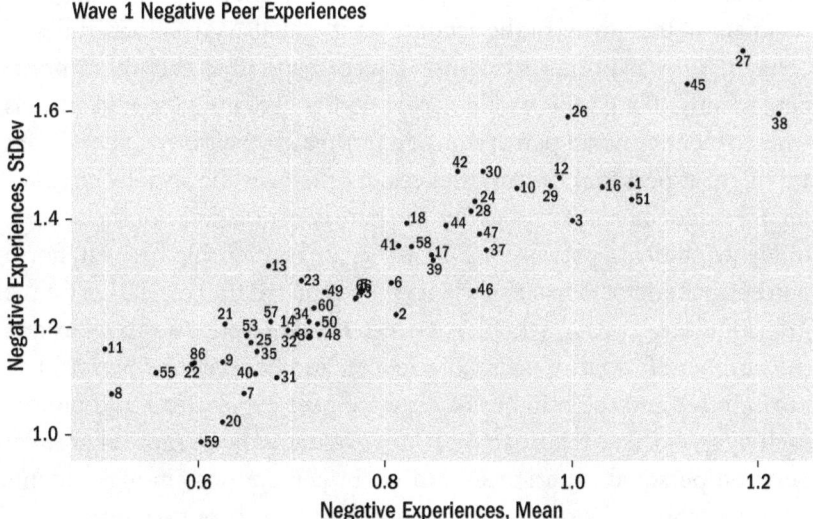

Figure 10.5. Negative Peer Experiences by School, Means and Standard Deviations

At schools 8, 11, and 55, students report a low number of negative peer experiences, and there is little variation between students in these low mean values. There is little evidence of experiences (and, presumably, behavior from other students) that support a culture of harassment at these schools. In contrast, at schools 45, 27, and 38, students report a very high number of negative peer experiences, and there is a great amount of variation among students in their experiences. At these schools, there is evidence of experiences that support a culture of harassment, though these experiences affect some students much more than others.

Alignment between Norms and Experiences

Once we examine the mean values of and extent of variation in norm perceptions and personal experiences within a school, we can furthermore ask whether students' experiences align with their perceptions of norms. According to an interactionist norm account, perceptions and behaviors are interrelated: when they are aligned, norm perceptions can increase behavior as behavior can strengthen norm perceptions; when they are not aligned, perceptions may change in the face of disconfirming behavior or behavior may change in response to norm perceptions.

In schools where students' norm perceptions match their own experiences, students may draw on firsthand experience as part of their assessment of the norms of the school. We might also guess that students' behaviors toward other students may correspond to their own norm perceptions, though this would merit additional examination. In schools where students' norm perceptions do not match their own experiences, we might expect that the experiences of others, or the socially circulating messages or narratives about the harassment culture of the school, influence students' perceptions. To assess the relationship between norm perceptions and personal experiences, I calculated the correlation (at the individual level, within schools) between the descriptive norm index and the number of negative peer experiences, and between the prescriptive norm index and the number of negative peer experiences and plotted each by school (see Figure 10.6). Higher values indicate more alignment between personal experiences and norm perceptions among students within a school (the overall correlation between these two measures of alignment among the schools is $r = .57$).

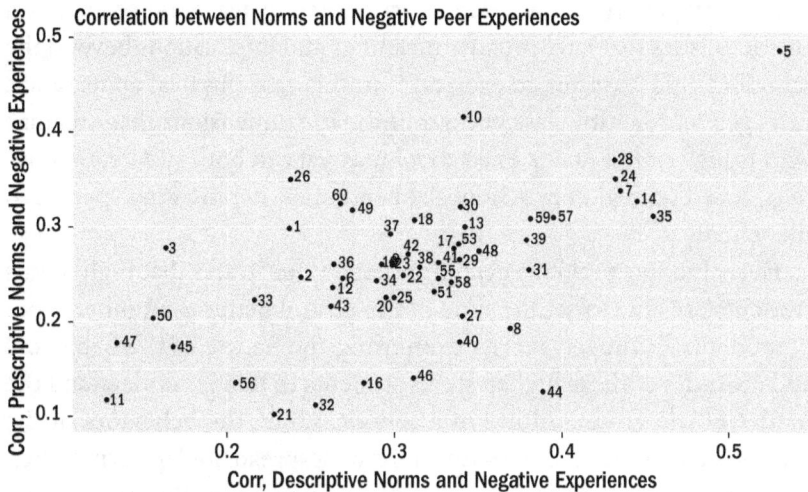

Figure 10.6. Relationship between Norm Perceptions and Negative Peer Experiences by School

We see variation between schools in the extent of alignment between personal experiences and norm perceptions; some schools are closely aligned (such as school 5), while others are largely unaligned (schools 11, 47, and 45). Researchers might examine what accounts for alignment or lack of alignment. We might expect greater change in norm perceptions or behavior among schools with less alignment between behavior and norm perceptions over time.

Behavior of High-Status Students

An interactionist norm approach to group cultures considers how behavior may not be evenly distributed throughout a group, producing different exposure to behavior and information about behavior based on patterns of interaction. Additionally, the behavior of some group members might exert a disproportionate effect on the norm perceptions and subsequent behaviors of others. Consequently, I examine the self-reported behavior and attitudes of high-status students in the group in order to better characterize the nature of group culture. Students may be high status in a particular school for a variety of reasons either specific to the school (e.g., participating in certain after-school activities, specific interaction patterns, how students are treated by teachers) or based on characteristics that have broader meanings and implications beyond the school (Tilly's "exterior categories,"[25] in this case physical appearance, race, gender identity, class background). The dimensions that organize who is high or low status in a school may vary in both systematic ways (e.g., based on region or school size) and idiosyncratic ways specific to the school.

Here, I follow previous evidence that demonstrates that high-status students are able to set the tone of the school better than other types of students.[26] Thus, it merits examining the nature of the behaviors and attitudes of these higher-status students to further understand the nature of the group culture of a school. When the behaviors of the high-status students align with more widespread social norms, then we would expect norm perceptions to be more easily transmitted, more widely shared, and less susceptible to change. When the behaviors of high-status students are not aligned with perceived norms, then we might expect cultural change. Following our previous work, here I consider high-status students to be those in the top 10 percent of their school in terms of the number of nominations they receive from other students as someone others chose to spend time with over the past two weeks.[27] Figure 10.7 plots the mean values among influential students in a school in terms of their self-reports of having conflict with other students (x-axis) and in terms of their attitudes about conflict at the school ("You have to be mean to survive at this school"; y-axis). Higher values indicate more negative behaviors and attitudes among these influential students (the relationship between these two measures is high, $r = .57$).

At schools 3 and 45, influential students say that they both are involved in conflict and endorse negative beliefs. This is not the case for the influential students in schools 16, 31, 43, 50, or 59, who report low values of both conflict and negative attitudes. Influential students in schools 1 and 44 report relatively little personal involvement in conflict but endorse the statement that you need to be mean to survive at the school. The behaviors and attitudes of these influential students may be an indicator of the beliefs and behaviors of other students, or they may indicate that it is more respected or acceptable to engage in such behaviors and attitudes.

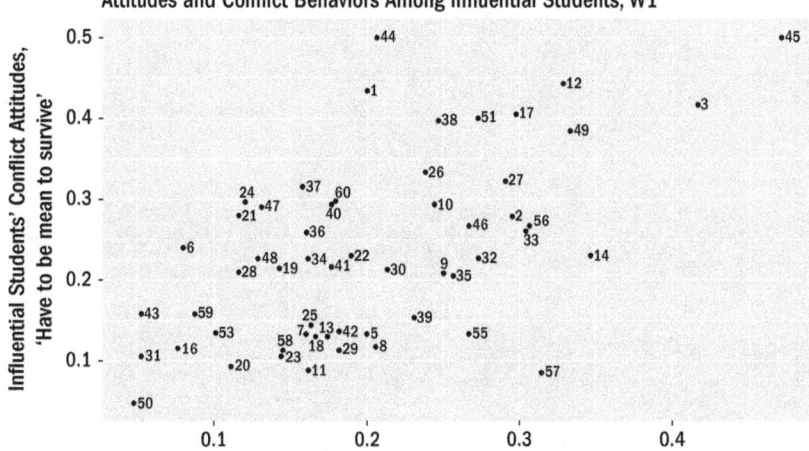

Figure 10.7. Attitudes and Behaviors of Influential Students by School

Transmission of Culture

A final dimension of culture that I consider here is the extent to which it becomes transmitted to new members as they join the group and how quickly. We can examine how different the perceptions of the culture are between new group members compared to group members who have been a part of the group for longer. In schools where there is a larger gap in perceptions between new members and existing members, we expect that acquiring the group culture takes more assimilation into the group in the sense that students cannot simply interpret their own immediate social experiences as a source of understanding the culture of the school, but need to understand other social cues. It may be that a smaller gap in perceptions between new members and existing group members indicates a faster transmission process, or a stronger set of signals about group culture. Another dimension of interest is whether new group members move toward the perceptions of existing members or not. When new group members move toward the perceptions of existing group members (or both groups move more toward each other), it may give us information about interactions within the group, or about the nature of the group culture itself. In most schools, presumably the composition of new members is roughly similar to the composition of

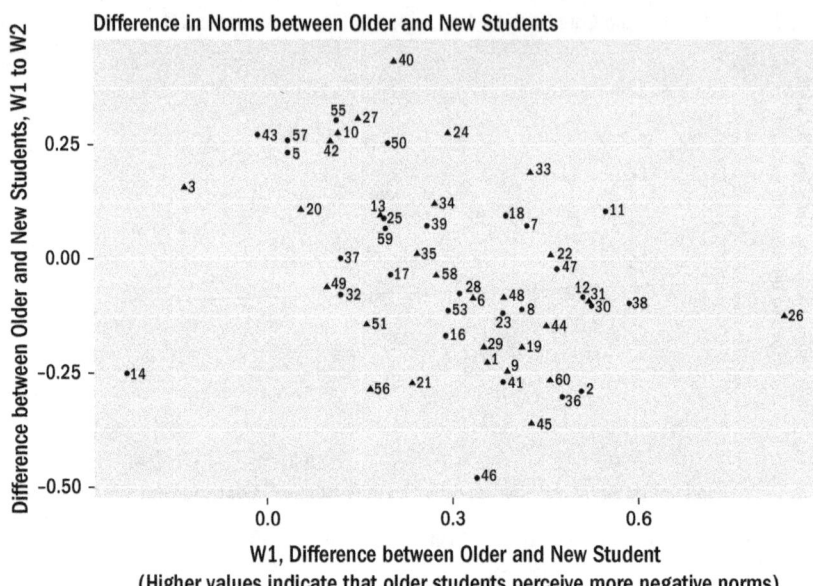

Figure 10.8. Differences in Norm Perceptions among New and Older Students by School

existing members, but in other groups or organizations, new members may be treated systematically differently, altering the process of the transmission of culture.

Figure 10.8 plots the distance in the fall (wave 1) between prescriptive norm perceptions among students new to the school and students in higher grades who are presumably returning to the school (x-axis), compared to the change in this difference between new students and other students between wave 1 and wave 2 (the y-axis).[28] Higher numbers along the x-axis indicate a greater difference in norm perceptions between new students and older students such that older students have more negative perceptions of the norms of the school. Numbers above zero along the y-axis indicate an increase in the distance between new students and older students such that their perceptions become more distinct over time; numbers below zero indicate a decrease in the distance between perceptions of norms between new students and older students, indicating that they become more similar over time.

At most schools, older students perceive more negative norms of peer harassment than do new students (schools 3, 14, and 43 are exceptions to this pattern). However, for about half of the schools, the magnitude of distance between these groups of students decreases over the course of the school year (those schools below the zero line along the y-axis), while for the other half the magnitude of the distance increases (above the zero line along the y-axis). For example, in school 11, which started with a relatively large gap between the norm perceptions of new students and older students, the size of that gap grew over the school year, while in school 38, also a control school and thus a school where norm perceptions were not being influenced by the intervention program, the relatively large gap between the norm perceptions of new students and those of older students got smaller. This graph does not tell us about the direction of the changes in perceptions,[29] but it indicates the nature of change between these two distinct groups of students in terms of their perceptions of norms at the schools. We might use this type of information to examine the processes by which new group members come to share perceptions with existing group members.

Differentiating School Cultures: School 14 and School 21

As a preliminary illustration of the value of considering these additional dimensions of school culture, compare school 14, where about 90 percent of the two hundred students are Latinx in a low-SES district, and school 21, a school where about 80 percent of the four hundred students are Latinx, also in a low-SES district. If we consider only the mean values for peer harassment norm perceptions (Figure 10.2) and negative experiences (Figure 10.5), these schools look very similar to one another; they are low to moderate in terms of their peer harassment culture. However, in school 14, the amount of variation in students' perceptions of prescriptive norms is high, indicating less agreement among students about the perceived norms, compared to low variation among students at school 21. There is also a high correlation between students' own experiences and their norm perceptions in school 14, while this correlation is low in school 21 (Figure 10.6). In school 14, the conflict behaviors and attitudes of the high-status students at the beginning of the school year are far more negative than are the conflict behaviors and attitudes of the high-status students in school 21 (Figure 10.7). Finally, there is little difference in the norm perceptions of new and older students in school 14 (and new students initially have more negative perceptions than do older students, which is unique in these data, and their perceptions get more negative while older students' perceptions stay the same), while in school 21 the perceptions of older students start more negative than those of the new students, and new students' perceptions become more negative to more closely match those of the older students (Figure 10.8).

These empirical differences suggest a number of open questions for researchers and practitioners. First, we might ask what the difference in the lived experience of being at these schools is for students and how these nuances in school culture relate to student achievement and well-being. Second, we might use existing patterns of relationships among students (local and school-level network structure) at each school to analyze the sources of these descriptive differences in student culture and to theorize about how student culture might develop over time. Finally, we might expect that different types of anti-harassment programs or interventions will be received differently and produce different results in these two schools because of the nuances in these student cultures. For example, programs that utilize the influence of high-status students as I describe below might be received very differently at the two schools, given the differences in the initial levels of conflict among high-status students at the two schools.

Student Culture and Community and School Characteristics

A persistent question in the study of group cultures is the extent to which culture is related to characteristics of the composition of the group and the environment in which the group operates. The legacy of the "culture of poverty" debate is that explanations for group cultures or the variation between group cultures are often reduced to the demographic characteristics of the individuals who make up the group, or assumptions about their immediate environment. An interactionist norm account of culture provides a different account, where community and group characteristics may create the context for patterns of interaction and action,

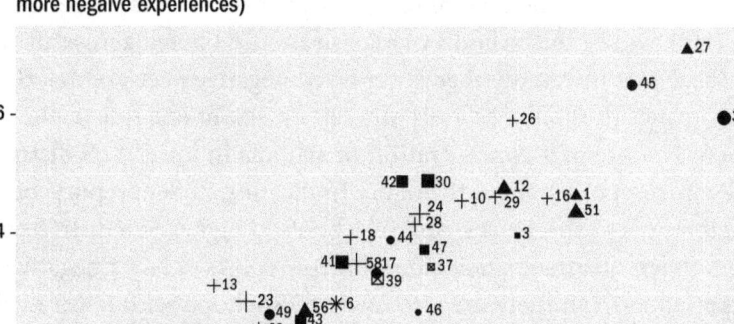

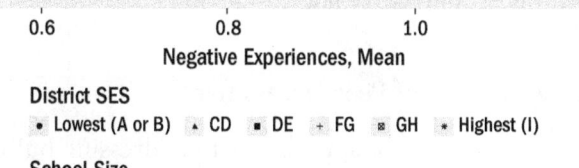

Figure 10.9. Negative Experiences and School Characteristics

but they are not sufficient to understand the type of change in group culture. But the type of explanation I provide here is not incompatible with approaches that account for the material and existing shared beliefs and behaviors of the larger physical, economic, political, and demographic contexts within which schools are embedded. One way in which material resources might interface with the account I provide here is through shaping the frequency and type of interactions between students. For example, underresourced schools are often physically crowded, which changes the conditions of interaction among students.[30]

I provide a description of the relationship between school size (the number of students), the SES of the community, and one dimension of peer harassment cultures, students' self-reported negative peer experiences, in Figure 10.9. Note that this is the same as Figure 10.5, with the points scaled by school size and shaped according to the New Jersey

Department of Education's assessment of community SES, the District Factor Grouping. The beginning of the alphabet indicates poorer districts.

Here, we see that schools of all size are distributed across all values of the x-axis (mean number of reported negative peer events); there is not a concentration of schools of a certain size at one side or the other. There is more of a concentration of schools in lower SES districts at the top-right quadrant of the figure (indicating student reports of more negative peer experiences) and of schools in higher SES districts at the bottom left quadrant (indicating student reports of fewer negative peer experiences), but there are also lower SES schools with fewer negative peer experiences (e.g., schools 21, 40, 14, 32) and higher SES schools with more negative peer experiences (e.g., schools 16, 26, 29).

I turn now to thinking about how student-driven culture based on interaction might be leveraged to change peer harassment in schools and how this fits into current anti-bullying efforts.

Changing Cultures of Peer Harassment

There are a multitude of approaches to addressing bullying and peer harassment in schools, many of which have been evaluated with neutral or modestly positive effects.[31] The majority of these approaches, however, do not privilege the role of students in driving peer harassment cultures of schools and focus on the role that adults play in setting expectations for behaviors. Using the example of two school-based field experiments that draw on the principles of the interactionist norm account of student culture described above, I illustrate how taking this type of approach might inform intervention efforts. Both interventions focused on making the prosocial behaviors of influential students—students who are particularly salient to other students in the school—visible to other students in order to change peer harassment behaviors. In our first intervention program, we examined change within one small high school; in our second program, we examined change within fifty-six New Jersey middle schools. Both of these intervention programs assumed, in contrast to many other anti-bullying efforts that rely on adults to shape messages about how to treat other students, that messaging about peer harassment is most effective when coming from students, in line with a conception of student-driven culture.

In the first program in the small high school, following a schoolwide network survey of students to assess the extent and type of relationships between students, a randomly selected group of influential students (those nominated most frequently by other students, which we referred to as *social referent* students) were asked to participate in and lead an assembly-based Anti-Defamation League program, "Names Can Really Hurt Us." The intervention students first participated in two training sessions to prepare for a schoolwide assembly. During that assembly, the intervention students described their own harassment experiences and invited other students to do the same. During the rest of the school year, the intervention students participated in a number of follow-up events (e.g., morning announcements, posters around the school, and wristbands) to reinforce the association between the intervention students and anti-harassment messages. We then assessed the effect of being connected to these intervention students on norm perceptions and harassment behaviors through the school year. We found that students with more social connections to intervention students had more positive prescriptive norm perceptions (beliefs about what other students considered acceptable or unacceptable behavior) over the school year, but having social connections to intervention students did not change personal beliefs about peer harassment. Importantly, peer-harassment-related behaviors (assessed through disciplinary records, teacher evaluations, and an intervention-generated behavior) decreased among students with more social connections to intervention students.[32] Additionally, students with social connections to especially well-respected intervention students (who were disproportionately male) had more positive perceived norms and fewer peer harassment behaviors.[33] These findings support the idea that students' norm perceptions and behaviors are influenced in particular by highly visible (social referent) group members and dependent on patterns of interaction in the school. Changes in the behaviors of high-profile group members can influence the nature of student culture.

In the second intervention program, we worked with fifty-six public middle schools in New Jersey. Half of the schools were randomly assigned to receive the intervention, and in each of these schools, we selected a group of students representing 15 percent of the school population to participate in the intervention program. We randomly assigned

50 percent of that group to be invited to participate in the anti-conflict program as intervention students. Within each treatment group at each school, a proportion were social referent students (in the top 10 percent of their school in connections reported by other students). In contrast to the first study, where all intervention students were social referent students, in this study the proportion of social referent students varied randomly by school, allowing us to test the effect of the proportion of social referent students on outcomes.

The program consisted of ten meetings of activities and discussions with the selected students from November to May of the school year in the twenty-eight intervention schools. Treatment students were encouraged to become the public face of opposition to these types of conflict. The ninth of the ten meetings at each treatment school was the culminating event of the intervention. The intervention model was similar to a grassroots campaign in which the treatment students took the lead in identifying the peer harassment issues at their school and generating responses to them. The intervention did not include an educational or persuasive unit regarding adult-defined problems at their school. To maintain a standardized intervention, the research assistants followed the same semistructured scripts and activity guides.

At the school level, we found that the intervention reduced disciplinary reports of peer conflict by 25 percent and that this effect varied by the proportion of social referent students in the intervention group. For example, when 20 percent of the students in the group were social referent students, disciplinary reports of peer conflict declined by up to 60 percent, demonstrating that particular group members are able to shift patterns of behavior in a group. At the individual level, those with a social connection to a social referent intervention student had less negative perceived norms. Again, patterns of interaction between students help us understand how behavior and norm perceptions spread in a group, and behavior change among high-profile students can lead to schoolwide culture and behavior changes.

Summary and Implications

The concept of culture suffers from both theoretical and methodological disagreement about what it is and how to measure it. This challenge is evident for scholars and practitioners who seek to understand cultures of peer harassment among students. I propose that we use a perspective on culture within schools that focuses on student perceptions of the norms of peer harassment and peer support behaviors among other students at the school and that assumes that cultures are produced through patterned interaction between group members. Interactions between individuals and patterns of interaction in groups are necessarily complex and dynamic. This approach to culture does not solve many of the important questions about group dynamics and the relationship between perceptions and behavior, but it does provide a starting point from which to ask different types of questions and pay attention to different forms of evidence.

Future research can take up some of the questions this approach raises. For example, what are the conditions that give rise to alignment between personal experiences and norm perceptions, and what are the consequences of such alignment? Is there a linear relationship between the extent of sharing of perceived norms among students and how consistently students comply with the norm, and does the form of this relationship vary by different types of peer harassment behaviors? How does social network segregation within a school along social identity lines change these processes? How does the larger context of a school shape interactions, the formation of norm perceptions, and behavior? How do signals about what is valued from adults, both in and outside of the school, interact with student-driven culture?

The type of empirical evidence I provide here can help researchers and practitioners distinguish between types of peer harassment cultures and highlight important questions for future qualitative research on student culture in schools. Additionally, we would expect that the conditions that create change in peer harassment behaviors will vary based on the nature of the student culture in a school, indicating that this type of empirical work can help us decide what type of intervention might be most important and effective.

Thinking about how interactions between people and the behavioral norms of a group impact behavior can also help us better understand very pressing questions about inequalities in experiences within schools and other organizations. For example, an interactionist norm account can help us understand why some identities might become targeted by peers in a school instead of others; when it becomes widespread that boys regularly make comments about how girls look or their dating behaviors; how widespread knowledge about and support for different gender identities might emerge or fail to emerge in a school; how white students in a school might develop a discourse about white privilege and antiracist practices or, conversely, white supremacist support; when students feel it is acceptable to shame others about their family or how expensive their clothes are; and how entrenched or malleable all of these peer dynamics are. This type of account also helps us understand social behavior in schools beyond peer harassment: when do students in a school focus on academic achievement, or why might students in a school tend to participate in social movements like the Sunrise Movement or the Black Lives Matter movement, while at other schools most students eschew such participation? Finally, we might apply this perspective beyond schools, to other groups and organizations, to better understand what conditions support behaviors that ameliorate forms of inequality and injustice, and when they uphold existing injustices.

NOTES

1. Coyle, 2008.
2. Deal and Peterson, 2016.
3. Olweus, 2001.
4. Bruner, 1990.
5. Espelage et al., 2000; Espelage, 2014.
6. Brank et al., 2012.
7. Wang et al., 2013.
8. Olweus, 1993.
9. Unnever and Cornell, 2003; Smith and Brain, 2000.
10. Unnever and Cornell, 2003.
11. See Olweus, 1993.
12. Juvonen and Galvan, 2008.
13. Juvonen and Graham, 2014; see also Salmivalli et al., 1996.
14. For a review of approaches to the study of culture, see Patterson, 2014.
15. Fine, 1979.
16. Fine and Tavory, 2019.
17. Cialdini et al., 1991; Elster, 2009.
18. Bradshaw and Waasdorp, 2009; Espelage, 2014.
19. Mackie, 1996.
20. See examples of such work by Feld, 1991; Friedkin, 2001; Kitts, 2003; Sgourev, 2006.

21 Shepherd, 2017.
22 Paluck et al., 2013.
23 These questions were selected based on previous literature and discussions with school administrators about what they saw in their school. I consider each of these to be different manifestations of peer harassment, and as such, I combined the ten items (reverse-coding the six peer support items) and divided by 10 to create a mean perceived norm value (from 0 to 5) for each individual, separately for wave 1 and wave 2.
24 Students were also asked about their positive peer experiences, but I do not consider them here in the interest of simplicity.
25 Tilly, 1998.
26 Paluck and Shepherd, 2012; Shepherd and Paluck, 2015; Paluck et al., 2016.
27 See Callejas and Shepherd (2020) for an alternative network-based measure of status in these schools and a discussion of the differences between the measures.
28 Some subset of these students will also be new, but here I focus on students who could not have potentially been at the school the preceding year due to their age. This description necessarily conflates younger age and new members, but most schools do not have enough older, new members for a sustained analysis. Future research should take up this issue.
29 For example, in school 11, the perceptions of older students from wave 1 to wave 2 became even more negative than did those of new students; in school 38, perceptions among new students became more negative than did perceptions among older students, decreasing the gap between the two groups.
30 See Shepherd and Garip (2021) for further explication of the role of context on patterns of interaction.
31 For example, see Bradshaw and Waasdorp, 2009; Flannery et al., 2016; Juvonen and Graham, 2014; Waasdorp et al., 2012.
32 Paluck and Shepherd, 2012.
33 Shepherd and Paluck, 2015.

REFERENCES

Bradshaw, Catherine P., and Tracy E. Waasdorp. 2009. "Measuring and Changing a 'Culture of Bullying.'" *School Psychology Review* 38 (3): 356–361.

Brank, Eve M., Lori A. Hoetger, and Katherine P. Hazen. 2012. "Bullying." *Annual Review of Law and Social Science* 8:213–230.

Bruner, Jerome. 1990. *Acts of Meaning.* Cambridge, MA: Harvard University Press.

Callejas, Laura, and Hana Shepherd. 2020. "Conflict as a Social Status Mobility Mechanism in Schools: A Network Approach." *Social Psychology Quarterly* 83:319–341.

Cialdini, Robert B., Carl A. Kallgren, and Raymond R. Reno. 1991. "A Focus Theory of Normative Conduct: A Theoretical Refinement and Reevaluation of the Role of Norms in Human Behavior." In *Advances in Experimental Social Psychology*, vol. 24, edited by Mark Zanna, pp. 201–234. New York: Academic Press.

Coyle, H. Elizabeth. 2008. "School Culture Benchmarks: Bridges and Barriers to Successful Bullying Prevention Program Implementation." *Journal of School Violence* 7 (2): 105–122.

Deal, Terrence E., and Kent D. Peterson. 2016. *Shaping School Culture*. New York: John Wiley.

Elster, Jon. 2009. "Norms." In *The Oxford Handbook of Analytical Sociology*, edited by Peter Hedstrom and Peter Bearman, 195–217. Oxford: Oxford University Press.

Espelage, Dorothy L. 2014. "Ecological Theory: Preventing Youth Bullying, Aggression, and Victimization." *Theory into Practice* 53 (4): 257–264.

Espelage, Dorothy L., Kris Bosworth, and Thomas R. Simon. 2000. "Examining the Social Context of Bullying Behaviors in Early Adolescence." *Journal of Counseling & Development* 78 (3): 326–333.

Feld, Scott L. 1991. "Why Your Friends Have More Friends Than You Do." *American Journal of Sociology* 96 (6): 1464–1477.

Fine, Gary Alan. 1979. "Small Groups and Culture Creation: The Idioculture of Little League Teams." *American Sociological Review* 44 (5): 733–745.

Fine, Gary Alan, and Iddo Tavory. 2019. "Interactionism in the Twenty-First Century: A Letter on Being-in-a-Meaningful-World." *Symbolic Interactionism* 42 (3): 457–467.

Flannery, Daniel J., Jonathan Todres, Catherine P. Bradshaw, Angela Frederick Amar, Sandra Graham, Mark Hatzenbuehler, Matthew Masiello, Megan Moreno, Regina Sullivan, Tracy Vaillancourt, Suzanne M. Le Menestrel, and Frederick Rivara. 2016. "Bullying Prevention: A Summary of the Report of the National Academies of Sciences, Engineering, and Medicine." *Prevention Science* 17:1044–1053.

Friedkin, Noah E. 2001. "Norm Formation in Social Influence Networks." *Social Networks* 23:167–189.

Juvonen, Jaana, and Adriana Galvan. 2008. "Peer Influence in Involuntary Social Groups: Lessons from Research on Bullying." In *Understanding Peer Influence in Children and Adolescents*, edited by Mitchell J. Prinstein and Kenneth A. Dodge, 225–244. New York: Guilford.

Juvonen, Jaana, and Sandra Graham. 2014. "Bullying in Schools: The Power of Bullies and the Plight of Victims." *Annual Review of Psychology* 65:159–185.

Kitts, James A. 2003. "Egocentric Bias or Information Management? Selective Disclosure and the Social Roots of Norm Misperception." *Social Psychology Quarterly* 66 (3): 222–237.

Mackie, Gerry. 1996. "Ending Footbinding and Infibulation: A Convention Account." *American Journal of Sociology* 61 (6): 999–1017.

Olweus, Dan. 1993. *Bullying at School: What We Know and What We Can Do*. Malden, MA: Blackwell.

———. 2001. "Peer Harassment: A Critical Analysis and Some Important Issues." In *Peer Harassment in School*, edited by Jaana Juvonen and Sandra Graham, 3–20. New York: Guilford.

Paluck, Elizabeth Levy, and Hana Shepherd. 2012. "The Salience of Social Referents: A Field Experiment on Collective Norms and Harassment Behavior in a School Social Network." *Journal of Personality and Social Psychology* 103 (6): 899–915.

Paluck, Elizabeth Levy, Hana Shepherd, and Peter M. Aronow. 2013. "Changing Climates of Conflict: A Social Network Experiment in 56 Schools, New Jersey." Ann Arbor, MI: Inter-university Consortium for Political and Social Research.

———. 2016. "Changing Climates of Conflict: A Social Network Experiment in 56 Schools." *Proceedings of the National Academy of Sciences* 113 (3): 566–571.

Patterson, Orlando. 2014. "Making Sense of Culture." *Annual Review of Sociology* 40:1–30.

Salmivalli, Christina, Kirsti Lagerspetz, Kaj Björkqvist, Karin Österman, and Ari Kaukiainen. 1996. "Bullying as a Group Process: Participant Roles and Their Relations to Social Status within the Group." *Aggressive Behavior* 22 (1): 1–15.

Sgourev, Stoyan V. 2006. "Lake Wobegon Upside Down: The Paradox of Status-Devaluation." *Social Forces* 84 (3): 1497–1519.

Shepherd, Hana. 2017. "The Structure of Perception: How Networks Shape Ideas of Norms." *Sociological Forum* 32 (1): 72–93.

Shepherd, Hana, and Filiz Garip. 2021. "On Inequality." In *Personal Networks: Classic Readings and New Directions in Ego-centric Analysis*, edited by Mario Small, Brea Perry, Berenice Pescosolido, and Ned Smith, 630–650. Cambridge: Cambridge University Press.

Shepherd, Hana, and Elizabeth Levy Paluck. 2015. "Stopping the Drama: Gendered Influence in a Network Field Experiment." *Social Psychology Quarterly* 78 (2): 173–193.

Smith, Peter K., and Paul Brain. 2000. "Bullying in Schools: Lessons from Two Decades of Research." *Aggressive Behavior* 26 (1): 1–9.

Tilly, Charles. 1998. *Durable Inequality*. Berkeley: University of California Press.

Unnever, James D., and Dewey G. Cornell. 2003. "The Culture of Bullying in Middle School." *Journal of School Violence* 2 (2): 5–27.

Waasdorp, Tracy E., Catherine P. Bradshaw, and Philip J. Leaf. 2012. "The Impact of Schoolwide Positive Behavioral Interventions and Supports on Bullying and Peer Rejection: A Randomized Controlled Effectiveness Trial." *Archives of Pediatrics & Adolescent Medicine* 166 (2): 149–156.

Wang, Cixin, Brandi Berry, and Susan M. Swearer. 2013. "The Critical Role of School Climate in Effective Bullying Prevention." *Theory Into Practice* 52 (4): 296–302.

11

The Anti-Bullying Myth

Bullying and Aggression in an Inhabited Institution

BRENT HARGER

Bullying is an inherently social problem that, since the late 1990s, has received increased public and academic attention due to high-profile school shootings and teen suicides as well as a variety of other negative effects.[1] Despite the social nature of bullying and other forms of aggression in schools, early research on these topics often featured individualistic framings that provided little insight into the social contexts in which these behaviors occur.[2] More recent research has addressed these shortcomings. The emphasis on social-ecological approaches to understanding the "individual, family, peer, school, and community contexts" of bullying is particularly useful for sociologists studying this topic and is reflected in much of the qualitative research in relation to bullying and aggression.[3]

The shift in academic approaches to bullying and aggression has not corresponded to a shift in public perspectives on these topics. Within schools, students and teachers are influenced by these public perspectives, sometimes falling back on media stereotypes and individualistic views of bullies.[4] As a result, bullying and aggression have proven difficult for schools to address as they respond with individual approaches to problems rooted in social interaction and school cultures. Meta-analyses of bullying intervention programs demonstrate the lack of efficacy in this area, finding relatively few significant changes in schools.[5]

In this chapter I address the question of why, given the widespread focus of bullying and aggression researchers on social contexts, teachers and school staff members would continue to approach these problems from an individualistic standpoint resulting in individualistic attempts at solutions. To answer this question, I draw on inhabited institutionalism and school culture approaches to examine ethnographic data from two elementary schools. The result is an in-depth look at the interactive processes by which students and adults in these schools dealt with the cultural myth of bullying, contributing to school cultures in which aggressive behaviors were normalized and individualistic definitions of bullying were preferred. I find that these processes allowed both students and adults to define their own behaviors in more favorable ways, with aggressive students defining themselves as non-bullies and adults claiming the effectiveness of their anti-bullying efforts. From the perspective of many in these schools, then, individualized approaches to bullying were appropriate because there were very few "bullies" to address.

Bullying and Aggression in Inhabited Institutions

Schools have long been of interest to institutional researchers. As Meyer notes, education is "a central element in the table of organization of society, constructing competencies and helping create professions and professionals."[6] Indeed, a crucial question in the rise of new institutionalism was why schools adopt similar organizational forms when these forms do not necessarily meet their functional needs, with Meyer and Rowan arguing that these forms increase legitimacy and the chance of survival at the cost of internal coordination and control.[7] As work along these lines developed, researchers frequently used large-scale quantitative studies to examine surface measures of organizational conformity to broad cultural "myths" that foster public legitimacy while turning away from examinations of the inner workings of organizations.[8]

In contrast to new institutionalism, recent scholars have examined not only the meanings that give organizations like schools legitimacy but also the ways that these meanings evolve through social interaction.[9] This inhabited institutionalism approach combines institutional theory and interactionist sociology, typically using ethnographic methods to explore the relationships between institutions, interactions, and organizations.[10] From this perspective, institutions have a double construction in which they "provide the guidelines for social interactions ('construct interactions'), but [they] are also constituted and propelled forward by interactions that provide them with force and meaning."[11] As a result, interactions become a central part of a larger mesosociological approach in which institutional pressures penetrate organizations but "the practical implications and meanings of these institutional pressures get worked out in social interactions."[12]

The *meaning* of this institutional pressure and how schools address this cultural myth, though, is worked out in social interactions between principals, teachers, staff members, and students within schools. Consider, for example, the definition of bullying. Researchers traditionally define bullying as repeated exposure to intentionally negative actions by one or more individuals in which there is an imbalance of power, taking the form of verbal abuse, physical abuse (or attempted physical abuse), or indirect abuse through hand gestures, facial expressions, or systematically ignoring, excluding, or isolating an individual.[13] Within schools, though, definitions of bullying often differ from those of researchers as teachers, students, and staff members construct meanings that work for them in the context of the school.[14]

Bullying in School Culture

Schools addressing the cultural myth of bullying, then, do so in a way that is informed by their meso-level group culture.[15] Gary Alan Fine has long explored the creation of culture through small-group interaction.[16] He defines culture as "a construction based upon the consensual meaning system of members; it comprises the interactional products that result from a verbal and behavioral representation of that meaning system."[17] Through interaction, then, students and teachers in schools create "a system of knowledge, beliefs, behaviors, and customs shared by members of an interacting group to which members refer and that they employ as the basis of further interaction."[18] In this way, interactions between and within groups of students and adults contribute to the perspectives of the school, which provides meaning for the actions of these groups.[19]

The presence of group cultures in schools demonstrates "how interactions and institutions combine through common recognition and intersubjective experience."[20] Pascoe's research with high school students provides an example of the maintenance of interaction norms within school cultures in response to the cultural myth of masculinity. Pascoe describes masculinity as a process in which male students use homophobic epithets like "fag" to insult others and assert their own masculine heterosexual identities.[21] Similarly, Klein asserts that "gay bashing" is used to police those who fail to meet masculinity expectations in schools, sometimes leading to violent responses by those who feel they need to prove their manhood.[22] For boys, verbal attacks on sexuality have been found to provoke stronger reactions than even physical abuse.[23]

These behaviors are normalized within the broader school culture not only by their frequency among students but also by the practices of the school itself. Pascoe states, "School ceremonies and authorities encouraged, engaged in, and reproduced the centrality of repudiation processes to adolescent masculinity."[24] Teachers contributed to the normalization of these behaviors by not intervening and, in some cases, by engaging in these behaviors themselves.[25] Indeed, recent research conducted in two middle schools argues that the norms that govern interactions between teachers are communicated to students through day-to-day interactions at school, setting unofficial standards for student behaviors that mirror those between adults.[26]

Approaching bullying from the perspective of school cultures also demonstrates the need for a broader focus on aggression in schools. For example, Finkelhor et al. note that Olweus's definition of bullying excludes peer aggression that occurs only once or between equals and that power imbalance is difficult to define and varies by context.[27] In chapter 8, Callejas argues for a broader definition of bullying that includes interpersonal conflict between students of similar levels of power and status, such as friends. Further, Espelage and Swearer argue that behaviors outside of this traditional definition "still have serious effects on their targets," and Callejas notes that interpersonal conflict can escalate to serious antisocial behavior if left unchecked.[28] Finally, traditional definitions of bullying neglect the roles that students, teachers, and other adults play in contributing to the school cultures in which bullying is created and sustained.[29] As a result, I focus broadly on aggressive behavior, which Faris and Felmlee define as "behavior directed toward harming or causing pain to another, including physical (e.g., hitting, shoving, and kicking), verbal (e.g., name-calling and threats), and indirect aggression (also called social or relational aggression). Indirect aggression is defined as harmful actions perpetrated outside of a victim's immediate purview, such as spreading rumors and ostracism."[30]

In this chapter I use inhabited institutionalism and school culture approaches to examine the ways that students, teachers, and staff members in two elementary schools address the cultural myth of bullying. Drawing on conclusions from my previous work, I argue that both the organizational approaches of the schools and interactional challenges affect adults' responses to bullying and aggression.[31] These responses contribute to school cultures in which aggressive behaviors were normalized and individualistic definitions of bullying were preferred, allowing both adults and aggressive students to protect themselves from the negative perceptions associated with this cultural myth.

Setting and Methods

The data in this chapter are drawn from a study of peer interaction among fifth grade students (ten and eleven years old) in two public elementary schools in the same school district: Hillside and Greenfield.[32] Located in a rural midwestern city of about fifteen thousand people, each school provides education for roughly 240 students in kindergarten through fifth grade. Students at both schools are largely white and from middle- or working-class families. At Hillside Elementary 98 percent of students are white and 30 percent receive free or reduced-price lunches, compared to 97 percent and 41 percent at Greenfield Elementary. During my data collection there were 45 fifth grade students in two classrooms at Hillside and 37 fifth grade students in two classrooms at Greenfield. In contrast to middle or high school, elementary school provides a set of relatively stable peer relationships for studying aggression. In a typical middle school, for example, students from a number of elementary schools come together for the first time, leading to struggles for social status that likely exacerbate aggressive behavior.[33] Most of the fifth graders whom I spent time with for this study, however, had attended school together since kindergarten.

During the 2007–2008 school year I conducted over 430 hours of participant observation at the two schools combined. In my observations I used an interpretive approach, viewing individuals as active agents who are influenced by social structures but take an active role in counteracting or modifying these structures.[34] Although I observed adults primarily in their interactions with students and my ability to obtain adult perspectives was largely limited to interviews and brief interactions before school, this limitation did not affect my ability to understand the roles of both adults and students in constructing a school culture through interaction with each other.

The roles that I took on in the schools were similar to those of Thorne, who conducted research with fourth and fifth graders.[35] In the classroom I spent most of my time sitting in the back of the room and observing, while I was more involved at lunch and recess and during classes like music, physical education, and art. During recess at the schools I twirled jump ropes, played basketball, four square, football, and tag, used the swings and the slides, and just walked around. My increased involvement at recess aided data collection. Early in my fieldwork I found that when observing from outside of student interactions I could see students getting angry with each other when playing games like basketball or tag, but I could not hear what was being said. Participating in these games provided me with a better vantage point while helping set me apart from other adults.

Setting myself apart from other adults was a key goal as I modeled my interactions with students on Corsaro's atypical adult and Eder, Evans, and Parker's quiet friend roles.[36] In addition to my participation in games at recess, students and teachers alike were initially surprised when I went to classes like music with the students rather than spending this time in the teachers' lounge. When interacting with students I typically remained quiet and participated only to the degree necessary for acceptance as part of the group. The students demonstrated their acceptance of me in a number of ways, such as ensuring that the teachers included me in classroom games and activities, asking me to protect objects for them, and teasing me. Students also repeatedly demonstrated that they did not view me as an authority figure by participating in behavior that could get them in trouble, such as swearing or playfully hitting each other, in my presence but stopping these behaviors when other adults walked by. In interviews, several adults also commended me on my ability to be accepted by their students.

In addition to participant observation, I interviewed 53 of the 82 fifth grade students, all four of the fifth grade teachers, both principals, and four school staff members who were frequently present during lunch and recess. Following Eder and Fingerson, the participant observation portion of my data collection preceded interviewing and was used to ground interview questions and observe communicative norms and patterns while developing a general understanding of the school culture.[37] All fifth grade students were invited to participate in interviews, and interviews were completed with all who returned signed parent and student informed consent statements. In total, I interviewed 24 of 37 fifth grade students at Hillside Elementary and 29 of 45 at Greenfield Elementary. Student interviews typically lasted for twenty-five to thirty minutes and took place during periods of free time approved by the teacher in empty classrooms. Adult interviews typically lasted between fifty and sixty minutes.

Data from field notes and interview transcripts were analyzed using ATLAS.ti, a qualitative data analysis program. In ATLAS.ti I identified patterns in the data and searched for negative cases. I looked particularly closely at interactions involving aggressive behaviors, but I was also careful to examine the school cultures as a whole and the ways that the actions of adults and students affected norms within the schools. Because I conducted my observations and interviews in two schools, I compared my findings from each, looking for similarities and differences. The result is an in-depth look at the interactive process by which students and adults in these schools dealt with the cultural myth of bullying. In the sections that follow I first explore the approaches of the two schools to the cultural myth of bullying and the challenges that adults faced when addressing this myth, contributing to the normalization of aggressive behavior. I then discuss the ramifications of these challenges for the definitions of bullying used by those in the schools and their contribution to individualistic definitions of bullying that allowed both adults and aggressive students to protect themselves from the negative perceptions associated with this cultural myth.

Organizational Approaches to the Cultural Myth of Bullying

Although anti-bullying programs were not mandated at the time I studied Greenfield and Hillside, the school district had adopted a program called CLASS (Connected Learning Assures Successful Students) as a preemptive measure to address potential concerns related to accountability.[38] According to Mrs. Knight, Hillside's principal, the school district adopted the CLASS program as the result of a grant because it would allow the district to have something in place that it could point to as a model for reform in the event of low student test scores or other potential accreditation problems. CLASS was implemented to various extents at each school. Its most prominent implementation was through Life Skills meetings with the principal at Hillside and through the morning routine at Greenfield, during which a different group of students each day would say, "Don't forget the Life Goals. Do the right thing, treat people right" and then recite the Pledge of Allegiance after the principal's morning announcements.

While the CLASS program included school climate and community aspects that helped the district deal with external expectations to address bullying, Hillside Elementary had also had a peer mediation program for the three years preceding my observations. This program, intended to reduce conflicts and violence by teaching students how to discuss and mediate their disagreements, was the result of a grant through the state bar association. Mrs. Knight, Hillside's principal, believed that the program was a success, describing how students responded to problems with peers during its implementation: "Last year, I think even if it was a situation where they weren't on the playground and they didn't have the clipboards to get the peer mediator to talk through it, they were kind of doing it anyway. You know, they were kind of forgiving each other. Talking through it and saying, well you know, all the things they had been taught, you know."

Despite Knight's positive assessment of the program, fifth grade teacher Mr. Hanson was less sure of its success: "The bottom line I think is that the teachers and the staff, the principals are responsible for taking care of problems like that. Uh, if other students can help and so forth, you know, that's okay but I'm not really sure how, how successful or how unsuccessful that was, I really don't know." These differing opinions highlight the way that meanings are formed through interactions in the school culture. It is important to note that as principal, Knight may have had a better vantage point on the program's success or failure because she was responsible for handling the conflicts that arise on the playground and in the cafeteria. While the program, and the presence of the home-school advisor who ran it, had ended by the time I entered the school, Mrs. Knight expressed hope that the students had learned from the experience and developed coping mechanisms as a result.

In addition to their different implementations of the CLASS program and the former presence of a peer mediation program at Hillside, the fifth grade teachers in the two schools also took different approaches to discipline. Consistent with inhabited institutionalism, both schools had similar rules regarding student behavior, but the meanings of "good" behavior adopted by adults differed based on interactions within the schools. Students in the fifth grade classes at both schools had developed reputations for being disruptive by the end of their fourth grade years. While Mrs. Lane at Greenfield Elementary noted that this caused her to "set on them harder because of how they were last year," however, neither Mr. Erickson nor Mr. Hanson at Hillside reported making similar considerations.[39] Possibly as a result, students at Greenfield were quieter in their classrooms, in the hallways, and when lining up at the end of recess. Further, Mrs. Hunter, one of Greenfield's supervisors stated that in contrast to those at Greenfield, the fifth graders at Hillside were "pretty much out of control."

Crucially, these contrasting approaches to enforcing school rules for order and quiet affected adult perceptions of student behavior but not the presence of aggressive interactions. I observed a roughly equal number of aggressive interactions at each school, and the number of interactions that were visibly perceived as negative by one or both participants were also roughly equal. Because one or two adults are often responsible for overseeing a large number of students, it can be difficult for adults in schools to observe student behavior, much less have an accurate gauge of peer interactions.[40] Below, I detail how adults and students jointly maintained a culture that normalized these interactions.

Interactional Challenges to Addressing the Myth

The Disciplinary Process

Although organizational approaches to implementing the CLASS program differed between schools, adults at both schools faced the same challenges with regard to the disciplinary process that affected their efforts to address the cultural myth of bullying. In the schools that I observed, both the ratio of students to adults and students' efforts to hide their behaviors contributed to the fact that adults observed only a small number of the total aggressive behaviors that took place and were heavily reliant on students to report these interactions. Interpersonal relationships played a key role in students' willingness to do so. Students described a willingness to report those who were not their friends and an unwillingness to report those who were. Students also sometimes used the rules themselves as weapons against each other by reporting the rule violations of peers that they disliked, reporting behavior against them without mentioning that this behavior was in retaliation for something that they had done, and, in some cases, reporting things that were entirely fabricated.[41] In each case the goal was to negatively affect another student through adult action.

The low likelihood of directly observing a behavior combined with the fact that students sometimes falsely reported aggressive behaviors made adults cautious about relying on a single student report. In order to discipline students, then, adults talked to multiple witnesses and weighed what each said, constructing a series of likely events. For example, when I asked Mrs. Wheeler, a lunch and recess supervisor at Hillside, how she dealt with student reports of aggressive behavior, she stated, "You just gotta play detective. You just kind of try to dig 'til you get to the bottom of it. . . . Like, if you come up and complain about somebody else I'll say okay, you go over there for a little bit while I talk to this person . . . and then you might even have to pull other people aside. I always say, 'Who was around? Who's seen or heard? Who was with you?' Again, they may lie. Who knows? You don't really know." Mrs. Wheeler also recognized that students might not report the whole truth: "They may come to me and say, 'so and so hit me with the ball.' And I'm like, 'That is really weird. I can't imagine that person hittin' 'em with the ball.' Well, that truly did happen *but* they left the first part off that they tripped 'em as they went by." This detective work was further complicated by relationships between students, which influenced their responses to adult questioning much like their decisions to report behaviors.

Adults' responses to these reports were strongly influenced by the knowledge, beliefs, and expectations that they held about individual students, leading them to punish repeat offenders more harshly than others. Mrs. Knight, Hillside's principal, discussed this in her interview: "Usually, in the end the truth will come out. But if it doesn't, I will tell them, 'I can't pick your side and I can't pick your side. Looking at your records, you had fifteen [punishments] this year, he's not had any. I have to believe him. Because I have to punish someone.'" Other adults also mentioned the use of students' prior behavior. As Mrs. Neely, a recess and lunch supervisor at Hillside Elementary, explained, "First-time offenders, depending on what it is, you are kind of more lenient about things than the people who are repeatedly in trouble. I mean, I'm not one to take recess all the time from somebody, but the repeat offenders, I sometimes don't think twice about making them go stand [for time out]." Mr. White, the Greenfield principal, similarly reported considering a student's reputation along with what he called the "witness accounts" he gathered through his detective work.

Students with good reputations were frequently called upon by adults to act as witnesses, while students with bad reputations were accused more frequently and could be used as scapegoats for others. For example, Sandy argued Mike "sorta has, not a bad reputation, but people know that he can get in trouble really easy. And so, if something comes up, then they're just like, 'Mike did it.'" Brian, who regularly teased, chased, and pushed others, reported being wrongly accused because of his reputation: "I know I've got told on for throwing a ball and I didn't throw it, and it hit somebody." Consistent with inhabited institutionalism, these examples show the importance of social interactions between students and adults in developing school cultures. In both, the reliance of adults on student reports gave students a large amount of influence over the disciplinary procedures and allowed them to protect some students while using the rules themselves as weapons against others.

The Frequency of Aggression

The challenges that adults faced when making disciplinary decisions would have been easier to deal with if aggressive behavior was infrequent. Instead, it was a near constant presence in my observations. This placed adults in a difficult position since most aggressive behavior violated school rules, but sending students to the office for every occurrence they observed would have resulted in nearly empty classrooms and investigating every report would have taken up all of their time. Instead, adults attempted to interpret the meaning of each interaction for the participants, exemplifying the way that institutions "provide the guidelines for social interactions ('construct interactions'), but [they] are also constituted and propelled forward by interactions that provide them with force and meaning."[42] For example, in one instance I wrote in my field notes that Jared jumped on Brad and pulled him down to the ground before running away. Brad chased him, pulling on Jared's shirt. Mrs. Wheeler, who observed the interaction between these two friends, said, "You better be playing!"

Adults also sometimes intervened to stop aggressive behaviors between friends that they felt were getting out of hand without punishing the students involved, as the following field note demonstrates:

> At the beginning of recess some of the girls decided that they were going to play American Idol and Joanna, Brittney, and Emily were the judges, with Chelsea starting out as the contestant and Jody and Joel waiting for a turn. Chelsea started by pretending to sing a bad rendition of a Carrie Underwood song. Later, she pretended to be a contestant who was mad at the judges and had to have security called, playfully attacking Joanna and hitting her. The aide in the room said "Chelsea. Chelsea! Chelsea, stop!" and Chelsea stopped. The aide said that they needed to settle down.

In these examples, the adults recognized that aggression can be used between friends, but they also reinforced the idea that these behaviors are an accepted part of the school culture.

The willingness of adults to overlook aggression within friendship groups had negative effects for some students because aggression within friendship groups was not distributed equally. Callejas, in chapter 8, highlights that conflict with friends is positively associated with social status throughout the school year for middle school boys. My own data support this. In one popular peer group, for example, a core group of three friends frequently interacted with two marginal members. This core group used aggression against the marginal members to reinforce the boundaries of their group and maintain their own status, while the marginal members could not respond in kind because of their lower status.

For example, near the end of the school year students took a field trip to the local middle school for a presentation about the school's fine arts program, which included band, orchestra, and choir, so that students could consider the groups that they might be interested in joining when they attended middle school in the fall. On the bus, I noted, "Brad and Joel were sitting next to each other. Brad said he wasn't going to be friends with Joel next year because it will hurt his image, then he moved up a row and sat by Dustin and Jared. Joel moved next to Ben, who told him to move away but he didn't. After this, they talked to Joel like normal." Regardless of how Joel felt in this situation, as a student on the margins of the group his only options were to accept this treatment or to limit his interactions to lower-status students. The two marginal members did, however, direct aggression at each other. As a result, those on the margins of this group were the targets of much more aggression than those at the core of the group.[43]

In addition to the acceptance of aggressive behaviors as a part of the school culture, adults' interpretations of whether these behaviors necessitated disciplinary action sometimes differed from those of students. When students reported aggressive behaviors to adults, then, they had to contend with the possibility that the adults would not treat their reports seriously. Adults noted that the interactions that were reported were not always the ones they felt were most important to deal with, especially given the time required to "play detective," and sometimes discouraged telling on others unless they had done something "really bad." In her interview, Hillside principal Mrs. Winter mentioned that "kids seem to tattle on the trivial stuff and then sometimes when it's the bigger stuff we don't know it. We had a little boy here who was Black and someone was calling him 'nigger.' I want to know this." By dedicating their time to investigating student reports of "trivial stuff," adults believed they would have less time to deal with issues that were truly important. Paradoxically, the reluctance of adults to investigate these reports may have reduced the likelihood that students would report more serious issues.

The messages of adults reinforced student-held beliefs against "tattling," a label that was typically applied to those who adhered more closely to formal school rules. For example, Jim said, "I don't like bein' a tattletale and stuff, and telling on somethin' that's not really that big of a deal." Similarly, Leann defined tattlers as those who see "little things that are like no problem, not going to be a problem, but you go and tell anyway." Like Mrs. Winter's statement against "trivial stuff," though, labeling those who reported "little things" as "tattletales" likely contributed to the pressure students faced to avoid reporting *any* negative interactions.[44] By calling attention to behaviors that were overlooked by others, including aggression, tattletales appeared to demonstrate that they were not "tough" enough to participate in the normalized school culture of aggression. The need to appear "tough" is also strongly related to norms of hegemonic masculinity within schools.[45]

Definitions of Bullying in the School Culture

The normalization of aggression in these schools is the combined result of the institutional pressures faced by adults and the meanings formed in the school culture by students, teachers, and staff members. Defining those who report "trivial stuff" or "little things" as tattletales allowed those in the schools to downplay aggressive behaviors and view their daily interactions as free of major problems. These definitions also allowed adults to believe that they were conforming to public expectations for schools by adequately addressing bullying. This is even clearer when considering the ways that the normalization of aggression allowed those at Greenfield and Hillside to *define* bullying.

When asked in interviews what bullying means to them, both students and adults provided definitions that were broadly in line with aspects of the definitions used by researchers such as Olweus. As shown in Figure 11.1, the majority of students and adults included physical and verbal components in their definitions of bullying, though students were less likely to consistently include these than their adult counterparts. Very few students, however, described indirect behaviors like exclusion, repeated behaviors, or a power imbalance between bullies and victims. Adults were more likely to mention indirect behaviors and a power imbalance, but only three of them mentioned repetitive behavior in describing bullying.[46]

These differences in definitions of bullying also manifested in an uncertainty among adults about the behaviors of students in their schools. In response to an interview question asking whether there were any

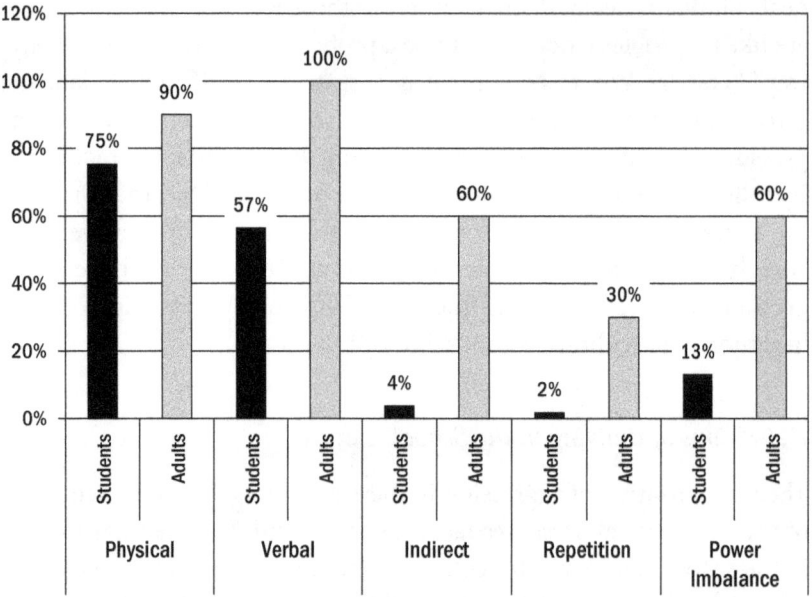

Figure 11.1. Percentage of Participants Providing Various Elements of Researchers' Bullying Definition

bullies in fifth grade in their school, the majority of students stated that there were, with about a third stating that there were not. Like their definitions of bullying, these statements were consistent between males and females and the two schools. In contrast to students, only three adults were sure that bullying occurred among fifth graders, with three stating that there were only minor issues with bullying in their school as a whole. Notably, some adults stated that they thought bullying was worse in some grades than others, but they disagreed as to *where* it was worse. Mr. White and Mrs. Lane at Greenfield stated that bullying was more overt among fifth graders. Also at Greenfield, Mrs. Hunter stated that she thought it was worse in lower grades, while Mrs. Adrian thought bullying was more prevalent in higher grades. That four adults in the same school would have such different perceptions of bullying is likely connected to the different definition applied by each.

Teachers at Hillside Elementary were more consistent in their answers, stating that they largely did not know how prevalent bullying was. Mr. Erickson and Mr. Hanson, Hillside's fifth grade teachers, noted that students are adept at hiding information from their teachers, with Mr. Hanson stating that a teacher is often "the last person to know." Mrs. Knight, Hillside's principal, noted that it was difficult to determine due to the differing perceptions between students, with more sensitive students perceiving higher levels of bullying than others. She stated, "I would love to believe that it's not even a percent. It's probably 90. These kids probably feel bullied." Like Mrs. Hunter at Greenfield, Mrs. Wheeler at Hillside stated that she thought bullying was more prevalent among younger students. Their positions as recess supervisors may have provided them with a broader perspective than the teachers, but their perceptions may also have been shaped by increased sophistication among fifth graders that made bullying harder to identify.

The behaviors of some students also made classification difficult. The behaviors of Kathy, a student at Hillside, exemplified this difficulty. Kathy frequently bothered others by pushing and arguing while playing sports at recess, touching students who were standing near her in the lunch line, and kicking those who sat across from her at the lunch table. Kathy was also a frequent target of other students who called her "fat," told her to "shut up" and "sit down" in the classroom, and pushed and kicked her while playing sports at recess. Mrs. Wheeler tried to make sense of this:

> They might have their little things in fifth, but I don't know if it's actually bullying, 'cause the Kathy thing you just kinda gotta take out, 'cause I don't know what all that is, and the things people will do back to her, I mean they're not, I don't know, you just gotta remove all that because I don't know what all that is. . . . Second grade, there's flat out two little bullies, I mean just always. They started up the other morning, because I do breakfast duty as well, seven forty in the morning . . . after each other. "Well he said this about my mom," you know and they're just *bullyin'* each other.

From Mrs. Wheeler's perspective, the clear-cut behaviors of these two second graders were easier to define as bullying than a fifth grader who did not fit the stereotypical image of a bully or a victim. Students tended to interpret Kathy's behavior depending on their own interactions with her, demonstrating the way that even supposedly clear behaviors like pushing could be interpreted differently by different students.

The Influence of Person-Centered Views

The fact that the definitions of students and adults in these schools shared elements with those of researchers did not mean that these definitions were applied evenly in the context of actual school interactions. The difficulty that both students and adults had in labeling the behavior of students like Kathy demonstrates just one way that these definitions of bullying were "worked out in social interactions" and affected the broader culture in both schools.[47] Further, the lack of a common definition of bullying allowed problematic conceptions of bullying to take hold. The stereotype of an older, larger student making life difficult for younger students is a part of the cultural milieu in the United States, and both students and adults used stereotypes such as these to create a person-centered view of bullies. In this view, bullying was seen as a dichotomy; an individual either *was* or *was not* a bully.

Through this person-centered view, students ignored the continuum of behaviors that ranges from bullying to non-bullying and the fact that a student might participate in bullying in one instance (e.g., pushing another student in the hallway, insulting someone) and non-bullying in another (e.g., doing well on a math test, joking with friends). Instead, they supported a false dichotomy that students either were bullies or were not and that a student's designation was based not on a single interaction but on the whole of his or her behaviors. Marshall at Hillside, for example, argued that he and his friends "usually, like, pick on kids" but were "probably not bullies 'cause we usually get As and Bs" and participate in extracurricular activities. Moving past this dichotomy allows us to see that Kathy was both a bully *and* a victim, depending on the situation, just as Marshall and his friends sometimes bullied others and other times participated in Math Bowl or choir.

This false dichotomy was shared by four adults (Mrs. Wheeler and Mrs. Knight at Hillside Elementary and Mrs. Scott and Mrs. Hunter at Greenfield Elementary). Mrs. Knight, Hillside's principal, stated that a student who was currently in high school whom she considered a bully was "mean by nature" and was "born that way." She noted that students such as this are rare and have typically been labeled emotionally disabled. At the time of our interview, Mrs. Knight proclaimed that there was only one student at Hillside whom she considered to be a bully:

He bullies the teacher; he bullies all the other kids. No one else can get a word in edgewise. He argues with his teacher. When she's talking he talks over her. He's at his desk, but then when he sees her pick up the telephone he goes back to interrupt. He sees another girl back there so he comes back there and starts talking, knocks her out of the way. I have one bully in my school right now, that I know of. Um, and I really, even as a teacher and being here nineteen years, I really can't think of five kids that I thought were bullies.

In this explanation she relies on the belief that in order for students to be considered bullies they must fit her ideal type of being "mean by nature" and thus *always* aggressive.

While those with person-centered views of bullying tended to reserve this label for students who fit media stereotypes, those who held action-centered views of bullying were more liberal in their usage of the term. For example, Mrs. Lane used media depictions to draw contrasts between outside perceptions and the reality of student life: "I don't see the old-fashioned bullying like what you'd see on *Leave it to Beaver*, you know, where he gets the black eye . . . it's more verbal, and it's subtle." Rather than attempting to identify patterns of behavior, those with action-centered definitions stated that bullying could take the form of small actions, even between friends. These examples demonstrate that one's definition of bullying can be in line with those of researchers, as Mrs. Knight's is, without the application of this definition following suit.

Discussion and Conclusion

The increased attention paid to bullying in the past two decades, by both researchers and the public, places pressure on schools to show that they are taking this topic seriously in order to be seen as legitimate.[48] If faced with questions by parents, both Greenfield and Hillside could point to the presence of the CLASS program in the district, which included school climate and community elements, as an indication that they were doing so. On its own, the presence of this program is an indication of the sort of organizational conformity to broad cultural myths that is consistent with new institutional theory.[49] However, an understanding of the *meanings* that this program had at Greenfield and Hillside, and the ways that these meanings influenced the schools' approaches to bullying and aggression, requires an examination of the interactions between students, teachers, and staff members that is consistent with inhabited institutionalism.[50]

At both Greenfield and Hillside, the CLASS program provided guidelines, but consistent with inhabited institutionalism, these guidelines were "propelled forward by interactions that provide them with force and meaning."[51] Because neither school provided clear and consistent definitions to teachers, students, and other staff members about what constituted bullying and how these behaviors should be addressed, many relied on definitions of bullying that were loosely connected to those used by researchers but that carved out exceptions for their own behaviors, including aggressive behaviors. Person-centered definitions like those held by Marshall allowed students to consistently "pick on kids" while arguing that factors such as grades or extracurricular activities prevented these attacks from being defined as bullying. These definitions also allowed adults in both schools to witness the frequent aggression between students while reassuring themselves that there were few "true" bullies present. In this way, both schools fulfilled Meyer and Rowan's assertion that "organizations must not only conform to myths but must also maintain the appearance that the myths actually work."[52]

The difficulty that both students and adults had in labeling the behavior of students like Kathy demonstrates just one way that these definitions of bullying were "worked out in social interactions" and affected the broader culture in both schools.[53] Many of the aggressive interactions that I observed between students met Olweus's definition of bullying by taking place repeatedly between students in which there was an imbalance of power but were not defined as bullying by adults or students in the setting.[54] Student and adult definitions of bullying, including person-centered views, resulted from, and contributed to, this normalization. By overlooking transgressions that did not fit their definitions of bullying and encouraging students to do the same, adults allowed aggression to be used among friends as well as enemies.

While a clear edict against aggressive behavior in general may have reduced the frequency of these behaviors, in the absence of this the sheer number of these interactions likely made it more difficult for adults to determine which should be addressed and which should not. The ability of students to hide aggressive behaviors also prevented adults from dealing with all of the interactions that were reported to them due to the time-consuming detective work that was necessary in the disciplinary process. Because of the time and effort involved in pursuing discipline, I observed several adults discouraging student reports, contributing to the stigmatization of reporting behaviors that were perceived as minor while effectively discouraging students from reporting aggressive behaviors to adults given the murky lines between acceptable and unacceptable interactions. Here, inhabited institutionalism provides insight into the ways that the meanings of aggressive behaviors are worked out through social interactions between students and adults.

In this context, and in line with person-centered views of behavior, students who were well behaved were perceived as being more trustworthy than others and had a greater influence on the disciplinary decisions of adults. Students who were often in trouble, on the other hand, sometimes found themselves accused of and even punished for things that they had not done. A reputation as a tattletale was another aspect of the school culture that was defined through interactions and could also reduce the likelihood that a student's reports would be taken seriously by adults. Furthermore, it is possible that some of the students who were known as tattletales were more sensitive to the behaviors that other students accepted as the norm, as Mrs. Knight noted.

Because they affected the broader school culture, the normalization of aggression and person-centered definitions of bullying affected students whether or not they personally held these definitions. Many of the students who reported the presence of bullies during interviews did not define bullying in this way but relied on those who did (including recess supervisors and Hillside's principal) when reporting negative interactions. As a result, the normalization of these behaviors in both schools and the belief by students that their behaviors did not constitute bullying because they did not fit their person-centered definitions suggest a need for broader views of aggression in schools.

Due to the relatively homogenous nature of Hillside and Greenfield and my focus on the broader school culture, this chapter largely sets aside the issue of inequality explored by others and given a central role in Pascoe's sociology of bullying.[55] As Pascoe notes, "When we call aggressive interactions between young people . . . bullying and ignore the messages about inequality (e.g., gender inequality, embedded serious and joking relationships), we risk divorcing what they are doing form larger issues of inequality and sexualized power."[56] Calarco also notes that inequalities "hinge on the activation of particular strategies of action and the interactive processes by which those strategies of action are interpreted and rewarded in institutional settings."[57] Although Paulle's finding that teachers in urban schools frequently let "minor" provocations slide suggests that school cultures in other types of schools may be similarly constructed, future researchers should apply inhabited institutionalism to bullying and aggression in other types of schools.[58] Future researchers should also explore how person-centered definitions of bullying and aggression may contribute to racial disparities in school discipline.[59]

The fact that these data were collected more than ten years ago provides an opportunity for research exploring the ways that increased access to communication technologies outside of schools affects the interactions of students within them. During my data collection many students had cell phones, some had online social networks on sites like MySpace, and a few played online games, but the interactions facilitated by these technologies outside of school did not typically affect their in-school interactions. This was likely a function of both technological access and age. Although the age at which kids first have access to these technologies has decreased in the intervening years, fifth graders in the United States today still appear to be near the transition point for technology use, with the average child getting his or her first phone at 10.3 years old and first social media account at 11.4 years old.[60] Future research should explore how increased access to smartphones and tablets affects the school cultures of preadolescents and how this access intersects with social status and other factors. It is also unknown how virtual learning environments affect these findings.

Researchers have long argued that successful anti-bullying programs need to address school cultures rather than individuals, yet schools such as Greenfield and Hillside continue to approach bullying in individualistic ways.[61] Given the external pressures to address bullying that schools and districts face, these findings show how, at least in these schools, person-centered definitions of bullying combined with the normalization of aggression allowed both students and adults to define their own behaviors in more favorable ways, with aggressive students defining themselves as non-bullies and adults claiming the legitimacy of their anti-bullying efforts. These benefits came at the expense of students who were the consistent targets of aggression by their peers and those who may have been more sensitive to aggression (stigmatized as tattletales). From the perspective of many at Greenfield and Hillside, then, despite widespread aggressive interactions between students, to define bullying as an issue to be addressed at the level of school culture would have been inconsistent with their belief that there were very few "bullies" to address.

NOTES
1. Parts of this chapter originally appeared in Harger (2016, 2019a, and 2019b).
2. Barboza et al., 2009; Faris and Felmlee, 2011; Viala, 2015.
3. Swearer and Espelage, 2004; Migliaccio and Raskauskas, 2015; Thornberg, 2011.
4. Migliaccio and Raskauskas, 2015; Harger, 2016.
5. Merrell et al., 2008; Evans et al., 2014; Jiménez-Barbero et al., 2016.
6. Meyer, 1977.
7. Meyer and Rowan, 1977.
8. Hallett and Hawbaker, 2019. Rather than implying that these ideas are "false," the use of "myth" in this context is intended to represent a widely shared cultural ideal providing a theory of how organizations should operate (Meyer and Rowan, 1977). These cultural ideals for organizations have been referred to as "institutional logics" by later researchers (Friedland and Alford, 1991).
9. Hallett and Ventresca, 2006; Hallett, 2010; Reyes, 2015.
10. Hallett and Ventresca, 2006; Hallett and Hawbaker, 2019.
11. Hallett and Ventresca, 2006.
12. Fine and Hallett, 2014.
13. Olweus, 1993.
14. Allen, 2015; Harger, 2016.
15. Fine and Hallett, 2014.
16. Fine, 1979, 2012.
17. Fine, 1979.
18. Fine, 2012.
19. Fine, 2003; Fine, 2012.
20. Fine and Hallett, 2014.
21. Pascoe, 2007.
22. Klein, 2012.
23. AAUW Educational Foundation, 2001.
24. Pascoe, 2007.

25 Pascoe, 2007; Klein, 2012.
26 Rafalow, 2017.
27 Finkelhor et al., 2012.
28 Espelage and Swearer, 2003; Callejas (chapter 8 of this volume).
29 Viala, 2015.
30 Faris and Felmlee, 2011.
31 Harger, 2016, 2019a, 2019b, 2019c.
32 Pseudonyms are used for all names and places.
33 Eder et al., 1995; Milner, 2004.
34 Mehan, 1992; Eder and Nenga, 2003.
35 Thorne, 1993.
36 Corsaro, 1985; Eder et al., 1995.
37 Eder and Fingerson, 2002.
38 See Hallett (2010) for a discussion of a principal's attempts to bring accountability to an urban elementary school.
39 Drawing conclusions about the behavior of adults based on gender is beyond the scope of my data. It is possible that the fact that both fifth grade teachers at Greenfield were women and both at Hillside were men contributed to the types of behavior they were willing to accept in their classrooms, but it is also possible that these differences had more to do with teaching styles or the approaches to discipline taken by their principals than with gender.
40 Leff et al., 1999.
41 Evaldsson and Svahn (2012) describe a similar situation in which a group of girls uses a school's bullying intervention program as a system of retaliation against a peer.
42 Fine and Hallett, 2014.
43 See Harger (2019b) for a more detailed description of the effects of aggression and masculinity within this peer group.
44 See Harger (2019c) for a more detailed description of students' decision-making processes regarding telling on others.
45 Connell, 1995; Evaldsson, 2002; Klein, 2012.
46 Vaillancourt et al., 2008.
47 Fine and Hallett, 2014.
48 Meyer and Rowan, 1977.
49 Meyer and Rowan, 1977; Hallett and Hawbaker, 2019.
50 Hallett and Ventresca, 2006; Hallett and Hawbaker, 2019.
51 Hallett and Ventresca, 2006.
52 Meyer and Rowan, 1977.
53 Fine and Hallett, 2014.
54 Olweus, 1993.
55 MacDonald and Swart, 2004; Calarco, 2014.
56 Pascoe, 2013.
57 Calarco, 2014.

58 Paulle, 2013.
59 Jacobsen et al., 2019.
60 Influence Central, 2016.
61 Olweus, 1993; Sullivan et al., 2004.

REFERENCES

AAUW Educational Foundation. 2001. "Hostile Hallways: Bullying, Teasing, and Sexual Harassment in School." Washington, DC: American Association of University Women Educational Foundation, 2001.

Allen, Kathleen P. 2015. "'We Don't Have Bullying, but We Have Drama': Understandings of Bullying and Related Constructs within the Social Milieu of a U.S. High School." *Journal of Human Behavior in the Social Environment* 25 (3): 159–181.

Barboza, Gia Elise, Lawrence B. Schiamberg, James Oehmke, Steven J. Korzeniewski, Lori A. Post, and Cedrick G. Heraux. 2009. "Individual Characteristics and the Multiple Contexts of Adolescent Bullying: An Ecological Perspective." *Journal of Youth and Adolescence* 38 (1): 101–121.

Calarco, Jessica McCrory. 2014. "The Inconsistent Curriculum: Cultural Tool Kits and Student Interpretations of Ambiguous Expectations." *Social Psychology Quarterly* 77 (2): 185–209.

Connell, R. W. 1995. *Masculinities*. Cambridge: Polity.

Corsaro, William A. 1985. *Friendship and Peer Culture in the Early Years*. Norwood, NJ: Ablex.

Eder, Donna, with Catherine Colleen Evans and Stephen Parker. 1995. *School Talk: Gender and Adolescent Culture*. New Brunswick, NJ: Rutgers University Press.

Eder, Donna, and Laura Fingerson. 2002. "Interviewing Children and Adolescents." In *Handbook of Interview Research: Context and Method*, edited by Jaber F. Gubrium and James A. Holstein, 181–201. Thousand Oaks, CA: Sage.

Eder, Donna, and Sandi Kawecka Nenga. 2003. "Socialization in Adolescence." In *Handbook of Social Psychology*, edited by John DeLamater, 157–182. New York: Kluwer.

Espelage, Dorothy L., and Susan M. Swearer. 2003. "Research on School Bullying and Victimization: What Have We Learned and Where Do We Go from Here?" *School Psychology Review* 32 (3): 365–383.

Evaldsson, Ann-Carita. 2002. "Boys' Gossip Telling: Staging Identities and Indexing (Non-acceptable) Masculine Behavior." *Text* 22 (2): 199–225.

Evaldsson, Ann-Carita, and Johanna Svahn. 2012. "School Bullying and the Micro-politics of Girls' Gossip Disputes." *Sociological Studies of Children and Youth* 15:297–323.

Evans, Caroline B. R., Mark W. Fraser, and Katie L. Cotter. 2014. "The Effectiveness of School-Based Bullying Prevention Programs: A Systematic Review." *Aggression and Violent Behavior* 19 (5): 532–544.

Faris, Robert, and Diane Felmlee. 2011. "Status Struggles: Network Centrality and Gender Segregation in Same- and Cross-Gender Aggression." *American Sociological Review* 76 (1): 48–73.

Fine, Gary Alan. 1979. "Small Groups and Culture Creation: The Idioculture of Little League Baseball Teams." *American Sociological Review* 44 (5): 733–745.

———. 2003. "Toward a Peopled Ethnography: Developing Theory from Group Life." *Ethnography* 4 (1): 41–60.

———. 2012. *Tiny Publics: A Theory of Group Action and Culture*. New York: Russell Sage.

Fine, Gary Alan, and Tim Hallett. 2014. "Group Cultures and the Everyday Life of Organizations: Interaction Orders and Meso-analysis." *Organization Studies* 35 (12): 1773–1792.

Finkelhor, David, Heather A. Turner, and Sherry Hamby. 2012. "Let's Prevent Peer Victimization, Not Just Bullying." *Child Abuse and Neglect* 36 (4): 271–274.

Friedland, Roger, and Robert R. Alford. 1991. "Bringing Society Back In: Symbols, Practices, and Institutional Contradictions." In *The New Institutionalism in Organizational Analysis*, edited by Walter W. Powell and Paul J. DiMaggio, 232–266. Chicago: University of Chicago Press.

Ghandour, Reem, Mary Overpeck, Zhihuan Huang, Michael Kogan, and Peter Scheidt. 2004. "Headache, Stomachache, Backache, and Morning Fatigue among Adolescent Girls in the United States." *Archives of Pediatrics and Adolescent Medicine* 158:797–803.

Hallett, Tim. 2010. "The Myth Incarnate: Recoupling Processes, Turmoil, and Inhabited Institutions in an Urban Elementary School." *American Sociological Review* 75 (1): 52–74.

Hallett, Tim, and Amelia Hawbaker. 2019. "Bringing Society Back in Again: The Importance of Social Interaction in an Inhabited Institution." *Research in the Sociology of Organizations* 65B:317–336.

Hallett, Tim, and Marc J. Ventresca. 2006. "Inhabited Institutions: Social Interactions and Organizational Forms in Gouldner's *Patterns of Industrial Bureaucracy*." *Theory and Society* 35 (2): 213–236.

Harger, Brent. 2016. "You Say Bully, I Say Bullied: School Culture and Definitions of Bullying in Two Elementary Schools." *Sociological Studies of Children and Youth* 20:95–123.

———. 2019a. "A Culture of Aggression: School Culture and the Normalization of Aggression in Two Elementary Schools." *British Journal of Sociology of Education* 40 (8): 1105–1120.

———. 2019b. "On the Margins of Friendship: Aggression in an Elementary School Peer Group." *Childhood* 26 (4): 476–490.

———. 2019c. "To Tell or Not to Tell: Student Responses to Negative Behavior in Elementary School." *Sociological Quarterly* 60 (3): 479–497.

Influence Central. 2016. "Kids & Tech: The Evolution of Today's Digital Natives." http://influence-central.com.

Jacobsen, Wade C., Garrett T. Pace, and Nayan G. Ramirez. 2019. "Punishment and Inequality at an Early Age: Exclusionary Discipline in Elementary School." *Social Forces* 97 (3): 973–998.

Jiménez-Barbero, José Antonio, José Antonio Ruiz-Hernández, Laura Llor-Zaragoza, María Pérez-García, and Bartolomé Llor-Esteban. 2016. "Effectiveness of Antibullying Programs: A Meta-analysis." *Children and Youth Services Review* 61:165–175.

Klein, Jessie. 2012. *The Bully Society: School Shootings and the Crisis of Bullying in America's Schools*. New York: New York University Press.

Leff, Stephen S., Thomas J. Power, Tracy E. Costigan, and Patricia H. Manz. 2003. "Assessing the Climate of the Playground and Lunchroom: Implications for Bullying Prevention Programming." *School Psychology Review* 32 (3): 418–430.

MacDonald, Helen, and Estelle Swart. 2004. "The Culture of Bullying at a Primary School." *Education as Change* 8 (2): 33–55.

Mehan, Hugh. 1992. "Understanding Inequality in Schools: The Contribution of Interpretive Studies." *Sociology of Education* 65 (1): 1–20.

Merrell, Kenneth W., Barbara A. Gueldner, Scott W. Ross, and Duane M. Isava. 2008. "How Effective Are School Bullying Intervention Programs? A Meta-analysis of Intervention Research." *School Psychology Quarterly* 23 (1): 26–42.

Meyer, John W. 1977. "The Effects of Education as an Institution." *American Journal of Sociology* 83 (1): 55–77.

Meyer, John, and Brian Rowan. 1977. "Institutionalized Organizations: Formal Structure as Myth and Ceremony." *American Journal of Sociology* 83 (2): 340–363.

Migliaccio, Todd, and Juliana Raskauskas. 2015. *Bullying as a Social Experience: Social Factors, Prevention, and Intervention*. Burlington, VT: Ashgate.

Milner, Murray, Jr. 2004. *Freaks, Geeks, and Cool Kids: American Teenagers, Schools, and the Culture of Consumption*. New York: Routledge.

Olweus, Dan. 1993. *Bullying at School: What We Know and What We Can Do*. Malden, MA: Blackwell.

Pascoe, C. J. 2007. *Dude, You're a Fag: Masculinity and Sexuality in High School*. Berkeley: University of California Press.

———. 2013. "Notes on a Sociology of Bullying: Young Men's Homophobia as Gender Socialization." *QED* 1 (1): 87–104.

Paulle, Bowen. 2013. *Toxic Schools: High-Poverty Education in New York and Amsterdam*. Chicago: University of Chicago Press.

Rafalow, Matt. 2017. "Bad Trees, Not Apples: School-Level Influences on Bullying." Paper presented at the annual meeting of the American Sociological Association, Montreal, Quebec, August 12.

Reyes, Daisy Verduzco. 2015. "Inhabiting Latino Politics: How Colleges Shape Students' Political Styles." *Sociology of Education* 88 (4): 302–319.

Sullivan, Keith, Mark Cleary, and Ginny Sullivan. 2004. *Bullying in Secondary Schools: What It Looks Like and How to Manage It*. Thousand Oaks, CA: Sage.

Swearer, Susan M., and Dorothy L. Espelage. 2004. "Introduction: A Social-Ecological Framework of Bullying Among Youth." In *Bullying in American Schools: A Social-Ecological Perspective on Prevention and Intervention*, edited by Dorothy L. Espelage and Susan M. Swearer, 1–12. Mahwah, NJ: Lawrence Erlbaum.

Takizawa, Ryu, Barbara Maughan, and Louise Arseneault. 2014. "Adult Health Outcomes of Childhood Bullying Victimization: Evidence from a Five-Decade Longitudinal British Birth Cohort." *American Journal of Psychiatry* 171 (7): 777–784.

Thornberg, Robert. 2011. "'She's Weird!'—The Social Construction of Bullying in School: A Review of Qualitative Research." *Children & Society* 25 (4): 258–267.

Thorne, Barrie. 1993. *Gender Play: Girls and Boys in School.* New Brunswick, NJ: Rutgers University Press.

Vaillancourt, Tracy, Patricia McDougall, Shelley Hymel, Amanda Krygsman, Jessie Miller, Kelley Stiver, and Clinton Davis. 2008. "Bullying: Are Researchers and Children/Youth Talking about the Same Thing?" *International Journal of Behavioral Development* 32 (6): 486–495.

Viala, Eva Silberschmidt. 2015. "The Fighter, the Punk and the Clown: How to Overcome the Position of Victim of Bullying?" *Childhood* 22 (2): 217–230.

12

Prevention and Intervention Programs for Bullying Perpetration and Victimization

DENISE WILSON, KIRSTEN L. WITHERUP, AND
ALLISON ANN PAYNE

Bullying perpetration and victimization continue to be a public health concern in the United States and abroad. Traditional interpersonal bullying (physical, social, and verbal) involves repetitive, unwanted behaviors that involve a power imbalance, whether real or perceived, between the bully and the victim. In addition to traditional interpersonal bullying, bullying has also moved into the realm of cyberspace; cyberbullying has been defined as "willful and repeated harm inflicted through the use of computers, cell phones, and other electronic devices."[1] A meta-analysis of eighty studies reporting bullying prevalence rates among adolescents found an average rate of 35 percent for traditional bullying and 15 percent for cyberbullying.[2] Bullying prevalence estimates have varied widely, likely due to differences in measurement.[3] For example, beyond the actual occurrence, interpersonal bullying and cyberbullying have also been associated with a host of other negative outcomes. While some are more immediate, such as depression, fighting, school disengagement, stunted academic progress, school avoidance and dropping out, and suicidal ideations and behaviors, other outcomes associated with bullying occur later in life, including social and psychological maladjustment as well as lower occupational stability and success.[4] Similarly, research has found cyberbullying victimization to be associated with depression, low self-esteem, school avoidance, and later mental health and relationship problems.[5] Given these negative consequences, prevention and intervention programs are crucial to reducing the incidence of bullying perpetration and risk of bullying victimization. This chapter reviews the evidence base for bullying prevention and intervention programs and discusses the most important areas for future research.

Research Overview

The first prevention program designed to specifically target bullying behaviors was developed by Dan Olweus in the mid-1980s.[6] Since that time, prevention programs targeting bullying have been on the rise and numerous prevention programs have been developed around the world to reduce bullying behaviors.[7] Despite there being many choices of programs to implement,[8] the evidence base for the most effective programs is limited. Several researchers have conducted systematic reviews and meta-analyses to determine what works in bullying prevention.[9] The results from these studies are mixed, likely due to differences in the methodology of both the specific prevention programs and the reviews' criteria for inclusion.[10] For example, Nickerson notes difficulty in drawing conclusions due to differences in program components, developmental stages at which the program is implemented, outcomes evaluated, and settings.[11] The overall conclusion is that while bullying prevention programs are effective, reductions in bullying behaviors and victimization have been relatively modest.[12] Moreover, the positive effects are often related to the attitudes, knowledge, and perceptions surrounding bullying, as compared to actual bullying perpetration and victimization behaviors.[13]

The most rigorous and widely cited[14] meta-analysis was conducted by Farrington and Ttofi[15] in 2009, with a follow-up on the effects of specific program components in 2011.[16] In the original study, they reported that program implementation, on average, was associated with a 20 to 23 percent decrease in bullying perpetration and a 17 to 20 percent decrease in bullying victimization.[17] Gaffney, Ttofi, and Farrington recently updated the analysis and included additional studies that had been published since the original review; they report slightly smaller reductions of 19 to 20 percent for bullying perpetration and 15 to 16 percent for bullying victimization.[18] Comparable effects were also found in another recent meta-analysis that looked specifically at school-based programs involving a parent component.[19] Therefore, even though the effects are moderate, consistent evidence suggests these programs can be effective.

The Whole-School Approach

When examining program structure, the consensus is that whole-school approaches that operate at multiple levels and include multiple components are the most successful at reducing bullying perpetration and victimization.[20] Indeed, a pivotal report by the National Academies recommends taking a multitiered approach similar to the National Research Council's public health model of mental health intervention.[21] This method includes indicated, selected, universal prevention/intervention strategies to reduce bullying behaviors.[22] Selective strategies are those that specifically target at-risk youth and may be a more intense version of a universal strategy, while an indicated approach would be directed toward those already engaged in bullying or who have a history of being bullied. Most programs to date, however, have taken a universal approach that targets all members of the population regardless of their risk for bullying, such as teaching social-emotional lessons to the entire student body. The National Academies report concluded that while many of these programs have been found to be effective, the results were modest.[23] By contrast, the National Academies report notes that selective and indicated prevention programs have been found to be effective for various youth behaviors, but there are few studies of these types of interventions that specifically target bullying.[24]

Olweus Bullying Prevention Program

The first and likely most well-known whole-school multitier program is the Olweus Bullying Prevention Program (OBPP).[25] This program builds on four principles based on aggression research to be used at the individual, classroom, and school levels. These principles focus on establishing a school environment characterized by (1) firm limitations on unacceptable behaviors; (2) consistent application of both nonphysical and nonpunitive sanctions for unacceptable behaviors or rule violations; (3) involvement, positive interest, and warmth from adults; and (4) adults who act as both authorities and positive role models.[26] Building a positive school climate, improving peer relations, and reducing opportunities and rewards for bullying are the main program strategies used to reduce bullying and prevent new bullying from occurring.[27]

Ttofi and Farrington examined the effectiveness in decreasing bullying of sixteen programs that were based on the Olweus model compared with twenty-five programs that were not and found programs inspired by OBPP to be the most effective models.[28] A more recent meta-analysis by Gaffney, Farrington, and Ttofi examined the moderating effect of four specific bullying programs (including OBPP) on bullying behaviors. Their results showed that the OBPP produced the largest effect sizes for reductions in bullying perpetration: on average, the OBPP was associated with a 26 percent reduction in bullying others.[29]

Olweus and Limber recently reviewed the research that has been conducted on the actual program in Norway and the United States.[30] In Norway, the program reduced bullying perpetration by 43 percent and bullying victimization by 33 percent. By contrast, early studies conducted in the United States found mixed results, showing some positive but also negative and nonsignificant effects. A more recent large-scale analysis of the program in Pennsylvania found reductions in bullying perpetration and victimization of about 3 percent.[31] A later study showed these results were consistent across specific types of bullying (i.e., verbal, physical, indirect, and sexual).[32] The program was also associated with an increase in empathy toward bully victims, a decrease in willingness to join in bullying of others, and the belief that teachers had increased their efforts to address bullying.[33] While the magnitude of these results is smaller than that in Norway, the authors suggest calls to create new approaches to bullying are premature and that the focus instead should be on the positive effects and improvement of the school climate.

While many support and recommend the OBPP, it is not without limitations. Temko recently conducted a content analysis of the program and criticized it for being overly individualistic.[34] He concludes that the program fails to address why bullying occurs in the first place and neglects the larger social context that produces and reproduces bullying. Further, he claims that the 2007 guidebooks and questionnaire are outdated and fail to include updates to the research and changes to society and culture. For example, just as a strong link exists between overall offending and victimization for both adults[35] and juveniles,[36] there is a correlation between bullying perpetration and victimization.[37] However, the OBPP materials silo students into bully, victim, or bystander categories, claiming these roles are fairly stable over time.[38] This conceptualization fails to capture the fluid nature of bullying, especially as cyberbullying has become a new phenomenon. Temko argues that in order to be more successful, the program needs to be updated to include the social context that influences individual variations in behavior.[39]

Social Ecological Framework

Whole-school multitier programs are typically discussed within the social ecological theoretical framework. The social ecological model embeds individuals within multiple levels of increasingly distal social contexts.[40] The most proximal context includes personal relationships such as with parents and peers, followed by the school and neighborhood, and finally social and cultural norms. Individuals' outcomes result from the complex interplay between individuals and their environments, which are further influenced by developmental and contextual periods of time.[41] Migliaccio also discusses the social ecological approach in chapter 9, highlighting the important role of culture that is often neglected in research that solely focuses on individual differences. These important moderating factors can shed light on individual differences in bullying behaviors. Programs that fail to include peers, families, schools, and the broader community are unlikely to make real and lasting changes to the prevalence of bullying. The following section discusses research on prevention programs guided by the social ecological model.

Individual

The individual is at the center of the social ecological approach, and individual differences in program effects may help to explain the overall moderate effects that have been found in meta-analyses. In order for bullying prevention programs to be effective, they must allow for individual differences in response to similar environments. This means that even though a whole-school program may be effective in the aggregate, there are likely students who would benefit from alternative strategies. Divecha and Brackett criticize many bullying prevention programs for omitting the person, claiming that "a program with a singular mechanism of change extrinsic to the child, like those that employ operant conditioning, zero-tolerance, or punishment as behavior change levers, may be ineffective simply because it fails to acknowledge individual differences."[42] For example, the well-established KiVa anti-bullying program has been found to be effective in reducing bullying perpetration and victimization;[43] however, recent analyses have found that program effects were moderated by individual characteristics such as gender, temperament, and environmental sensitivity.[44]

Research also suggests that programs should move beyond the primary focus on consequences and intervention to also highlight the promotion of positive skills at the individual level.[45] For instance, Hinduja and Patchin found that students with higher levels of resilience (i.e., the ability to bounce back from adversity) were less likely to report having been bullied, and of those who were bullied, those with higher resiliency experienced less academic and emotional disruption at school.[46] Accordingly, they discuss this need to promote internal positive youth development in addition to improving the external environment and call for a specific emphasis on resilience as a protective factor that could help prevent bullying and lessen the impacts on those who are bullied.

Parents and Family

Parents and other immediate family members are the most proximal influences on the individual. Ttofi and Farrington examined the specific program and intervention elements to determine what caused the greatest reductions in bullying.[47] Of the twenty included components, parent training/meetings was most strongly correlated with reductions in bullying perpetration and the third most correlated component with reductions in bullying victimization. Huang et al. also discuss the importance of parental involvement but note there are few empirical investigations of actual effects.[48] They conducted a meta-analysis of school-based programs that involved a parental component, grouping parent involvement into four groups: parent trainings/workshops, written information, in-person communication, and home activities that involve parents. While the results did not show a difference in effect size based on type of involvement, they did highlight the importance of parent involvement overall.

Axford et al. reviewed the research on school-based programs that included a parent component, specifying that these programs typically involve parents by providing information and/or holding parent-teacher meetings.[49] The idea is that through education and support, parents will be more likely to inform the school if they suspect their child is being bullied and that the provided information will be a resource to help parents intervene at home. They also note the importance of including parents in bullying prevention and intervention components because of the established link between negative parenting and bullying behaviors.[50]

Peers

Although peers are clearly an important part of bullying prevention, there is little support for stand-alone peer-led interventions, such as peer conflict resolution. The Ttofi and Farrington meta-analysis found that peer-oriented strategies such as peer mediation, peer mentoring, and encouraging bystander intervention to prevent bullying were associated with an increase in victimization.[51] While peer-led programs often fail to decrease bullying, and sometimes even increase both attitudes supportive of bullying and bullying behaviors,[52] whole-school methods show much better outcomes in terms of both misbehavior and academic achievement.[53] The main difference is the comprehensive nature of these approaches, which address not just student behavior but the entire school climate as well.[54]

School

Given that youth spend a large amount of their time in school, that most interpersonal bullying occurs on school grounds, and that a strong relationship exists between school factors and bullying behaviors, it is not surprising that the school is the setting for most prevention and intervention programs.[55] As mentioned above, whole-school programs that reflect a culture of positivity and support have been found to be the most successful in reducing bullying. A positive school climate has also been associated with other positive outcomes, including lower levels of absenteeism, truancy, dropping out, fear, victimization, substance use, aggression, deviance, delinquency, and violence.[56]

While researchers have linked a positive school climate to lower incidences of bullying, the mediating mechanisms between these variables are unclear. In a recent study, Acosta et al. examined whether school connectedness, peer attachment, and social skills (i.e., assertion and empathy) mediated the relationship between four perceived school climate variables (i.e., clarity and consistency, teacher support, positive peer interactions, and student input) and three types of bullying (i.e., physical, emotional, and cyber).[57] Generally, they found support for their hypothesis that the link between a positive school climate and less bullying would be mediated by higher school connection, peer support, and social skills.

In a whole-school prevention program, teachers are essential to positive outcomes.[58] They are often the intervention agents in the classroom, suggesting success hinges on their ability to implement programs. In an evaluation of the OBPP, Goncy et al. found that both high observer-rated procedural adherence and quality of delivery were associated with increased student responsiveness.[59] In addition to successful quality implementation of prevention programs, teachers need to be able to identify and respond to bullying behaviors. Pas et al. implemented an adapted version of the Classroom Check-Up to see whether coaching could improve teachers' detection of bullying, use of preventative strategies, and response to bullying.[60] Compared with their control counterparts, intervention teachers were more likely to report responding to bullies with referrals to counselors and other staff, to intervene with those involved in bullying, and to report that they do not believe other adults at school do enough to address bullying. There was no significant difference in the detection of bullying.

Such support among teachers—support that facilitates communication and collaboration between the whole school and wider community—lends itself to the implementation of practices that move away from traditional discipline measures exemplified by confrontation to those that emphasize restoration and prevention. Among more promising contemporary directions for bullying intervention and prevention in schools is restorative justice. As discussed in Hutzell and Payne, schools around the world have implemented restorative justice approaches as a reaction to bullying and other incidents of student misconduct.[61] These initiatives seek to "restore the relationship between the victim and the offender by using the reintegrative shaming techniques proposed by Braithwaite,[62] as well as forgiveness and reconciliation, to reduce incidents of bullying."[63] Through restorative processes, negative actions and conflict are transformed into cooperative behaviors.[64] Such outcomes seek to promote feelings of safety and security among school community members and behavioral changes among students. Although the implementation of this comprehensive framework will require considerable adjustments across all school levels, the potential for effective outcomes for bullying victims, perpetrators, and the school community encourages the employment of restorative processes.[65] Restorative justice programs that approach bullying victimization specifically use forgiveness, reconciliation, and reintegrative shaming techniques proposed by Braithwaite[66] to restore the relationship between the bully and the bully victim.[67] Research exploring the impact of these programs finds that prevention and intervention efforts developed from this framework are meaningful and hold important implications for policy and practice aiming to reduce bullying and victimization in schools.[68]

These whole-school restorative approaches show positive outcomes in terms of both misbehavior and academic achievement.[69] The important factor is the comprehensive nature of these methods, which address not just student behavior but the entire school climate as well.[70] Studies have demonstrated that such an approach will produce positive results only when restorative justice values are adopted as a philosophy by the entire school community rather than implemented as one practice or program.[71]

Law and Policy

One critical aspect of the broader social context is the laws and policies associated with bullying. In the United States, all states have anti-bullying laws and policies that encourage schools to combat this behavior.[72] However, the content of these laws varies, and many states allow schools the discretion to decide which anti-bullying programs to implement. Furthermore, most studies of these policies have been limited to content analyses, with only a few studies examining their actual effectiveness.[73] Using the 2011 Youth Risk Behavior Surveillance System study, Hatzenbuehler et al. conducted a cross-sectional analysis of Department of Education legislative components and their effects on student bullying and cyberbullying victimization.[74] They found that students from states with at least one legislative component had a 24 percent reduced odds of reported bullying victimization and a 20 percent reduced odds of reported cyberbullying victimization. Statement of scope, description of prohibited behaviors, and requirements for school districts to develop and implement local policies were most consistently associated with reduced odds of being bullied. This study is one of the first to empirically support the beneficial effects that legislation can have on lower rates of bullying. While this study is important, more research is needed on specific components of legislation and the mechanisms that are associated with less bullying. Research is also needed on the effects of policies on bullying perpetration.

Cyberbullying

Although many researchers use the social ecological model as a framework for discussing bullying, Divecha and Brackett criticize those who fail to include Bronfenbrenner's reformulation of the model that specifies the developing person (discussed above), historical and developmental time, and interpersonal relationships.[75] A historical component that is critical to the discussion of prevention and intervention programs is the evolution of cyberbullying. The National Academies report states that, second to schools, the online context is likely the most common area where bullying occurs.[76] Unfortunately, research surrounding the effectiveness of cyberbullying interventions is scarce. A recent meta-analysis of cyberbullying intervention and prevention programs found only twenty-four studies that met inclusion criteria, and the earliest study included was published in 2012.[77] This suggests that cyberbullying intervention and prevention programs—and the evaluation of them—are still in their infancy. Furthermore, the research that has been conducted on these programs lacks scientific merit.[78] Specifically, a systematic review of cyberbullying prevention programs found most interventions are "one-time initiatives that lack sustained or integrated programming."[79] Despite this, results were similar to the meta-analysis of school-based programs,[80] albeit showing smaller effects. Programs were associated with an approximate 9 to 15 percent reduction in online bullying perpetration and a 14 to 15 percent reduction in online bullying victimization.[81]

One important consideration is whether cyberbullying-specific prevention and intervention programs are necessary or whether programs targeting traditional interpersonal bullying can be adapted to target cyberbullying as well. In other words, does the setting actually matter? Certain characteristics distinguish cyberbullying from traditional bullying, namely anonymity, permanency, lack of supervision, social dissemination by others, and an infinite audience. Some believe that due to these characteristics, it is necessary to develop programs that specifically target cyberbullying,[82] while other researchers argue it would be more effective to adapt established programs originally created for interpersonal bullying.[83] Modecki et al. conducted a meta-analysis of prevalence rates for both interpersonal bullying and cyberbullying and found a high degree of overlap in these behaviors.[84] Ultimately, they proposed that interventions should focus on behavior rather than a specific setting. Furthermore, evidence suggests that some traditional bullying prevention programs, such as OBPP, KiVa, ViSC, NoTrap!, and Cyber-Friendly Schools, have successfully reduced cyberbullying.[85] Chaux et al. also proposed considering whether interventions should take a developmental approach where traditional bullying is targeted at younger ages, followed by an enhanced focus on cyberbullying at older ages, when youth are more likely to have access to electronic devices and social media.[86] The National Academies report reinforces this idea, concluding that different types of bullying behaviors may emerge or be more prominent at different developmental stages.[87]

Future Research and Best Practices

Given the number of established programs targeting bullying and their moderate success, more research is needed to improve and adapt them based on the specific needs of all levels of the social ecological model.[88] The following section highlights the most important areas for future research.

Cyberbullying

While some argue for cyberbullying-specific prevention programs, the consensus seems to be that existing whole-school programs should be adapted to target cyberbullying. More importantly, it is likely that a developmental approach to targeting cyberbullying is necessary since this specific mode of bullying is more common in the teenage years when individuals are more likely to own and use electronic devices including access to social media sites. The training of teachers and school staff is necessary to help them learn how to intervene in cyberbullying.[89] Moreover, since teachers may not be as helpful in supporting youth in the online context, it is important that social media companies become actively involved in the prevention of bullying.[90] Research is needed to document and empirically examine the role of online resources and social marketing of bullying prevention and intervention campaigns to determine their effectiveness. Finally, family factors such as parenting style and parental monitoring of children's internet use are important risk factors for cyberbullying perpetration and victimization.[91] Parenting influences also differ by factors such as socioeconomic status and education, thus research on effective techniques to help parents with various backgrounds monitor internet use is needed.

Programs Targeting Similar Behaviors

There is a strong correlation between all forms of bullying and other problem behaviors such as aggression, violence, and delinquency.[92] In contrast to bullying, there is a long history of high-quality research detailing the strong effectiveness of various aggression and violence prevention programs. While work on these programs has recently expanded to look at impacts on bullying, more research (specifically randomized controlled trials) is needed to determine whether and how they can affect bullying.[93] This is particularly important considering the limited resources schools face, in terms of both time and finances. A study by Gottfredson and Gottfredson reported that, on average, schools are using about fourteen strategies or programs to prevent negative behaviors and promote a positive school environment.[94] Consolidating and integrating programs to create one whole-school multilevel system of support that is implemented with fidelity is likely a better approach than creating a new program for every new problem that arises. For example, Espelage, King, and Colbert reviewed the research on risk and protective factors of bullying involvement and concluded that many of these factors are related to emotional intelligence (EI) and social-emotional learning (SEL).[95] They further reviewed prevention programs that align with the EI and SEL concepts, suggesting that these programs can have positive impacts on bullying behavior. Considering the added benefits in affecting other related behaviors (e.g., academic performance, mental health), they argue this broader approach is likely to be more effective than a narrower one focusing specifically on bullying behaviors. More research is needed on the ability of SEL programs to prevent and reduce bullying behaviors and how these programs can maximize their impacts on bullying-specific behaviors.

Most Effective Components

Given that multilevel, whole-school approaches that target various aspects of the social ecological framework are recommended, it is important to determine which components are most and least effective as well as to identify components that may produce negative outcomes.[96] According to the National Academies, there is limited information on the specific components of programs that are most effective in reducing and preventing the incidence of bullying behaviors.[97] As mentioned above, Ttofi and Farrington attempted to shed light on some of the most effective program features in reducing bullying;[98] however, critics of this analysis suggest that the selected categories lack the required detail to determine the true effectiveness of such components.[99] In their updated review of the 2009 and 2011 studies, Gaffney, Ttofi, and Farrington call for a similar analysis of the studies included in their meta-analysis and plan to code intervention components in greater detail to more definitively identify what works.[100] However, it is important to note that the described relationships are correlational, and therefore causal conclusions cannot be inferred from the data. As such, primary studies of bullying prevention programs should conduct more in-depth analyses of individual program components. For example, Huang et al. note that while parental involvement is often recommended as a component, it is rarely subject to empirical investigation.[101]

Moderators

It is also important to explore how intervention and prevention program effectiveness varies by individual and more distal (i.e., school and parenting) factors. Research has shown that various risk and protective factors are related to involvement in bullying behaviors.[102] Examining whether program effectiveness aligns with these factors is paramount in understanding and supporting the overall effectiveness of bullying intervention and prevention efforts. For example, while some programs are found to be more effective with younger students (i.e., below eighth grade),[103] others demonstrate a greater impact among adolescents.[104] Perhaps all bullying intervention and prevention programs (i.e., both interpersonal and cyberbullying) need to be adapted to target a particular context in order to be more impactful. That is, as previously discussed, a focus on interpersonal bullying at younger ages and cyberbullying in adolescence may be necessary. Moreover, in building a foundation of evidence for particular programs, some studies have found that certain individual characteristics are more strongly related to positive outcomes. In two studies of the KiVa anti-bullying program, both environmental sensitivity and temperament are suggested to be important moderators of program effectiveness.[105]

High-Quality Implementation

Although the process is seldom documented, high-quality program implementation is fundamental to success.[106] The National Academies highlights that regardless of the program of choice, assessing both the program itself and the strategies to help administrators and staff engage in high-quality implementation are critical to desired outcomes.[107] For instance, when examining fidelity of implementation of the OBPP in the United States, Goncy et al. found that both high observer-rated procedural adherence and quality of delivery were positively associated with increased student responsiveness.[108]

Research across disciplines consistently shows that implementation challenges and problems moderate program effectiveness.[109] In a recent review of research on the OBPP, Olweus and Limber document common implementation issues including resistance and doubt from administration and staff, a focus on simple, short-term solutions, lack of preparedness to tackle a comprehensive program, administrative turnover, and poor fidelity of implementation.[110] These implementation issues may vary by location of the school. Schools in more urban, low-income areas may not have as many resources, resulting in individual differences in bullying outcomes.

Cost-Benefit Analyses

Another important evaluation that is rarely used in relation to bullying prevention and intervention programs is cost-benefit analysis.[111] A small number of cost-benefit analyses have been conducted on the Friends, OBPP, and KiVa bullying prevention programs. The studies revealed that these programs show promise for cost-effectiveness.[112] Additionally, in a large-scale cost-benefit evaluation of the OBPP in Pennsylvania, the Highmark Foundation found that benefits exceeded costs in relation to academic, health care, and societal outcomes.[113]

It is important to note that bullying intervention and prevention programs, particularly multilevel, whole-school approaches, are costly to implement in terms of both time and finances. While direct program costs are easy to calculate, the short- and particularly long-term benefits are more difficult. Future research should continue to examine the costs versus benefits of bullying programs, particularly the long-term benefits, as providing policy makers and funding agencies with this information is crucial to their support and buy-in for initial and continued program implementation.

Culture and Context

An important aspect of the social ecological model that is often overlooked is that individuals are embedded within multiple layers of social contexts. Individual characteristics are important in predicting who is more likely to report bullying behaviors, as are the most immediate layers such as family, peers, and the school. However, the broader cultural and social contexts of where the program is implemented are also important influences on behavior. When researchers generalize about the effects of programs, they ignore cultural and contextual differences that are likely to influence outcomes.[114] Two main areas that are often discussed in this regard are program location and stigma-based bullying.

Research has demonstrated that program location matters and that not all programs are equally effective in all places without some adaptation to local norms. For example, in an evaluation of intervention and prevention program features, Ttofi and Farrington found programs implemented in Norway were more successful than those implemented in the United States and Canada.[115] Gaffney, Farrington, and Ttofi also found differences in the effectiveness of programs by country and region.[116] Moreover, research on specific programs has found differences in effectiveness by location. For example, the OBPP has been found to be more effective in Norway compared with evaluations conducted in the United States.[117] While the reasons behind these differences are not clear, findings suggest that cultural differences are likely an important consideration in the development of appropriate strategies and program implementation.

Much of the research in this area has looked at individual and relational aspects of bullying. However, structural-level influences that are part of the social ecological model, such as stigma and bias, have been largely neglected with regard to bullying research.[118] What existing literature does suggest is that motivations for bullying and a greater likelihood of being victimized may be related to socially devalued identities, characteristics, or attributes that are reflected in the social dominance, stereotypes, and prejudices that vary by social context.[119] The National Academies recommended existing interventions should recognize the role that stigma-based bullying could play in bullying behaviors.[120] In response, Earnshaw et al. conducted a systematic review of stigma-based bullying interventions, concluding that while such efforts are becoming more numerous, they are unevenly distributed across stigmas, location, and organization.[121] They suggest stigma-based bullying intervention programs need to be multicomponent and guided by a theoretical framework.

While it is important not to ignore this type of bullying, evidence suggests that stigma may be limited in its explanatory power for victimization. Gardella et al. examined students' open-ended responses about reasons for why they were bullied.[122] While these broader social structural rationales were mentioned, they represented a small number of student responses. Thus, one could argue that existing programs could be adapted to target stigma-based bullying along with bullying behaviors motivated by other reasons.

Conclusion

This chapter provides a review of evidence for traditional interpersonal bullying and cyberbullying intervention and prevention programs. It also highlights future directions for research—ways to adapt and improve upon established programs—guided by the theoretical framework of the social ecological model. Given the negative consequences associated with traditional interpersonal bullying and cyberbullying, as well as the link between them,[123] it is crucial that specific, identified needs at all levels of the social ecological model are addressed to reduce bullying perpetration and victimization. The recommendations for future research provided in this chapter with regard to cyberbullying, programs that target behaviors similar to those associated with bullying (e.g., aggression and violence), the most effective program components, moderating factors, the quality of implementation, cost-effectiveness, as well as cultural and contextual influences seek to encourage the development and implementation of the most effective programs. Moreover, with additional research that supports a greater understanding of such initiatives, school districts can better manage the strategic use of limited school resources as they navigate between education and the widespread demand for school safety.

NOTES
1 Hinduja and Patchin, 2014, 11.
2 Modecki et al., 2014, 607.
3 Olweus and Limber, 2018, 140; Smith, 2019, 4–5.
4 Hutzell and Payne, 2018, 215–217; National Academies, 2016, 113–160.
5 Hinduja and Patchin, 2010, 214–216; Payne and Hutzell, 2017, 1164; Ybarra et al., 2006, e1173.

6 Olweus et al., 2019, 71.
7 Bradshaw, 2015, 322; National Academies, 2016, 179.
8 For overviews of specific bullying prevention and intervention programs, see Divecha and Brackett, 2020; Gaffney, Farrington, et al., 2019; Menesini, 2019; National Academies, 2016; Nickerson, 2019; Smith, 2016, 142–164; Smith, 2017, 1–13; Smith, 2019; Zych, Farrington, et al., 2017.
9 Baldry and Farrington, 2007; Cantone et al., 2015; Della Cioppa et al., 2015; Earnshaw et al., 2018; Farrington and Ttofi, 2009; Ferguson et al., 2007; Gaffney, Farrington, Espelage, et al., 2019; Gaffney, Farrington, et al., 2019; Gaffney, Ttofi, et al., 2019; Hall, 2017; Huang et al., 2019, 32–44; Hutson et al., 2018; Jiménez-Barbero et al., 2016; Lancaster, 2018; Lee et al., 2015; Merrell et al., 2008; Mishna et al., 2009; Smith et al., 2004; Ttofi and Farrington, 2011; Vreeman and Carroll, 2007; Yeager et al., 2015; Zych et al., 2015.
10 Bradshaw, 2015, 322; Nickerson, 2019, 16–18.
11 Nickerson, 2019, 18.
12 Bradshaw, 2015, 323; Jiménez-Barbero et al., 2016, 173; Lee et al., 2015, 150; National Academies, 2016, 236; Nickerson, 2019, 18; Smith, 2016, 150; Smith, 2017; Smith, 2019, 15; Zych, Farrington, et al., 2017, 66.
13 Lancaster, 2018, 594–595; National Academies, 2016, 234; Nickerson, 2019, 18.
14 National Academies, 2016, 188; Zych et al., 2015, 19.
15 Farrington and Ttofi, 2009, 322–326.
16 Ttofi and Farrington, 2011.
17 Farrington and Ttofi, 2009, 322–323.
18 Gaffney, Ttofi, et al., 2019, 124–125.
19 Huang et al., 2019, 41.
20 Bradshaw, 2015, 325–326; Cantone et al., 2015, 74; Divecha and Brackett, 2020, 106; Flannery et al., 2016, 1049; National Academies, 2016, 235; Smith, 2019, 212.
21 National Academies, 2016, 180.
22 National Academies, 2016, 181–184.
23 National Academies, 2016, 236.
24 National Academies, 2016, 236.
25 Olweus et al., 2019, 71; Olweus et al., 2019.
26 Olweus, 2003, 15.
27 Olweus and Limber, 2019, 29.
28 Ttofi and Farrington, 2011, 41–42.
29 Gaffney, Farrington, et al., 2019, 22.
30 Olweus and Limber, 2019, 30–36.
31 Limber et al., 2018, 69.
32 Olweus et al., 2019, 81–82.
33 Limber et al., 2018, 67–68.
34 Temko, 2019, 3.
35 Singer, 1981, 786.
36 Lauritsen, Sampson, and Laub, 1991, 286.

37 Kowalski et al., 2014, 1123–1124; Parault et al., 2007, 149–150.
38 Temko, 2019, 5.
39 Temko, 2019, 9.
40 Bronfenbrenner, 1979; Swearer and Hymel, 2015, 344.
41 Bronfenbrenner, 2005.
42 Divecha and Brackett, 2020, 99.
43 Sainio et al., 2019, 58–60.
44 Nocentini et al., 2018, 855–857; Nocentini et al., 2019, 395.
45 Divecha and Brackett, 2020, 106.
46 Hinduja and Patchin, 2017, 57.
47 Ttofi and Farrington, 2011, 41–42.
48 Huang et al., 2019, 33.
49 Axford et al., 2015, 244.
50 Axford et al., 2015, 248; Zych, Baldry, et al., 2017, 122–124.
51 Ttofi and Farrington, 2011, 42–43.
52 National Academies, 2016, 221–222; Ttofi and Farrington, 2011, 42–43.
53 Gardella, 2015; Morrison and Vaandering, 2012, 144–145.
54 Bazemore and Schiff, 2010; Cremin, 2010; Gregory et al., 2014.
55 Flannery et al., 2016, 1046; Lee et al., 2015, 137.
56 See Payne and Hutzell, 2017, for extensive discussion.
57 Acosta et al., 2019, 211–212.
58 Pas et al., 2019, 59.
59 Goncy et al., 2015, 446–448.
60 Pas et al., 2019, 64–65.
61 Hutzell and Payne, 2018, 224.
62 Braithwaite, 1989.
63 Ferguson et al., 2007, 403.
64 McDonald and Moore, 2001.
65 Calhoun and Daniels, 2008, 44.
66 Braithwaite, 1989.
67 Ferguson et al., 2007, 403.
68 Ahmed and Braithwaite, 2006, 365–366.
69 Gardella, 2015; Morrison and Vaandering, 2012, 144–145.
70 Bazemore and Schiff, 2010; Cremin, 2010; Gregory et al., 2014.
71 Fields, 2003, 44; González, 2012; Morrison et al., 2005.
72 Bradshaw, 2015, 322; National Academies, 2016, 261; USDOE, 2011.
73 Flannery et al., 2016, 1048; National Academies, 2016, 269.
74 Hatzenbuehler et al., 2015, e152411–e152419.
75 Divecha and Brackett, 2020, 97.
76 National Academies, 2016, 299–300.
77 Gaffney, Farrington, Espelage, et al., 2019, 146.
78 Della Cioppa et al., 2015, 67; Gaffney, Farrington, Espelage, et al., 2019, 138–139; National Academies, 2016, 96–97.

79 Della Cioppa et al., 2015, 67.
80 Gaffney, Farrington, et al., 2019, 23.
81 Gaffney, Farrington, Espelage, et al., 2019, 146.
82 Della Cioppa et al., 2015, 61–62.
83 Agatston and Limber, 2018, 88–89; Modecki et al., 2014, 608; Slonje et al., 2013, 31.
84 Modecki et al., 2014, 605.
85 Campbell, 2019, 182–184; Olweus and Limber, 2019, 34.
86 Chaux et al., 2016, 163.
87 National Academies, 2016, 292.
88 Farrington et al., 2017, 102; Zych, Farrington, et al., 2017, 81–83.
89 Agatston and Limber, 2018, 86.
90 National Academies, 2016, 299–300.
91 Wilson et al., 2019, 10–12.
92 Wilson et al., 2019, 10.
93 Bradshaw, 2015, 324; Flannery et al., 2016, 1049; National Academies, 2016, 295–299.
94 Gottfredson and Gottfredson, 2001, 323.
95 Espelage et al., 2018, 235–236.
96 Bradshaw, 2015, 328–329.
97 National Academies, 2016, 193, 279.
98 Ttofi and Farrington, 2011.
99 Gaffney, Ttofi, et al., 2019, 127; Smith et al., 2012, 439.
100 Gaffney, Ttofi, et al., 2019, 127–128.
101 Huang et al., 2019, 33.
102 National Academies, 2016, 69–102; Wilson et al., 2019; Zych, Baldry, et al., 2017, 119–124.
103 Yeager et al., 2015, 47.
104 Lee et al., 2015, 149; Ttofi and Farrington, 2011, 42.
105 Nocentini et al., 2018, 855–857; Nocentini et al., 2019, 395.
106 Bradshaw, 2015, 327; Huang et al., 2019, 35; Nickerson, 2019, 18.
107 National Academies, 2016, 223–224.
108 Goncy et al., 2015, 446–448.
109 Durlak et al., 2011, 418.
110 Olweus and Limber, 2019, 36–40.
111 Bradshaw, 2015, 328; Masiello et al., 2012; Smith, 2019, 215.
112 Smith, 2019, 215–216.
113 Masiello et al., 2012.
114 Bradshaw, 2015, 329; Earnshaw et al., 2018; National Academies, 2016; Temko, 2019.
115 Ttofi and Farrington, 2011, 42.
116 Gaffney, Farrington, et al., 2019, 21.
117 Olweus and Limber, 2019, 32.
118 Earnshaw et al., 2018, 179; National Academies, 2016, 5.

119 Earnshaw et al., 2018, 180; Gardella et al., 2020, 3–4.
120 National Academies, 2016, 102.
121 Earnshaw et al., 2018, 193–194.
122 Gardella et al., 2020, 9.
123 Wilson et al., 2019, 4–6.

REFERENCES

Acosta, Joie, Matthew Chinman, Patricia Ebener, Patrick S. Malone, Andrea Phillips, and Asa Wilks. 2019. "Understanding the Relationship between Perceived School Climate and Bullying: A Mediator Analysis." *Journal of School Violence* 18 (2): 200–215.

Agatston, Patricia, and Susan Limber. 2018. "Cyberbullying Prevention and Intervention: Promising Approaches and Recommendations for Further Evaluation." In *Bullying Prevention and Intervention at School*, edited by Jacob U. Gordon, 73–93. Cham, Switzerland: Springer.

Ahmed, Eliza, and Valerie Braithwaite. 2006. "Forgiveness, Reconciliation, and Shame: Three Key Variables in Reducing School Bullying." *Journal of Social Issues* 62 (2): 347–370.

Axford, Nick, David P. Farrington, Suzy Clarkson, Gretchen J. Bjornstad, Zoe Wrigley, and Judy Hutchings. 2015. "Involving Parents in School-Based Programmes to Prevent and Reduce Bullying: What Effect Does it Have?" *Journal of Children's Services* 10 (3): 242–251.

Baldry, Anna C., and David P. Farrington. 2007. "Effectiveness of Programs to Prevent School Bullying." *Victims and Offenders* 2 (2): 183–204.

Bazemore, Gordon, and Mara Schiff. 2010. "No Time to Talk: A Cautiously Optimistic Tale of Restorative Justice and Related Approaches to School Discipline." In *Contemporary Issues in Criminological Theory and Research*, edited by Richard Rosenfeld, Kenna Quinet, and Crystal A. Garcia, 77–86. Belmont, CA: Wadsworth.

Bradshaw, Catherine P. 2015. "Translating Research to Practice in Bullying Prevention." *American Psychologist* 70 (4): 322–332.

Braithwaite, John. 1989. *Crime, Shame and Reintegration*. Cambridge: Cambridge University Press.

Bronfenbrenner, Urie. 1979. *The Ecology of Human Development: Experiments by Nature and Design*. Cambridge, MA: Harvard University Press.

———. 2005. *Making Human Beings Human: Bioecological Perspectives on Human Development*. Thousand Oaks, CA: Sage.

Calhoun, Avery, and Gail Daniels. 2008. "Accountability in School Responses to Harmful Incidents." *Journal of School Violence* 7 (4): 21–47.

Campbell, Marilyn. 2019. "Specific Interventions Against Cyberbullying." In *Making an Impact on School Bullying: Interventions and Recommendations*, edited by Peter K. Smith, 177–201. New York: Routledge.

Cantone, Elisa, Anna P. Piras, Marcello Vellante, Antonello Preti, Sigrun Daníelsdóttir, Ernesto D'Aloja, Sigita Lesinskiene, Mathhias C. Angermeyer, Mauro G. Carta, and

Dinesh Bhugra. 2015. "Interventions on Bullying and Cyberbullying in Schools: A Systematic Review." *Clinical Practice and Epidemiology in Mental Health* 11 (Suppl 1 M4): 58–76.

Chaux, Enrique, Ana María Velásquez, Anja Schultze-Krumbholz, and Herbert Scheithauer. 2016. "Effects of the Cyberbullying Prevention Program Media Heroes (Medienhelden) on Traditional Bullying." *Aggressive Behavior* 42 (2): 157–165.

Cremin, Hilary. 2010. "Talking Back to Bazemore and Schiff: A Discussion of Restorative Justice Interventions in Schools." Paper presented at the meeting of the American Society of Criminology, San Francisco.

Della Cioppa, Victoria, Amy O'Neil, and Wendy Craig. 2015. "Learning from Traditional Bullying Interventions: A Review of Research on Cyberbullying and Best Practice." *Aggression and Violent Behavior* 23:61–68.

Divecha, Diana, and Marc Brackett. 2020. "Rethinking School-Based Bullying Prevention through the Lens of Social and Emotional Learning: A Bioecological Perspective." *International Journal of Bullying Prevention* 2:93–113.

Durlak, Joseph A., Roger P. Weissberg, Allison B. Dymnicki, Rebecca D. Taylor, and Kriston B. Schellinger. 2011. "The Impact of Enhancing Students' Social and Emotional Learning: A Meta-analysis of School-Based Universal Interventions." *Child Development* 82 (1): 405–432.

Earnshaw, Valerie A., Sari L. Reisner, David D. Menino, V. Paul Poteat, Laura M. Bogart, Tia N. Barnes, and Mark A. Schuster. 2018. "Stigma-Based Bullying Interventions: A Systematic Review." *Developmental Review* 48:178–200.

Espelage, Dorothy L., Matthew T. King, and Cassandra L. Colbert. 2018. "Emotional Intelligence and School-Based Bullying Prevention and Intervention." In *Emotional Intelligence in Education*, edited by Kateryna V. Keefer, James D. A. Parker, and Donald H. Saklofske, 217–242. Cham, Switzerland: Springer.

Farrington, David P., Hannah Gaffney, Friedrich Lösel, and Maria M. Ttofi. 2017. "Systematic Reviews of the Effectiveness of Developmental Prevention Programs in Reducing Delinquency, Aggression, and Bullying." *Aggression and Violent Behavior* 33:91–106.

Farrington, David P., and Maria M. Ttofi. 2009. "How to Reduce School Bullying." *Victims and Offenders* 4 (4): 321–326.

Ferguson, Christopher J., Claudia San Miguel, John C. Kilburn Jr., and Patricia Sanchez. 2007. "The Effectiveness of School-Based Anti-bullying Programs: A Meta-analytic Review." *Criminal Justice Review* 32 (4): 401–414.

Fields, Barry A. 2003. "Restitution and Restorative Justice in Juvenile Justice and School Discipline." *Youth Studies Australia* 22 (4): 44–51.

Flannery, Daniel J., Jonathan Todres, Catherine P. Bradshaw, Angela Frederick Amar, Sandra Graham, Mark Hatzenbuehler, Matthew Masiello, et al. 2016. "Bullying Prevention: A Summary of the Report of the National Academies of Sciences, Engineering, and Medicine." *Prevention Science* 17 (8): 1044–1053.

Gaffney, Hannah, David P. Farrington, Dorothy L. Espelage, and Maria M. Ttofi. 2019. "Are Cyberbullying Intervention and Prevention Programs Effective? A Systematic and Meta-analytical Review." *Aggression and Violent Behavior* 45:134–153.

Gaffney, Hannah, David P. Farrington, and Maria M. Ttofi. 2019. "Examining the Effectiveness of School-Bullying Intervention Programs Globally: A Meta-analysis." *International Journal of Bullying Prevention* 1 (1): 14–31.
Gaffney, Hannah, Maria M. Ttofi, and David P. Farrington. 2019. "Evaluating the Effectiveness of School-Bullying Prevention Programs: An Updated Meta-analytical Review." *Aggression and Violent Behavior* 45:111–133.
Gardella, Joseph H. 2015. "Restorative Practices: For School Administrators Considering Implementation." Nashville, TN: Vanderbilt University.
Gardella, Joseph H., Benjamin W. Fisher, Abbie R. Teurbe-Tolon, Brian Ketner, and Maury Nation. 2020. "Students' Reasons for Why They Were Targeted for In-School Victimization and Bullying." *International Journal of Bullying Prevention* 2:114–128.
Goncy, Elizabeth A., Kevin S. Sutherland, Albert D. Farrell, Terri N. Sullivan, and Sarah T. Doyle. 2015. "Measuring Teacher Implementation in Delivery of a Bullying Prevention Program: The Impact of Instructional and Procedural Adherence and Competence on Student Responsiveness." *Prevention Science* 16 (3): 440–450.
González, Thalia. 2012. "Keeping Kids in Schools: Restorative Justice, Punitive Discipline, and the School to Prison Pipeline." *Journal of Law & Education* 41:281–335.
Gottfredson, Gary D., and Denise C. Gottfredson. 2001. "What Schools Do to Prevent Problem Behavior and Promote Safe Environments." *Journal of Educational and Psychological Consultation* 12 (4): 313–344.
Gregory, Anne, Joseph P. Allen, Amori Yee Mikami, Christopher A. Hafen, and Robert C. Pianta. 2014. "The Promise of a Teacher Professional Development Program in Reducing Racial Disparity in Classroom Exclusionary Discipline." In *Closing the School Discipline Gap: Equitable Remedies for Excessive Exclusion*, edited by Daniel J. Losen, 166–179. New York: Teachers College Press.
Hall, William. 2017. "The Effectiveness of Policy Interventions for School Bullying: A Systematic Review." *Journal of the Society for Social Work and Research* 8 (1): 45–69.
Hatzenbuehler, Mark L., Laura Schwab-Reese, Shabbar I. Ranapurwala, Marci F. Hertz, and Marizen R. Ramirez. 2015. "Associations between Antibullying Policies and Bullying in 25 States." *JAMA Pediatrics* 169 (10): e152411.
Hinduja, Sameer, and Justin W. Patchin. 2010. "Bullying, Cyberbullying, and Suicide." *Archives of Suicide Research* 14 (3): 206–221.
———. 2014. *Bullying Beyond the Schoolyard: Preventing and Responding to Cyberbullying*. Thousand Oaks, CA: Corwin Press.
———. 2017. "Cultivating Youth Resilience to Prevent Bullying and Cyberbullying Victimization." *Child Abuse & Neglect* 73:51–62.
Huang, Yuanhong, Dorothy L. Espelage, Joshua R. Polanin, and Jun Sung Hong. 2019. "A Meta-analytic Review of School-Based Anti-bullying Programs with a Parent Component." *International Journal of Bullying Prevention* 1 (1): 32–44.
Hutson, Elizabeth, Stephanie Kelly, and Lisa K. Militello. 2018. "Systematic Review of Cyberbullying Interventions for Youth and Parents with Implications for Evidence-Based Practice." *Worldviews on Evidence-Based Nursing* 15 (1): 72–79.

Hutzell, Kirsten L., and Allison Ann Payne. 2018. "The Relationship between Bullying Victimization and School Avoidance: An Examination of Direct Associations, Protective Influences, and Aggravating Factors." *Journal of School Violence* 17 (2): 210–226.

Jiménez-Barbero, José Antonio, José Antonio Ruiz-Hernández, Laura Llor-Zaragoza, María Pérez-García, and Bartolomé Llor-Esteban. 2016. "Effectiveness of Antibullying School Programs: A Meta-analysis." *Children and Youth Services Review* 61:165–175.

Kowalski, Robin M., Gary W. Giumetti, Amber N. Schroeder, and Micah R. Lattanner. 2014. "Bullying in the Digital Age: A Critical Review and Meta-analysis of Cyberbullying Research among Youth." *Psychological Bulletin* 140 (4): 1073–1137.

Lancaster, Morgan. 2018. "A Systematic Research Synthesis on Cyberbullying Interventions in the United States." *Cyberpsychology, Behavior, and Social Networking* 21 (10): 593–602.

Lauritsen, Janet L., Robert J. Sampson, and John H. Laub. 1991. "The Link between Offending and Victimization among Adolescents." *Criminology* 29 (2): 265–292.

Lee, Sunhee, Chun-Ja Kim, and Dong Hee Kim. 2015. "A Meta-analysis of the Effect of School-Based Anti-bullying Programs." *Journal of Child Health Care* 19 (2): 136–153.

Limber, Susan P., Dan Olweus, Weijun Wang, Matthew Masiello, and Kyrre Breivik. 2018. "Evaluation of the Olweus Bullying Prevention Program: A Large Scale Study of US Students in Grades 3–11." *Journal of School Psychology* 69:56–72.

Masiello, Matt, Diana Schroeder, Shiryl Barto, Karla Good, Charvonne Holliday, LaShae Jeffers, Allison Messina, and Betsy Schroeder. 2012. "The Cost Benefit: A First-Time Analysis of Savings." Highmark Foundation. www.highmarkfoundation.org.

McDonald, John, and David Moore. 2001. "Community Conferencing as a Special Case of Conflict Transformation." In *Restorative Justice and Civil Society*, edited by Heather Strang and John Braithwaite, 130–148. Cambridge: Cambridge University Press.

Menesini, Ersilia. 2019. "Translating Knowledge into Interventions: An 'Individual by Context' Approach to Bullying." *European Journal of Developmental Psychology* 16 (3): 245–267.

Merrell, Kenneth W., Barbara A. Gueldner, Scott W. Ross, and Duane M. Isava. 2008. "How Effective Are School Bullying Intervention Programs? A Meta-analysis of Intervention Research." *School Psychology Quarterly* 23 (1): 26–42.

Mishna, Faye, Charlene Cook, Michael Saini, Meng-Jia Wu, and Robert MacFadden. 2009. "Interventions for Children, Youth, and Parents to Prevent and Reduce Cyber Abuse." *Campbell Systematic Reviews* 2.

Modecki, Kathryn L., Jeannie Minchin, Allen G. Harbaugh, Nancy G. Guerra, and Kevin C. Runions. 2014. "Bullying Prevalence across Contexts: A Meta-analysis Measuring Cyber and Traditional Bullying." *Journal of Adolescent Health* 55 (5): 602–611.

Morrison, Brenda, Peta Blood, and Margaret Thorsborne. 2005. "Practicing Restorative Justice in School Communities: Addressing the Challenge of Culture Change." *Public Organization Review* 5 (4): 335–357.

Morrison, Brenda E., and Dorothy Vaandering. 2012. "Restorative Justice: Pedagogy, Praxis, and Discipline." *Journal of School Violence* 11 (2): 138–155.

National Academies of Sciences, Engineering, and Medicine. 2016. "Preventing Bullying through Science, Policy, and Practice." Washington, DC: National Academies Press.

Nickerson, Amanda B. 2019. "Preventing and Intervening with Bullying in Schools: A Framework for Evidence-Based Practice." *School Mental Health* 11 (1): 15–28.

Nocentini, Annalaura, Ersilia Menesini, and Michael Pluess. 2018. "The Personality Trait of Environmental Sensitivity Predicts Children's Positive Response to School-Based Antibullying Intervention." *Clinical Psychological Science* 6 (6): 848–859.

Nocentini, Annalaura, Benedetta Emanuela Palladino, and Ersilia Menesini. 2019. "For Whom Is Anti-bullying Intervention Most Effective? The Role of Temperament." *International Journal of Environmental Research and Public Health* 16 (3): 388–400.

Olweus, Dan. 2003. "A Profile of Bullying at School." *Educational Leadership* 60 (6): 12–17.

Olweus, Dan, and Susan P. Limber. 2018. "Some Problems with Cyberbullying Research." *Current Opinion in Psychology* 19:139–143.

———. 2019. "The Olweus Bullying Prevention Program (OBPP)." In *Making an Impact on School Bullying: Interventions and Recommendations*, edited by Peter K. Smith, 23–44. New York: Routledge.

Olweus, Dan, Susan P. Limber, and Kyrre Breivik. 2019. "Addressing Specific Forms of Bullying: A Large-Scale Evaluation of the Olweus Bullying Prevention Program." *International Journal of Bullying Prevention* 1 (1): 70–84.

Olweus, Dan, Sue Limber, and S. F. Mihalic. 1999. *Blueprints for Violence Prevention, Book Nine: Bullying Prevention Program*. Boulder, CO: Center for the Study and Prevention of Violence.

Parault, Susan J., Heather A. Davis, and Anthony D. Pellegrini. 2007. "The Social Contexts of Bullying and Victimization." *Journal of Early Adolescence* 27 (2): 145–174.

Pas, Elise T., Tracy E. Waasdorp, and Catherine P. Bradshaw. 2019. "Coaching Teachers to Detect, Prevent, and Respond to Bullying Using Mixed Reality Simulation: An Efficacy Study in Middle Schools." *International Journal of Bullying Prevention* 1 (1): 58–69.

Payne, Allison Ann, and Kirsten L. Hutzell. 2017. "Old Wine, New Bottle? Comparing Interpersonal Bullying and Cyberbullying Victimization." *Youth & Society* 49 (8): 1149–1178.

Sainio, Miia, Sanna Herkama, Mari Kontio, and Christina Salmivalli. 2019. "KiVa Antibullying Programme." In *Making an Impact on School Bullying: Interventions and Recommendations*, edited by Peter K. Smith, 45–66. New York: Routledge.

Singer, Simon I. 1981. "Homogeneous Victim-Offender Populations: A Review and Some Research Implications." *Journal of Criminal Law and Criminology* 72:779–788.

Slonje, Robert, Peter K. Smith, and Ann Frisén. 2013. "The Nature of Cyberbullying, and Strategies for Prevention." *Computers in Human Behavior* 29 (1): 26–32.

Smith, J. David, Barry H. Schneider, Peter K. Smith, and Katerina Ananiadou. 2004. "The Effectiveness of Whole-School Antibullying Programs: A Synthesis of Evaluation Research." *School Psychology Review* 33 (4): 547–560.

Smith, Peter K. 2016. "School-Based Interventions to Address Bullying." *Eesti Hariduseaduste Ajakiri / Estonian Journal of Education* 4 (2): 142–164.

———. 2017. "School-Wide Interventions for Bullying: What Works?" *The Wiley Handbook of Violence and Aggression*, edited by Peter Sturmey, 1–13. New York: John Wiley.

———, ed. 2019. *Making an Impact on School Bullying: Interventions and Recommendations*. New York: Routledge.

Smith, Peter K., Christina Salmivalli, and Helen Cowie. 2012. "Effectiveness of School-Based Programs to Reduce Bullying: A Commentary." *Journal of Experimental Criminology* 8 (4): 433–441.

Swearer, Susan M., and Shelley Hymel. 2015. "Understanding the Psychology of Bullying: Moving toward a Social-Ecological Diathesis–Stress Model." *American Psychologist* 70 (4): 344–353.

Temko, Ezra. 2019. "Missing Structure: A Critical Content Analysis of the Olweus Bullying Prevention Program." *Children & Society* 33 (1): 1–12.

Ttofi, Maria M., and David P. Farrington. 2011. "Effectiveness of School-Based Programs to Reduce Bullying: A Systematic and Meta-analytic Review." *Journal of Experimental Criminology* 7 (1): 27–56.

U.S. Department of Education Office of Planning, Evaluation and Policy Development, Policy and Program Studies Service (USDOE). 2011. "Analysis of State Bullying Laws and Policies." www2.ed.gov.

Vreeman, Rachel C., and Aaron E. Carroll. 2007. "A Systematic Review of School-Based Interventions to Prevent Bullying." *Archives of Pediatrics & Adolescent Medicine* 161 (1): 78–88.

Wilson, Denise, Kirsten Witherup, and Allison Ann Payne. 2019. "Risk and Protective Factors for Cyberbullying Perpetration and Victimization." In *The Palgrave Handbook of International Cybercrime and Cyberdeviance*, edited by Thomas Holt and Adam Bossler, 1257–1282. Cham, Switzerland: Palgrave Macmillan.

Ybarra, Michele L., Kimberly J. Mitchell, Janis Wolak, and David Finkelhor. 2006. "Examining Characteristics and Associated Distress Related to Internet Harassment: Findings from the Second Youth Internet Safety Survey." *Pediatrics* 118 (4): e1169–e1177.

Yeager, David Scott, Carlton J. Fong, Hae Yeon Lee, and Dorothy L. Espelage. 2015. "Declines in Efficacy of Anti-bullying Programs among Older Adolescents: Theory and a Three-Level Meta-analysis." *Journal of Applied Developmental Psychology* 37:36–51.

Zych, Izabela, Anna C. Baldry, and David P. Farrington. 2017. "School Bullying and Cyberbullying: Prevalence, Characteristics, Outcomes, and Prevention." In *Handbook of Behavioral Criminology*, edited by Vincent B. Van Hasselt and Michael L. Bourke, 113–138. Cham, Switzerland: Springer.

Zych, Izabela, David P. Farrington, Vicente J. Llorent, and Maria M. Ttofi. 2017. *Protecting Children Against Bullying and Its Consequences*. Basel, Switzerland: Springer.

Zych, Izabela, Rosario Ortega-Ruiz, and Rosario Del Rey. 2015. "Systematic Review of Theoretical Studies on Bullying and Cyberbullying: Facts, Knowledge, Prevention, and Intervention." *Aggression and Violent Behavior* 23:1–21.

13

Understanding Culture to Combat Bullying

A Mixed-Methods Approach

ALICIA RAIA-HAWRYLAK

Researchers and school-based practitioners typically use schoolwide surveys to measure perceptions of bullying and related aspects of school climate. The ability of schools to collect and act upon these critical data has depended on access to a quality instrument and sufficient data collection tools and resources, and the presence of staff with necessary data literacy and related competencies. Some states have recently invested in open-access online dashboards to encourage or even require schools to collect school climate data, including items and/or dimensions focused on bullying behavior. The requirement to collect school climate and bullying data, and provision of tools to do so, promotes access to information that can be used to identify problem areas and monitor progress in addressing them over time. The data, when compared across and within schools, can serve to highlight equity concerns related to unequal learning conditions in schools and classrooms. Disproportionate exposure to aggression and victimization is a barrier to learning that can limit opportunities for vulnerable groups. Understanding the nature, extent, causes, correlates, and consequences of bullying behavior is critical to closing persistent achievement gaps.

Following a year embedded as a mixed-methods researcher, I was surprised to find that the survey data I collected from a high-income high school and a low-income high school told a relatively similar surface-level story about bullying. At the same time, the lived experiences of aggressive behavior I recorded through ethnographic observations and interviews at the two schools were anything but similar. In this chapter I present a case for the need for mixed-methods approaches to the sociological study of bullying and peer interpersonal aggression. I argue that to fully understand and address the cultural factors shaping the context for aggression in schools, researchers must take a grounded approach to link quantitative patterns to observed interactions and student narratives. While tremendous resources are needed to gather qualitative data in schools, the mixed-methods approach is necessary for the effective measurement and understanding of bullying patterns. Without these rich data, it is not possible to implement effective interventions or adequately measure progress in combating bullying over time.

Addressing bullying, aggressive behaviors, and the schoolwide organizational and group-level factors that produce them is essential to the pursuit of educational equity. Experiencing bullying, whether subtle or overt, diminishes the conditions for learning and has the potential to impact individual students in a range of negative ways, as has been well documented in the research literature and other chapters in this volume. The field of sociology should support effective and targeted efforts to combat bullying patterns by developing local understandings of the cultures and norms that produce them. Using qualitative, grounded methodology to further understand quantitative patterns of victimization holds tremendous promise for better understanding and intervening to reduce peer aggression. By combining an understanding of schoolwide victimization patterns from surveys with observations within smaller groups, like classrooms, sociologists can paint a detailed picture of the process of aggression. This process accounts for ecological levels of the school and includes inquiry into the formation and enactment of schoolwide culture and classroom idiocultures.[1]

In 2015, I spent a full year attending classes in two high schools in New Jersey alongside students to better understand how patterns of bullying and aggressive behavior unfold. I selected a higher income high school, referred to as Hilltop High School, and a lower income high school, referred to as Hughes High School, which were located about an hour from one another. I attended language arts and mathematics classes with students in different ability-level groupings, observing the same twenty-nine classrooms for peer interpersonal aggressive behavior. Toward the end of the school year, I conducted a survey in both schools to measure self-reported victimization, peer social norms, and personal investment in academic and social goals. These survey data were designed to reflect schoolwide patterns in experiences as well as to capture certain group-level experiences through the disaggregation of data by demographic factors and other individual factors, such as personal investment in academic success. Finally, I conducted in-depth interviews with a sample of the students I had observed. These interviews enabled me to probe into the process of bullying and aggression further and to zoom in from the macro or schoolwide view of bullying from survey data to the small-group process in classrooms. Speaking directly with students allowed me to connect events I observed to the understandings of individual students who experienced them directly. Their narratives uncovered less visible patterns of interaction and situated my observations in the broader cultural reality they experienced throughout and beyond the school day.

The Sociological Study of Bullying

Both within and outside of the field of sociology, much existing bullying research uses cross-sectional survey data to uncover patterns in aggression and victimization as they relate to group membership, identity, and other characteristics. Surveys typically measure bullying or aggressive behavior by asking students how frequently they have experienced particular types of aggression, such as verbal, physical, social, or cyber. These data reveal the perceptions and experiences of individuals at a given point in time, which aggregated can reflect a limited sense of the generalized experience of students within a school. The results can inform an understanding of differences in patterns of aggression across organizations and can also demonstrate differences within them if the data can be disaggregated by characteristics such as grade level, gender, and race or ethnicity. Yet these data do not uncover local contextual factors that shape students' actions, nor do they unpack how period effects or current events, whether local, national, or global, shape patterns over time. Survey data lack specific, key details of interactions, such as the relationships of participants and the intentions behind their interactions.

Schools, which are typically similar in their design and goals, provide differential contexts for bullying and aggressive behavior among students. Situated in these contexts are specific actors that inhabit them at various times, as students move through schools and graduate. These actors interact with, shape, and redefine cultural contexts at the schoolwide level and in small groups, such as classrooms. Their interactions lead to differential patterns of bullying both across schools and within schools, varying by cohort, social group, classrooms, and other micro contexts within the school building. This points to the need that Shepherd identified in chapter 10 to develop "a process account of culture," illustrating how the interactions of students are critically shaped by their local educational contexts. Local cultures must be studied through research protocols accounting for these processes at both the organizational and group levels, in order to effectively address bullying.

Qualitative methods are essential to understanding the content, process, and social significance of aggressive student interactions, while providing clues to their causes and implications. Observations account for the potential self-selection bias and timing bias of students taking a voluntary, cross-sectional survey. Ethnography allows for rich description and reveals variation in patterns over time. Interviews facilitate personal narration and sense making of events by respondents. In addition, combining the use of quantitative survey methodology with observations and interviews enables sociologists to understand the formation and enactment of cultural norms across levels of the school organization. A few examples of existing sociological work have begun to demonstrate the benefits of incorporating quantitative methods as part of a mixed-methods approach to exploring how school culture informs students' experiences of aggression.[2]

All forms of interpersonal aggressive behavior vary in their motivation and consequences; the relationships between actors vary as well. The very definition of any of these behaviors as "bullying" in a legal sense or under school policy depends on how these behaviors fit within a hierarchy, or power differential, and whether the behavior was part of a repeated pattern. Mandated reporting and investigations of harassment, intimidation, and bullying lead to the aggregation of qualitative bullying data in states such as New Jersey, but these data represent only those cases that rise to the level of reporting. Often this qualification is based on the power differential or repetitive nature of incidents, thus excluding from the record and study myriad other bullying behaviors and interactions embedded within the local culture.

The study of bullying alone fails to take account of other forms of aggression that do not meet the formal definition. In studying generalized aggressive interactions through a mixed-methods approach, it is possible to expand beyond the traditional definition of bullying, which depicts the behavior as an outcome of individual-level psychological or behavioral problems, and to understand these interactions and intervene to prevent them in a way that accounts for context. The typical definition of bullying requires a power differential between victim and aggressor and that the aggressive behaviors be chronic and repeated.[3] This definition fails to consider those behaviors that are not chronic and do not include a power differential but that may be just as harmful and disruptive to learning. Mixed-methods approaches that marry self-reported victimization rates from surveys with observations can capture a wider range of aggressive behaviors and typical conflict in schools.[4]

I combine survey data, ethnographic observations, and interviews to better understand the cultural factors impacting exposure to and engagement in aggressive behaviors at the level of the school, the classroom, and, to an extent, the individual student. Since the definition of bullying varies conceptually and use of the term "bullying" itself can suppress or bias self-reporting, I do not specifically measure bullying but instead capture a range of aggressive behaviors regardless of the power dynamics, content, or frequency with which they occur. I followed Donoghue and Raia-Hawrylak by focusing on generalized aggression as an alternative to bullying, as it is reported on surveys, observed in classrooms, and described in the words of students.[5]

I use an original research tool called the School Climate Understanding and Building Aspirations (SCUBA) Survey, which measures the types, frequencies, temporal and spatial locations, relational dynamics, and personal traits associated with victimization. To witness the grounded process of aggressive interactions and the influence of classroom-based idiocultures, and to understand more nuanced variation in experiences within the same school and across school contexts, I conducted ethnographic observations in two high schools across a full academic year. I observed general spaces (e.g., cafeterias, hallways) and a total of twenty-nine classrooms of varying ability levels, mainly representing students in the ninth and eleventh grades. I also conducted in-depth interviews with two randomly selected students (one classified as male, one female) from each of the classrooms I observed to get a richer sense of how culture and behavior norms are understood and enacted by individual students.

SCUBA Survey data suggest that self-reported victimization does not vary greatly across the two schools studied in terms of the percentage of respondents who report experiencing it within the prior thirty days. For example, students in both schools were equally likely to say that they had been verbally victimized. However, in Hughes, the lower-income school, students were much more likely to experience victimization in academic classrooms and for the language or content of statements to be related to a protected category (e.g., race or gender). The students were only slightly more likely to report physical victimization in Hughes compared to the higher-income Hilltop High School. Yet the nature and content of observed physical forms of victimization vary greatly. These incidents include forms of sexual harassment, such as unwanted touching; slapping, hitting, or restraining a romantic partner as a form of dating violence; "play fighting" or practice fighting with a friend that goes too far; body slamming someone in the hallway as a joke or threat; or stabbing a classmate with a pen during instruction. The targets of bullying and aggressive behavior vary greatly as well, according to the norms that guide the formation of social hierarchies in schools and classrooms. For example, norm reinforcement around gender may appear to be an issue from survey data, but observations are required to notice that transgender students are particularly vulnerable in a given setting. Similarly, various other aspects of student identity may be more or less salient as reasons for victimization. Without access to complete information about how cultural context shapes the specific norms that are enforced among peers, adults may not be able to intervene in the most targeted or appropriate ways. The mixed-methods findings, when triangulated to tell a full story, reflect important nuances in the experiences of students and in turn help to support an understanding of the causes of aggressive interactions and their impacts. Understanding the causes and correlates of aggressive interactions leads to more efficient prevention and mitigation techniques. In addition, understanding the impact of these patterns leads to more effective resource allocation when it comes to supporting students who have been victimized.

Classrooms and Small-Group Cultures

Current research on bullying does not sufficiently consider variation in exposure to aggression among students in the same school context. I consider how the schoolwide organizational culture works in concert with what I call classroom idiocultures to shape both the context of aggressive behaviors and the behaviors themselves. According to Fine and Hallett, "Culture is a form of practice, linked to local understandings, everyday interactions, and ongoing social relations . . . culture is not merely cognitive, but is revealed in action."[6] I argue that classrooms are the primary location where much cultural work occurs, and they play a vital role in structuring various interactional micro dynamics, and especially aggressive behavior. Fine argues that the small group is an understudied yet powerful force in organizing interaction, given that "the outcomes that are often attributed to large-scale social forces originate within small-scale domains."[7] The role of the small group, or classroom, in shaping students' school-based experiences is also understudied relative to bullying behavior. In particular, the extent to which academic tracking practices impact how aggressive behavior is experienced by secondary students has not been adequately considered, among other group-level factors.

Within schools, classroom groups quickly develop "routinized interaction," which fosters the socialization of individuals to common standards and the establishment of communal standards and expectations.[8] In these spaces status processes and identities become concrete, yet the norms and values that sustain social hierarchies in classrooms may vary.[9] To understand how peer interpersonal behaviors are influenced and shaped in small groups, particularly classrooms, I employ the concept of small-group idiocultures, or "microcultures that are developed from a group's opening moments and that depend on a shared recognition of solidified meaning and perspective," leading to "local cultural understandings."[10] Classrooms develop persistent idiocultures that can be analyzed efficiently through micro-ethnographic study,[11] given the time-bounded and predictable nature of the group and its goals. These idiocultures are best documented and analyzed through ethnographic observation. Clear, unspoken, persistent expectations emerged quickly in all of the classrooms I observed, remaining predictable even in the face of members' absence or replacement. Through observational data I explore how norms regarding interpersonal behavior are shaped at the organizational level of the school and how they are communicated, enacted, and sometimes challenged at the level of the small group in classrooms.

The school culture at the organizational level provides overarching norms, beliefs, and practices that shape the development of classroom-based idiocultures. Classroom-based idiocultures are developed as local understandings and shared expectations emerge, particularly as they relate to interpersonal behaviors. Students move through a variety of classroom-based idiocultures. Within these varying contexts, students exercise agency regarding their involvement in aggression, invoking their own cultural toolkits[12] and the social capital they have developed both outside and inside of school. In adhering to or challenging aspects of the school organizational culture, norms, or classroom-based idiocultures, individual students may also influence and shape the culture and context for aggression. The process by which this interpersonal negotiation takes place can best be understood through the employment of mixed-methods approaches.

As part of a mixed-methods approach, youth must be engaged directly in the measurement and investigation of bullying. Involving students in the design of survey instruments and soliciting their feedback on the appropriateness of questions and wording, when possible, is a way to improve the effectiveness of new and existing instruments. In addition to collecting quantitative data from all stakeholders (students, staff, and families when appropriate), researchers should explore other local sources of data indicating patterns of behavior. These include reviewing disciplinary data and bullying reports carefully, with the understanding that various institutional pressures and other realities may skew reporting over time. Qualitative data gathered through ethnographic observations and in-depth interviews should be used to clarify and further articulate patterns observed at the schoolwide level through survey data and to elicit the sense making of a diverse group of student respondents. Selecting as many students as possible, to represent diverse stakeholder groups within the school, will yield the most useful and complete data.

If students have become familiar with an outside researcher during extended periods of ethnographic observation, they may be more comfortable and candid in sharing their perspectives and experiences related to bullying and aggression. Ideally, researchers will supplement quantitative reports and ethnographic observations by conducting iterative interviews with students to probe further into patterns revealed through quantitative data or observations. Student focus groups may be more feasible from a resource perspective, but very careful assignment of participants and advanced norm setting are required to create a safe space where students can be candid. Observations and interviews can help researchers move beyond "what" kind of aggression is occurring to better understand who is involved, when it occurs, why it occurs (intentions and targets), and how it occurs.

Interviews with youth about bullying experiences are also essential for understanding behavioral adaptations to strict anti-bullying rules and laws for a variety of reasons. For example, anti-bullying legislation may have unintended effects on how schools and students talk about and address aggressive behaviors, which are best revealed and interpreted qualitatively.[13] Strict rules may increase or suppress reports of bullying depending on reporting norms that evolve locally among students and adults. As such, bullying reports and other less standardized disciplinary data are difficult to compare across schools, or even in the same school over time. In addition, the threat of punishment under anti-bullying legislation may cause students to adopt more covert strategies to avoid detection of bullying behaviors, such as engaging in cyber rather than visible forms of aggression in front of supervising adults.[14] Students experiencing covert victimization may not receive adequate attention or support from adults, and the best way to capture their stories may be through interviews about their experiences in a variety of settings or digital spaces.

Findings from Mixed-Methods Research on Aggressive Behavior

Survey data from the two schools provided a cross-sectional snapshot of the perceptions, attitudes, and experiences during the spring. On the surface, victimization rates were similar across the schools. About 39 percent of students in both schools reported experiencing verbal victimization. Social forms of victimization were the second most reported, with about 27 percent in Hughes and 23 percent in Hilltop indicating it occurred at least once. Threats were the next most common in Hughes, with 18 percent, where three times more respondents indicated that this occurred in the last month compared to Hilltop. Physical victimization was reported by 17 percent of students in Hughes compared with 14 percent in Hilltop. Damage to property is the least likely form of victimization, reported by 9 percent of students in Hughes and 4 percent in Hilltop. Students in Hughes are more likely to experience almost all forms of cyber victimization compared to Hilltop. Students in Hughes had significantly higher scores on a scale measuring victimization of all types.

Comparing the percentages of students who have reported victimization is not sufficient to fully understand the nature of behavior and its variation at the schoolwide and group levels. While the extent of victimization appears to be similar across the two schools, the severity and duration of interactions falling under these definitions varied extensively and systematically between the schools. As I immersed myself in the daily classroom observations, I immediately noticed significant and consistent differences in the patterns of overt aggression and victimization. The classroom occurrences I witnessed fell into relatively predictable and consistent patterns of interaction once the routines, practices, and interpersonal dynamics of the group were established. These disparities impacted the learning conditions and outcomes for students within classrooms significantly.

Students in Hughes were more likely to experience victimization in classrooms, and it was typically much more visible, severe in nature, and sustained and, for those reasons, more disruptive to learning even for those uninvolved. For example, while occasional hitting or punching occurred beyond the supervision of adults in Hilltop classrooms, behaviors including hair pulling, smacking, punching, and tripping were frequently done in Hughes classrooms in full view of adults and with little response. Often these physical forms of victimization result in continuing interactions, including provocation and response, which escalate until one party or the other backs off. In rare cases, the interactions result in physical fighting, but more often they fizzle out, though not before potentially putting all classroom members into a biophysical defense state of "fight or flight" that challenges the learning process.[15] It is also important to note that in Hilltop, students have access to laptops and phones during class time and can engage in covert interpersonal interactions using social media as a means to displace visible forms of aggression. These less visible interactions are further explained through interviewing. In Hughes, cell phones are prohibited in classrooms, and related rules are prioritized for enforcement, resulting in more visible and disruptive aggressive behaviors.

Connecting schoolwide trends to observations of grounded realities uncovered how norms are formed and communicated at the schoolwide level and enacted by staff and students within the classroom group. Academic expectations at the schoolwide level play a role in the development of idiocultures in classrooms and in turn influence norms about student interaction. In Hughes High School a majority of students (53 percent) disagreed or strongly disagreed with the statement that the school prepares them for college; in Hilltop, 90 percent of students agreed or strongly agreed with the statement. However, students in Hughes were equally invested in attitudinal scales related to academic goals compared to Hilltop. Students in Hughes were significantly more likely to perceive that other students think it is normal or funny to get in trouble. Competing norms around the normalcy of getting in trouble shaped the context for aggression in content area classes. Observations reveal that much visible aggression and victimization behavior was ignored by teachers or met with warnings in Hughes; because the behaviors were so frequent and ubiquitous, reacting to every instance would take up much of the available class time.

I observed three main elements of school organizational culture and classroom-based idiocultures that shape the contexts in which aggressive interactions unfold at both levels. These are the ways academic and aspirational norms, disciplinary norms, policies, and informal practices, and the unique "everyday practices" or routines emerge among specific classroom groups. While it is possible to measure perceptions of academic culture and discipline at the schoolwide level via survey, these data do not reflect how norms and practices related to these factors are enacted differently in various spaces, shaping the interactional field for bullying behavior in important ways within individual classrooms. For example, disciplinary policies may exist in a schoolwide code of conduct but may be differentially applied in different classrooms; one teacher may ignore a particular behavior, while another may meet it with a harsh, zero-tolerance response. Similarly, while the academic culture was not as strong at the organizational level in lower-income Hughes High School, there were teachers who fostered a strong motivation to learn and succeed among students, regardless of ability level. The ways teachers structure time, the norms of playfulness among peers, and other predictable patterns of behavior developed and sustained in small classroom groups shaped exposure to victimization.

At the classroom level, key factors that further differentiate outcomes are academic tracking, the classroom teacher(s), and the student peer culture that emerges in a particular group, which can be understood and documented only within that specific group. At this time, very little research exists on how academic tracking is related to victimization. As a function of shared understandings and expectations in classrooms emphasizing high academic aspirations, students in these classrooms are theoretically most likely to refrain from visible bullying or to strategically displace it outside of the classroom. They seek to maximize achievement and avoid getting in trouble. Students in lower-tracked classrooms are more willing to risk punishment if aggressive behaviors or interactions are seen as a gateway to higher social status.[16] Research on disciplinary climate explores the relationship between students' schoolwide perceptions of fairness and legitimacy and school climate outcomes including bullying.[17] More mixed-methods or qualitative research is needed to document inconsistencies or disparities between real-time observations in classrooms reflecting which behaviors are ignored and which are addressed and the nature of the disciplinary or restorative response. Doing so can help hold school leaders accountable for disproportionate responses to aggressive behavior and reduce racial disparities in punishment, while also making visible racialized forms of victimization that may have gone underreported or unaddressed in some contexts. Interviews with students provide a narrative description and sense making for how the schoolwide norms around discipline and adult intervention are enacted differently not only in the classrooms observed but also in other unobserved classrooms attended by that student for comparison.

Qualitative research, when paired with quantitative data or reports, helps counter the idea that there are "bad schools" with rampant bullying and better schools where less bullying takes place. Instead, the data reveal the ways in which students have varied experiences depending on their classroom assignment and academic tracking. Hilltop High School, an organized and well-resourced, academically rigorous school, where most students have high academic aspirations, still houses classrooms that possess divergent academic and behavioral expectations that, in turn, lead to disproportionately high exposure to aggressive behavior. In Hughes High School, which is underresourced and generally chaotic in terms of behavior, it is less clearly messaged that students are expected to achieve academically and attend college at the schoolwide level. Yet there are classrooms there in which teachers promote higher expectations and less aggressive behavior, even compared to certain settings within Hilltop High School.

The qualitative findings also counter the idea that there are "bad students" or "bullies" who act out regardless of contextual factors. Specific students whom I observed engaging in aggressive interactions in one classroom behaved quite differently in other classrooms. Acknowledging that student behavior varies according to small-group culture grants more agency to students as individual actors with unique cultural repertoires they can invoke during various points in the school day. It suggests that targeted behavioral interventions, which typically take place at the level of individual students whose aggression is most visible, are not enough. Instead, interventions should involve examination of both the macro- and micro-level contexts in which problematic behaviors are enacted. To fully understand and reduce patterns of aggression in schools, the organizational culture, classroom idiocultures, and individual "cultural toolkits" of students must be explored and theorized in concert.

Recommendations and Interventions

Education policy is beginning to move away from anti-bullying approaches that simply discourage negative interpersonal behaviors to a focus on overall school climate and related learning conditions as shaping victimization and other outcomes. The assessment of culture and climate at both the organizational and group levels is necessary for identifying data-driven needs, but at this time most school climate reform efforts rely on cross-sectional, aggregated data to pinpoint areas for intervention. Disaggregation of responses by subgroups of students can highlight equity issues, but it is also important to account for the process by which engrained culture is informing stakeholder interactions and impacting climate. Sociologists can contribute by creating and deploying study designs and metrics that seek to understand how culture informs climate at various levels, putting quantitative and qualitative data in conversation to reveal common behavioral patterns and identify targeted areas of need.

Expanding youth interpersonal behaviors of interest to sociologists and others beyond "bullying" to include the full range of youth interpersonal aggressive behaviors, is a first step to improving our understanding of these behaviors and our ability to prevent various forms of victimization. Eliminating the term "bullying" from surveys and interviews may help sociologists gather data on a wider range of negative behaviors, as has been shown to increase reporting compared with tools that use the word.[18] Observing victimization allows researchers to conceptualize additional analytical categories that do not meet the strict definition of bullying but still carry potentially negative consequences for involved students. It is important to distinguish between isolated incidents and those that occur ritualistically and are predictable within the local culture. More difficult is distinguishing between playful interactions and those that are intentionally harmful, although body language and relational dynamics support adults' abilities to interpret intent and follow-up questions or interviews can clarify further.

In this study, analytical categories of aggressive behavior that emerge from ethnographic observations include playful and isolated incidents, playful and ritualistic incidents, intentionally harmful and isolated incidents, and intentionally harmful and ritualistic incidents. These observational categories may help distinguish between bullying and conflict and to better understand their roots in culture. Assigning incidents or observations into these categories requires an understanding of how they fit in a larger pattern of behavior, through a grounded approach. Providing training to teachers and staff members as qualitative researchers with a sociological lens reduces the amount of resources necessary to fully uncover patterns of aggression and makes it feasible for these practices to be scaled in schools. Doing so empowers adults to use observational data to interrogate their own presumptions about bullying patterns in their school and to guide interventions to prevent specific forms of bullying within different settings in the building. Training school-based staff to document interactions as researchers and understand the differences will also better equip them to address the aggressive behavior with students directly and system-wide at the organizational level, depending on which patterns emerge.

School staff should be also trained in the use of standardized instruments for collecting qualitative classroom climate data through systematic classroom observation protocols. Once these data are collected, they must be systematically analyzed to identify needs and plan for evidence-based interventions to reduce problematic peer behaviors. A major barrier for most schools is carving out the time needed for leaders to engage in data analysis and strategic planning for bullying reduction and school climate improvement. Yet the time dedicated to designing and delivering instruction will be squandered if the interpersonal conditions for successful learning are not in place. Teacher preparation programs should focus on the development of educators' inquiry skills around the collection and analysis of local data (both quantitative and qualitative) from their classrooms. This training would equip educators to gather data to understand how everyday dynamics in their classrooms set the context for interpersonal behaviors.

By grounding research on aggression in theories related to culture and power, sociologists can also uncover how differences in cultural background between educators and students may lead to misunderstandings and disproportionate punishment of students of color. When educators become more aware of their own biases and are able to reflect on qualitative data that reveal these biases in action, they will be better able to understand how their responses to student behaviors are situated within a system of oppression. Using data to make educators more aware of their biases and reactions to perceived misbehavior could reduce disciplinary disparities related to aggressive behaviors and foster higher expectations for all students, which in turn builds a stronger academic and aspirational culture and reduces the context for aggression.

Emdin recommends techniques that empower students to participate in a dialogue about how to improve their classroom environments, similar to the use of interviewing or focus groups by researchers.[19] Emdin terms such dialogue as a "cogen" or cogenerative dialogue to generate plans for action for improving the classroom and assist in bridging divides between students and teachers, and students of different backgrounds.[20] The "cogen" model may provide a rich source of qualitative data for understanding bullying and aggression, guiding interventions, and monitoring progress over time.

Interventions to reduce bullying must shift from a punitive approach to a more culturally sustaining and restorative approach. Anti-bullying legislation frequently focuses on the reduction or prevention of problem behaviors, without identifying the root causes of the behaviors or equipping students (and staff) with positive skills or competencies to respond to conflict or interact positively with their peers. As the short- and long-term positive outcomes associated with organizational and instructional competency-building approaches become better understood,[21] schools should consider competency-building approaches that also seek to create more restorative cultural norms and practices as an alternative to harsh discipline. These approaches should be equity informed and should involve efforts to build the cultural competence of educators in order to reduce disproportionate punishment and avoid perpetuating institutional bias toward predominantly white and middle-class behaviors. Efforts to build peer interventions and student leadership, as described by Shepherd in chapter 10, are also essential for changing the organizational and group cultures that shape aggressive behaviors.

Disparities in learning conditions and environments should be regarded as a major unaddressed barrier to achieving educational equity and access for all students. The current focus on bullying, through research and policy, fails to capture more common forms of interpersonal peer aggression. Efforts to reduce aggressive behaviors and improve school climate fall short of measuring and understanding cultural factors that shape climate and conditions for learning. Sociologists must be engaged in the problem-solving process related to improving school culture and climate in order to fully account for the structural, organizational, and group-level factors that determine opportunities students receive in various settings. Sociologically informed systems-level change should drive the development of contextually specifically reform efforts, with the goals of reducing peer aggression and improving learning opportunities for all students.

Education and youth experiences were radically reshaped by events in 2019 and 2020. The COVID-19 pandemic and the racial reckoning that followed the George Floyd murder, situated within the intensely divisive political rhetoric of the 2020 presidential election, amounted to period effects drastically shaping the context and content of youth aggression. The sociological lens is particularly important for understanding how these events have disrupted and shaped bullying patterns in schools.

While some schools observed an increase in reported bullying incidents during the COVID-19 pandemic, many recorded a decrease in these incidents during the same period. The aggregation of statistics on bullying incidents during this time will ultimately shed light on whether *reported* incidents of bullying were different when students were not together in face-to-face instruction. In this analysis, it will be critical to uncover the process by which aggressive attitudes and behaviors occur in virtual and hybrid instruction, and this requires in-depth, mixed-methods data collection.

Mixed-methods approaches will also be critical to documenting and understanding the ways in which youth interpersonal norms and behaviors are changing during this transitional and transformative moment in education and society at large. The post-COVID-19 return to "normalcy" and in-person schooling will also likely reset previous social hierarchies, norms, and patterns of behavior in ways that will require new forms of assessment and use of varied research methods to adequately understand and address the context for victimization.

NOTES

1 Doll et al., 2004.
2 Milner, 2004; Crosnoe, 2011; Harger, 2019.
3 Gladden et al., 2014; Olweus, 1992.
4 Collins, 2011; Paluck et al., 2016.
5 Donoghue and Raia-Hawrylak, 2016.
6 Fine and Hallett, 2014.
7 Fine, 1987, 2012.
8 Fine, 1987, 2012.
9 Faris and Felmlee, 2011.
10 Fine, 1987, 2012.
11 Fine, 1987, 2012; Fischer, 1968.
12 Swidler, 1986.
13 Raia-Hawrylak and Donoghue, 2016.
14 Raia-Hawrylak and Donoghue, 2016.
15 Vogel and Schwabe, 2016.

16 Milner, 2004; Faris and Felmlee, 2011.
17 Konold and Cornell, 2015.
18 Kert et al., 2010.
19 Emdin, 2016.
20 Emdin, 2016.
21 Domitrovich et al., 2017; Durlak et al., 2011; Gregory and Fergus, 2017; Portnow et al., 2018.

REFERENCES

Collins, Randall. 2011. "The Inflation of Bullying: From Fagging to Cyber-effervescent Scapegoating." *Sociological Eye*, July 7. http://sociological-eye.blogspot.com.

Crosnoe, Robert. 2011. *Fitting In, Standing Out: Navigating the Social Challenges of High School to Get an Education*. Cambridge: Cambridge University Press.

Doll, Beth, Samuel Song, and Erin Siemers. 2004. "Classroom Ecologies That Support or Discourage Bullying." In *Bullying in American Schools: A Social-Ecological Perspective on Prevention and Intervention*, edited by Dorothy L. Espelage and Susan M. Swearer, 161–183. Mahwah, NJ: Lawrence Erlbaum.

Domitrovich, Celene E., Joseph A. Durlak, Katharine C. Staley, and Roger P. Weissberg. 2017. "Social-Emotional Competence: An Essential Factor for Promoting Positive Adjustment and Reducing Risk in School Children." *Child Development* 88 (2): 408–416.

Donoghue, Christopher, and Alicia Raia-Hawrylak. 2016. "Moving beyond the Emphasis on Bullying: A Generalized Approach to Peer Aggression in High School." *Children & Schools* 38 (1): 30–39.

Durlak, Joseph A., Roger P. Weissberg, Allison B. Dymnicki, Rebecca D. Taylor, and Kriston B. Schellinger. 2011. "The Impact of Enhancing Students' Social and Emotional Learning: A Meta-analysis of School-Based Universal Interventions." *Child Development* 82 (1): 405–432.

Emdin, Christopher. 2016. *For White Folks Who Teach in the Hood: And the Rest of Y'all Too*. Boston: Beacon.

Faris, Robert, and Diane Felmlee. 2011. "Status Struggles: Network Centrality and Gender Segregation in Same- and Cross-Gender Aggression." *American Sociological Review* 76 (1): 48–73.

Fine, Gary Alan. 1987. *With the Boys: Little League Baseball and Preadolescent Culture*. Chicago: University of Chicago Press.

———. 2012. *Tiny Publics: A Theory of Group Action and Culture*. New York: Russell Sage Foundation.

Fine, Gary Alan, and Tim Hallett. 2014. "Group Cultures and the Everyday Life of Organizations: Interaction Orders and Meso-analysis." *Organization Studies* 35 (12): 1773–1792.

Fischer, John L. 1968. "Microethnology: Small-Scale Comparative Studies." In *Introduction to Cultural Anthropology: Essays in the Scope and Methods of the Science of Man*, edited by James A. Clifton, 374–401. Boston: Houghton Mifflin.

Gladden, R. Matthew, Alana M. Vivolo-Kantor, Merle E. Hamburger, and Corey D. Lumpkin. 2014. "Bullying Surveillance among Youths: Uniform Definitions for Public Health and Recommended Data Elements. Version 1.0." Centers for Disease Control and Prevention. www.cdc.gov.

Gregory, Anne, and Edward Fergus. 2017. "Social and Emotional Learning and Equity in School Discipline." *Future of Children* 27:117–136.

Harger, Brent. 2019. "A Culture of Aggression: School Culture and the Normalization of Aggression in Two Elementary Schools." *British Journal of Sociology of Education* 40 (8): 1105–1120.

Kert, Allison S., Robin S. Codding, Georgiana Shick Tryon, and Mariya Shiyko. 2010. "Impact of the Word 'Bully' on the Reported Rate of Bullying Behavior." *Psychology in the Schools* 47 (2): 193–204.

Konold, Timothy R., and Dewey Cornell. 2015. "Measurement and Structural Relations of an Authoritative School Climate Model: A Multi-level Latent Variable Investigation." *Journal of School Psychology* 53 (6): 447–461.

Milner, Murray. 2004. *Freaks, Geeks, and Cool Kids: American Teenagers, Schools, and the Culture of Consumption.* New York: Routledge.

Olweus, Dan. 1992. "Bullying among Schoolchildren: Intervention and Prevention." In *Aggression and Violence throughout the Life Span*, edited by Ray D. Peters, Robert J. McMahon, and Vernon Quinsey, 100–125. Newbury Park, CA: Sage.

Paluck, Elizabeth Levy, Hana Shepherd, and Peter M. Aronow. 2016. "Changing Climates of Conflict: A Social Network Experiment in 56 Schools." *Proceedings of the National Academy of Sciences* 113 (3): 566–571.

Portnow, Sam, Jason T. Downer, and Joshua Brown. 2018. "Reductions in Aggressive Behavior within the Context of a Universal, Social Emotional Learning Program: Classroom- and Student-Level Mechanisms." *Journal of School Psychology* 68:38–52.

Raia-Hawrylak, Alicia, and Christopher Donoghue. 2016. "Assessing the Impact of Emerging Anti-bullying Legislation on Children and Youth." *Sociological Studies of Children and Youth* 20:167–184.

Swidler, Ann. 1986. "Culture in Action: Symbols and Strategies." *American Sociological Review* 51:273–286.

Vogel, Susanne, and Lars Schwabe. 2016. "Learning and Memory under Stress: Implications for the Classroom." *NPJ Science of Learning* 1 (1): 1–10.

14

Full of Bull

Militarized Capitalism, Education, and Psychologists

YALE R. MAGRASS AND CHARLES DERBER

Bullying has been a means of controlling people, putting them in "their place," for perhaps as long as there have been humans.[1] Until about twenty years ago, it was dismissed as "normal," a rite of passage that children and adolescents must go through and "get over." Some endure relatively little of it—perhaps they are bullies themselves—and it leaves them with little long-term impact. For others, it is a trauma that leaves lifelong scars.

Bullying affects people of all ages, but in America children and adolescents are being prepared for a bullying society, which we call militarized capitalism, one that needs people who are simultaneously aggressive and docile—in other words, bullies and victims. In militarized capitalism, institutions and their leaders bully while the young must learn their place within a hierarchy—some on top, some on the bottom. Among adolescents there will be jockeying for position, with the most successful becoming bullies, the least dominant becoming victims, and others in the middle who can bully those below them but are forced to submit to those above. Bullying will not end by simply telling people to "Stop Bullying!," just as Nancy Reagan's "Just Say No!" campaign failed to end drug addiction. Rather, reducing bullying will require a fundamental social transformation—turning away from militarized capitalism, which is actually the essence of American society.

We live in a state of militarized capitalism. Capitalism assumes competition—winners and losers. Militarism requires violence, aggression, and submission to authority. Bullying builds these very traits. Psychology is inadequate to understand the cause and power of bullying. Indeed, bullying is about power, and psychology hardly has a concept of power. It focuses on individuals, their attitudes, their mental disorders, and therapeutic change, and neglects how they are constrained by institutional imperatives.

The psychological approach to bullying overlooks the root of the problem. When children or adults bully, they are responding to the norms or incentives of their companies and their militarized society. They are not "sick" or maladjusted or "under-socialized"; they are rather already well adjusted to the larger system and don't need therapy to become further adjusted.

Bullying is the means through which the corporate empires were built. Carnegie and Rockefeller intimidated and threatened their rival capitalists to cede them an ever-larger share of the market. They brought in Pinkerton goons to beat striking workers into submission. Workers were forced to either sign "yellow dog" contracts and pledge not to join unions or be thrown into the street. Similar bullying practices continue today. Corporations warn entire communities they will shut down factories and undermine the local economy if they do not accept low wages and minimal regulations. Banks entice consumers to borrow through predatory loans and then raise interest rates and threaten foreclosure. Through advertising, children and adolescents are told they must have the coolest toys and clothes. Otherwise they will not be "with it" but instead will be outcasts who deserve to be shunned and bullied.

Capitalism is a ruthlessly competitive system in which all capitalists—whether corporations or individual entrepreneurs—have no choice but to compete furiously. Karl Marx argued that capitalists who do not compete with the ferocity of sharks, going for the kill, will be destroyed by rivals who are committed to the economic battlefield and to winning at all costs. This is an economic version of militarism, and it mirrors the world of the schoolyard bully—dominate or die.

This systemic competition incentivizes even "nice" capitalists toward bullying workers, consumers, and fellow capitalists. Corporations that do not bully workers—by paying low wages and breaking unions and constantly bullying those who seek to challenge the power of the companies—will typically be at competitive disadvantage with those who do, since bullying leads to high corporate profits, as in McDonald's and other fast-food giants, thus attracting more capital from the financial markets. Investors follow the money, just as sharks follow blood in the water. Corporations that do not bleed their workers by cutting wages and benefits—and intimidating those who challenge their degradation—will tend to see reduced profits and lose out to their competitors in the capital markets. This is a structural reality faced by all capitalists whatever their personality—and shows the need to move from a psychological paradigm to one focusing on structural imperatives.

There is hope. An anti-bullying movement is developing in parts of U.S. society. Even as power and wealth inequalities grow larger, we are seeing a revulsion in significant sectors of U.S. society against personal bullying, especially among children. In America, a debate is emerging over bullying, which may be a reflection of a larger "culture war." One side identifies with a tough great nation with whom nobody dares mess. These people fear creating a "wimpy" generation and would want the young to learn bullying. On the other side, there is a counterculture that emphasizes values of compassion, equality, nonviolence, simple living associated with a rejection of consumerism and materialism, and peace, as well as harmony with nature. This counterculture has helped nourish a strong "anti-bullying" sensibility in parts of the population.

However, the anti-bullying movement appears to be constrained by the micro, individual paradigm of bullying that we have critiqued. It focuses on personal bullying and mainly seeks conversations and policies that deal with young people and the schools. Its discourse is largely captured by the psychological and therapeutic view of bullying, failing to reflect the sociological imagination and our macro paradigm that sees bullying as a product of militarism and corporate capitalism. For the anti-bullying movement to succeed, it must recognize it is not enough to focus on interpersonal bullying, especially among children, but must instead challenge the militarized capitalist institutions that nourish bullying. The anti-bullying movement must be one to transform all of American society, from top to bottom.

Participation in social movements by young people, such as the hundreds of thousands of schoolchildren in the United States who have engaged in "climate strikes" by refusing to go to school, points to one possible way to build a more meaningful anti-bullying culture. Following the example of sixteen-year-old Greta Thunberg, the Swedish teenager who sparked a global student climate movement by going on strike outside her own high school, is a symbol of such a possibility. Thunberg, who talks about her Asperger syndrome as an empowering asset, was bullied in elementary school. She became isolated and depressed. But Thunberg, supported by a Swedish culture that has not embraced militarized capitalism, began learning about climate change and became totally focused on how the adult generation was, in a sense, bullying her own generation into passive acceptance of a violent system attacking people and the environment. Sensing that she and her fellow students would not live a full or healthy life as the environment declined, Greta took power into her own hands. By 2020 she had become a leader of millions of schoolchildren who were launching their own school strikes and building a "climate justice" movement around the world, focused on changing the social system. It is emerging as a global movement that is increasingly intersectional, looking at climate change as a result of capitalist greed, endless wars, racism, and discrimination. Thunberg talks of a system that uses violence against vulnerable and powerless people, such as kids like herself who have been bullied, and she sees the solution not in therapy but in movements to transform society. Thunberg and her fellow teenaged activists may not have read C. Wright Mills, but they are inspired by the sociological imagination. They may offer the best example of how not just to reduce bullying but to save the planet.

NOTES

Editor's Note: For a response to this essay, see chapter 15 by Ann Farrell and Tracy Vaillancourt.

1   Some of the material in this chapter has been drawn from our book *Bully Nation* and several of our published articles and interviews in *Truthout*, including Derber and Magrass, "Trump Card: The Bully Who Exposes Our Bully Nation," *Truthout*, May 17, 2016, and Mark Karlin, "How Capitalism Fosters Bullying," *Truthout*, October 16, 2016.

15

Bullying from a Psychological Perspective

A Response to Magrass and Derber

ANN H. FARRELL AND TRACY VAILLANCOURT

As highlighted in the introductory chapters, bullying is examined across multiple disciplines, including education, medicine, epidemiology, criminology, social work, and, of relevance to this response, sociology and psychology. There are several similarities between sociological and psychological research on this topic. For example, as discussed by Faris and Faris in chapter 2, the most recognized definition of bullying includes intentionally harmful and repetitive behavior that occurs in the context of a power imbalance.[1] Although the original definition advanced by Olweus centered on more overt aspects of power such as age, size, and physical strength, like sociologists, psychologists have expanded the definition of power to include less visible forms, with the most salient one being social power. Therefore, contrary to the claim made by Magrass and Derber in chapter 14 that psychology does not have a concept of power, we argue that not only does psychology have a concept of social power, but the understanding of power dynamics is a critical component of psychologists' efforts to investigate and prevent bullying.

The Importance of Social Power

As discussed by Magrass and Derber, social hierarchy is a fundamental component of human society. Individuals often engage in zero-sum competitions for positions at the top of the hierarchy in order to secure social power. Sociologists and psychologists share the important value placed on social power for understanding bullying. For example, findings from Vaillancourt et al.'s seminal psychological study demonstrate the significance of investigating social power by revealing a dual taxonomy of bullying perpetration.[2] Using peer nominations, Vaillancourt et al. found that all bullies had some degree of explicit power, which was achieved through coercive methods that elicited fear, compliance, and submission. What differentiated subtypes of bullies however was the degree to which they exerted implicit power. Implicit power was afforded to bullies who possessed characteristics valued by the peer group such as physical attractiveness, wealth, and athleticism. Results indicated that it was the mélange of explicit and implicit power that engendered peer approval, respect, and admiration (i.e., peer-perceived popularity). Vaillancourt et al. found that only a minority of perpetrators (less than 10 percent), in contrast to high-status bullies, relied exclusively on explicit power. These bullies were cruel and rejected, socially impeded, and psychologically maladjusted. They were also low on peer-perceived popularity and were rated much lower on admired and desired features. It is worthy to note that it is this minority group of low-status bullies from whom many of the misconceptions about psychological maladjustment are born.[3] Moreover, because this group is so impaired and so obvious, they garner most of the attention of the general public and, unfortunately, that of educators as well. Considering that only a small fraction of bullies are in fact maladjusted, we disagree with the argument made by Magrass and Derber in their chapter that psychological bullying research focuses only on mental disorders and therapeutic approaches.

Since this publication by Vaillancourt et al.,[4] researchers from around the world have replicated the strong link between bullying perpetration and peer-perceived popularity[5] and the role that peer-valued characteristics play in this association.[6] Researchers have also documented the challenges of reducing bullying, which center on Vaillancourt et al.'s assertion that it is difficult to persuade individuals to give up their source of power. Indeed, because bullying behavior serves a utilitarian purpose, it tends to be resistant to the most ardent efforts at curtailing it.[7] This point is well illustrated by Garandeau et al., who found that the bullies most impervious to the effects of their anti-bullying interventions were those who wielded the most power in their social group.[8] Therefore, we agree with Magrass and Derber that interpersonal features of bullying along with macro-level institutions that reinforce the utilitarian abuse of power must be targeted in order to effectively reduce bullying.

In sum, psychologists recognize that bullying involves an interaction between individuals' characteristics and their peer group, with social power afforded and reinforced by the peer group.[9]

The Role of Individual Differences

As noted by Magrass and Derber, one area of bullying research in psychology that differs considerably from bullying research in sociology pertains to the role of individual differences. Some psychologists examine whether perpetrators of bullying are likely to possess certain temperament or personality traits. The most prominent traits associated with bullying perpetration reflect antisocial tendencies characterized by exploitativeness and a lack of empathy,[10] including specific traits such as psychopathy,[11] narcissism,[12] and Machiavellianism.[13]

Although Magrass and Derber criticize psychological studies on bullying and personality, psychologists acknowledge that individual differences are one of many important and interacting factors that contribute to bullying. Accordingly, three important caveats should be recognized. First, these traits are examined as variations of "normal" personality traits rather than pathological personality disorders. For example, individuals higher on narcissism may be more likely to engage in bullying perpetration, but this does not necessarily mean that these individuals have narcissistic personality disorder, a clinical disorder that has specific features and impairments. Second, these associations do not mean that an individual higher on a trait such as narcissism will engage in bullying. Instead, these associations mean that a person with higher levels of antisocial traits such as narcissism is more likely to use bullying for social power relative to a person with lower levels of narcissism. In contrast, an individual with lower levels of narcissism might prefer to use prosocial strategies to gain power such as being helpful, at least relative to an individual with higher levels of narcissism. Third, these findings with personality make sense considering the broader social context of that specific individual. To understand the broader social context, Bronfenbrenner's social-ecological theory[14] has been a popular framework applied to psychological research on bullying.[15]

Bronfenbrenner's model recognizes that a child's development occurs within a series of nested systems, with the most immediate system comprising the child, their characteristics, and their immediate social settings (e.g., family, teachers, peers). Applied to bullying, a child is more likely to use bullying in a school classroom that has a competitive climate characterized by an asymmetrical distribution of power than within a classroom characterized by peer intolerance of bullying behavior.[16] Indeed, Machiavellianism was more strongly associated with bullying perpetration in classrooms with higher prestige norms for relational aggression.[17] In addition, classrooms with anti-bullying norms had bullies who were lower on popularity and victims who were more likely to be defended by peers.[18] Therefore, social environments can affect the expression of underlying traits through the use of bullying, and individual behavior can shape the social norms in a given environment.

Complex models that incorporate a social-ecological perspective are used increasingly as a framework when examining the range of factors that contribute to bullying.[19] These complexities have been important considerations for bullying interventions. For example, the KiVa bullying prevention program researched by both sociologists and psychologists focuses on ways of empowering bystanders in a peer group to intervene and reduce the social power afforded to perpetrators.[20]

Moving Forward to Understand and Prevent Bullying

We believe that bullying is an individual behavior and a social behavior. Both views of bullying behavior are needed for a comprehensive understanding and effective prevention. These goals can be obtained through the joint efforts of psychologists and sociologists who can bring together their overlapping and unique perspectives. For example, as highlighted by Magrass and Derber, we agree that one area that lacks in psychological research is a more thorough understanding of structural power beyond the school community. Although broader societal factors are recognized in the macro system of the social-ecological model, they are rarely studied in psychological school bullying research. In fact, Magrass and Derber discuss the ways that institutions embedded within society such as corporations can promote systemic competition and the abuse of power. As evident throughout the chapters of this book, sociological research is crucial to fully understand how bullying can result from inequalities in social, political, cultural, and economic structures. It is integral to understand how these structures set everyday norms that in turn directly or indirectly sanction bullying behavior. We also agree with Magrass and Derber that there is hope for bullying prevention through youth-led initiatives that promote a culture of compassion. Our future is in our children who socialize, learn, and live in these very structures. The integration of research from multiple disciplines including sociology and psychology is needed along with youth participation and leadership to effectively eliminate and prevent bullying in all domains of society.

NOTES

1. Olweus, 1991, 1994.
2. Vaillancourt et al., 2003.
3. Vaillancourt et al., 2010.
4. See Vaillancourt et al., 2003.
5. De Bruyn et al., 2010; Duffy et al., 2017; Pouwels et al., 2018; Thunfors and Cornell, 2008.
6. Pouwels et al., 2016; Nelson et al., 2019; Vaillancourt and Hymel, 2006.
7. Vaillancourt, 2001; Vaillancourt et al., 2003; Vaillancourt et al., 2010; Volk et al., 2012; Volk et al., 2014.
8. Garandeau et al., 2014a.
9. See Vaillancourt et al., 2003 and Vaillancourt et al., 2010.
10. Book et al., 2012; Caravita et al., 2009.
11. Fanti and Kimonis, 2012.
12. Farrell and Vaillancourt, 2020.
13. Sutton and Keogh, 2000.
14. Bronfenbrenner, 1979.
15. Espelage et al., 2018; Farrell et al., 2020; Merrin et al., 2018; Swearer et al., 2010.
16. Garandeau et al., 2014b.
17. Berger and Caravita, 2016.
18. Romera et al., 2019; Peets et al., 2015.
19. See Espelage et al., 2018; Farrell et al., 2020; Merrin et al., 2018; Swearer et al., 2010.
20. Kärnä et al., 2011.

REFERENCES

Berger, Christian, and Simona Caravita. 2016. "Why Do Early Adolescents Bully? Exploring the Influence of Prestige Norms on Social and Psychological Motives to Bully." *Journal of Adolescence* 46:45–56.

Book, Angela S., Anthony A. Volk, and Ashley Hosker. 2012. "Adolescent Bullying and Personality: An Adaptive Approach." *Personality and Individual Differences* 52 (2): 218–223.

Bronfenbrenner, Urie. 1979. *The Ecology of Human Development: Experiments by Nature and Design*. Cambridge, MA: Harvard University Press.

Caravita, Simona C. S., Paola Di Blasio, and Christina Salmivalli. 2009. "Unique and Interactive Effects of Empathy and Social Status on Involvement in Bullying." *Social Development* 18 (1): 140–163.

de Bruyn, Eddy H., Antonius H. N. Cillessen, and Inge B. Wissink. 2010. "Associations of Peer Acceptance and Perceived Popularity with Bullying and Victimization in Early Adolescence." *Journal of Early Adolescence* 30 (4): 543–566.

Duffy, Amanda L., Sarah Penn, Drew Nesdale, and Melanie J. Zimmer-Gembeck. 2017. "Popularity: Does It Magnify Associations between Popularity Prioritization and the Bullying and Defending Behavior of Early Adolescent Boys and Girls?" *Social Development* 26 (2): 263–277.

Espelage, Dorothy L., Mark J. Van Ryzin, and Melissa K. Holt. 2018. "Trajectories of Bully Perpetration across Early Adolescence: Static Risk Factors, Dynamic Covariates, and Longitudinal Outcomes." *Psychology of Violence* 8 (2): 141–150.

Fanti, Kostas A., and Eva R. Kimonis. 2012. "Bullying and Victimization: The Role of Conduct Problems and Psychopathic Traits." *Journal of Research on Adolescence* 22 (4): 617–631.

Farrell, Ann H., and Tracy Vaillancourt. 2020. "Bullying Perpetration and Narcissistic Personality Traits across Adolescence: Joint Trajectories and Childhood Risk Factors." *Frontiers in Psychiatry* 11:1193.

Farrell, Ann H., Anthony A. Volk, and Tracy Vaillancourt. 2020. "Empathy, Exploitation, and Adolescent Bullying Perpetration: A Longitudinal Social-Ecological Investigation." *Journal of Psychopathology and Behavioral Assessment* 42 (3): 436–449.

Garandeau, Claire F., Ihno A. Lee, and Christina Salmivalli. 2014a. "Differential Effects of the KiVa Anti-bullying Program on Popular and Unpopular Bullies." *Journal of Applied Developmental Psychology* 35 (1): 44–50.

———. 2014b. "Inequality Matters: Classroom Status Hierarchy and Adolescents' Bullying." *Journal of Youth and Adolescence* 43 (7): 1123–1133.

Kärnä, Antti, Marinus Voeten, Todd D. Little, Elisa Poskiparta, Anne Kaljonen, and Christina Salmivalli. 2011. "A Large-Scale Evaluation of the KiVa Antibullying Program: Grades 4–6." *Child Development* 82 (1): 311–330.

Merrin, Gabriel J., Dorothy L. Espelage, and Jun Sung Hong. 2018. "Applying the Social-Ecological Framework to Understand the Associations of Bullying Perpetration among High School Students: A Multilevel Analysis." *Psychology of Violence* 8 (1): 43–56.

Nelson, Helen J., Sharyn K. Burns, Garth E. Kendall, and Kimberly A. Schonert-Reichl. 2019. "Preadolescent Children's Perception of Power Imbalance in Bullying: A Thematic Analysis." *PLOS ONE* 14 (3): e0211124.

Olweus, Dan. 1991. "Bully/Victim Problems among Schoolchildren: Basic Facts and Effects of a School-Based Intervention Program." In *The Development and Treatment of Childhood Aggression*, edited by Kenneth H. Rubin and Debra J. Pepler, 411–448. Hillsdale, NJ: Lawrence Erlbaum.

———. 1994. "Bullying at School: Basic Facts and Effects of a School-Based Intervention Program." *Journal of Child Psychology and Psychiatry* 35 (7): 1171–1190.

Peets, Kätlin, Virpi Pöyhönen, Jaana Juvonen, and Christina Salmivalli. 2015. "Classroom Norms of Bullying Alter the Degree to Which Children Defend in Response to Their Affective Empathy and Power." *Developmental Psychology* 51 (7): 913–920.

Pouwels, J. Loes, Tessa A. M. Lansu, and Antonius H. N. Cillessen. 2016. "Participant Roles of Bullying in Adolescence: Status Characteristics, Social Behavior, and Assignment Criteria." *Aggressive Behavior* 42 (3): 239–253.

———. 2018. "A Developmental Perspective on Popularity and the Group Process of Bullying." *Aggression and Violent Behavior* 43:64–70.

Romera, Eva M., Ana Bravo, Rosario Ortega-Ruiz, and René Veenstra. 2019. "Differences in Perceived Popularity and Social Preference between Bullying Roles and Class Norms." *PLOS ONE* 14 (10): e0223499.

Sutton, Jon, and Edmund Keogh. 2000. "Social Competition in School: Relationships with Bullying, Machiavellianism and Personality." *British Journal of Educational Psychology* 70 (3): 443–456.

Swearer, Susan M., Dorothy L. Espelage, Tracy Vaillancourt, and Shelley Hymel. 2010. "What Can Be Done about School Bullying? Linking Research to Educational Practice." *Educational Researcher* 39 (1): 38–47.

Thunfors, Peter, and Dewey Cornell. 2008. "The Popularity of Middle School Bullies." *Journal of School Violence* 7 (1): 65–82.

Vaillancourt, Tracy. 2001. "Competing for Hegemony during Adolescence: A Link between Aggression and Social Status." PhD diss., University of British Columbia.

Vaillancourt, Tracy, and Shelley Hymel. 2006. "Aggression and Social Status: The Moderating Roles of Sex and Peer-Valued Characteristics." *Aggressive Behavior* 32 (4): 396–408.

Vaillancourt, Tracy, Shelley Hymel, and Patricia McDougall. 2003. "Bullying Is Power: Implications for School-Based Intervention Strategies." *Journal of Applied School Psychology* 19 (2): 157–176.

Vaillancourt, Tracy, Patricia McDougall, Shelley Hymel, and Shafik Sunderani. 2010. "Respect or Fear? The Relationship between Power and Bullying." In *Handbook of Bullying in Schools: An International Perspective*, edited by Shane R. Jimerson, Susan M. Swearer, and Dorothy L. Espelage, 211–222. New York: Routledge.

Volk, Anthony A., Joseph A. Camilleri, Andrew V. Dane, and Zopito A. Marini. 2012. "Is Adolescent Bullying an Evolutionary Adaptation?" *Aggressive Behavior* 38 (3): 222–238.

Volk, Anthony A., Andrew V. Dane, and Zopito A. Marini. 2014. "What Is Bullying? A Theoretical Redefinition." *Developmental Review* 34 (4): 327–343.

ACKNOWLEDGMENTS

This book is the product of not only many labors but also sacrifices and contributions made by many people, first of whom is my wife, Lisa Donoghue. Her support and critical input into the things I try to create is what makes my ideas become realities. My daughter, Amanda Donoghue, offered me a view into the world of adolescence when she was an adolescent herself. She tells me when I'm right about something, but more importantly she tells me when I'm wrong. This project may be a good test of what I have learned or failed to learn from her about young people, and needless to say, my fingers are crossed. My mother, Teresa Donoghue, taught me to be a pretty tough critic of my own work. I will always be grateful for that, especially when I finish something and release it to others.

Our editor, Ilene Kalish and our assistant editor, Sonia Tsuruoka, supported this project tremendously from day one. They made everything we hoped to accomplish become real and possible. Bob Faris, Todd Migliaccio, Tracy Vaillancourt, and Ann Farrell served as the secret brain trust behind all major decisions with this text, and there were many to be made. So I thank them for their time and interest in the project. Likewise, the many other authors were so engaged from the start. They put a great deal of energy and thoughtfulness into their work and kept us on target to finish the book despite the tremendous challenges of the COVID-19 pandemic, during which nearly all of the writing was done. My three editorial assistants, Melanie Mulhern, Noushig Ohanian, and Ashley Steimle, also performed many hours of reading, talking, and editing with me. Their efforts were crucial for keeping the moving parts of the book together, and I am so grateful to them for that.

Many people read drafts of this book and offered advice and feedback. Among them are the anonymous reviewers, but also Taulant Asani, Lauren Calabrese, Ian Callahan, Amanda Donoghue, Lisa Donoghue, James Gamvas, Melissa Gonzalez, Kevin Ha, Kylinn Kraemer,

Crystal Magallon, Kahiya McDaniels, Arianna Menendez, Richard Reinschmidt, Stephen Shahin, Tayler Szabo, Victoria Vazquez, and Zack Weland. Their critical eyes were crucial to the editing process. They helped us to make the work more relevant to young people.

Former students and colleagues at Montclair State University, Kean University, and Rutgers University performed a great deal of the legwork that went into my school climate and bullying research over the years, and this has greatly affected the way I think about bullying. They include David Brandwein, Alicia Raia-Hawrylak, my dear friend Barry Mascari whom we recently lost, Dina Rosen, Angela Almeida, Barbara Prempeh, Danisha Moodie, Luis Bernal, Rey Sentina, Noel Rozier, Ian Callahan, Rachel Druker, and the entire SCUBA team. I also owe many thanks to Brian Lowe and Arnaud Kurze for their early contributions and advice on this project.

During the writing of this book, the disciplines of sociology and psychology lost two of their most influential writers on the topic of bullying, Murray Milner and Dan Olweus. It is the hope of all the contributors on this book that their legacies will continue on and their sociological and psychological work on peer aggression among adolescents will be understood as complements to one another.

A former superior once told me that a person who was mercilessly abusing me was a *bully*. You can imagine my surprise since my scholarship was on bullying at the time, and yet I didn't see this despite my endless suffering as a victim. I will forever be indebted to him because he believed me when I spoke up and he made me feel like a person again.

ABOUT THE CONTRIBUTORS

AMY L. BEST is Professor of Sociology at George Mason University. Her research focuses on the study of youth and gender identity formation, social inequalities, youth, school and consumer culture. She holds expertise in qualitative and feminist approaches to social research and program evaluation based on observation. She is author of *Prom Night: Youth, Schools and Popular Culture* (2000), selected for the 2002 American Educational Studies Association Critics' Choice Award, *Fast Cars, Cool Rides: The Accelerating World of Youth and Their Cars* (2006), and *Fast-Food Kids: French Fries, Lunch Lines, and School Ties* (2017), selected for the 2018 Morris Rosenberg Award by the DC Sociological Society. She is editor of *Representing Youth: Methodological Issues in Critical Youth Studies* (2007) and series co-editor for NYU Press's books series Critical Perspective on Youth.

LAURA CALLEJAS is a consultant with the School Climate Transformation Project (SCTP), a multiyear initiative that provides support to K–12 New Jersey schools in developing and sustaining a positive and inclusive school climate through data-driven strategic planning and customized consultation. The SCTP is a partnership between the Graduate School for Applied and Professional Psychology at Rutgers University and the New Jersey Department of Education. She earned her PhD in sociology at Rutgers University in 2020. Her dissertation research examines the relationship between social status mobility and interpersonal conflict among adolescents in middle schools using social network data. Her recent co-authored work appears in *Social Psychology Quarterly*.

RANDALL COLLINS is Professor of Sociology Emeritus at the University of Pennsylvania. His books include *Interaction Ritual Chains* (2004); *Violence: A Micro-sociological Theory* (2008); a sociological novel, *Civil*

War Two (2018); and, most recently, *Charisma: Micro-sociology of Power and Influence* (2020).

ROBERT CROSNOE is Associate Dean of Liberal Arts and Rapoport Centennial Professor of Sociology at the University of Texas at Austin, where he also is a faculty member in the Department of Psychology (by courtesy) and Population Research Center. He received a PhD in sociology from Stanford University and completed postdoctoral fellowships at the University of North Carolina at Chapel Hill. His mixed-methods research explores the connections among health, child/adolescent development, and education and the contributions of these connections to socioeconomic and immigration-related inequalities in American society. A few of his book titles are *The Starting Line: Latina/o Children, Texas Schools, and National Debates about Early Education*; *Fitting In, Standing Out: Navigating the Social Challenges of High School to Get an Education*; *Debating Early Child Care: The Relationship between Developmental Science and the Media*; and *Families Now: Diversity, Demography, and Development*. He is Co-Director of the Interdisciplinary Collaborative on Development in Context, Past President of the Society for Research on Adolescence, a trustee of the Population Reference Bureau, and a member of the Executive Board of the Council on Contemporary Families.

CHARLES DERBER, Professor of Sociology at Boston College, is the author of twenty-five books, including *The Wilding of America*, *The Pursuit of Attention*, *Corporation Nation*, *People Before Profit*, and *Welcome to the Revolution*—translated into twelve languages. He is a public sociologist and lifelong activist who writes about structural and cultural analysis of capitalism and social movements seeking transformational systemic change.

JOHN FARIS was Associate Professor of Sociology at Towson University in Baltimore. In his subsequent career he did applied sociology with British Railways, Boeing, the Bill & Melinda Gates Foundation, University of Washington, Washington Biotechnology & Biomedical Association, Pacific Northwest Research Institute, Landesa, and other organizations.

ROBERT FARIS is Professor of Sociology at the University of California, Davis. His research uses social network analysis to investigate how violence, bullying, and aggression shape social hierarchies and has appeared in the *American Sociological Review,* the *American Journal of Sociology, Social Forces, Social Networks,* and *Social Psychology Quarterly.* He recently served as a Fulbright Specialist working in Israel with its largest anti-bullying NGO.

ANN H. FARRELL is an Assistant Professor in the Department of Child and Youth Studies at Brock University. Her research examines the longitudinal associations between youth bullying and personality, including the social environmental contexts that contribute to these associations.

BRENT HARGER is Associate Professor of Sociology at Gettysburg College in Gettysburg, Pennsylvania. He earned his PhD in sociology at Indiana University. His primary research has examined the ways that peer interactions are defined and interpreted by students, teachers, and staff members within elementary schools. He has also conducted research on the use of gossip in school staff meetings, the depictions of professors in popular films, and the scholarship of teaching and learning. With Ingrid Castro and Melissa Swauger, he co-edited *Researching Children and Youth: Methodological Issues, Strategies, and Innovations.* His current projects focus on college students, including an exploration of their experiences during the COVID-19 pandemic.

YALE R. MAGRASS endured continual bullying in elementary, middle, and high school. He then became involved in the new left, especially the movement against the American invasion of Vietnam. He continued in his academic career to investigate how militaristic capitalism warps individual lives, results in continual wars, destroys community, produces gross inequality, and threatens the viability of the planet. One of its impacts is a culture in which bullying becomes a normal mode for people to interact with one another. He is currently Chancellor Professor of Sociology/Anthropology at the University of Massachusetts–Dartmouth. He is the author of over sixty articles and eight books, seven of which were co-authored with Charles Derber. Among those books are *Bully Nation*, *Capitalism: Should You Buy It*, and *Glorious Causes*.

TODD MIGLIACCIO, Associate Dean of Academic Affairs at Penn State University, Berks, has researched bullying and the subsequent development of prevention and intervention programs in K–12 grades for the past eleven-plus years. His focus has been on the social interactions that sustain and/or challenge the existence and persistence of bullying, including students, staff, and faculty. He has, along with a colleague, developed materials to assist educators, all of which are located for free online (www.csus.edu/cbm). He also, along with a colleague, wrote a book on bullying, *Bullying as a Social Experience: Social Factors, Prevention and Intervention*, that integrated comparative findings from different countries, theoretical underpinnings of bullying, and best intervention practices. His focus in all his endeavors is engaging bullying in a comprehensive manner to thoroughly address it as a social problem. Recently, he has begun studying bullying within academia.

SARAH A. MILLER is an ethnographer whose research focuses on the sociology of gender, sexuality, education, and new media. Her current book project, "The Tolerance Generation: Growing Up Online in an Anti-Bullying Era," explores how youth grapple with inequality, conflict, and the pressures of digital culture in the anti-bullying era. Her upcoming study focuses on the gendered and racialized dimensions of school shooting threats and their impacts on school communities. Her research has been published in *Gender & Society*, *Sexualities*, and the *Journal of Youth and Adolescence* and funded by the National Academy of Education / Spencer Foundation, National Science Foundation, American Sociological Association, and the Center for Research on Families. As a public sociologist, she has worked on a variety of initiatives focused on advancing adolescent health and sexuality education policy in collaboration with the Public Engagement Project, Futures of Sex Education, and Advocates for Youth. She is a full-time lecturer at Boston University in the Department of Sociology and the Women's, Gender, and Sexuality Studies Program.

C. J. PASCOE is Associate Professor of Sociology and affiliate faculty in Women's, Gender and Sexuality Studies and the Department of Education Studies. Her research focuses on inequality in adolescence, with a specific focus on gender and sexual inequalities in schools. Her award-winning book *Dude, You're a Fag: Masculinity and Sexuality in High School* examines the central role homophobic and heterosexist harassment plays in contemporary understandings of masculinity. Along with Tristan Bridges she is the co-editor of *Exploring Masculinities: Identity, Inequality, Continuity and Change*. Her forthcoming book, *American High School: Coming of Age in an Unequal Time*, examines how inequalities in adolescence are reproduced or challenged both interactionally and institutionally. She has worked with numerous organizations to address aggression, bullying, and inequality in public schools.

ALLISON ANN PAYNE is a Professor in the Department of Sociology and Criminology at Villanova University. Her research interests include school disorder and climate, school discipline and security, crime and delinquency prevention, and criminological theory. She has recently researched the impact of school climate on teacher victimization, the relationship between student ethnic composition and school discipline, predictors of bullying perpetration and victimization, and the effects of student racial and ethnic composition on school security and discipline. She has been published in multiple journals, including *Criminology, Social Problems, Journal of Research in Crime and Delinquency*, and *Social Science Research*.

ELIZABETHE PAYNE is Founder and Director of QuERI—the Queering Education Research Institute—and is Education Faculty at the City University of New York. QuERI is dedicated to bridging the gaps between research, policy, and practice in support of LGBTQ+ students. She is a sociologist of education with a focus on gender and sexual minorities. Her research explores anti-bullying discourses, state-level LGBT-inclusive anti-bullying policy and its implementation, educator experiences working with gender and sexual minority students, and the school experiences of LGBTQ+ young people. Currently, she is conducting a ten-year evaluation study of the implementation of New York's anti-bullying law. She serves on the New York State Dignity for All Students Act Task Force and works directly with the New York State Education Department and the state legislature toward more effective research-based policy for LGBTQ students and families. She also worked with the U.S. Department of Justice on the historic application of Title IX to LGBTQ student harassment cases. Her applied work additionally addresses state-level sex education and HIV education policy, and policies related to teacher education and school climate. She is a member of the board of the International Gender and Education Association. She teaches courses in LGBTQ issues in education, public policy, qualitative research methods, and sociology of education. With co-author Melissa Smith, her forthcoming edited volume, *Queer Kids, School Violence, and the Limits of "Bullying,"* brings together leading international scholars to challenge the limits of current anti-bullying efforts in support of gender and sexual minority students. She was a high school English teacher in Houston, Texas, before completing her PhD.

ALICIA RAIA-HAWRYLAK is Project Manager and Supervisor of Evaluation with the School Climate Transformation Project (SCTP), a partnership between the Graduate School for Applied and Professional Psychology at Rutgers University and the New Jersey Department of Education. SCTP supports New Jersey schools in using data to drive school climate improvement. She earned her PhD in sociology at Rutgers University. Her recent research uses a mixed-methods approach to explore how peer interpersonal aggression varies between and within high schools. She is particularly interested in exploring the formation of positive and supportive learning environments through data-driven school climate improvement efforts and implementation of evidence-based and equity-oriented social and emotional learning. She also contributed to the evaluation of the LGBTQ-Inclusive Lessons and Resources Pilot Program in New Jersey, examining the supportive conditions, implementation experiences, and outcomes associated with integrating curricula focused on the social, political, and economic contributions of members of LGBTQ+ individuals in grades 5–12. She is a former middle school language arts teacher in New York City and Asbury Park, New Jersey. Her research has been published in *Sociological Studies of Children and Youth*, *Children and Schools*, and the *Journal for Educational and Psychological Consultation*.

HANA SHEPHERD is Associate Professor of Sociology at Rutgers University–New Brunswick. She studies culture and cognition, social networks, and organizations, in the service of better understanding the creation and persistence of inequality. In addition to her interest in culture and cultural change in schools, she is working on a book project about how local government agencies enforce employment protections like minimum wage and paid sick leave standards (with Janice Fine). Her other work examines how organizational practices shape networks in low-wage jobs, both within workplaces and online, and the implications of such networks for collective action. Her work appears in outlets such as *Poetics*, *Social Psychology Quarterly*, *Social Science Research*, *Sociological Science*, and the *Proceedings of the National Academy of Sciences*.

MELISSA J. SMITH is Associate Professor of English Education at University of Central Arkansas and Associate Director of Research for the Queering Education Research Institute (QuERI). Her research focuses on educators' engagement with LGBTQ+ inclusion in K–12 education. She has published research in journals including *Equity and Excellence in Education*, *Educational Administration Quarterly*, and *Educational Studies*. In collaboration with Elizabethe Payne, she is editing a forthcoming volume, *Queer Kids, School Violence, and the Limits of "Bullying,"* which brings together leading international scholars to interrogate the limitations of anti-bullying interventions in support of gender and sexual minority students.

LIANN TUCKER is a PhD candidate in sociology at Duke University who uses social network analysis to study adolescent mental health and health-risk behaviors. Her dissertation focuses on the causes and consequences of adolescent friendship stability.

TRACY VAILLANCOURT is Tier 1 Canada Research Chair in School-Based Mental Health and Violence Prevention at the University of Ottawa, where she is cross-appointed as Full Professor in Counselling Psychology, Faculty of Education and the School of Psychology, Faculty of Social Sciences. She is President-Elect of the International Society for Research on Aggression, Associate Editor for *Aggressive Behavior*, and an elected member of the College of the Royal Society of Canada. Her research examines the links between bullying and mental health, with a particular focus on social neuroscience. Her research is routinely highlighted in the media including the *New York Times*, *The Times*, *Forbes* magazine, *The Atlantic*, the *Huffington Post*, BBC World News, and CNN and was recently featured in the Steven Spielberg and Alex Gibney (producers) documentary *Why We Hate*. She has impacted research, practice, and policy working with committees such as the Royal Society of Canada COVID-19 task force; Canada's Mental Health Strategy; U.S. National Academies of Sciences, Engineering, and Medicine; and the European Standards of Care for Newborn Health. She is currently funded by the Canadian Institutes of Health Research and the Social Sciences and Humanities Council of Canada.

DENISE WILSON is Research Associate for the Department of Sociology and Criminology at Villanova University. Previously she worked for the Pew Charitable Trusts in Washington, DC. She received her master's degree in criminology and criminal justice from the University of Maryland, College Park. She is a generalist and has researched a wide range of topics in the areas of sociology, criminology, and state policy.

KIRSTEN L. WITHERUP is an Associate Professor in the Department of Criminology and Criminal Justice at York College of Pennsylvania. She graduated with her doctor of philosophy degree in criminology, law, and society from George Mason University. Her research interests include school disorder and violence, crime and delinquency prevention, program evaluation and research methodology, restorative justice, and criminological theory.

ABOUT THE EDITOR

CHRISTOPHER DONOGHUE is Associate Professor in the Department of Sociology and Coordinator of the Master of Arts in Social Research and Analysis at Montclair State University in New Jersey. He earned his PhD in sociology at Fordham University. His research in educational settings spans the areas of adolescent bullying, sex education, and ethnic and racial prejudice. This work has appeared in journals such as *Journal of Adolescence, Sex Education, Sociological Studies of Children & Youth, Children and Schools, Qualitative Research in Education, Sociological Forum*, and the *Social Science Journal*. His research on bullying has focused on the ways that middle school and high school students define the term "bullying" and how they cope with its effects on their lives, including the ways that it affects their sleep. In collaboration with schools, colleagues, and college students, he has conducted many school climate and bullying surveys in middle and high schools. He has also studied the impact of messages from socializing agents on the decisions that high school students make about when to engage in sexual intercourse. Among college students he has carried out the last two national replications of the Bogardus Social Distance Survey, one of the oldest statistical measures still in use by the discipline, to examine long-term trends in ethnic and racial prejudice. He has served as an educational consultant for public and private schools in New Jersey, assisting in their efforts to address school climate, bullying, ethnic and racial prejudice, sexual risk taking, and multicultural education. Prior to his work on young people, his focus was on older adults, disabilities, and long-term care facilities. This work has appeared in journals such as *The Gerontologist, Research on Aging, Journal of Applied Gerontology, Health Care Management Review, Journal of Health and Social Policy*, and *Disability and Society*. He is also the co-author of *Statistics: A Tool for Social Research and Data Analysis* (11th ed.), with Joseph Healey.

INDEX

Page numbers in *italics* indicate Figures and Tables.

Abels, Margot, 97
Acosta, Joie, 254
adults, 2, 6; in anti-bullying myth, 223, 225, 228, *234*, 234–35, 242n39; gender norms and, 10–11; misunderstanding by, 23–24; in peer harassment, 188; theory of instrumental aggression and, 122
adults compared to teenagers, 121–22
African Americans, 168–69; Black Lives Matter and, 175, 176, 216; in North Carolina study, 125–26, *127*
age appearance, 149, *152*, *154*, 156
aggression, 3, 7–8, 98, 249–50; bullying queer youth related to, 48, 52–53; of friends, 231–32; of girls, 101–3; indirect, 223–24; in middle school friends, 140, 141, 142, 143, 146; normalization of, 233–34, 238–39; peer, 11; popularity and, 131
aggression frequency, 230–33
aggression patterns, 276
aggressive behavior, 2, 223–24
aggressive behavior mixed-methods research findings, 282–86
aggressive interactions, 228
alcohol, ix–x
analytic technique, 146–47
anti-bullying campaigns, 1–2, 6, 10–11; in bullying queer youth, 57; effectiveness of, 13, 131; KiVa as, 131; mixed-methods research for, 13; responsibility in, 112–13; school climate in, 13; school-wide surveys in, 13; whole-school approaches in, 13. *See also* Operation Nice; Project Cyber Safety
anti-bullying myth: adults in, 223, 225, 228, *234*, 234–35, 242n39; aggression frequency in, 230–33; aggressive interactions in, 228; behaviors continuum and, 236–37; bullying definitions in, 222–24, 233–35, *234*, 238, 241; classification in, 235–36; CLASS in, 226–27, 228–29, 237–38; communication technologies in, 240; construct interactions in, 231; data analysis on, 226; "detective work" in, 229, 232, 239; disciplinary process and, 228–30, 242n39, 242n41; discussion on, 237–40; ethnographic data on, 220–21; false dichotomy in, 236–37; friends in, 231–32; gay bashing in, 222–23; individualistic approach and, 220–21, 226; inequality in, 239–40; inhabited institutionalism and, 221–22; institutionalism and, 221–22, 240; interpretive approach on, 224–25; intervention in, 231; interviews on, 225–26; masculinity in, 222–23; meta-analyses related to, 220; morning routine and, 227; myth in, 221, 241n8; normalization of aggression in, 233–34, 238–39; observation on, 224–25; organizational approaches to, 226–28; peer mediation program and, 227–28; person-centered influence on, 236–37, 239–42;

318 | INDEX

anti-bullying myth (cont.)
principal and, 227–28; public perspectives on, 220, 221; repeat offenders in, 229–30; researcher role related to, 225; scapegoats in, 230; in school culture, 222–24, 240–41; setting and methods in, 224–26; social-ecological approaches and, 220; status in, 231–32; stereotypes related to, 236–37; student characteristics and, 224, 236; student fabrications in, 229; student reports in, 229, 230, 231–33, 239; witnesses in, 229–30
antisocial behavior, 51–52
Aristotle, 25
Asian, 170
Asperger syndrome, 295–96
Axford, Nick, 253

bad names, 54
Banerjee, Robin, 172
bathrooms, 90–91
behavior management, 49, 282–86
behaviors continuum, 236–37
betweenness centrality, 11
bias, 9–10, 12
binge drinking, ix–x
Black Lives Matter, 175, 176, 216
boys. See specific topics
Brackett, Marc, 251–52, 256
Braithwaite, John, 255
brokerage status, 145, 146, 151; betweenness centrality of, 147–48; for boys, 152, 155, 156; for girls, 152, 153, 154
brokerage status mobility, 153, 154
Bronfenbrenner, Urie, 5, 121, 256, 299–300
Bullies and Whipping Boys (Olweus), 26
bullying: language for, 4; term use of, 8. See also specific topics
bullying definitions, 12, 23; in anti-bullying myth, 222–24, 233–35, 234, 238, 241; in bullying queer youth, 55–56; narrowness and broadness in, 27–28, 30; of Olweus, 3–4, 8–9, 25–28, 52, 139; problem of, 7–8; repetition in, 27–28, 32n12; in understanding of culture, 278
bullying inflation, 23–24; fagging in, 19; individual honor contests in, 20–21; insult contests and, 21–22; intergroup fights and, 21; malicious gossip and, 22; mass-participation ritual in, 20; mid-level in, 19–20; ongoing relationship in, 19–20; scapegoats and, 20; in total institutions, 20; tradition compared to, 19
bullying queer youth: aggression related to, 48, 52–53; anti-bullying programs in, 57; antisocial behavior and, 51–52; bad names in, 54; behavior management and, 49; bullying definition in, 55–56; changing bullying conversation of, 50–51; conversation change and, 50–51; critique related to, 51; cultural systems and, 49; culture in, 57–58; daily routines in, 54; data sources on, 58–59; dominant bullying discourse and, 48; gender categories and, 48; gender differences regulation in, 53–56; gender policing in, 54–55, 57; hetero-gender normativity and, 50–51; heteronormative gender expectations in, 54; holistic school culture for, 51; inclusive schools' implications for, 57–58; in LGBTQ-inclusive schools, 57–58; mainstream value systems and, 48; normative cruelties in, 53; Olweus Bullying Prevention Program and, 52; personal qualities for, 51–52; policies and practices related to, 51; power related to, 52; professional development and, 49–50; regulator for, 53–56; safety problems and, 50; schools in, 53–56; social for, 51–53; social function in, 69; social norm violations in, 53–54; social status in, 55; sociocultural approach

for, 50–51; status quo in, 55; targets in, 56; value system related to, 49
bullying queer youth PD: belonging related to, 63; DASA in, 61; heteronormativity in, 59–60, 63; language in, 61, 62–63; normalized gender policing in, 62; optimism related to, 63; proactive strategies in, 61–62; research design on, 59–60; risk in, 60; root cause and, 59; safety related to, 59; school climate and school culture in, 61–62, 69–70; status quo in, 60–61; stigma in, 60; takeaways on, 61–62
bullying queer youth state-level policy, 49–50; affirming spaces in, 68–69; categories in, 64–65, 67–68; DASA in, 63–64, 65, 66, 67; difference in, 64; Dignity Act Coordinators in, 66; marginalization in, 68–69; proactive approaches in, 64; reactive compared to proactive in, 67; social norms in, 68–69; State Education Department in, 65–66; university coursework related to, 68; U.S. Supreme Court on, 64
bullying theories: adults compared to teenagers in, 121–22; criminological theories in, 121; interactionist norm account of culture theory, 12, 189, 191–93, 196, 199–200, 204–5, 210, 212–15; paradox in, 120, 132n1; popularity in, 120–21; psychology in, 120; punching up in, 123; short social distances in, 123; social ecological perspective on bullying, ix, 5–6, 11, 13–14, 121, 166–68, 176–77, 189, 220, 251, 256, 258–59, 261–63, 275, 299–300; status-motivated behavior in, 121–22; theory of instrumental aggression, 120, 122–23, 131; theory of status relations, 40, 42, 44, 45; victimization in, 120, 122–23; vulnerabilities in, 120
The Bully Society (Klein), 6

Calarco, Jessica McCrory, 240
capitalistic ethic, xi; militarized capitalism and, 5–6, 14. *See also* militarized capitalism, education, and psychologists
Centers for Disease Control and Prevention, 27
Chaux, Enrique, 257
Chinese footbinding, 194
CLASS. *See* Connected Learning Assures Successful Students
class and income: materialism and, 172, 173; number of friends related to, 172–73; school economic inequality and, 173; SES as, 172–73; victimization related to, 173
classification, 235–36
Classroom Check-Up, 254
classroom level, 285
classroom observations, 275
classrooms and small-group cultures, 280–82
classroom victimization, 283–84
Clementi, Tyler, 27, 32
climate justice movement, 295–96
cluelessness, 11
Colbert, Cassandra L., 259
Collins, Jim, 103
Columbine High School mass shooting, vii
communication technologies, 240. *See also* social media
competition: in middle school friends, 139–40, 143, 146; in militarized capitalism, education, and psychologists, 293–95; in Operation Nice, 103; for social status, ix–xi; in status systems, 40
complaints, 7
concept creep, 29, 30
conflict engagement, 11, 158. *See also specific topics*
conflict resolutions skills, 159
conformity, 41–42, 45

Connected Learning Assures Successful Students (CLASS), 226–27, 228–29, 237–38
construct interactions, 231
content analyses, 255–56
Cornell, Dewey, 174, 190
corporate empires, 294
Corsaro, William A., 225
cost-benefit analysis, 261
counterculture, 295
COVID-19, 289–90; middle school friends related to, 139, 159–60
criminal justice systems, 29, 32n17
criminal records, 109–10
criminological theories, 121
Cross-Lagged Linear Model of Retained Friends, Status Valuation, Close Friend Valuation, and Centrality, 128–29, *130*
Cross-Lagged Linear Model Path Diagram, 126, *129*
cruelty, 30–32. *See also* mean girls and tough guys
culture: in bullying queer youth, 57–58; hip-hop, 82; idiocultures, 191, 280–81. aggression patterns in, 276; 251; aggressive behavior mixed-methods research findings in, 282–86; bullying definition in, 278; classroom level in, 285; classroom observations in, 275; classrooms and small-group cultures in, 280–82; classroom victimization in, 283–84; cogenerative dialogue in, 288–89; competency-building approaches in, 289; COVID-19 in, 289–90; cross-sectional survey data in, 276; disciplinary climate in, 285; disciplinary policies in, 284–85; disproportionate exposure in, 274; ecological levels in, 275; educational equity in, 275; ethnography in, 274, 277, 278, 281–82; gender in, 279; group-level experiences of, 275–76, 287–88; high- and low-income school in, 274–76, 279; idiocultures in, 280–81, 284, 286; interaction severity and duration in, 283; interviews in, 274, 276, 277, 278–79, 282, 287; local cultures in, 277; norms communication in, 284; observational categories in, 287–88; observations for, 274–75, 277; open-access online dashboards in, 274; power differential in, 277–78; qualitative research in, 285–86, 288; quantitative patterns in, 274–75, 277; racial disparities in, 285, 288, 289–90; recommendations and interventions in, 286–90; school climate in, 287, 289; school staff training in, 287–88; SCUBA in, 278–79; sexual harassment in, 279; small groups in, 286; social capital in, 281; social media in, 283–84; sociological study in, 276–79; students' role in, 276–77, 281–82; survey data in, 274–76; victimization in, 279, 282–84, 285, 287
culture and context, 261–63
culture definition, 214–15, 222
culture meaning, 190–91
cultures change, 212–14
culture theory, 192
culture transmission, 207–9, *208*, 217nn28–29
cyberbullying, 1, 3, 78; in prevention and intervention programs, 247, 256–57, 258, 263; in Project Cyber Safety, 107–8

Daigle, Leah, 169
Darwin, Charles, 25
DASA. *See* Dignity for All Students Act
D'Asta, Mark, 103–4
debunked theories, vii
descriptive and prescriptive social norms, 200–203, *201*, *202*
"detective work," 229, 232, 239
developmental psychologists, viii
Diagnostic and Statistical Manual, 25

Dignity for All Students Act (DASA), 58–59, 71n42; in bullying queer youth PD, 61; in bullying queer youth state-level policy, 63–64, 65, 66, 67
Dioscorides, 25
disabilities, 2–3, 167, 169, 188–89
disciplinary data, 150
disciplinary policies, 284–85
disciplinary process, 228–30, 242n39, 242n41
Dittmar, Helga, 172
Divecha, Diana, 251–52, 256
documentary, 102–4
dominant bullying discourse, 48
dominant story line, viii–x
Dude, You're a Fag (Pascoe), 10
dummy variables, 148, 149–50
Durkin, Kevin, 174

Earnshaw, Valerie A., 262
ecological levels, 275
Ecological theory, ecology. *See* social-ecological perspective
Eder, Donna, 226
EI. *See* emotional intelligence
Emdin, Christopher, 288–89
Eminem Exception, 80
emotional intelligence (EI), 259
empirical approach, 199–200
empirical variation, 196–97
Espelage, Dorothy L., 223, 259
ethnic minorities, 2–3
ethnography, 220–21, 274, 277, 278, 281–82
Evaldsson, Ann-Carita, 242n41
expressive relations, 43

face saving, 32n18
fag discourse, 82, 83
fagging, 19
"fag" term use, 79–80, 81, 82
false dichotomy, 236–37
family, 252–53
Farrington, David P., 248, 250, 253
Felmlee, Diane, 142, 143, 223

Fine, Gary Alan, 191, 222, 280
Fingerson, Laura, 226
Finkelhor, David, 223
Fitting In, Standing Out (Crosnoe), 9–10
football players, 76, 80, 92
Freaks, Geeks, and Cool Kids (Milner), ix. *See also* status system
friends, 231–32; in theory of instrumental aggression, 123, 124–25. *See also specific topics*
friendship network centrality, 125, 128, *129*
friendship stability, 124–25
friendship termination, 124
friendship ties, conflict and social status, 142–44, 158–59

Gaffney, Hannah, 248, 250
Garandeau, Claire F., 298
gay bashing, 222–23
Gay-Straight Alliance (GSA), 85
gender, 1, 48, 50–51, 279; of middle school friends, 142, 145–46, 147, 158; status systems and, 22
gender differences regulation, 53–56
gendered norm enforcement, 83–84
gender inequalities, 111–12
gender norms, 83–84; adults and, 10–11
gender policing, 54–55, 57
gender socialization, 82
gender socialization process, 83–84
girl-on-girl crime, 103
girls: aggression of, 101–2, 101–3; brokerage status for, *152*, 153, *154*; of color, 98, 103; in middle school results, 151, *152*, 153, *153*, *154*, 215–16; in Operation Nice, 103, 106–7; in Project Cyber Safety, 106–11
Glass, Ira, 42
goal, 14
Goffman, Erving, 43
Goncy, Elizabeth A., 254
gossip, 22, 30
Gottfredson, Denise C., 258
Gottfredson, Gary D., 258

Gould, Roger V., 32n18, 139, 141, 144–45
Greenberg, Max, 96
group culture, 189
GSA. *See* Gay-Straight Alliance
Gusler, Stephanie, 169–70

Hallett, Tim, 280
hate crimes, 174
haters, 188–89
Hatzenbuehler, Mark L., 256
health research, 4, 249
heroic masculinity, 99
hetero-gender normativity, 50–51
heteronormative gender expectations, 54
heteronormativity, 9–10, 59–60, 63.
    See also institutional heteronormativity
hierarchy, x–xi
high- and low-income school, 274–76, 279
high status: behavior of, 205–6, *207*; nominations of, 199
high-status student behavior, 193, 205–6, *207*, 209–10
Hinduja, Sameer, 252
hip-hop culture, 82
Hite, Cynthia, 172
Hite, Robert, 172
Hoffman, Chrystina, 169
home, bullying at, 2–3
homophobia levels decline, 77–78
Huang, Francis, 173–74
Huang, Yuanhong, 252–53
Huli tribe, Papua New Guinea, 32n17
Hutzell, Kirsten L., 254–55

identities, 85, 87, 89, 100
idiocultures, 191; in understanding of culture, 280–81, 284, 286
Importance of Close Friends and Being Popular, 126, *127*, 128
incentives, xii
inclusive schools' implications, 57–58
indirect aggression, 223–24
indirect bullying, 234

individual honor contests, 20–21
individualism, viii, 38–39
individualistic approach, 220–21, 226
individualization, 96, 97
individual paradigm, 4–5
inequality, 96–100, 111–12, 173; in anti-bullying myth, 239–40
influential students, 206, *207*
informal status hierarchies, 141
inhabited institutionalism, 221–22
Instagram, 28, 107, 149, *152*, *154*, 156, 197
institutional bias, 12
institutional heteronormativity, 84–92; anti-bullying messages in, 84; bathrooms in, 90–91; challenges in, 88–89; community response in, 87–88; district policy document in, 89–90; drag show in, 85–88; framing in, 91–92; GSA in, 85, 87–88, 89–90; identities in, 85, 87, 89; kindness in, 84, 92; open mindedness in, 84; permission slips in, 90; pronouns in, 88; Queen Quixotic in, 86, 87; sexism in, 84; Transsexual Menace in, 86–87; trans students in, 85–88, 90; trans teacher in, 86–87, 88; victimization in, 91
institutionalism, 221–22, 240
institutionalized racism, 176
institutions, 2
instrumental aggression, theory of, 120, 122–23, 131; adults and, 122; friends in, 123, 124–25; popularity in, 124–25; psychological antecedents in, 120; status in, 121, 122–23, 124
instrumental relations, 43. *See also* status motivation, network stability, and instrumental cruelty
insult contests, 21–22
intelligible masculinity, 99
intentionality, 3–4, 27
interactional homophobia, 10, 78–84, 92; Eminem Exception in, 80; fag

discourse in, 82, 83; "fag" term use in, 79–80, 81, 82; gendered norm enforcement in, 83–84; gender socialization in, 82; as gender socialization process, 83–84; hip-hop culture in, 82; homophobic harassment in, 79; imitations in, 79, 81; insults in, 82; joking in, 81; masculinity in, 80–82; no homo in, 82–83; sexuality in, 80; Twitter and, 82; vulnerability in, 81
interactionism. See peer harassment
interactionist account, 189, 191–94, *193*
interactionist norm account of culture theory, 12, 189, 191–93, 196, 199–200, 204–5, 210, 212–15
interaction patterns, 194–95
interactions repetition for norms perception, 194–96
intergroup fights, 21
interpretive approach, 224–25
intervention, xi–xii, 231. See also prevention and intervention programs
interviews, 100; on anti-bullying myth, 225–26; understanding of culture, 274, 276, 277, 278–79, 282, 287

Jackman, Kasey, 169
Just Say No to Bullying!, 5

Kiang, Lisa, 169–70
King, Matthew T., 259
KiVa, 131, 252
Klein, Jessie, 6, 223
Konold, Timothy, 169

language, 4; in bullying queer youth PD, 61, 62–63
La Salle, Tamika P., 170
Latinos, 168–69, 171
law and policy, 169, 174, 255–56. See also bullying queer youth state-level policy
LGBTQ, 1, 9–10. See also bullying queer youth

LGBTQ-inclusive schools, 57–58. See also bullying queer youth PD
Limber, Susan P., 250
Linear Model Path Diagram, 126, *129*
locker room talk, 108–9

Machiavellianism, 300
macro and micro factors, 166–67, *167*
macrosociological perspective, 8, 9
male cheerleader, 76
malicious gossip, 22
marginalization, 96, 177; in bullying queer youth state-level policy, 68–69
Marx, Karl, 294
masculinity, 76, 96, 99; in anti-bullying myth, 222–23; in interactional homophobia, 80–82
mass-participation ritual, 20
mean girl archetype, 97–99
Mean Girls (film), 101
mean girls and tough guys: anti-bullying and inequality in, 96–100; anti-bullying texts in, 97; boys' violence in, 99; bullycides in, 98; cultures change related to, 212–14; heroic masculinity in, 99; hidden culture of indirection in, 98; horizontal aggression in, 98; implications of, 214–16; individualization in, 96, 97; inequalities reinforcement in, 99–100; inequality in, 97, 98; intelligible masculinity in, 99; interviews of, 100; marginalization in, 96; without "mean boys," 99; mean girl archetype in, 97–99; methods related to, 100; normalized masculine violence in, 96, 99; norms in, 97; Operation Nice and, 95, 99–105, 111–12; posters in, 95; privileged girls in, 98; separate cultures in, 99–100; sexting in, 95–96; sexual identities in, 100; structural inequality in, 97; topless photo in, 95, 96. See also Project Cyber Safety
meanness, 30–32

media coverage, 8
meta-analyses, 220; in prevention and intervention programs, 247–48
Meyer, Faye, 97
Meyer, John W., 221, 238
middle school friends: activities and dating in, 149–50; age appearance in, 149, 152, 154; aggression in, 140, 141, 142, 143, 146; analytic technique on, 146–47; background of, 142; bullying definition and, 139; competition in, 139–40, 143, 146; conclusion on, 157–60; conflict resolutions skills and, 159; control variables in, 150–51; COVID-19 related to, 139, 159–60; data on, 141–42, 146–47, 150; disciplinary data in, 150; dummy variables in, 148, 149–50; friends and non-friends conflict variables in, 148–49; friendship ties, conflict and social status in, 142–44, 158–59; gender of, 142, 145–46, 147, 158; hypotheses in, 145, 146; informal status hierarchies in, 141; interactionist norm and, 212–16; interpersonal conflict definition in, 139; measures, 147–51; opportunities for, 140–41; political divisiveness related to, 160; popularity in, 140, 142; psychologists on, 140; race/ethnicity in, 159, 215–16; reference category in, 148, 149–50, 153, 154; school year start in, 150, 151, 155; social movements and, 216; social status in, 139–42, 143–44; stable dominance in, 148–49; status ambiguity and interpersonal conflict in, 144–45, 158, 159; status variable in, 147–48; student-driven culture and, 212–16; wave 1 variables in, 150–51, 152, 153, 153, 154. See also brokerage status
middle school results, 213–14; age appearance in, 154, 156; boys in, 151, 152, 153, 154, 155–57, 215–16; brokerage status mobility in, 153, 154; future research related to, 215; girls in, 151, 152, 153, 153, 154, 215–16; Instagram in, 154, 156; new members in, 207–9, 208, 210, 217nn28–29; nonphysical altercations in, 154, 156; older members, 207–9, 208, 210, 217nn28–29; SES in, 203, 211, 211–12; social referent students in, 214; status mobility in, 154, 155–57, 158; student culture and community and school characteristics in, 210–12, 211; targets in, 156; time and attention in, 156–57
militarized capitalism, 5–6, 14
militarized capitalism, education, and psychologists: climate justice movement in, 295–96; competition in, 293–95; control in, 293; corporate empires in, 294; counterculture in, 295; power in, 293–94; social movements in, 295–96; social status in, 293; social transformation in, 293; trauma of, 293
Milner, Murry, ix, x, 2. See also status system
Mishna, Faye, 99
mixed-methods approach. See understanding of culture
mixed-methods research, 13, 282–86
Modecki, Kathryn L., 257
moderators, 260
morning routine, 227
motivation. See structure and motivation
mugging victim, 30–31

National Academies, 249, 257, 263
national politics, 11–12, 173–77
National School Crime and Victimization Survey, 2
Native Americans, 168
network isolates, 8, 23
network nominations, 199
network structures, 23–24
new members, 207–9, 208, 210, 217nn28–29

New York state. *See* bullying queer youth state-level policy
Nickerson, Amanda B., 248
normal behavior, 2
normalization of aggression, 233–34, 238–39
normalized masculine violence, 96, 99
normative beliefs, 190
normative dichotomies, 167
normative femininity, 101
normative perception, 195–96
norm perceptions, 200–202, *201, 202,* 204–5, *205*
norms and experiences alignment, 204–5, *205*
North Carolina study, 125–26, *127*
Norway, 250, 262
nudes, 109–10, 111

OBPP. *See* Olweus Bullying Prevention Program
observational categories, 287–88
observations: on anti-bullying myth, 224–25; for understanding of culture, 274–75, 277
older members, 207–9, *208,* 210, 217nn28–29
Olweus, Dan, 248, 250; bullying definitions of, 3–4, 8–9, 25–28, 52, 139
Olweus Bullying Prevention Program (OBPP): criticism of, 250–51; definition in, 52; meta-analysis on, 250; outcomes of, 13; program strategies of, 249–50
Operation Nice, 95, 99, 111–12; advertising of, 101; boys in, 103–5; competition in, 103; discomfort with, 104–5; documentary in, 102–4; emotionality and responsibility in, 101; girls in, 103, 106–7; girls of color in, 103; low-income girls in, 103; national campaign of, 100–101; normalized sexual violence and, 105; normative femininity in, 101; privilege in, 102–3; reactions to, 104–5; reputation in, 106–7; responsibility in, 101, 104; universal relational aggression in, 101–3; "you can sit with us" button in, 101, 104
optimism, 63
organizational approaches, 226–28

Papua New Guinea, 32n17
parents and family, 169, 252–53
Pas, Elise T., 254
Pascoe, C. J., 222–23, 239–40
Patchin, Justin W., 252
patriarchy, 97; in Project Cyber Safety, 112
patriotism, 12
Paulle, Bowen, 240
Payne, Allison Ann, 254–55
PD. *See* professional development
peer aggression, 11
peer harassment: access and exposure in, 195; adults in, 188; behavior reception in, 196; changing cultures in, 212–14; Chinese footbinding related to, 194; chronic interactions in, 195; correlations in, 199–200, 204–5, *205*; culture meaning in, 190–91; culture theory in, 192; culture transmission in, 207–9, *208,* 217nn28–29; data on, 196–97; descriptive and prescriptive social norms in, 200–203, *201, 202*; descriptive norms in, 197, 198, 199, 200–202, *201, 202*; ecology of, 189; empirical approach on, 199–200; empirical variation in, 196–97; exterior categories in, 205–6; group culture in, 189; haters in, 188–89; high-status student behavior in, 193, 205–6, *207,* 209–10; idioculture in, 191; implications of, 214–16; influential students on, 206, *207*; interactionist account of, 189, 191–94, *193*; interaction patterns in, 194–95; interactions repetition for norms perception in, 194–96;

peer harassment (*cont.*)
  linear process of, 194; mean values on, 200, *201*, *203*, 203–4, 206, *207*; measures on, 197–99; negative peer experiences in, 198, 217n24; network nominations in, 199; normative beliefs in, 190; normative perception in, 195–96; norm perceptions in, 200–202, *201*, *202*, 204–5, *205*; norms and experiences alignment in, 204–5, *205*; own behavior and attitudes in, 198–99; peer harassment term use in, 189; perceived norms in, 192–94, 197–98, 217n23; perception updating in, 193–94; personal experiences in, 197, 202–4, *203*; prescriptive norms in, 197, 199, 200–203, *201*, *202*; quantitative measures on, 196–97; random assignment on, 196; school characteristics in, 197, 199; school climate in, 190; school culture and community and school characteristics in, 210–12, *211*; school cultures differentiation in, *201*, *203*, *205*, *207*, 209–10; school cultures in, 188, 190; school-level behavioral patterns in, 192–93; social norms in, 190–91, 192; standard deviations in, 203, *203*; starting drama in, 188; student-driven cultures and, 188
peer harassment term use, 189
peer mediation program, 227–28
peers, 253
Peguero, Anthony A., 169
Pennsylvania, 250
perceived norms, 192–94, 197–98, 217n23
perception updating, 193–94
person-centered influence, 236–37, 239–42
Peskin, Melissa Fleschler, 169
physical bullying, 108, *234*
physically aggressive behavior, 3
popular culture, 4–5
popularity, 6; aggression and, 131; in bullying theories, 120–21; cross-lagged linear model of, 128–29, *129*, *130*; descriptive statistics on, 126, *127*; importance of, 126, *127*, 131; in middle school friends, 140, 142; retained friends and, *127*, 128–29, *129*, *130*, 133n39; in theory of instrumental aggression, 124–25; valued over time, 126, 128, *128*, 131
power, viii–ix, 293–94; bullying queer youth related to, 52; imbalance of, 27; rewards related to, 2; social status related to, 9; of system, x–xi; in Trump era, 174, 176–77
power imbalance, *234*, 277–78
prescriptive norms: definition of, 197; descriptive and, 200–203, *201*, *202*; of peer conduct, 199
prevalence rates, 123–24
prevention and intervention, xi–xii
prevention and intervention programs: aggression research principles in, 249–50; bullying prevalence estimates and, 247; Classroom Check-Up in, 254; conclusions from, 248; content analyses in, 255–56; cost-benefit analysis in, 261; culture and context in, 261–63; culture in, 251; cyberbullying in, 247, 256–57, 258, 263; definitions in, 247; future research and best practices in, 257–63; high-quality implementation in, 260–61; individual in, 251–52; law and policy in, 255–56; meta-analyses in, 247–48; moderators in, 260; most effective components in, 259–60; National Academies on, 249, 257, 259, 260, 262, 263; in Norway, 250, 262; OBPP in, 249–51; outcomes and, 247, 249; parents and family in, 252–53; peers in, 253; in Pennsylvania, 250; programs targeting similar behaviors in, 258–59; public health model of mental health in, 249; resilience in, 252; restorative justice in, 254–55; school climate

in, 253–54; school in, 253–55; social ecological framework in, 251–57, 263; stigma-based intervention in, 262–63; structural-level influences in, 262; traditional bullying prevention programs in, 257; whole-school approach in, 249, 251, 254
principal, 227–28
privilege, 54, 68, 98; in Operation Nice, 102–3
proactive strategies, 61–62
professional development (PD), 49–50. *See also* bullying queer youth PD
Project Cyber Safety, 95–96, 99–100; beginning of, 105; boys in, 106, 108, 113; criminal records in, 109–10; cyberbullying in, 107–8; "don't be stupid" in, 106; extortion in, 110; gender inequalities in, 111–12; girls in, 106–11; locker room talk in, 108–9; manly physical bullying in, 108; nondominant teens in, 112; nudes in, 109–10, 111; patriarchy in, 112; propositions in, 110–11; public service announcement in, 107; reputations in, 106–7, 110–11, 112; responsibility in, 112–13; sexting in, 108–9, 110–11; sexual propriety in, 106–7; sisters in, 109; slut continuum in, 107
pronouns, 88
Proportion Valuing Popularity and Close Friends over Time, 126, *128*
psychological paradigm, 3; individual differences in, 299–300; moving forward on, 300–301; social power importance in, 297–99
psychology, viii, 120
psychology versus sociology, 7; definition related to, 3–4; health research in, 4; individual paradigm in, 4–5; militarized capitalism in, 5–6; popular culture and, 4–5; quantitative research in, 4; school climate in, 4; social ecological theory in, 5; social factors in, 5; social forces in, 5–6; social power in, 5; symbolic interactionism in, 5
public health model of mental health, 249
public perspectives, 220, 221
punching up, 123

qualitative research, 285–86, 288
quantitative measures, 196–97
Queen Quixotic, 86, 87
Queering Education Research Institute (QuERI), 58. *See also* bullying queer youth

race, 2–3; social ecology in, 11–12; status systems and, 44
race/ethnicity: African Americans in, 168–69; Asian in, 170; diversity within, 170; intervention programs and, 170; Latinos in, 168–69, 171; in middle school friends, 159, 215–16; Native Americans in, 168; oppositional conclusions on, 168–69; parents in, 169; school statistical minority in, 170–71; sexual-minority students in, 169; in social differentness, 168–72; suicide related to, 170; whites in, 168–69, 171; white supremacy in, 171–72
random assignment, 196
Raskauskas, Juliana, 6–7
Reagan, Nancy, 293
Reay, Diane, 99
reciprocity, 22–23
Reduction of Stigma in Schools (RSIS), 58, 59, 60, 61
religious school, 1
Renold, E. J., 99
repetition, 26–28, 32n12, 234; cruelty in, 31–32; punishment related to, 229–30
reputations, 106–7, 110–11, 112
researcher role, 225
research methodology in difference, 22–23
resilience, 252
response rates, 125

responsibility: in Operation Nice, 101, 104; in Project Cyber Safety, 112
restorative justice, 254–55
retained friends, 125, *127*, 128–29, *129*, *130*, 133n39
rewards, xi, 2, 64, 120, 131
Ringrose, Jessica, 99
River High School. *See* interactional homophobia
role of status. *See* status systems
Rowan, Brian, 221, 238
RSIS. *See* Reduction of Stigma in Schools

SafeOregon, 77, 78
same-sex marriage, 77–78
scaffolding, 38
scandals, 20
scapegoats, 30; in anti-bullying myth, 230; bullying inflation and, 20
school characteristics, 197, 199
school climate, 61; in anti-bullying campaigns, 13; in peer harassment, 190; in prevention and intervention programs, 253–54; in psychology versus sociology, 4; in Trump era, 174–75; in understanding of culture, 287, 289
school climate and school culture, 61–62, 69–70
School Climate Understanding and Building Aspirations (SCUBA), 278–79
school cultures, 51, 61–62, 69–70; anti-bullying myth in, 222–24, 240–41; community and school characteristics, 210–12, *211*; in peer harassment, 188, 190
school cultures differentiation, *201*, *203*, *205*, *207*, 209–10
school staff training, 287–88
school statistical minority, 170–71
school status systems, 44, 45, 46
school year start, 150, 151, 155
SCUBA. *See* School Climate Understanding and Building Aspirations
SEL. *See* social-emotional learning
SES. *See* socioeconomic status
sexism, 84
sexting, 95–96; in Project Cyber Safety, 108–9, 110–11
sexual harassment, 4, 279
sexual identities, 100
sexuality, 80
sexual-minority students, 169
sexual propriety, 106–7
Shen Nung, 25
single teen mom, 103
1619 Project, 12
slut continuum, 107
small-group cultures, 280–82
social bullying, 3
social circles, vii
social climbing, 6
social differentness: class and income in, 172–73; feedback loop in, 177; marginalization in, 177; race/ethnicity in, 168–72; social ecological perspective in, 166–68, *167*; in South, 177; Trump era in, 173–76
social ecological perspective on bullying, ix, 5–6, 11, 13–14, 121, 166–68, 176–77, 189, 220, 251, 256, 258–59, 261–63, 275, 299–300; culture and agency in, 168; macro and micro factors in, 166–67, *167*; normative dichotomies and, 167; policies and interventions related to, 168; power in, 167–68; resources in, 167; systems theory as, 166
social-emotional learning (SEL), 259
social forces, 5–6
social media: Instagram, 28, 42, 107, 149, *152*, *154*, 156, 197; Twitter, 80, 82, 107, 149, 150–51, *154*
social network research, 9
social network theories, 6, 8, 11
social norms, 68–69. *See also* peer harassment

social norm violations, 53–54
social power, 5, 297–99
social problem: cultural shift in, 76, 77–78; cyberbullying in, 78; homophobia levels decline in, 77–78; institutional heteronormativity in, 84–92; interactional homophobia in, 78–84; male cheerleader in, 76; SafeOregon in, 77, 78; same-sex marriage and, 77–78
social rewards, 2
social status, vii, 158–59, 293; in bullying queer youth, 55; competition for, ix–xi; in middle school friends, 139–42, 143–44; obsession with, 6; power related to, 9
social systems, ix; concentric circles of, xi; individual bullying and, 3; schools as, x–xi; thinking in, x
social transformation, 293
sociocultural approach, 50–51
socioeconomic status (SES): as class and income, 172–73; in middle school results, *203, 211,* 211–12
sociologically informed approaches. *See* bullying queer youth
sociological understanding as public understanding, xi
sociologists, 2
sociology, 7–8
Southern Poverty Law Center, 169, 174
Standardized Total Effects on Tertiary Outcomes, 129, *130*
starting drama, 188
state-level policy. *See* bullying queer youth state-level policy
status, 231–32; in theory of instrumental aggression, 121, 122–23, 124
status mobility, *154,* 155–57, 158
status motivation, network stability, and instrumental cruelty: bullying theories in, 120–23; data and methods in, 125–26; results in, 126, *127, 128,* 128–29, *129, 130*; structure and motivation in, 123–25;

theory of instrumental aggression, 120, 121, 122, 123–24, 131
status quo, 55; in bullying queer youth PD, 60–61
status relations, theory of, 40, 42, 44, 45
status systems: associations in, 41–42, 45; bottom in, 39–40; boundaries in, 42–43; competition in, 40; conformity in, 41–42, 45; consumer capitalism and, 44–45; crowds and cliques in, 39; disenfranchisement in, 39; exclusion in, 39; expressive relations in, 43; faith-based centers and, 46–47; food in, 41; gender and, 22; as inalienable, 40–41, 45; individualism and, 38–39; inexpansibility in, 40–41, 45; instrumental relations in, 43; multidimensionality and, 46–47; online, 42; organization and, 43; pattern in, 40; project-based learning and, 47; race and, 44; resources and, 46–47; scaffolding related to, 38; in schools, 44, 45, 46; stigma in, 41; structure of, 39; theory related to, 38, 45; traditions related to, 46; working assumptions in, 39
stereotypes, vii, 12; anti-bullying myth related to, 236–37
stigma, 9–10, 41, 262–63; RSIS and, 58, 59, 60, 61
strategic jockeying, xi
structure and motivation: friendship stability in, 124–25; friendship termination in, 124; mobility opportunities in, 124; prevalence rates in, 123–24
student characteristics, 224, 236
student fabrications, 229
student reports, 229, 230, 231–33, 239
suicide, 27, 60, 68, 92, 157, 170, 220
Supreme Court, U.S., 64
surface compliance, 23
Svahn, Johanna, 242n41
Swearer, Susan M., 223
Swedish culture, 295–96

symbolic interactionist theories, 6, 8
systems theory, 166

targets, 56, 156
Tavory, Iddo, 191
taxonomy of harm: concept creep in, 29, 30; cruelty in, 30–32; lumping in, 25, 28–29; plants and, 25; retaliation in, 29; splitting in, 25, 29; status and, 28–29, 30; systematic differences in, 29, 32n18; thin alternative in, 29–31; trauma of, 29, 31
teachers, 23; in prevention and intervention programs, 254
Temko, Ezra, 250–51
thinking, x
Thorne, Barrie, 225
Thunberg, Greta, 295–96
Tippett, Neil N., 173
total institutions, 20
Township High School. *See* mean girls and tough guys
tradition: bullying inflation compared to, 19
traditional bullying prevention programs, 257
traditional schools, 44
Transsexual Menace, 86–87
trans students, 85–88, 90
trans teacher, 86–87, 88
trauma, 293; degrees of, 29; of mugging victim, 30–31
Trump, Donald, 11–12
Trump era: Black Lives Matter in, 175; community values and, 176; curriculum relevance in, 175; hate crimes in, 174; immigrant criminalization in, 174; institutionalized racism in, 176; patriotism in, 175; power in, 174, 176–77; rhetoric in, 173–74; school climate in, 174–75; student voice in, 175; white supremacy in, 176
truth, xiii
Ttofi, Maria M., 248, 250, 253
TV sitcom, 76
Twitter, 80, 82, 107, 149, 150–51, 154
two-sided conflicts, 32n18

universal relational aggression, 101–3
Unnever, James, 190

verbal abuse, 3
verbal bullying, 234
victimization, 2, 30–31; in bullying theories, 120, 122–23; class and income related to, 173; in institutional heteronormativity, 91; in understanding of culture, 279, 282–84, 285, 287
village courts, 32n17

white supremacy, 171–72, 176
whole-school approaches, 6–7, 13; in prevention and intervention programs, 249, 251, 254
Williams, Lisa M., 169
winning, xi, 294
witnesses, 229–30
Wolke, Dieter, 173

"you can sit with us" button, 101, 104
Youth Risk Behavior Surveillance System, 256

www.ingramcontent.com/pod-product-compliance
Lightning Source LLC
Chambersburg PA
CBHW020244030426
42336CB00010B/610